RUNNING A PERFECT INTRANET

Written by

Rich Casselberry   Kannan Ramasubramanian
David Baker   Jeff Rigg
Gordon Benett   Krishna Sankar
Jane Calabria   David Schramm
Simeon Greene   Ian Verschuren
Jim O'Donnel   Joe Weber

Running a Perfect Intranet

Credits

President
Roland Elgey

Publisher
Joseph B. Wikert

Publishing Manager
Jim Minatel

Editorial Services Director
Elizabeth Keaffaber

Managing Editor
Sandy Doell

Director of Marketing
Lynn E. Zingraf

Acquisitions Editor
Stephanie Gould

Product Director
Mark Cierzniak

Editors
Sydney Jones
Anne Owen

Product Marketing Manager
Kim Margolius

Assistant Product Marketing Manager
Christy Miller

Technical Editors
Troy D. Holwerda
Russ Jacobs
Glenn Smith

Acquisitions Coordinator
Jane K. Brownlow

Software Relations Coordinator
Patty Brooks

Editorial Assistant
Andrea Duvall

Book Designer
Ruth Harvey

Cover Designer
Dan Armstrong

Production Team
Stephen Adams
Debra Bolhuis
Marcia Brizendine
DiMonique Ford
Trey Frank
Amy Gornik
Jason Hand
Daniel Harris
Casey Price
Laura Robbins
Bobbi Satterfield
Sossity Smith

Indexer
Craig Small

Composed in *Stone Serif* and *MCPdigital* by Que Corporation.

We'd Like to Hear from You!

As part of our continuing effort to produce books of the highest possible quality, Que would like to hear your comments. To stay competitive, we *really* want you, as a computer book reader and user, to let us know what you like or dislike most about this book or other Que products.

You can mail comments, ideas, or suggestions for improving future editions to the address below, or send us a fax at (317) 581-4663. For the online inclined, Macmillan Computer Publishing has a forum on CompuServe (type **GO QUEBOOKS** at any prompt) through which our staff and authors are available for questions and comments. The address of our Internet site is **http://www.mcp.com** (World Wide Web).

Thanks in advance—your comments will help us to continue publishing the best books available on computer topics in today's market.

Mark Cierzniak
Product Development Specialist
Que Corporation
201 W. 103rd Street
Indianapolis, Indiana 46290
USA

Contents at a Glance

Introduction

Writing HTML

Setting Up Software

Maintenance

Appendix

Contents

III Writing HTML for the Intranet   199

9 Basic HTML and Simple Pages   201

10 Graphics, Imagemaps, and Tools   223

15 Search Engines and Annotation Systems   337

16 Database Access and Applications Integration Using Scripts   363

17 Commercial Applications   395

18 Groupware Applications 419

IV Maintenance and Security   441

19 Using Multimedia   443

20 Usage Statistics and Log Analysis   467

Appendix   543

A What's on the CD-ROM?   545

Introduction

The Internet has been growing in popularity at a phenomenal rate. Many television ads now contain URLs (Uniform Resource Locators) such as CNN's **http://www.cnn.com** and surveys commonly ask for an e-mail address. An even faster growing phenomenon, though, is the use of the Intranet.

An Intranet is an IP network designed for internal use. The growth of Intranets has been silent but rapid, and is actually where most sales of Web servers are used.

Intranets are used in many types of companies from high-tech computer firms to real estate companies to oil refineries. Everyone can benefit from the technology available.

Intranet technology is used in many different ways. It can be used to set up a central document repository or workgroup server. It can be used to integrate with existing databases, either by writing custom software or using commercial applications. Most database vendors currently have or are working on WWW interfaces to their products.

Intranets can also be used as a client/server combination, allowing quick building of distributed applications. Use of the Web can also allow developers to quickly build cross-platform tools. Because HTML is an open standard, almost any computer will have a browser that can be used as a graphical user interface, or GUI.

Intranet-based tools also allow groupware applications to be integrated. Groupware applications can be built using free software, or commercial applications such as Lotus can be purchased and integrated.

What Does This Book Cover?

Part I "Introduction to the Intranet"

Chapter 1, "The WWW and the Intranet," introduces the World Wide Web and gives a good overview of the HyperText Transfer Protocol (HTTP) and HyperText Markup Language (HTML). The first chapter also explains how WWW technology fits into an internal network and covers what some good uses for an Intranet are. Chapter 1 also introduces Web servers and discusses the HTTP, plus discusses the secure versions of HTTP, Secure Sockets Layer (SSL), and Secure HTTP (SHTTP).

Part II "Choosing Software and Setting Up"

Chapter 2, "Choosing a Server Platform," discusses choosing a server. It covers what is important when integrating into an existing network and what sort of features are useful. Servers for UNIX networks, Microsoft NT networks, Netware networks, and Lotus Notes networks are all covered.

Chapter 3, "Installing and Configuring HTTPD for UNIX," covers installation and configuration of Apache HTTPD for UNIX. Apache is a free Web server that is very popular for UNIX machines. This chapter covers downloading, building, and configuring Apache as well as a section on troubleshooting and testing.

Chapter 4, "Installing and Configuring IIS," covers Microsoft's Internet Information Server (IIS). This server adds WWW, plus, FTP (File Transfer Protocol) and Gopher are covered as well. Installation, configuration, and troubleshooting IIS is covered in this chapter.

Chapter 5, "Installing and Configuring Netscape Enterprise Server and LiveWire," covers installation and configuration of both Windows NT and UNIX platforms. This chapter also covers some Netscape specific options, such as searching and editing features.

Chapter 6, "Installing and Configuring Novell Netware Web Server," covers Novell's Netware Web Server. It covers hardware and software requirements, installation, and configuration.

Lotus InterNotes, WebPublisher, and HTTP server are explained and discussed in Chapter 7, "Installing and Configuring Lotus Notes Web Publishing Products." Installation, configuration, and troubleshooting of these packages are covered in detail. This chapter also covers some specific examples, such as querying Notes databases.

Chapter 8, "Installing and Configuring Browser Software," covers how browsers work and what to look for in a browser. This chapter also discusses IP (Internet Protocol) networking. A troubleshooting section is also included to help fix common browser problems.

Part III "Writing HTML for the Intranet"

Chapter 9, "Basic HTML and Simple Pages," covers basic HTML as well as HTML 2.0, 3.0, and the Netscape extensions. HTML editors such as HotDog, HotMetal, and FrontPage are covered and explained. HTML converters, which can be used to convert existing documents to be used on your Intranet, are discussed in this chapter.

Chapter 10, "Graphics, Imagemaps, and Tools," explains graphic formats used on an Intranet. It also covers imagemaps and gives some examples when to use them in an Intranet. Tools to help you create graphic files and imagemaps are also covered in this chapter.

Chapter 11, "HTML Forms," covers HTML forms. It explains how to create an easy-to-use form that can be used to replace paper-based forms. This chapter also discusses when to use forms and when not to use forms.

Chapter 12, "CGI and Perl," covers using the Perl language to create pages on the fly, process forms, and perform actions. It discusses CGI's uses as well as Server Side Includes (SSI).

Chapter 13, "Java and JavaScript" explains the Java language and how it relates to JavaScript. It also covers how to configure Netscape servers to use JavaScript and how to write an application using these tools.

Chapter 14, "VB Script and ActiveX Controls," covers scripting languages from Microsoft, VB Script, and ActiveX Controls. It explains what they are and how to use them to develop intranet applications. This chapter also discusses Object Linking and Embedding (OLE).

Chapter 15, "Search Engines and Annotation Systems," covers simple full text searches, search engines, annotation systems, and, covers how they can be used in an Intranet.

Chapter 16, "Database Access and Application Integration Using Scripts," covers accessing databases and integrating currently used applications into the Intranet using scripts. This chapter also discusses when you should rewrite an application and when you should integrate the application.

Chapter 17, "Commercial Applications," covers commercial options available to help integrate your Intranet with existing applications and databases. Microsoft BackOffice and Oracle Universal Server and Web System are covered in detail in this chapter.

Chapter 18, "Groupware Applications," covers groupware and the use of groupware in an Intranet. It covers Lotus Notes, Usenet, and mailing lists.

Part IV "Maintenance and Security"

Chapter 19, "Using Multimedia," focuses on multimedia applications and their uses. It covers the different multimedia formats, such as mpeg and RealAudio, and then goes on to discuss the viewers required to support them. This chapter also discusses how network bandwidth is affected and offers strategies on how to reduce network saturation. The chapter ends with some exciting real-life uses for multimedia.

Chapter 20, "Usage Statistics and Log Analysis," covers usage statistics and log file analysis and explains how to convince management of the benefits of using an Intranet. Usage statistic tools are covered and explained.

Chapter 21, "Maintaining the Server and Documents," covers maintaining the server and documents. It describes how to organize your file structure for ease of maintenance, as well as access control. It defines various tools, such as link checkers and HTML validators. The last section covers using Server Side Includes to make maintaining the documents easier.

Chapter 22, "Sharing the Intranet with the World," outlines how to safely allow remote users, customers, or everyone access to part of the Intranet server. This chapter also covers linking to outside servers.

Chapter 23, "Intranet Security," covers keeping intruders from abusing the Intranet. It covers such topics as defining a security policy, using obscurity to help hide the site, using software security, and firewalls. This chapter also covers limiting what employees can get to. It covers defining what is allowed via policy and discusses technical ways to enforce this policy.

Who Should Read This Book?

This book is designed to help network or system managers deal with the myriad of issues involved in designing and running an internal Web site. Webmasters who are designing sites, or portions of sites, for internal use will also find this book valuable.

Because Intranets are IP-based, it is assumed that the network is running some sort of IP network. The reader should be familiar with basic IP network issues as well as the network design at the site.

This book covers many different scenarios and includes different operating systems. Familiarity with one of the following is required:

- Microsoft NT
- Novel Netware
- A version of UNIX, such as Solaris 2.5, IRIX, BSDI, HPUX, SunOS, or Linux
- Lotus Notes

Various programming languages are covered and knowledge of one or more will be helpful but are not necessary. These languages include:

- Perl
- Visual Basic
- Java
- JavaScript
- ActiveX

Any other programming experience will be helpful, especially when integrating databases or using CGI scripts.

Basic HTML is covered in Part II but at a very rapid pace. We are including on the CD-ROM the book *Special Edition Using HTML*, 2nd Edition from Que for additional HTML coverage.

What Will You Learn?

After reading this book you should be able to understand what is required from an Intranet server, as well as configure a server that fits into your existing network topology. You will also be able to do the following:

- Intelligently choose software for your Intranet, such as browsers, servers, and viewers
- Build and maintain your Intranet
- Make your Intranet safe from outside intruders
- Add existing documents to your Intranet
- Add useful features to your Intranet such as groupware, database integration, and search tools

This book will help you to develop and maintain a successful Intranet for your company. It will also help you to expand your knowledge and create more complex applications that match your company's needs.

Conventions Used in This Book

As you read this book you will notice some sections of the text that stand out. New terms are in *italics*. Words that you should type and site addresses are in **boldface**. Screen displays and on-screen messages appear in a special monospace typeface.

> **Note**
>
> Notes contain additional information or "reminders" of important information you should know.

> **Tip**
>
> Tips are bits of advice that help you solve a problem or learn the best way to do something.

> **Caution**
>
> Cautions alert you to potentially dangerous consequences of a procedure or practice.

Part I

Introduction to the Intranet

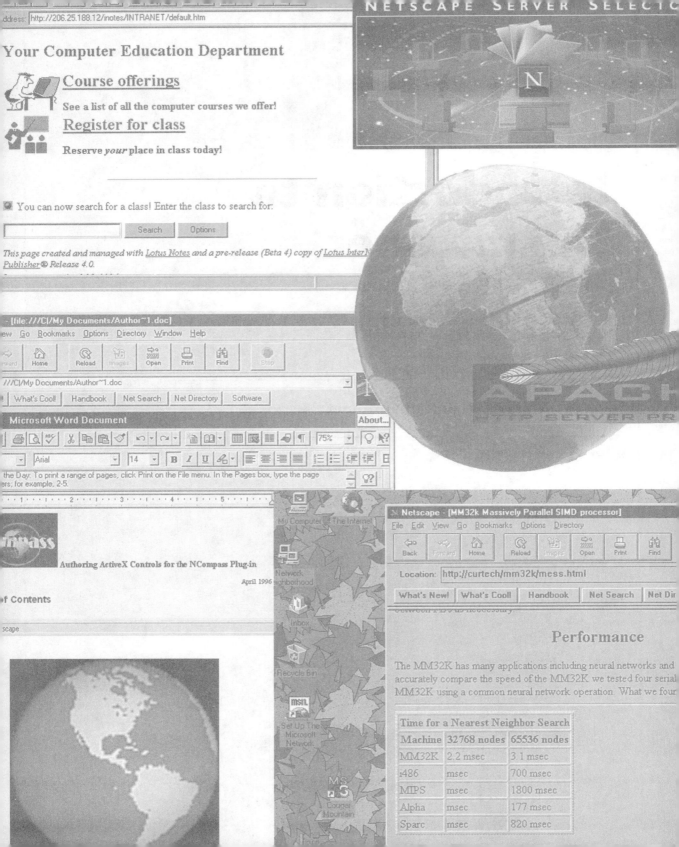

Your Computer Education Department

Course offerings

See a list of all the computer courses we offer!

Register for class

Reserve *your* place in class today!

☑ You can now search for a class! Enter the class to search for:

| | Search | Options |

This page created and managed with Lotus Notes and a pre-release (Beta 4) copy of Lotus InterN
Publisher® Release 4.0.

[file:///C|/My Documents/Author~1.doc]

ew Go Bookmarks Options Directory Window Help

| | | | | | | |
| Forward | Home | Reload | Images | Open | Print | Find | Stop |

///C|/My Documents/Author~1.doc

| What's Cool! | Handbook | Net Search | Net Directory | Software |

Microsoft Word Document   About...

Arial   14   **B** *I* U

the Day: To print a range of pages, click Print on the File menu. In the Pages box, type the page
ers; for example, 2-5.

NETSCAPE SERVER SELEC

APACH
HTTP SERVER PR

---

mpass

Authoring ActiveX Controls for the NCompass Plug-in

April 1996

f Contents

scape

My Computer The Internet

Network
eighborhood

Inbox

Recycle Bin

msn.

Set Up The
Microsoft
Network

MS
S

Cougar
Mountain

Netscape - [MM32k Massively Parallel SIMD processor]

File Edit View Go Bookmarks Options Directory

| | | | | | | |
| Back | Forward | Home | Reload | Images | Open | Print | Find |

Location: http://curtech/mm32k/mess.html

| What's New! | What's Cool! | Handbook | Net Search | Net Dir |

etween PEs is necessary

Performance

The MM32K has many applications including neural networks and
accurately compare the speed of the MM32K we tested four serial
MM32K using a common neural network operation. What we four

Time for a Nearest Neighbor Search		
Machine	32768 nodes	65536 nodes
MM32K	2.2 msec	3.1 msec
i486	msec	700 msec
MIPS	msec	1800 msec
Alpha	msec	177 msec
Sparc	msec	820 msec

## CHAPTER 1

The WWW and the Intranet

The World Wide Web and the Intranet are closely joined but there are some differences. The WWW is designed to be used by everyone while the Intranet is used primarily for company employees.

This chapter describes the underlying technology used by both the WWW and the Intranet. We will also discuss how they work and what can be done to make your Intranet more usable.

In this chapter, you will learn:

- What IP, HTTP, and HTML are and how they work
- What can be done in an Intranet
- Why you should build an Intranet
- What a Web server does
- How everything works together

World Wide Web versus Intranet

The growth of the Internet in the past few years has been explosive, in fact, the growth has been so rapid the exact number of users is still not known. While the media has touted the Internet as the greatest computing invention ever, Intranets, internal Internets usually complete with WWW servers and mailing lists, are the big hit in many companies. Intranets are easier and cheaper to set up and maintain than proprietary systems.

A recent survey by "International Treasurer" shows that 40 percent of U.S. multinational companies have an Intranet. Other studies estimate that one out of four Fortune 1000 companies have an Intranet, and two-thirds of all large companies have Intranets.

> **Note**
>
> The term Intranet refers to an internal network designed to be used by company employees. This network commonly consists of a WWW server but can also be made up of other servers such as usenet servers, FTP servers, database servers or other applications. In the text, we may use the term Web server to mean Intranet server.

IP Networks

Intranets are IP networks, like the Internet, designed to be used inside of a company. IP networks are already in use in many companies because they are based on an open standard. This allows many software companies to adopt IP technology and incorporate it into their products. In fact, IP networks have become so popular in the past few years, companies who developed competing standards, such as Novell and Microsoft, have given in to the market's demand and added IP as a networking option.

IP networking is now included in Microsoft Windows 95, Microsoft Windows NT, OS/2 Warp, Warp Server, and Novell Netware. It is also available for Windows for Workgroups, Windows 3.x and Macintosh clients. IP networking has been in almost all UNIX software for years, and it would be hard to find a UNIX vendor that shipped a current operating system without IP networking.

> **TCP/IP and UDP/IP**
>
> IP is used in many applications such as FTP (File Transfer Protocol), NFS (Network File Sharing), SMTP (Email), and rlogin (Remote Login). IP networks use two main types of networking, Transmission Control Protocol (TCP) and User Datagram Protocol (UDP). Most user programs such as telnet, rlogin, or FTP use TCP layered on top of IP, hence the popular name TCP/IP networks. UDP is used mostly in file systems, such as NFS, and name servers, such as DNS.
>
> In addition to TCP and UDP, there is a third called ICMP for Internet Control Message Protocol. The most popular user program to use ICMP is ping. Ping tests network connections between two hosts.

IP is unique in several ways but one of the most important things about IP is the fact that it is a layered protocol, see figure 1.1. IP networks were designed to be used in a heterogeneous network and can be run on any type of machine and over almost any type of network topology. Whether a company uses Token Ring, Ethernet or almost any other network topology, IP can work with it.

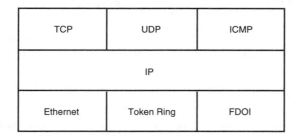

Fig. 1.1
IP networks are layered to be more flexible.

Since IP networks are layered they also work over WAN links such as 56kbps dedicated lines, or T1 lines. This feature also allows companies to use IP between corporate sites. So IP works very well as a LAN and a WAN transport.

IP also works over common dial-up lines and can be used to easily allow remote users to dial in using a modem. This connection is usually a PPP (Point- to-Point Protocol) link or SLIP (Serial Line IP) connection, see figure 1.2. Software exists for almost any computer to use PPP or SLIP to connect to a LAN. ˙

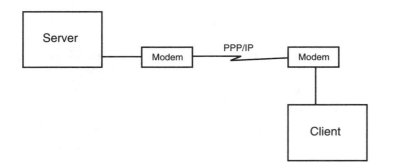

Fig. 1.2
IP can be used over modems to allow remote network connections.

HTTP

HTTP, which stands for HyperText Transfer Protocol, is what allows the World Wide Web to communicate. Like IP, HTTP is also an open standard and any computer that talks TCP/IP can talk HTTP, assuming someone has written the software.

HTTP is a connectionless protocol, which allows many quick connections without having to hold ports open. With WWW traffic originally grabbing only a few Kbytes for each page, and then often connecting to a different server, this design decision made sense.

Connectionless protocols have one flaw in a commercial environment; they are stateless. This means users can't be tracked through a site since they open a new connection each time to get a page. For many connections to the same site, having to set up and break down a new TCP connection for each page can cause a significant amount of overhead.

> **Note**
>
> Although we use the term *page* to refer to a single access, there may be multiple connections to an actual viewed page. Each hit actually uses one connection. A *hit* is a file access, whether that file is text, image, or sound, and requires a TCP setup and breakdown to occur.

HTTP allows two way communication, which allows the browser to send information to the server as well as vice versa. The specification also can allow content negotiation between the server and browser though this is not currently in use.

Commands

The HTTP supports several commands. These include, GET for retrieving pages, HEAD, which gets the headers of a document, POST for sending in information, PUT for placing information on a server, DELETE for removing a page, and TRACE for debugging.

These commands are part of the HTTP 1.1 specification. The most popular commands are GET, HEAD, and POST. DELETE and TRACE are rarely used.

Headers

The HTTP specification specifies different headers that are required to be sent. The Web server and browser use these headers to pass information back and forth. Some servers will allow the Web developer to read the header and use information in it to make decisions based on this information. Some of the headers include:

- Accept, Accept-Charset, Accept-Encoding, Accept-Language. These are used by some clients to define what mime-types, character sets, encoding, and languages they can handle.

- Authorization. Used to tell the server what type of authorization is being used. Only Basic is supported.
- Content-Encoding, Content-Language, Content-Length, Content-Type. This tells the client what type of encoding, language, length, and type is being used.
- Date. Sent from the server to tell when a response was generated.
- Expires. Used to tell clients when a page must be recached.
- Host. Used to define which host the URL is pointing to.
- If-Modified-Since. Used to get a document if it has changed since this date.
- If-Unmodified-Since. Used to get a document if it hasn't changed since this date.
- Last-Modified. Sent from the server to let the client know when the document last changed.
- Location. Used to tell the client the document has moved.
- Referer. Sent from the client to tell the server the name of the previously accessed document.
- Server. Tells what server is running.
- User-Agent. Sent from the client to tell the server what kind of client it is.
- WWW-Authenticate. Sent from the server to tell the client authentication is required.

These header fields are the most often used ones. There are other ones as well. For more information on headers, consult the HTTP specification.

Basic Authentication

The HTTP also allows for basic authentication. This allows the server to require a username and password for each security domain defined. Normally, a server would have only one security domain but it could possibly have multiple domains.

Clients normally store the username and password for each domain during each session. This keeps the user from having to type in this information for each access.

Basic authentication is a fairly simple procedure; when the client requests a page, the server sends back a reply saying it needs to be authenticated. The client then pops up a username and password prompt to the user. Once the user enters the correct information, the client resends the request with the username and password included. The server then decides if it is the correct password or not. If not, it returns a message saying the password or username was wrong. If the username and password are okay it returns the document.

Caution

Basic authentication does not allow for encrypted usernames or passwords. This would allow a system cracker to sniff the passwords over the network if they were attached to a network that carried the traffic between the client and server.

If this is not enough security then a stronger protocol such as Secure Sockets Layer (SSL) or Secure HTTP (S-HTTP) is required. SSL and S-HTTP are covered in the section named "Secure Protocols."

Content Negotiation

Content negotiation is also specified in the HTTP specification. This allows clients and servers to negotiate on file formats, languages or other specifics.

Content negotiation is one of the important but underused aspects of the HTTP. How it works is like this: The client requests an image and sends a list of what formats it can handle. The server looks at the list and returns the best format for the browser.

Client negotiation also allows servers and clients to agree on different languages or multimedia formats.

Note

Currently, no browsers support content negotiation and scripts are often written to decide which features a particular browser should get.

This makes it harder for Web developers and could be avoided if browsers would support the standard for negotiating content.

Caching

Since the WWW can be used across the Internet, the performance can be greatly improved by using caches to store recently retrieved documents. Caching must be done carefully since Web documents change frequently.

Caching can also be used in an Intranet to help reduce network load. Many networks are made up of multiple segments. Some segments are connected via fast links others may be connected over slower links. Caching can help to reduce the amount of traffic going across the slower links and also help reduce total network traffic.

The HTTP specification contains many headers that are used to determine if a document in a cache can be used and for how long. These headers are discussed in the header section.

Caching works like this: the client requests a page from the proxy server. The proxy server checks to see if it has the page in its cache or not. If so, and it is current, it gets sent directly from the cache and never has to query the actual server for it. If it is not in the cache, then the proxy server gets the page and stores it in its cache.

There is also an expire header that tells cache servers how long to use a document without retrieving a new one. This is useful for dated documents and can also be used to automatically expire script documents.

Caching is very useful for reducing bandwidth for commonly accessed documents. Some browsers do caching both in memory and to local disk. Others only cache to memory or not at all.

Secure Protocols

Since HTTP is so flexible and popular, many companies are trying to use HTTP to transfer sensitive data. Examples of this data would be credit card numbers, purchase order numbers, or confidential data, such as personnel records.

Some studies show 80 percent of all computer attacks come from inside the company so it's easy to see why security would be important inside an Intranet as well as over the Internet. Plus, securing the Intranet makes it harder for someone to get information. Most companies have almost no security in place except for a firewall. Once an intruder gets past the firewall, they have full reign over what they can see and do. Having a secure Intranet helps to solve this problem.

HTTP, unfortunately, is not a secure protocol, it is prone to different attacks such as:

■ IP Spoofing. This is where someone trying to break in, commonly called a cracker, pretends to be someone else in order to submit commands to a server. It is often used to open other doors for the cracker to get in. IP spoofing is not specific to HTTP, it is inherent in any IP connection.

■ Man in the Middle attacks. These are attacks where the cracker is between the client and server. These allow the cracker to take over a network session. This is also an IP limitation.

■ Eavesdropping. This allows a cracker to watch for certain types of information on a network. It requires the cracker to be on a network segment that the traffic goes through. This information can be credit card numbers, passwords, or other sensitive information.

In order to make HTTP safe enough for confidential traffic to pass over a network, a means of encrypting and authenticating data connections is required. This is handled by using a secure protocol to transfer information between the server and client. There are currently two popular secure protocols in use.

One protocol is called SSL for Secure Sockets Layer. It is more popular since it can be used with protocols other than http. The other protocol is S-HTTP, for Secure HTTP. These protocols are discussed in the next two sections.

SSL

SSL or Secure Sockets Layer is a protocol that sits between HTTP, or another protocol, and the TCP/IP stack. It allows secure connections using digital certificates. It allows for authentication, encryption, and data integrity.

> **Note**
>
> Authentication allows clients and servers to be sure who they are talking to.
>
> Encryption ensures no one else can read a document or eavesdrop on a transaction.
>
> Data integrity makes sure the document hasn't been altered during transmission.

SSL is available on the Netscape Enterprise Server, but not the Netscape FastTrack server. If you need secure transactions, you have to purchase the Enterprise server. SSL is also available on Microsoft IIS and a version of Apache called ApacheSSL.

> **Caution**
>
> SSL servers only work with browsers that understand SSL. If a browser doesn't understand SSL, it can't communicate with an SSL-secured server.

How SSL Works

SSL requires a digital certificate. This is an encrypted piece of data that contains specific certificate information such as the name of the server, the server's public key, the expiration date and the name of the Certificate Authority (CA).

The other part of the digital certificate is the signature. The digital signature is an unforgetable piece of data proving the certificate has been signed by the certificate authority. The certificate authority is a server that is known and trusted by many other servers. The CA is used to verify the relationship between a server and its public key.

To obtain a certificate you must generate a public and private key. The private key is stored and kept secret and the public key is sent to the CA along with proof of the servers identity and some other information such as:

- Common Name. Usually the fully qualified domain name (FQDN) of the server.
- E-mail address. Used to correspond with you in case the CA needs further information.
- Organization. The name of your business or institution.
- Locality. Where your business is located, for example Boston.
- State or Province. Where your business is located. Most CAs won't accept abbreviations.
- Country. The abbreviated country your business is in.

The CA then generates a digital signature for the server and sends back a signed certificate. This certificate is then published or attached to messages that the server sends out.

> **Note**
>
> Anyone can see this certificate since it contains the server's public key. Any documents that encrypt using the public key in the certificate can only be read by using the private key. The public key in the certificate can't be changed without ruining the signature.

Users can then verify the certificate using the digital signature and the public key of the CA who signed the certificate. Once the certificate has been verified, the data inside the certificate can be trusted.

In use, the client will send a connection request to the server. The server will return a signed digital certificate. The client then authenticates the certificate using the digital signature and the public key of the CA.

If the certificate is not authentic the connection is dropped. If it is authentic then the client sends a session key and encrypts the data using the servers public key. This ensures only the server can read it since decrypting requires knowing the servers private key. This is why the private key must be kept secret.

Once the server has the session key, it can use this to encrypt and decrypt data with the client. Since the data sent between the client and server is encrypted, it can't be read by anyone else.

Using SSL

To enable SSL you must do the following:

1. Generate a keypair. Netscape servers can generate a keypair by filling out a form in server manager. The form is located under the configuration area under "Generate a key." On IIS, you can use the command keygen. The syntax for keygen is: keygen password keypair.txt certreq.txt "C=US, S=Massachusetts, L=Boston, O=org, OU=Sales, CN=www.company.com". The information in quotes corresponds to the information required by the CA as shown in the list above. With ApacheSSL you use the command "req" with the newkey option.

2. Generate a certificate request. Netscape servers have a form under Server Manager that must be filled out to request a certificate. It is located under the link labeled "Request or Renew a Certificate." IIS and APacheSSL automatically generate a certificate request when creating a keypair.

3. Install the signed certificate. Once the certificate comes back from being signed you need to tell your server where it is located. Netscape can be told from the Server Manager under the "Install a Certificate" link. IIS uses the setkey command. The syntax is: setkey Password keypair.txt certif.txt. Password and keypair.txt were used in the keygen command. certif.txt is the file that we saved the signed certificate in. ApacheSSL needs to be told via the SslCertificateFile directive in the httpd.conf file.

4. Add SSL security for the server. Netscape again uses the Server Manager to add this. Select the link "Activate Security and verify ciphers" and fill out the information. This includes the path to the files we used, the port (default is 443), and which ciphers to use. IIS needs to be told to use SSL in the Internet Server Manager. Select the directory and click the "Requires Secure SSL" box.

S-HTTP

Secure HTTP is a version of HTTP that provides secure transactions. It allows for Data integrity, encryption, and authentication. Secure HTTP or S-HTTP, unlike SSL can be used in conjunction with http. It does this by recognizing the fact that the browser can't handle secure transactions and either refusing to communicate or by notifying the user that the transaction is insecure.

S-HTTP allows browsers to perform several cryptographic functions.

- Encryption or decryption of traffic. This eliminates man in the middle attacks as well as makes your traffic unreadable.
- Client side digital signatures. This proves to the server that the request actually came from the client. This requires a digital certificate from a certificate authority.
- Server digital signature verification. This proves that the server actually sent the message. Using server digital signatures requires a certificate authority.

How S-HTTP Works

The default cryptographic behavior is for the client to encrypt traffic but not sign it. The server transmits in the clear. The idea behind this default is to allow the client to encrypt payment information, such as credit card numbers. The server normally responds with a page saying the order has been placed. This is not considered sensitive enough to be encrypted.

Normally, when a client receives a form that needs to be securely submitted, it will also receive the Distinguished Name (DN) of the server. The client can tell if it is a secure form by the Action form. If the Action URL has HTTP as the protocol it does not get encrypted, if it is S-HTTP then it needs to be encrypted. The DN allows the client to look up the servers public key.

Once the client has the server public key, it can encrypt the message using that. However, using that encryption key would be very slow, so what the client does is generate a symmetric key, which is faster to decrypt and more secure. The client then encrypts the message with the symmetric key and then encrypts the symmetric key with the servers public key. Since the message can only be decrypted using the private key, only the server can get the symmetric key.

Once the server receives the message, it decrypts the symmetric key and then the rest of the message.

The Webmaster can also force the return document to be encrypted, authenticated, or signed. This is done using the Privacy-Enhancement header. This header can force the server to encrypt, authenticate, or sign.

The client can also be requested to sign, authenticate, or encrypt by adding a CRYPTOPTS block in the FORM tag. The CRYPTOPTS can have a field defining how the form should be submitted. The syntax would be CRYPTOPTS "Shttp-Privacy-Enhancements: recv-required=sign." The client could also be asked to authenticate or encrypt by separating them by commas.

When signing a form submission, the client is required to have a digital certificate. This digital certificate is used the same way that SSL uses it. The client attaches its signed certificate. When the server receives that certificate it verifies its authenticity. If it is authentic then the server can be assured it was really the client that submitted it.

The same is true when the server signs a document. The client verifies the signature and if it is authentic can be assured the server really sent it.

Secure http can also handle out of band key exchanges. This allows a client and server to have a shared secret that has been pre-arranged either by phone or other media. This allows for faster encryption/decryption then public key encryption.

Using Shttp

Shttp isn't as popular as SSL and very few browsers and servers support it. One of the browsers is Secure Mosaic, and a server that supports shttp is Secure NCSA httpd. More servers and browsers may be coming out that support shttp, but most companies seem to be more interested in SSL.

You can get more information on Secure Mosaic from **http://www.commerce.net/software/SMosaic**. More information for Secure HTTPD from NCSA is available from **http://www.ncsa.uiuc.edu/**.

HTML

HTML or HyperText Markup Language allows browsers to display documents based on the logical layout of the document. It does not allow exact formatting since different screens would display things differently. Instead, HTML allows you to describe what the document is and allows the browser the flexibility to display the text however it looks best on the screen. This allows, for example, a employee handbook to be created that can be read on any size screen on any type of machine.

One disadvantage of HTML is the fact that the formatting is not as exact as it would be using a programming language such as Visual Basic, or a word processor such as FrameMaker. Newer HTML standards are working on this issue and much more can be done using HTML 3.0 tags and external viewers, than could be previously done. HTML 3.0 is still being defined and may still have changes before it is the official standard. The current HTML standard is 2.0.

HTML also allows hypertext links, or hyperlinks, in the article. These special areas in the text tell the browser to get a different document to display. This document however doesn't need to be text, it can be pictures, sounds or video.

Open Standards

Open standards and Internet technology can also be used to make corporate networks more efficient, in fact, many companies are doing exactly that. Using Web technology for internal use is a natural evolution for several reasons:

- IP networks are easy to integrate over LANs as well as WANs. This allows companies to use the same technology to communicate across the room, or across the world.

- Web technology allows cross platform development. Since HTML looks the same on a Mac as it does on any other machine, developers can concentrate on developing new technology instead of porting existing programs.

- The WWW is inherently client server based. Companies have been looking for ways to take advantage of client server technology for years. The WWW makes this easy to do.

- Web technology is also cost effective. The Web browser and server market is very competitive with many companies trying to get a piece of the action. This makes the technology cheap, plus, since it is all open standards, there is an abundance of free software available.

- Web technology scales well. Web servers can start small with only one machine and a few HTML pages, and can grow to hundreds of servers and thousands of pages.

In the "Why Intranets Make Sense" section we will discuss in detail why companies are finding Intranet technology so useful.

What Are Some Intranet Applications?

Intranets are used in many different types of companies, from high tech computer companies, to real estate firms to oil refineries. Intranets aren't just useful in large companies either, smaller companies can gain a competitive advantage by using their Intranet to deliver information to the right people faster. Intranets can also make development time quicker and can help save costs.

This section will cover some uses of Intranets and give some examples of what can be done using Intranets. Different companies will have different needs and this is by no means a definitive list of what can be done. It is merely a list of ideas that may fit in with your company, or help to give you new ideas of what can be done.

Almost all Intranet applications fall into three main categories:

- Publishing applications or applications that allow one person or group to talk to many.
- Discussion applications which allow many people to talk to many people.
- Interactive applications or applications that interact with a program or other document.

Publishing Applications

These are the usual first steps in creating an Intranet. These applications are easy to setup and may not even require a WWW server.

> **Note**
>
> It is possible to view simple static HTML files without a WWW server. Most browsers allow you to open a local file and view it. The name local file simply means it is not delivered over http. The file can be remotely mounted, or shared from a server.

Document Repository

Intranets were originally used to allow groups of people to share documents. This make sense since that is what the WWW was originally developed for. Using a Web server for a central document repository allows employees to quickly locate documents and save time searching for a particular piece of information. Also, since the documents are all stored in one place, changes are easier to make, plus changing one copy changes everyone's copy.

Since HTML documents don't need to be simply text, companies can also store graphics, audio, or even video. This allows almost any type of information to be centrally located and easily found.

Documents may include, employee handbooks, company newsletters or policies, design specifications, phone or e-mail lists, manuals, or job postings.

Bulletin Boards

Most companies have bulletin boards where company notices are placed and employees can place "for sale" items. Bulletin boards converted to HTML allow employees to get to a central bulletin board from their desks. This is helpful if the company is spread among different building or countries.

Having a Web server act as a bulletin board also makes sense for other reasons, searching capabilities and ease of maintenance. Since HTML is text-based, it is easy to set up a search program. This would allow employees to easily search for items of interest, for example "Car for sale."

Since the bulletin boards items would be files on a Web server, standard tools can be used to remove them after a certain period of time. Plus, since they are protected by the operating system, people can't simply remove them or change them.

Workgroup Server

The Web can be used to share information between group members as well as between different groups. For some companies, it might make sense to have each workgroup have an area where they can discuss what they are working on, who they are and what they know. This can help groups get to know each other and can help find out who knows about a particular type of software or component.

Workgroup servers can also be used to track project status. This can be done by having a team leader make changes to a page containing project schedules. Workgroup servers can also be used to store design specifications, notes, memos, or other information useful to the group.

Workgroup servers can also be used to introduce new team members and could be a central area for them to gather information on what has been done.

> **Note**
>
> Some of these applications actually could also be considered discussion or interactive applications.

Group Bookmarks

The Internet has many useful Web pages but they aren't always easy to find so setting up an area pointing to external links often allows users to quickly find information they are looking for. This bookmark page is often how Web sites start, one person may be designated as an Internet Researcher who builds a directory of useful pages for others to use.

Introduction

Discussion Applications

Intranets can do more than simply store documents, they can also be used as a front end for group discussions. Different ways to do this could be as simple to set up as writable pages or as complex as real-time chat servers.

Usenet News servers also work nicely to facilitate communication between group members, or different departments. News servers are readily available, and most browsers allows reading of news without the need for a special program. Mailing list software can also be used to allow groups to communicate together.

Discussion lists can include many topics from design specifications to the best restaurants in town. Some discussion topics can include software products, engineering issues, outages and problems, corporate policy, and general discussion. Since lack of communication is one of the biggest problems in many corporations, allowing groups to communicate is one of the important uses of an Intranet server.

Good communication can save money in many ways such as:

- Reuse of technology. Engineers or other power users may not be able to use some older machines, such as 486 class PCs but for an employee in data entry, it might be just the right machine.

- Reduced development costs. Many times different groups are working on the same or similar projects. Instead of duplicating efforts, good communication would allow different groups to be aware of what else is happening and reuse what others know.

- Better prices on purchased items. Communicating needs to the purchasing department can allow them to buy in bigger quantity and get better prices.

- Reduced support costs. People communicating among each other can help reduce calls to a support team. Setting up an area for users of a particular software to talk to others will allow them to help each other out.

Interactive Applications

Interactive applications are the applications that do work. These applications are used to query or search databases or to view what is happening on the network. You can, for example, see which machines are busy or what is running on a server. Interactive applications are handled by using CGI or Java or another programming language. These topics are covered in detail in Part III "Writing HTML for the Intranet."

Standard User Interface

Using HTML as a standard front end to existing software will allow users to use any type of machine to access the system. Since HTML makes things look the same on different machines, users will be more comfortable using different types of hardware.

Creating HTML front ends also makes it easier to develop sophisticated looking applications without having to learn a complicated programming language such as C++. Reducing the time it takes to develop applications means more work gets done.

Central Form Submission

Many companies have different forms for different requirements. When a new person starts, his manager usually needs to fill out a new user account form, a request for a network drop, a request for a phone and other forms.

HTML allows forms to be built and accessed via a WWW browser. Creating a central form area can make getting equipment or services much easier and in some cases automatic. Even if the form can't be handled automatically, having it submitted electronically can help eliminate forms getting lost or misdirected.

Caution

Acting on data received from an HTML form can be a time saver but it can also be dangerous. Automatically creating user account or making other changes may save time but it can also cause many problems if used improperly. Data of this sort should be forwarded to an administrator who can verify it and then act on it if required.

Almost any form can be converted to HTML and placed on a Web server. Some examples are, new user account forms, time off requests, equipment request forms, and problem tracking forms.

Development Platform

With the introduction of Sun Microsystem's Java to the Web, developers can start building applications that are cross platform and distributed. Java allows the same piece of code to run on any machine that has a Java virtual machine ported to it. Examples of such machines are Solaris 2.x, Windows NT and Windows 95, and soon to be Macintosh system 7.x.

Building Java applications or "applets" allows developers to not only develop the same code for multiple platforms, it is also true distributed computing.

The processing is done on each client machine, not on the server. This allows the server to be dedicated to I/O applications instead of CPU processing and can help reduce costs. Adding Java applets can increase network traffic since each time someone uses an applet they must download it again. However Java applets can also reduce traffic by eliminating the need for a client to send all processing requests to the server.

System Status Tools

Different operating systems have different ways to query print queues and other system-specific information. By creating an HTML front end to these applications, any user on any system can easily check out what is going on, without having to know the correct command or syntax.

Almost any command that can be done from a command line can easily be converted to an HTML page. Some examples of status or monitoring tools are:

- Print queue monitor. Having a page for all the printers in a workgroup, building or company wide, will allow users to see which printers are busy or when their jobs are done. It will also allow support personnel to monitor when printers are jammed up or overloaded.

- System load monitor. In a distributed environment jobs can be run on different machines. By having a page show the system load, users can go to a machine that it being less used. This also offers a system manager a view of all the systems so he or she can see which machines are being over utilized or need to be upgraded.

- Network status. Networks are becoming more reliable but occasionally have problems, setting up a page showing which servers are responding can give users a view of what is wrong and can avoid frustration in case of outages. This also allows system managers to see which parts of a network are not working properly.

- Process status. Setting up a page to show running programs can help users tell when their reports are done. It can also allow system managers a view of what is going on and help them to reschedule large jobs for nighttime runs.

Why Intranets Make Sense

This section will cover why it makes sense to create an Intranet server for your company. With Internet servers, many companies decide they need to get on the Net because everyone else is. Whether this is reason enough to create an external Web server is not known but publicity is a reason for some companies to develop an Internet presence. Intranets however are not created for publicity reasons and, if done properly, no one outside of your company will even know you have one. Therefore there must be a better reason to create one. This section will discuss some reasons to integrate an Intranet into your existing or new network.

Using the Intranet to Merge Technology

Many software products work with specific operating systems. Microsoft BackOffice works great with NT servers or other Microsoft products but not as well with UNIX machines. Likewise for Novel's Groupwise product. It works really well on a Novell network but when integrating with other platforms can be troublesome.

Intranets, however, can integrate with Microsoft products as well as products from Novell, Lotus, or UNIX vendors. Intranets can be used as the middleware to allow you to merge your disparate systems into one homogenous computing environment, see figure 1.3.

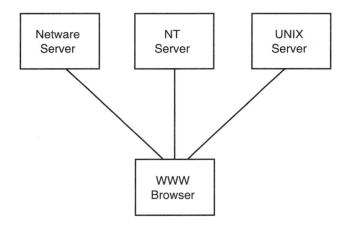

Fig. 1.3
Using the WWW can allow users to talk to different types of systems.

Companies with multiple databases such as Oracle, Sybase, or Microsoft SQL server can use the Web as a front end for all of them. Users no longer will need to learn syntax for extracting data from each one or even where it all comes from.

Even different types of file servers can be combined into one seamless Web of information. Web servers can run on Netware servers, NT servers, or UNIX servers and can be set up to allow users to get information from them without knowing what type of server they are talking to.

There are other products that allow communication between different types of systems but none are as universally accepted as the combination of HTTP and HTML.

Intranets can allow many different systems to talk the same language. This can lead to many benefits including:

- Single point of access to multiple databases. Oracle, Sybase, and SQL servers all can talk to the Web allowing users to get information from or to them from a Web browser.
- Allows users to get information from different types of platforms such as a file from a Netware server or a document from a UNIX machine.
- Applications can be accessed from systems other than the ones they were designed for. A Netware server could send a request to a remote process running on a UNIX machine.

Saving Money with Intranets

Intranets are cost effective. The Web server and browser markets are very competitive, making prices and features very competitive.

Web browsers range in price from nothing for Mosaic or Microsoft Internet Explorer, to under a hundred dollars for Netscape or Lotus Internotes. Web servers such as Apache or IIS are free; others, such as Netscape Enterprise server or Netware Web server, are under a few thousand dollars.

Browsers and servers are also available for almost every platform in use today. This means existing servers can be utilized, saving both hardware costs and management costs. These costs must be considered when comparing Web servers to other technology since the costs to administer a new server can add up quickly.

Programmers can quickly be taught to adapt to programming for the Web since the biggest change is in how data is presented. Data from a Web page is usually passed in environment variables or on the command line instead of read from the keyboard. Output must also be formatted to meet the HTML specification. These are trivial changes and most programmers should be able to pick this up in a short time.

Many converters and other useful utility programs are free for downloading over the Internet. These include programs to convert word processor files or spreadsheets to HTML. Other utilities are link checkers, to make sure that links point to another page, and HTML editors, to make creating HTML pages easier.

Expandability

Web servers can start out small, with just a few pages, and expand to several thousand pages very easily. Since HTML allows links to point to pages on separate servers, it is easy to add a new server when one gets to busy.

This allows groups to have separate departmental servers and have a central corporate server act as a main directory. This allows great scalability, limited only by network bandwidth and the amount of machines available.

The fact that Web servers can start out small allows even small companies to try using Intranets and expand only as needed. It also allows large companies to grow as large as needed without expensive per user charges (see figure 1.4).

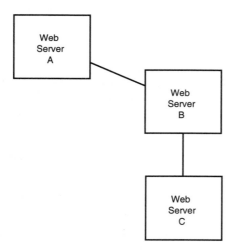

Fig. 1.4
Using Web servers allows unlimited scalability.

User Friendliness

World Wide Web technology is designed to take complicated tasks and make them accessible from one user interface. The original WWW browser, Mosaic, allowed users to ftp, read news, connect to gopher servers, and view HTML files all from the same GUI. This made it easy for non power users to get information easily.

Web browsers have only gotten better. In addition to everything Mosaic allowed WWW pioneers to do, new browsers allow posting of News articles, reading and sending e-mail, and many other things.

Using HTML as a front end for different processes makes it easy for users to learn new things since they don't need to relearn the look and feel of the software. It also makes users more at ease since they are familiar with the environment. Even on a different hardware platform the Web looks the same. Standardizing on a corporate browser makes it even easier since then the browser is exactly the same regardless of system software.

Note
Many new releases of programs are coming with either an HTML interface or HTML output. Online help is also commonly written in HTML to allow easy reading.

Reduced Development Time

Using CGI interfaces and HTML can help developers create front-end interfaces to complex programs quickly and easily. Best of all, if there is an HTML interface any browser can take advantage of it, reducing porting time and cost. Less time spent on GUI design allows developers to spend more time optimizing internal code.

Since the WWW is client-server, the company can take advantage of the benefits of this flexible environment without having to understand all the details of it.

Using Java can allow the company to go a step further than client-server to true distributed computing. Java downloads the applets to the client and uses the processing power of the client instead of the server. This greatly reduces the load on the server, especially if the applets are CPU intensive programs.

Java programming is more sophisticated than standard CGI programming since Java is a separate language. CGI programs can be written in any language the programmer is comfortable with, as long as they can output HTML and receive input from environment variables or the command line. Programmers familiar with object oriented languages, such as C++, will be able to fairly easily learn Java.

> **Caution**
>
> Not all browsers support Java so care must be taken when choosing a browser. This is covered in Chapter 8 "Choosing and Configuring Browser Software." Java will also not run on all platforms, so care must be taken when deciding to develop applications in Java.

What Are Web Servers?

Web servers are programs that can understand and talk the HTTP. They are used to answer HTTP requests and respond with HTTP answers. A basic Web server can be used to perform any HTTP operation and return the correct headers and documents. More sophisticated servers though have many features that make it easier to server HTML documents.

Some of the more popular features include ways to allow the server to parse the files or run external programs, more sophisticated authentication such as using DBM files instead of text files, advanced logging features, or access controls to limit by IP address.

Server Parsed Files

In order to make something besides static HTML files it is required for the server to parse files or to run external programs. There are many ways this is done but the two most common are Server Side Includes and CGI programs.

Server Side Includes or SSIs allow an HTML page to include different things at the time the file is downloaded. This allows, for instance, programs to run and insert their output. One common use for SSI is to generate a header and footer. This allows you to customize the look and feel of a site by changing one or two files, instead of having to change every file.

CGI or Common Gateway Interface, allows programs to be run. These can be used to do almost anything any other program can do. The only real difference between CGI programming and other types of programming is the input and output the program uses. CGI normally passes input as command line options or environment variables. The output should be valid HTML.

Authentication

The HTTP specification allows for basic authentication, which allows the server to require a username and password. How these are verified is up to the Web server.

Most Web servers allow basic authentication to be done by verifying the username and password from a text file. This text file however stores the passwords in clear text. While no one should be able to see this file, it is possible to misconfigure and expose your passwords to the Internet. Searching a text file for a password is OK for a small amount of users, but when you start getting a few hundred it gets to be too slow.

More sophisticated servers allow other ways to verify passwords. Some allow you to use DBM password files, which are mush faster than straight text files. Others allow native lookups. An example of this is the NDS authentication that the Netware Web server uses.

Logging

Many sites need to know who is using their Web server. This may be used for billing or for helping to decide what features users are after. For whatever reason, logging features are one of the most important features a Web server can have.

Most Web servers now support the common log format. This logs many different things, including the client's machine name, the user ID and group ID (if authenticated) the date and time, the http request, the status of the request and the number of bytes transferred.

There are also other log file formats that may log more information. Netscape proxy server also offers extended log file formats and extended-2 log file formats. These include other details about the transaction such as communications between the proxy and server and transfer times. Apache allows users to create new logging modules to log any header information that they want.

Access Controls

Many Web servers allow the administrator to create access lists on what machines or what users can connect to different parts of the server.

This allows you to isolate your Intranet server from the Internet, based on IP addresses.

Administrative Interface

Web servers can get very complicated to administer and one of the important aspects of a Web server is the administration of it. Early Web servers required editing the configuration files by hand and knowing what all the options did and how they worked together.

Newer Web servers can be administered via a GUI. This GUI helps to keep you from doing things that could cause problems. It also makes it easier to change different options. Netscape's administrative interface is shown in figure 1.5.

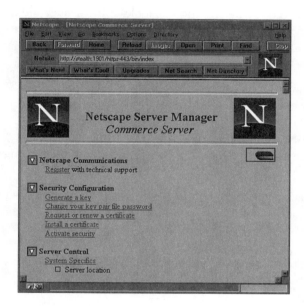

Fig. 1.5
Netscape's server manager can be used to administer the server.

How It All Works

Web servers and browsers talk using the HTTP, but how do they work? This simple example will help to explain the process that happens when a browser requests a document.

- The user sends a request to get a document. In this case, the URL is **http://www.company.com/**.

- The browser connects to the default HTTP port 80, and requests the / document by sending "GET /". Telling the server to "GET /" means to get the top document usually index.html.

- The server sees the request since it is listening on port 80, and looks at the / document. The server checks its configuration to see which document that is. Normally, DocumentRoot/DirectoryIndex.

- The server now checks to make sure there are no access restrictions on that file. If there are restrictions and the client can't get it, it returns an error status.

- If the client is allowed to get the document, then the server generates a header. This header contains the file-type, for example "text/html". This tells the client what type of file it is. It then sends the header and the file.

- The client gets the header and file, looks at the header and decides how to display the file. If the client knows how to display the file, it displays it. If the client can't handle the mime-type then an external viewer is started or the file is saved to disk.

In this example, we mentioned file types and helper applications. The next section discusses mime-types and helper applications in more detail.

Mime-types

Mime-types are used to tell a remote client what sort of file is being sent. The server usually has a file called mime-types.

This file acts as a reference to tell the server which files can be used with which applications. This is usually done by looking at the file extension. A sample mime-types file would look like:

```
application/postscript    eps ps
application/zip           zip
image/gif                 gif
video/mpeg                mpeg mpg mpe
text/html                 html htm
text/plain                txt
```

What the server does when it sends a document is attach a Content-Type header with the defined mime-type along with it. For example, if the server were sending index.html it would tell the client to display it as text/html.

The client also has a lookup table similar to the servers. It knows that it can display text/html in the browser without having to start an external viewer so it does. If however it has a file-type of video/mpeg and can't display mpeg video, it will look for an external viewer to use to display it, or prompt the user to save the file.

This allows great flexibility, especially in Intranets. For example if your company develops an application, say bar, that takes as input .foo files, you could set up a mime-type to handle them. On the server you would set up a mime-type that looked like:

```
application/bar           foo
```

On the clients, you would tell the software when it gets an application/bar mime type to use the external viewer bar. Now you have an easy way to distribute foo files to your company. ❖

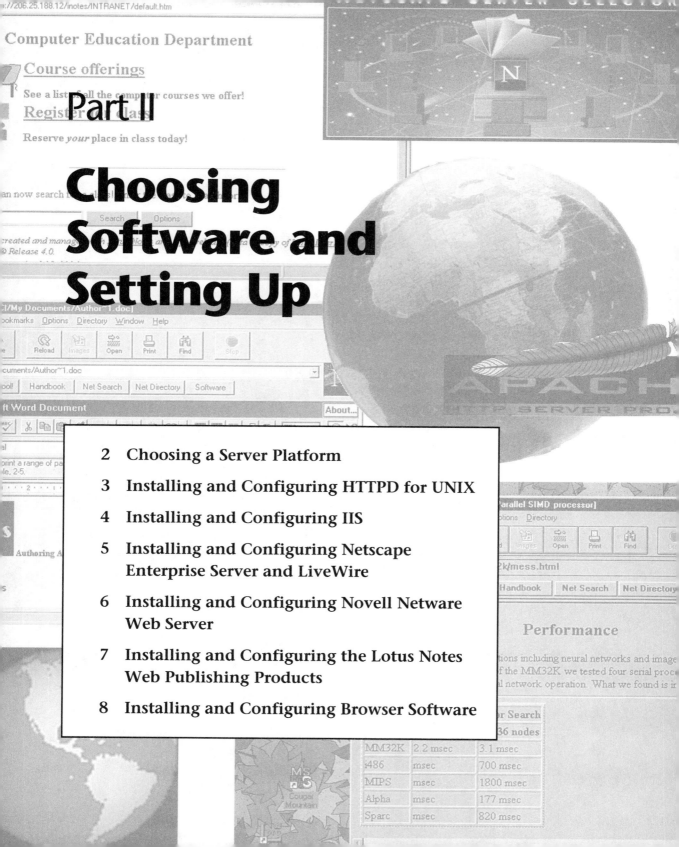

Part II

Choosing Software and Setting Up

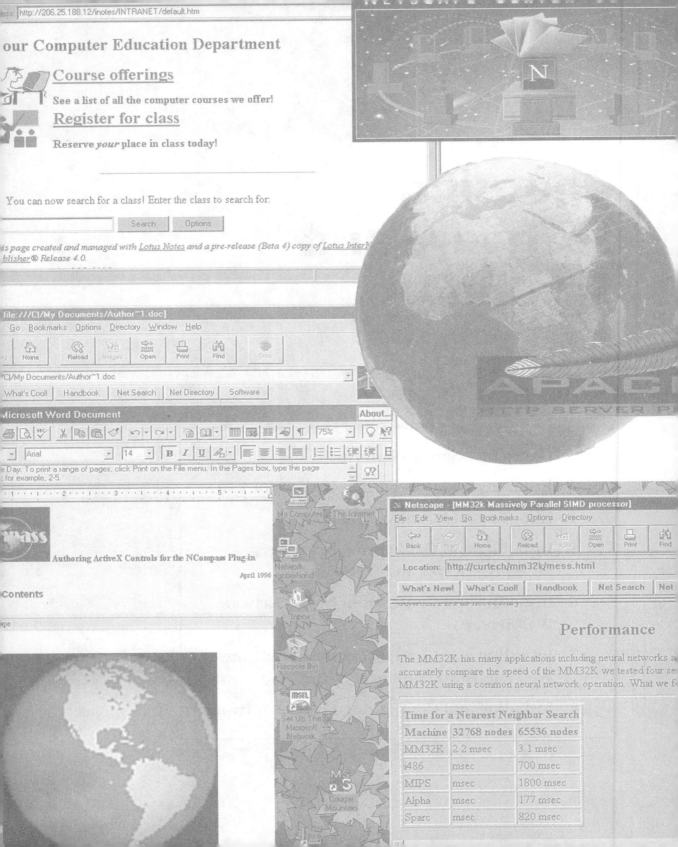

ess: http://206.25.188.12/inotes/INTRANET/default.htm

our Computer Education Department

Course offerings
See a list of all the computer courses we offer!

Register for class
Reserve *your* place in class today!

You can now search for a class! Enter the class to search for:

[   ] Search   Options

is page created and managed with *Lotus Notes* and a pre-release (Beta 4) copy of *Lotus InterN*
blisher ® Release 4.0.

---

file:///Cl/My Documents/Author~1.doc]

Go Bookmarks Options Directory Window Help

| Home | Reload | Images | Open | Print | Find | Stop |

Cl/My Documents/Author~1.doc

What's Cool! | Handbook | Net Search | Net Directory | Software

Microsoft Word Document   About...

Arial   14   B I U   75%

e Day: To print a range of pages, click Print on the File menu. In the Pages box, type the page
for example, 2-5.

---

pass

Authoring ActiveX Controls for the NCompass Plug-in
April 1996

Contents

Netscape - [MM32k Massively Parallel SIMD processor]

File Edit View Go Bookmarks Options Directory

| Back | Forward | Home | Reload | Images | Open | Print | Find |

Location: http://curtech/mm32k/mess.html

What's New! | What's Cool! | Handbook | Net Search | Net

Performance

The MM32K has many applications including neural networks a
accurately compare the speed of the MM32K we tested four se
MM32K using a common neural network operation. What we f

Time for a Nearest Neighbor Search		
Machine	32768 nodes	65536 nodes
MM32K	2.2 msec	3.1 msec
i486	msec	700 msec
MIPS	msec	1800 msec
Alpha	msec	177 msec
Sparc	msec	820 msec

CHAPTER 2
Choosing a Server Platform

In computer jargon, the word *platform* can refer to many things: The type of hardware being used, the operating system, a set of network protocols, or some combination of these.

In this book we define a computing platform as the matched set of hardware and operating system used to run selected software applications. In particular, an Intranet server is the combination of hardware, operating system and HTTP software used to run an internal Web. Because of its openness and wide availability, HTTP has been ported to almost every computer platform, including 16-bit environments like Microsoft Windows 3.x and Apple MacOS. The latter lack the memory protection and multithreading of 32-bit systems and are therefore not suitable for critical business use. But they can be a good place to learn Web server basics.

Here, the focus is on robust, 32-bit Web servers with preemptive multitasking. Three operating systems dominate this market, shown next together with the hardware they support.

Operating system	Runs on
UNIX (many brands)	RISC processors, Intel PCs, Apple Macintosh
Windows NT	Intel PCs, selected RISC machines (for example, Digital Alpha, Hewlett-Packard PA-RISC)
Novell NetWare	Intel PCs. Limited support for RISC systems

As you can see, UNIX runs on the widest variety of hardware, from high-performance RISC machines to Intel-based PCs. As an example, Sun Microsystems offers versions of its Solaris operating system for both its native SPARC processor and for Intel hardware. To compete with such diversity, Microsoft has had to step outside the Intel box, porting Windows NT to several vendors' RISC systems as well as Intel PCs. Novell, meanwhile, continues to aim its market-leading NetWare product at Intel-based networks, reserving multi-platform support for its UNIX brand (UNIXWare).

Note

RISC stands for Reduced Instruction Set Computer, a type of microprocessor design associated with high-performance UNIX workstations. Examples of popular RISC processors are Digital Alpha, Silicon General MIPS, and IBM PowerPC.

Early Intel processors such as the 80286 used a different, slower design called CISC, for Complex Instruction Set Computer. But with the addition of RISC features to its Pentium class processors, Intel has blurred the RISC/CISC distinction— in both design and performance.

In this chapter you learn about the following:

- Key concepts involved in choosing an Intranet server, with specific examples based on UNIX, NT, and NetWare platforms
- Features to look for in a Web server, including basic technology and enhancements such as server-side includes, access control, and integration with other programs
- Apache, an increasingly popular freeware server for UNIX systems
- Netscape's expanding line of commercial UNIX and NT Web server software
- Microsoft's Internet Information Server (IIS), which is bundled free with Windows NT
- The platform-specific NetWare Web Server from Novell

Note

The products mentioned in this chapter are just a sampling of the many commercial, shareware, and freeware Web servers available to meet your needs. For a complete, up-to-date listing, visit **http://www.webcompare.com/**.

Essential and Desirable Features of a Web Server

The purpose of a Web server is to respond to HTTP requests from Web clients (that is, browsers) by delivering a requested file, or executing a requested script. At a minimum, then, all Web servers must be able to interpret standard HyperText Transfer Protocol (HTTP) commands. In addition, to run programs, a server must conform to the Common Gateway Interface (CGI) standard. You can assume HTTP and CGI are present in any software calling itself a Web server.

Another essential server feature is the ability to recognize various file content types. This is necessary in order for the server to return the appropriate content-type header to the client, identifying the nature of the response. Web servers carry out this *content negotiation*, as the process is called, by mapping certain file extensions (such as .MPEG or .HTML) to standard MIME, Multipurpose Internet Mail Extensions,content types. Every Web server must accordingly maintain a configuration file showing this mapping.

Occasionally new document types become available, such as the RealAudio format for streaming audio over the Internet. A server administrator can add new types and extensions to the MIME configuration file, enabling the server to handle them. Table 2.1 shows part of a typical MIME configuration.

Table 2.1 MIME Content Types and Associated File Extensions	
MIME Type	**File Extension**
audio/basic	au snd
audio/x-aiff	aif aiff aifc
audio/wav	wav
image/gif	gif
image/jpeg	jpeg jpg jpe
image/tiff	tiff tif
text/html	html htm
text/plain	txt
text/richtext	rtx
video/mpeg	mpeg mpg mpe
video/quicktime	qt mov
video/msvideo	avi

II

Setting Up Software

All Web servers have the ability to record HTTP transactions in a log file. For now, the industry has settled on the so-called common log format. Conformance to this standard ensures logs can be read by third-party utilities, such as log analysis and reporting tools.

In addition to HTTP, CGI, MIME and logging, a Web server may offer one or more of the following enhancements:

- Server-side includes
- Access control
- Proxy and caching services
- Special database or application connectivity

Each of these is discussed briefly in the following sections.

Server-Side Includes (SSI)

SSI is an extension to standard HTTP that enables HTML *authors* to embed executable commands in their Web pages. These commands execute on the server after a page is requested, but before it's sent to the client. The embedded commands are called *server-side includes*.

> **Note**
>
> The essential reference for SSI is at NCSA's Web site: **http://hoohoo.ncsa. uiuc.edu/docs/tutorials/includes.html**.

SSI is a simple and direct form of interaction with a Web server. It makes possible in a few lines of self-explanatory code effects much trickier to achieve with CGI scripting. For instance, the following code snippet causes the current date/time to be displayed on a Web page:

```
<p>
Local intranet time is: <!--#echo="DATE_LOCAL"-->.
</p>
```

Those familiar with HTML will recognize what looks like a comment (anything set off with <!--*comment* -->) in the middle of the text. SSI command syntax is the same as that for comments, except that the keyword must be one of six allowable words and preceded by a '#' sign. SSI-capable server software also makes available a set of *SSI environment variables*, including DATE_LOCAL as shown above. Others record the IP address or domain name of the client. The complete list of standard SSI commands is posted on NCSA's Web site.

This seems like a pretty good way to greet users by name, report the current time, or check for a certain browser version. And it is. But as with most neat tricks, there's a catch.

Two catches, actually. SSI loads the Web server heavily, requiring the server to scan each document for SSI code before transporting it. On top of that, it's the least secure of all the interactive modes. SSI in effect allows users to run embedded code on the server *without restriction*.

To mitigate these risks, server software typically provides configuration options for disallowing some or all SSI commands, selectively enabling SSI by user or directory. Further, to alleviate the parsing burden on the server, a MIME configuration option is available to identify those files that should be scanned for SSI code.

As an example the following line tells the UNIX-based NCSA HTTPd server to parse files ending in *.SHTML for includes:

```
AddType text/x-server-parsed-html .shtml
```

The NCSA documentation contains additional details.

Authentication, Authorization, and Encryption

HTTP servers pose unique security problems for network administrators, stemming from the fact that file permissions have to be fairly open to enable users to access Web pages and run CGI scripts. For instance, processes launched on a server from a Web browser can delete files, send e-mail, even format disks. Scripts therefore represent a major security hole on any Web. Fortunately, techniques for closing this hole are well-documented. For a thorough treatment check out Lincoln Stein's comprehensive *WWW Security FAQ* at **http://www-genome.wi.mit.edu/WWW/faqs/www-security-faq.html**.

In addition to writing secure scripts, you may want to restrict access at the Web server based on a client's IP address or username. Most server software provides some type of *access control* mechanism by which "authorized" users receive access to protected information and others are denied.

For this to work, the server needs to ascertain two things: that a user is who she says she is, and that the user has permission to access the requested document. The process of verifying the identity of a user is called *authentication*. The process of verifying an authenticated user's rights is called *authorization*. The server software described later in this chapter can do both.

Access control is an essential facet of Intranet security, but it leaves a flank exposed. All exchanges on a Web, even those with restricted access, consist of open data transmissions on the network. It is technically trivial to monitor these transmissions, in essence neutralizing access control schemes.

Enter *encryption*. "In a multi-user setting," writes RSA Laboratories, a leading source of cryptographic tools and services, "encryption allows secure communication over an insecure channel."

Encryption works by encoding the text of a message with a key, which is just a very long number. Typical keys are 40, 64, 80 or 128 digits long, with the longer keys affording stronger encryption. In the parlance of cryptographers, a key's *strength* refers to the amount of computation required to crack it. The idea is that strong keys require more computing power to crack than can be practically harnessed.

Secure Web servers provide encryption using a particularly strong technique called *public keys*. In a public key system, everyone owns a unique pair of keys. One is called the *public key*, and is widely distributed to anyone who wants a copy. The other, called the *private key*, is kept secret.

Under this system, a person who needs to send a message to a recipient encrypts the message with the recipient's public key. So encrypted, the message can only be read by decrypting it with—you guessed it—the recipient's *private* key. This way, anyone can send a secure message, but only the intended party can read it. This solves the problem of message interception, as well as a few other subtler ones. If you plan to carry sensitive material on your Intranet, consider installing a secure Web server (one with public key encryption) from the outset.

Proxy Services

Many organizations find that the value of Intranet and Internet technology is maximized when they work together across a firewall. The *firewall* is a device, typically a router or server, that provides secure communications between private, trusted networks (such as an Intranet), and public, untrusted networks (such as the Internet). Firewalls can also mediate between workgroups *within* an organization. This might be useful, for instance, in a business with regulated and unregulated subsidiaries that share some resources, but are obligated to maintain a "Chinese wall" between others.

Importantly, the firewall can provide secure access to most Internet services, including HTTP, FTP, DNS (domain name services) and SMTP (e-mail). Each service provided in this way is called a *proxy*.

Technically, a proxy is a program that lives on the firewall and can see both sides of the interface, Intranet and Internet. Requests for outbound services from within the organization, such as a Web browser pointing at a remote URL, are caught by the proxy (HTTP, in this case) and, if allowed by the firewall's rule base, passed onto the Internet. Conversely, traffic from the Internet headed into the organization, such as e-mail, is captured by the proxy (SMTP, in this case) and, if allowed by the firewall's rule base, passed to the Intranet. A further advantage of firewall/proxy servers is that all services accessed through the firewall are logged, providing a built-in audit trail for transactions with the outside world.

Not all Web servers can act as proxies. For instance, CERN HTTPd can, but NCSA HTTPd cannot. If proxy services are important for your Intranet, add them to your checklist. Except for Apache the servers discussed next can function as proxies.

The remainder of this chapter illustrates how Web server software can provide essential and enhanced Intranet services, whether on UNIX, Windows NT or Novell NetWare.

Web Origins: UNIX HTTPd

There is no one UNIX. Rather, a welter of UNIX brands continues the tradition of open network computing begun at Bell Labs in 1969. Sun Microsystems Solaris, IBM AIX, Hewlett-Packard HP/UX, and freeware Linux issue from this common tradition.

But regardless of brand, every version of UNIX has a special relationship to the Internet, because the Internet was built on a UNIX foundation. TCP/IP is integral to the UNIX kernel, for instance, replete with the services commonly associated with cyberspace. And because the WWW began as a service of the Internet, it too has roots in UNIX soil.

As a matter of fact, the first Web server software was written to run on UNIX. From this tradition emerged two freeware programs that remain popular today: NCSA HTTPd, from the University of Illinois, and CERN HTTPd, maintained at MIT by the W3 Consortium.

Most commercial Web servers derive from these early programs. Netscape's server line and Microsoft IIS, for instance, build on NCSA HTTPd, adding secure transaction and proxy support. The freeware Apache HTTPd, too, is a descendant that aims to improve on the NCSA original. The next section will show you how.

Native to UNIX: The Apache Project

> **Note**
>
> See how popular your favorite server is on the Netcraft survey report, available on the WWW at **http://www.netcraft.co.uk/Survey/Reports/**.

Since August 1995 Netcraft, a British Web and network consultancy, has conducted a monthly survey of Web server software usage on Internet-connected computers. The May 1996 results show an astonishing 30 percent of 193,000 survey respondents using some version of Apache HTTPd. (NCSA HTTPd accounts for the next largest chunk at 25 percent, followed by Netscape, with a 15 percent share of respondents.)

The Apache project was organized in March 1995 in an attempt to answer some of the concerns regarding active development of a public domain HTTP server. According to the project's Web site at <http://www.apache.org/>, "the goal of the project is to provide a secure, efficient and extensible server that provides HTTP services in sync with the current HTTP standards." The home page is shown in figure 2.1.

Fig. 2.1
The Apache Project's home page.

The software runs on UNIX and builds directly on the NCSA source code. It therefore meets conventional Web standards. Apache aims to provide superior speed and stability over the NCSA server, as well as enhanced features. Most of these are technical, such as the use of UNIX-standard DBM databases for authentication to improve server performance with large number of authorized users.

> **Note**
>
> The online documentation for Apache SSI complements the NCSA specification. See **http://www.apache.org/docs/mod_include.html**.

Apache supports SSI in the same manner as NCSA HTTPd. Security is also similar, with improvements as noted previously. The current production release (1.0.5) does not support encryption or proxies. A general API to allow native program interactions is under development.

From the decision-maker's standpoint, Apache is a better NCSA server with a large and growing following. Both are currently free. The Apache project, however, reports that NCSA is in the process of changing its license terms, and makes a point of stating that Apache will never charge for use or redistribution. If low cost is prominent on your checklist, this may be a selling point.

Offsetting this advantage somewhat is the lack of product support for freeware in general. Apache is supported mainly through the *comp.infosystems.www.servers.unix* newsgroup. The software comes in source code form; you must compile at the UNIX command line. Apache will therefore be most suitable in shops with good UNIX skills, where the sweat equity required in lieu of a purchase is not too burdensome.

Netscape on the Server

> **Note**
>
> Complete information on Netscape's server platforms is available at **http://home.netscape.com/comprod/server_central/index.html**.

II

Setting Up Software

The company best known for its market-leading Web browser also has an impressive line of server software. Netscape recently reoriented its server offerings to meet a broader spectrum of business needs. All products are available for both major UNIX platforms and Windows NT.

At the top of the line is Netscape Enterprise Server, a high performance, secure Web server intended as a hub for client/server application systems. Out of the box the server comes integrated with a full-text search engine and multi-user version control.

On the World Wide Web Netscape has earned a reputation for driving the HTML standard forward with its popular, proprietary extensions. The same thing is happening with Netscape's HTTP implementation. For instance, in addition to standard server-side includes, Enterprise Server supports a range of server-parsed enhancements. These are suitable for adding dynamic data to Web pages, such as live stock quotes, weather data, or manufacturing data from an assembly line. Netscape's vision is clearly to make the Web server a real-time decision support resource.

The Netscape Server API (NSAPI) is a means of extending or customizing the core functionality of the Netscape Web server. NSAPI provides a scaleable, efficient mechanism for building interfaces between the HTTP server and back-end applications.

Note

In its white paper, "The NSAPI versus the CGI Interface," Netscape points out many NSAPI advantages, such as the ability to customize server behavior regarding on-the-fly document translation, non-standard encryption, or custom error handling. Netscape's paper is online at **http://home.netscape.com/newsref/std/nsapi_vs_cgi.html**.

Netscape's emphatic point concerning the implementation of NSAPI is that it *modularizes* their server product, in the spirit of user-configurable software. While Netscape has no intention of giving away its source code, NSAPI offers users almost the same discretion in tailoring product behavior. All of Netscape's servers support NSAPI. NSAPI, in turn, supports JavaScript on the server, making possible ODBC connections to relational databases.

In the areas of authentication, authorization and encryption, few vendors can rival Netscape, which drafted many of the Web security standards in current use. These include Secure Sockets Layer (SSL), a Netscape proposal widely adopted for Internet commerce.

Netscape Proxy Server, a peer product to Enterprise Server, enables companies to optimize Web performance across network boundaries, both Internet and internal. Proxy Server provides the basic gateway and security services mentioned earlier. In addition, Netscape has added replication to this server, making it a powerful tool for segmenting and controlling access to large webs. Automated replication is an important capability for distributed data systems. It accounts for a much of the appeal of groupware products such as Lotus Notes. By offering replication at the Web server, Netscape further marginalizes these traditional venues.

Responding to the demand for integrated solutions, Netscape bundles Enterprise Server and Proxy Server with other Internet software in a package called SuiteSpot. The server suite also comes with Netscape's new Web development platform, LiveWire Pro.

For smaller installations Netscape offers FastTrack Server, optimized for easy setup and maintenance. The $295 product complements its enterprise-strength siblings at the workgroup or departmental level. FastTrack Server supports secure Web communications through the Secure Sockets Layer (SSL). The server also supports NSAPI, JavaScript and ODBC, in keeping with Netscape's Internet Application Framework.

Besides these recent releases, Netscape still supports its original product line, including Netscape Communications Server and Commerce Server. However, these employ previous-generation technology and should not be considered for new projects.

Gaining Fast: Windows NT Webs

Microsoft was late to market with the Internet. Server authors such as Rob Denny (now at O'Reilly & Associates) ported NCSA to Windows long before February 1996, when Microsoft finally released its Internet Information Server (IIS).

But timing is a second-order effect when a giant jumps in the pool. The splash is what gets your attention.

IIS is creating a splash for three reasons. First, Microsoft is giving it away through its WWW site at <www.microsoft.com>. As competitors have been

II

Setting Up Software

quick to point out, Microsoft's fee-based support offsets the zero initial cost; but a freebie is compelling nonetheless. Second, IIS was designed from the ground up to run under Windows NT. The week of its release, reviewers were already acclaiming its superb performance, a consequence of single-minded design. Third, IIS bundles many of the tools needed to implement high-functioning Intranets out of the box. With most Web servers, the onus is on the developer to assemble a tool kit, learn multiple languages, and integrate them all to the customer's satisfaction. With IIS, most of this is turnkey.

These advantages come with the same Faustian bargain as all Microsoft products—namely, vendor-dependence. Where the free market (acting on the open technology of UNIX) brought about a rainbow of variants, there is only one Windows NT. And it has the assembled might of a $2B software giant and its army of VARs and technical partners behind it.

As an IT decision-maker assessing platforms, your chief concern is whether NT-based Web servers will meet your needs. The answer is that technically, they are at least the equal of UNIX httpd, although NT employs different methods to achieve the same ends. On the other hand, deciding whether the Microsoft Way is a good fit for your organization is "left as an exercise for the reader."

Intranets Based on Windows NT

Make no mistake: buying into IIS is a fork in the road. Many of the tools and standards synonymous with Web technology under UNIX—which is to say, canonical standards—are weakly supported or non-existent in the NT world.

For instance, the language of choice for many programming tasks under UNIX is Perl, a powerful and concise scripting language. While versions of the Perl interpreter have been written for many non-UNIX platforms, including NT, they tend to have bugs and lack key features of the UNIX original. Kinks like this are often smoothed with time. But the problem remains that Perl is *a UNIX tool*, requiring mastery of *UNIX* syntax and programming concepts (such as regular expressions) largely irrelevant to NT. So, while NT Perl may be a useful stepping stone for *UNIX* programmers making the leap to Windows, it will never be the language of choice for IIS.

> **Note**
>
> Investigate NT Perl yourself by downloading it from **http://www.process.com/ resource/perl.htp** (version 4.036, the classic) or **http://www.perl.hip.com/** (v5.001, the latest).

If this were the only gap between IIS and *UNIX* HTTP, the two roads would run much closer. As it turns out, however, Perl dysfunction is just a symptom of the non-standard way all Windows-based HTTP servers implement the Web's programming interface, CGI.

Windows CGI ("Win-CGI") is Microsoft's native interface, that enables Web forms to launch processes and display result sets. The specification for Windows CGI v1.3a begins with the following disclaimer:

> "It is not intended for this specification to enter the Internet standards track, as it is platform-specific to Microsoft Windows 95 and Windows NT." [Courtesy: Rob Denny]

Essentially Microsoft is writing a new standard in its own image. This won't come as a surprise to anyone who has watched IT vendors duke it out for the last ten years. Leveraging the low cost of open technology to dominate the market with proprietary enhancements is a winning strategy. It's precisely what Netscape has done with its browser—all those <FONT> and <CENTER> tags run roughshod over the HTML standards. Microsoft is merely following the leader with its own (different, naturally) browser extensions. The same holds true for its effort to redefine CGI.

> **Note**
>
> Anyone serious about creating an NT-based Intranet should read Rob Denny's Win-CGI specification, available online at **http://solo.dc3.com/wsdocs/32demo/windows-cgi.html**.

The Power of Proprietary Thinking

For some organizations, the idea that Microsoft will be the one-stop place to shop is comforting. Open standards put a lot of responsibility on the customer to understand technology components and integrate them. In an age of information overload, proprietary thinking may be just what the doctor ordered.

NT-based servers have some powerful features over their UNIX cousins. We'll focus on Microsoft IIS here, but many of these features are available with other products as well.

> **Note**
>
> For a fair-minded overview of the offerings, consult the list of Win32 servers and features online at **http://www.webcompare.com/server-win.html**.

The virtues of IIS fall into two categories: administrative ease and open database access. Setting up an NT-based server is straightforward. You simply follow the instructions, filling out a sequence of online forms while the server does the hard work behind the scenes. This is a distinct advantage over UNIX-based servers, which usually require some character-based dialogue via the command line. An NT server can be maintained graphically as well.

Enabling users to access data distributed throughout the enterprise is the Holy Grail of networking, and the IIS makes a real contribution towards this goal. It does this in two ways. First, the proprietary Win-CGI interface described above provides a pipeline to so-called Rapid Application Development (RAD) tools like Visual Basic and PowerBuilder. These programming environments bring with them rich libraries of components that solve many standard problems, such as exchanging data with a database. In addition to this, IIS comes with its own Internet Database Connector (IDC).

IDC enables the developer to create templates for data access and retrieval. The problem with Web-to-database connectivity so far has been the need to maintain custom scripts for formatting query results in HTML tables. IDC automates this labor-intensive process. Furthermore, in conjunction with other IIS enhancements (namely, Microsoft's proprietary ISAPI), IDC promises to improve database access performance as well.

On balance, Microsoft's IIS is a very strong product that can solve major Intranet problems, albeit with proprietary solutions. For the price (free), it's well worth comparing to other NT-based servers.

Leveraging the Novell LAN: NetWare Web Server

> **Note**
>
> For more information on NetWare Web Server, visit Novell's Web site at **http:// iamg.novell.com/iamg/internet/nws.htm**.

If your enterprise LAN is based on Netware 4.1, you need to consider Novell's Web Server for Netware. (Novell has no plans to support earlier versions of Netware). Implemented as a set of NetWare Loadable Modules (NLMs), NetWare Web Server can host HTML files natively, eliminating the need for a UNIX or NT platform. It ships with a native Perl interpreter and features CGI support, access control and logging.

In its current release (2.1), Web Server for Netware lacks a couple of desirable features, such as the ability to support multiple IP addresses on one server ("multi-homing") and proxy support. These will come, according to Novell.

Where the product shines, not surprisingly, is in the area of network integration. The Web Server authenticates users against NetWare Directory Services (NDS) simplifying security administration. The Web Server also supports standard NCSA-style Web security. SMTP gateways are available from Novell and other vendors to enable the Web server to process "mailto:" requests.

Many of the features for which NetWare is justly famous carry over to the Web server. For instance, you can ensure scalability in your Intranet—the ability to add processors without replacing whole machines—by hosting it on a NetWare 4.1 Symmetric MultiProcessing (SMP) platform. Alternatively, if your primary need is 24-hour, 7-day availability with no downtime, you can run the Web server on NetWare SFT III, Novell's highly rated fault-tolerant platform.

> ### Note
>
> Several companies besides Novell make server software for NetWare. Two you may wish to consider are:
>
> American Internet Corporation (Bedford MA). AIC offers SiteBuilder™, a complete Web server solution for NetWare with features similar to Novell's entry. However, SiteBuilder runs on NetWare 3.11 or later, good news if you run a legacy LAN. Find out more at <http://www.american.com/>.
>
> Electronic Dimensions (Australia), makers of Edime™ WebWare™, a line of Web servers for NetWare. Distinguishing features include powerful non-standard extensions to SSI, access to server serial ports for Web-based process control, automatic formatting of database query results as HTML tables. An Enterprise Version adds support for SQL and EDI (Electronic Data Interchange) transactions. For more information consult Edime's Web site at **http://www.edime.com.au/webware.html**.

## CHAPTER 3

Installing and Configuring HTTPD for UNIX

If your site is running UNIX and looking for a free Web server, then you are probably looking for Apache. Apache is currently the most popular free server for UNIX machines. It is also a drop in replacement for the Web server from NCSA.

Apache runs on most versions of UNIX and comes in source code form so it can be easily compiled for other platforms. Having source code also makes it easy for a programmer to make changes to the program.

In this chapter, you will learn the following:

- The hardware and software requirements
- Where to get Apache
- How to build Apache from source code
- How to configure the Apache server
- How to test and troubleshoot the Web server

Apache

Apache is a high performance UNIX based httpd server. It is developed by the Apache Group and is available free of charge under the normal free software terms.

Apache is a drop in replacement for NCSA httpd server. If you are already running NCSA, you can simply compile Apache and replace the httpd binary from NCSA with the new Apache binary.

Apache comes in source form and can be compiled on many platforms such as, AIX, HPUX, IRIX, Linux, SCO UNIX, SunOS, NeXT, BSDI, FreeBSD, and Solaris.

There is also a version of Apache for OS/2. It is available from SoftLink Services (**http://www.slink.com**). There is also a version of Apache that supports Secure Sockets Layer, called ApacheSSL. It is available from Community Connexion (**http://apachessl.c2.org**).

Apache is currently one of the leading UNIX Web servers. NCSA httpd can be installed using almost the same instructions as the Apache httpd. These instructions along with the NCSA documentation will allow you to install that server as well. There are also other UNIX Web servers, that have similar instructions for installing, by using this chapter in conjunction with the instructions that come with the other servers you should have no problem installing them.

You can download Apache from many sites including:

- **http://www.apache.org**
- **http://sunsite.doc.ic.ac.uk/packages/**
- **http://www.ukweb.com/apache/**

Once you have the file saved, you need to unzip and untar it to get at the files. The filename should be apache_1.1.tar.gz. To unzip the file you use the program gunzip. The syntax is "gunzip apache_1.1.tar.gz", this will create a file called apache_1.1.tar. This tar file can be untarred using "tar xvf apache_1.1.tar". This will extract the files into a directory called apache_1.1. CD.

> **Note**
>
> Some WWW browsers can automatically unzip a file for you. If you don't have a .gz file, check to see if it is already unzipped.
>
> Gunzip is available from most GNU mirrors. The main GNU site is **ftp://prep.ai.mit.edu/pub/gnu**.

Compiling Apache

It is recommended that you use gcc for compilation though any ANSI C compiler should work. If you need gcc, it is available from the GNU archives at **ftp://prep.ai.mit.edu/pub/gnu**.

The first step in building Apache is to edit the configuration file. To start, cd into the src directory and copy "Configuration.tmpl" to "Configuration." This file contains compiler directives and other Makefile lines, such as CFLAGS, CC, and LFLAGS. These allow you to compile in options that are machine specific. This file is commented very well and by reading, you can easily set the right options for your system.

Module Definitions

After the Makefile rules come the module definitions. Apache is very customizable and you can add or remove modules that you don't want. By removing any unused modules you can have a very small, fast server.

The different modules vary depending on the release, but for the current release 1.1, the following basic modules are present:

- mime_module. This module is used to allow Apache to handle mime types.
- access_module. This is used to provide access restriction by IP address.
- auth_module. This module is used to perform basic authentication.
- negotiation_module. This module allows Apache to perform content negotiation.
- includes_module. This allows you to use Server Side Includes (SSI).
- dir_module. This module allows directory handling.
- cgi_module. This module is for CGI support.
- userdir_module. This is used to allow users to have HTTP directories.
- alias_module. This allows directory aliasing.
- common_log_module. This is used to handle the common log format.

These basic modules should probably be left in unless you are sure you do not need them. There are also some other useful modules that can be commented out if not being used. These include:

- asis_module. Used for ASIS files. ASIS files are files that should be sent just as they are. They can be used to send different HTTP headers.
- imap_module. This allows server side imagemaps.
- action_module. This is used to allow the server to perform certain actions on a set of files. For example you could force Apache to append a footer to every html file. See also the Action and AddHandler directives in the srm.conf file.
- cern_meta_module. This can be used to send additional HTTP headers.
- env_module. This is used to pass environment variables to scripts such as CGI scripts or Server Side Includes.

II

Setting Up Software

- cookies_module. This is used to handle Netscape style cookies. Cookies can be used to track status through a Web site or to store information on a user.

- status_module. This is used to allow the server to display details on how well it is performing and what it is doing. You might also want to add DSTATUS in the Configuration file.

- dbm_auth_module. This is used to allow authorization using DBM files instead of ASCII files.

- db_auth_module. This is another authorization file format.

- msql_auth_module. Yet another authorization file format. This allows you to store the passwords and usernames in a Microsoft SQL server.

- agent_log_module. Used to be compatible with NCSA. This adds the user_agent to the log file.

- referrer_log_module. Also used to keep compatible with NCSA. This logs the HTTP_REFERRER variable to the log file.

There are also experimental modules. These are probably okay if you are running a test server and like debugging programs. For a server that people are depending on though these probably should be used sparingly.

Note

Once you define which modules you want, the defaults will work if you don't want to worry about them yet, you need to run Configure. This makes changes to the Makefile and creates a file called modules.c which is where the modules get included. One of the popular features of Apache is the ability to add new modules. This should be done only be someone who is very familiar with the "C" language and how the server works. There is very good documentation on this on the Apache Groups Web server, **http://www.apache.org/**.

After Configure finishes, typing **make** will build Apache. This may take a few minutes. If you get any errors during the compiling or linking phase you will need to fix them before trying to run Apache.

Once Apache finishes building you should end up with a binary file called httpd. If you are switching from NCSA httpd to Apache you can simply copy this file over your existing one and restart.

> **Note**
>
> A simple test to make sure httpd built OK is to run httpd -v. This should tell you what version it is. If this doesn't work, stop and try to find out why the program doesn't work before going further.

If you are installing Apache from scratch, there are a few things you need to do before you can test it out.

- Create the ServerRoot directory. This is usually /usr/local/etc/httpd. You need to create the following directories under that tree. "conf," "htdocs," "cgi-bin," "logs", and "icons."

- Copy the files in the conf distribution directory to the ServerRoot/conf files. Rename them so they don't have the "-dist" ending. You should end up with access.conf, httpd.conf, mime.types, and srm.conf.

- Edit httpd.conf and set the different attributes such as port number and user. These are all covered in the Configuration section. Even more detail is available in the Apache documentation.

- Edit access.conf. If you are using a ServerRoot other than /usr/local/etc/ httpd, you will need to make changes here since this tells Apache which services are allowed for each directory. It normally sets standard services to the directories under /usr/local/etc/httpd.

- You may also need to edit srm.conf if you aren't using the default ServerRoot. This file tells Apache how filesystem directories map to Web space. It defaults to having DocumentRoot set to /usr/local/etc/httpd/ htdocs. You will also need to check any aliases that by default point to directories in /usr/local/etc/httpd.

Testing It Out

First create a "Home Page". This is simply an HTML file called index.html in the ServerRoot/htdocs directory. If you aren't familiar with HTML, then you can simply add this to the index.html file:

```
<HTML>
<HEAD>
<Title>It works!</TITLE>
</HEAD>
<BODY>
Apache is running!!!!
</BODY?
</HTML>
```

Start httpd, unless you changed the port in the httpd.conf file, it will run on port 80. This will require you to be logged in as root. If you receive any errors, go back and check your configuration files. Also check to make sure your httpd is running. On SunOS and BSD based UNIXes you can use "ps -aux | grep httpd" to see if the process is still running. On SystemV based UNIX versions you might need to use "ps -aef | grep httpd".

If it seems to be running OK, then point your Web browser to **http:// server/**. You should see your index.html file displayed in your browser.

> **Note**
>
> If you don't have a WWW browser you can test out the server using telnet. Simply "telnet server 80" and type "GET /" after you are connected. This should return your index.html file to you and close the connection.

Apache logs errors to ServerRoot/logs/error_log. If you have problems you should check in this file to try to find the cause. ServerRoot normally is /usr/local/etc/httpd.

Configuration

In addition to the compile time module definitions and other compile time options, there are many runtime options that you need to decide on. These include running as a standalone server or via inetd, where the server should reside, how many processes to start, and many other options.

These options are covered in the next few sections. They are split up by file to make it easier to reference later.

access.conf file

The access.conf file defines what features are available to the users. It is defined on a directory by directory basis using directives.

A directory directive is made up of several lines. The first line must contain:

```
<Directory [directory/name]>
```

[directory/name] is the absolute path to the directory, for example /usr/local/ etc/httpd/htdocs.

The directory directive ends with a line that looks like:

```
</Directory>
```

Inside these directives can be Options or Limit.

Options can be one of the following:

- None. No special options are available.
- All. All options except Multiviews are available.
- Indexes. This creates an automatic index of the directory, if the index.html file is missing.
- Includes. This allows files in this directory to have Server Side Includes.
- FollowSymLinks. Normally apache doesn't follow symbolic links. Using this option tells Apache to follow them.
- ExecCGI. Allow CGI programs to be run from this directory.
- MultiViews. This is used along with content negotiation to allow different views. This can be used to allow for different languages.

The Limit directive allows you to limit who can get what from this directory. This can be used to limit which IP addresses have access to this directory.

The Limit directive must start with a line like:

```
<Limit [access]>
```

[access] can be GET, PUT, POST, or DELETE.

The limit directive must end with:

```
</Limit>
```

Limit directives can contain:

- order. The order to parse the directive. The first match is used so the order can be important, if for example you allow 123.123.123.* and deny 123.123.123.4. You would want the order to be deny allow.
- allow. Which hosts are allowed access. These can be by hostname or IP address. Matching is supported so that .company.com can be used to match any machine in the company.com network. You can also use none or all.
- deny. Which hosts are denied access. This uses the same syntax and the same restrictions as the allow directive.

XBITHACK is used to tell Apache that text/html files with the owner execute bit set to be server parsed. To use XBITHACK you must have compiled with the -DXBITHACK flag set. There are three different options to XBITHACK:

- Off. This disables XBITHACK.
- On. This enables XBITHACK.

II

Setting Up Software

- Full. This tells Apache to send a Last-Modified header if the group execute bit is set.

AllowOveride tells Apache which options can be overridden by the .htaccess file. Uses the same names as Options. This can be used with the AuthConfig directive to allow authentication files and methods to be overridden on a per directory basis.

httpd.conf

The httpd.conf file describes the server process and other global parameters. It has directives for:

- ServerType. This is either standalone or inetd. If it is set to inetd then you need to define it in the /etc/inetd.conf file otherwise you need to define the Port directive. Inetd can be used to automatically start the server and can also be used with security packages, such as TCP_Wrappers, to restrict access and perform additional logging.

- Port. This is the port that httpd listens on. By default this is 80 but may be changed for security reasons.

- HostnameLookups. This is either on or off. If it is on, Apache logs client names, otherwise it logs the IP address. If your machine is really busy, this may cause a strain on your DNS servers, shutting this off may give you better performance.

- User. The UID httpd runs as. It must initially run as root to open port 80 but then switches to this user. For security reasons you should set this to a separate ID that basically has no permissions.

- Group. The group ID httpd will run under.

- ServerAdmin. This is the e-mail address of the server administrator. This is where problem notification should go.

- ServerRoot. This is the root directory for everything related to httpd. Normally /usr/local/etc/httpd. If you change this, you also need to make changes to srm.conf and access.conf

- BindAddress. This is used to tell Apache which IP address to listen on. It is used to support virtual hosts. * is valid and means listen on all interfaces.

- ErrorLog. Where the error log messages should go. If it is a relative name, (no leading /) then it is assumed to be relative from ServerRoot. Defaults to logs/error_log.

- TransferLog. Similar to ErrorLog. Tells Apache where the transfer log file should go. Defaults to logs/access_log.

- PidFile. Similar to ErrorLog. Tells Apache where to log its process ID number (pid). Defaults to logs/httpd.pid.

- ScoreBoardFile. This is used for internal process information. Defaults to log/apache_status.

- ServerName. This can be used to tell Apache to use a different hostname. For example to return www.server.com instead of the actual hostname. Must be a valid, fully qualified domain name (FQDN).

- CacheNegotiatedDocs. If this is uncommented, then any documents that have been negotiated can be cached. Normally negotiated documents aren't cached.

- Timeout. This is how long to wait for a send or receive message before giving up and timing out. Default is 400. If this is not in the file, the compile time default is 1200.

- KeepAlive. This tells Apache how many times a client can request to keep the connection open. Default is 5. If you set this to zero, then the KeepAlive option is disabled.

- MinSpareServers. Apache tries to keep a certain amount of servers running to keep up with sudden increases. This is the least amount of servers that will be waiting for a connection. Default is 5.

- MaxSpareServers. This is the maximum amount of spare servers that will be kept around. Default is 10.

- MaxClients. This is used to limit how many httpd processes there can be. This can help to keep your machine from being slowed to a crawl by a denial of service attack. Default is 150. If you expect more then 150 simultaneous users, this needs to be changed.

- MaxRequestsPerChild. Normally a child process will run forever but some machines have memory leaks that will eventually consume all available memory and crash the system. This tells Apache how many requests a process can handle before it is killed. Default is 30.

- ProxyRequests. This is either on or off. If it is on and uncommented, then Apache acts as a proxy server. Otherwise it does not.

- CacheRoot. This is used to enable caching as well as proxy support. This is the root directory for the cache files. Normally disabled.

II

Setting Up Software

- CacheSize. This is the size in Kb that the cache can use. Defaults to 5Kb. If you use caching you probably want to change this to something more reasonable like 100,000. (100MB)

- CacheGcInterval. The amount of time, in hours, before garbage collection runs. Garbage collection is used to keep the cache clean. Default is 4.

- CacheMaxExpire. This is the maximum time in hours before removing a document from the cache. Defaults to 24.

- CacheLastModifiedFactor. This is used to determine the expires date from the last modified date. The default is 0.1.

- CacheDefaultExpire. This is the default number of hours to keep a document in cache. Default is 1.

- Listen. Used to tell Apache to listen on another port as well as the default. Can be a port number or an IP address:port combination.

- Virtual Host. This is used to have one Apache server act as a server for different machines or domains. Anything that is valid in httpd.conf or srm.conf can be used in here.

Note

Virtual hosting is used by many ISPs to allow companies who don't have a WWW server to have a virtual one. This would allow one machine to be configured with multiple IP addresses and multiple Apache servers running and acting as though they were separate machines.

Here is a sample VirtualHost directive:

```
<VirtualHost virtual.company.com>
ServerAdmin webmaster@virtual.company.com
DocumentRoot /virtual/httpd/htdocs
ServerName virtual.company.com
</VirtualHost>
```

The first line tells Apache this directive applies to **virtual.company.com**. This is the address that the request came in from. See BindAddress. The ServerAdmin for this server is **webmaster@virtual.company.com**. The DocumentRoot is /virtual/httpd/htdocs and the ServerName should be **virtual.company.com**.

---

srm.conf

The srm.conf file is used to tell Apache how to handle requests. It defines such things as user HTTP directories, icon definitions, and languages.

Some of the directives in srm.conf are:

- DocumentRoot. This tells Apache where to look when someone references /. It is usually /usr/local/etc/httpd/htdocs.

- UserDir. This is the name of the directory in users home directories look at when they are referenced. User home directories are normally referenced with a URL like "http://www.server.com/~username." The default name is public_html. So files in public_html in richc's home directory can be retrieved using the base URL "http://www.server.com/~richc."

- DirectoryIndex. This is used as the default page or index of a directory. If this is not present the user gets a list of the files in the directory. If this page exists, it is displayed. If there is more then one DirectoryIndex, they need to be separated by spaces. Apache will try to access each one starting at the first one and going until one is found.

- FancyIndexing is either on or off. This defines how the index is created if DirectoryIndex does not exist. Figure 3.1 shows an index using fancy indexing on.

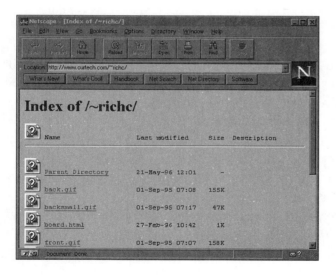

Fig. 3.1
Fancy indexing can be used to show more details.

- AddIcon. This is used to tell Apache what image to place next to the file to show what type of file it is. This is only used if FancyIndexing is on. The syntax is AddIcon [path/to/image] [ext1 ext2], for example AddIcon /images/text.gif .txt.

- DefaultIcon is the image file used if there is no AddIcon definition for a file type.

- AddDescription. This is a short text description of a file. It is used by the server when generating fancy indexes. The syntax is AddDescription "Descriptive text" filename.

- ReadmeName. This is the file that Apache will look for to use as the readme file. The syntax is ReadmeName filename. The default is README.

- HeaderName. This is the file that Apache prepends to directory indexes. The syntax is HeaderName filename. The default is HEADER.

- IndexIgnore. This is a set of filenames and wildcards, which should not show up in a server generated index.

- AccessFileName. This file allows users to override options set in the access.conf file. The default is .htaccess.

- DefaultType. If Apache can't figure out what type of file is being sent, it will send this mime-type. The default is text/plain.

- AddLanguage. This is used in content-negotiation. It defines which file extensions go with which languages. The syntax is AddLanguage [keyword] [suffix].

- LanguagePriority. This is also used in content-negotiation and is consulted in case there is a tie between two languages. This should be a list of languages, separated by spaces, starting with the most preferred.

- Redirect. This is used to tell clients that a document has moved. The syntax is Redirect [fakename] [url].

- Alias. This allows an alias for a filename. The syntax is Alias [fakename] [realname].

- ScriptAlias. This is an alias for a script directory. It uses the same syntax as Alias.

- AddType. Can be used to get around editing mime-types or to force a file to be a specific type.

- AddHandler. This can be used to pass off files with certain extensions to handlers. These handlers can be custom ones or standard handlers.

- Action. This can be used in conjunction with AddHandler to perform common functions to a file. For example to append a footer to html files you could add:

```
AddHandler footer-action html
Action footer-action /cgi-bin/footer
```

This tells Apache when it sees a file with a "html" extension to also run the Action command which is "/cgi-bin/footer".

- ErrorDocument. This directive is used to customize error messages. They can be handled by plain text, local redirects, or external redirects.

Mime-Types

The mime-types file maps extensions to file types. These file types are then used on the client to assign a viewer to be used. There are many "standard" mime-types and you may never need to add a new one. If you want to add a custom mime-type, it is very easy to add one to the mime-types files.

The format for the mime-types file is simple:

```
File-type    file-extension1 file-extension2
```

Adding a new mime-type is as simple as adding a line to mime-types and re-starting the server. For example to add a mime-type called "foo" that deals with files ending with ".bar" you would add the following line to mime-types:

```
application/foo    bar
```

You would also need to configure the client software to start an external viewer to view the .bar files. This is done differently on different browsers but most are either controlled by a GUI or a mime-types file.

Running Apache

Once Apache is installed and configured there is not much to do to keep it running. It must be started when the machine boots, the log files should be checked and any problems troubleshot and fixed.

This section will cover these topics and help to give you an overview of how to run a Web server.

Starting Apache

It is possible with most systems to have programs start automatically when the machine starts up. In UNIX there are three basic ways:

- Inittab
- RC Scripts
- Inetd

These ways may not all be available on your version of UNIX but at least one of them should be.

The first way we will discuss is starting the server via inittab. Inittab is a file init used to start programs at certain run levels. The most common levels are 1 or S for single user mode, 0 for halted, and 2 for multiuser mode. Init is the first program started and always has the process id of 1.

The inittab file normally consists of lines made up of:

```
id:rstate:action:process
```

id is a unique identifier. state is the run level that the process should run in. If a process is not defined for a run level, it is terminated. A process can be defined to be run in multiple run levels by adding another level. Multiple run levels are not separated.

The action field tells init how to run the process. Common action fields are:

- respawn. If the process dies it is restarted by init. If the process is running nothing happens. Once the process is started init continues its work.
- wait. When init starts this process it waits until the process completes before continuing on. The process is only run once.
- once. The process is started but not waited for. Once it finishes it is not restarted.

The process is the program and arguments that should be run.

To start Apache from inittab we need to add a line for run level 2. We can use the respawn or once action. A normal inittab line would look like:

```
as:2:once:/usr/local/etc/httpd
```

It is also possible to start Apache from RC scripts. These are commonly located in /etc/rc.local or in a separate directory under /etc, such as /etc/rc2.d.

These scripts are run at bootup. To start Apache using RC scripts like /etc/rc.local you would simply add a line at the end of the file such as:

```
/usr/local/etc/httpd
```

If your system has separate directories, you need to create a start script. The directories are named using the syntax rc#.d, where # is replaced with the run level. In the case of Apache the run level directory would be /etc/rc2.d. The script names usually begin with S and a number, followed by a name. One example would be S99Apache. The scripts are run by numerical order so you can place the script wherever you need to in the startup process.

To start Apache with a script you would create a file called /etc/rc.d/ S99Apache. In it would be:

```
#!/bin/sh
/usr/local/etc/httpd
```

The last way to start Apache automatically is via inetd. Inetd is a process that listens on network ports, when it gets a connection it starts the correct server. Inetd looks at a configuration file called inetd.conf. This is usually in /etc or /etc/inet.

The lines in inetd.conf consist of comments or server lines. The server line has a number of fields that are separated by spaces or tabs. They may vary from UNIX to UNIX but they are usually:

- service-name. The service name as found in /etc/services.
- endpoint-type. This is either stream, dgram, raw, seqpacket or tli.
- protocol. This is usually either tcp or udp.
- wait-status. This is usually nowait. Occasionally if a program holds the socket for a specific period of time it will be wait.
- uid. This is the user id the server should run as.
- server-program. This is the program name.
- server-arguments. This is the program name followed by the arguments.

To get Apache to run from inetd we also need to look at the services file. This is usually in /etc or /etc/inet. It consists of lines of the form:

```
service-name  port/protocol   aliases
```

Service name is the name of the service. This is used by inetd and must be spelled the same in both the inetd.conf file and the services file. Port/protocol is the port number and the protocol, for example 80/tcp. Aliases are other names the service might be known as.

In the services file we need to add a line that looks like:

```
httpd    80/tcp
```

In inetd.conf we need to add the following line:

```
httpd    stream  tcp  nowait  nobody /usr/local/etc/httpd/httpd
httpd
```

Note

Don't forget to change the httpd.conf file in DocumentRoot. The ServerType directive must be changed to inetd.

Troubleshooting Apache

Occasionally, Apache will have problems running. These problems are often related to other processes and rebooting the machine eliminates them. Other times though rebooting either is not possible or simply doesn't work. This section will cover some common error messages and how to fix them.

- Browsers can't connect to the server. The first step in troubleshooting this is to make sure Apache is running. The ps command is used to look for a process called httpd. For example on SunOS you would use the command ps -auxw | grep httpd. System V based UNIXes might need to use ps -aef | grep httpd. If Apache is not running, you can restart it by hand. If Apache is supposed to start automatically, you should reread the section titled "Starting Apache".

- The server is running but a browser can't connect. It is possible that the network between the two machines is not working properly. Use another network command such as ping to check and make sure the server is reachable.

- I can ping but still can't connect. Check to make sure the URL is correct. It is possible that you are using the wrong port. An easy way to make sure Apache is working right is to use telnet on the Web server to connect to the port, and get a file. For example on SunOS you would use "telnet localhost 80", then after you connected type **GET /**. This should get your home page. If so, Apache is running OK. If not, then the server is having problems.

- Apache isn't running or dies on startup. Check the error logs, usually DocumentRoot/logs/error_log. This should give you a more specific error message or point you to a configuration problem. You might also want to check the system error log, this can be /var/log/syslog or /var/adm/messages or other files depending on which version of UNIX you are running. You might also want to verify that httpd -v works okay. If this doesn't work, you probably have a problem with the program and it will need to be recompiled.

- I get server unknown when I try to connect. This is usually caused by a DNS configuration problem. Check to make sure you can telnet or ping the host by name. If not you can get around this by using the server IP address instead of the hostname. This workaround should only be used until you can get the DNS fixed.

These are, of course, just the more common error messages. It is possible to have other messages that aren't listed. If so, you need to try to narrow down the problem.

Checking to see if the server is compiled okay is a good first step to narrowing down the problem. If httpd -v works, it is probably compiled okay. It is also very common for the network to have problems. Telnetting to the port from the localhost eliminates the network. If it appears to be compiled okay and eliminating the network doesn't fix the problem, then it is most likely a configuration problem.

Note

It is fairly uncommon for a compiler problem to show no errors when compiling and running the -v flag properly. This does happen though. If you can't find the problem, you may have a bug. Bugs or suggestions can be submitted to the Apache group at **apache-bugs@mail.apache.org**.

If you aren't sure if you have a bug or just a problem, you should check out the Usenet newsgroup **comp.infosystems.www.servers.unix**. Many people on this newsgroup are very helpful and knowledgeable.

File Pruning

Apache logs connections and error messages. These log files continue to grow until they are removed or truncated. Simply removing the file though isn't enough since Apache references the files by inode. When you move the file it may appear to be different in a listing, but it isn't really closed until the server restarts (and Apache will happily continue writing to the moved file). If you truncate the file, you will find that Apache will keep writing in the same spot it was in and simply fill the file with blanks up to the size of the original log file. There is an easy way to truncate log files though.

- Normally you want to move the logfiles that are in use. This allows you to analyze them later. To move the log files you can use the command "mv", for example "mv error_log error_log.0". If you don't care about the files, you can remove them after that.

- Next you need to tell Apache to look for a new log file. This is done by sending the HUP signal the httpd processes. You can use the following command to do this on SunOS **kill -HUP 'cat /usr/local/etc/ httpd/pid.file**.

- Apache will automatically create new log files and start writing to them.

In addition to the log files, if you are using Apache as a caching proxy server, the disk space used for cache needs to be maintained.

This is normally done automatically by Apache as long as you set the CacheMaxSize and CacheGC directives correctly.

CacheMaxSize tells the server how much space it can use. If you set CacheMaxSize too high, you will use all of your diskspace for cache. If you set it too low, you will not have good cache performance. Experimentation is required to get an acceptable compromise of space and speed.

CacheGC tells the server how often to clean out the cache's old files. If CacheGC doesn't run often enough, you will have a stale cache. If it runs too often, you may have performance problems. It is important to experiment and find the best value for this parameter. ❖

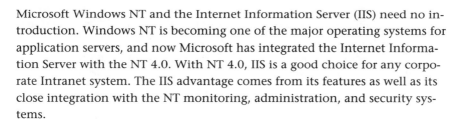

## CHAPTER 4

Installing and Configuring IIS

Microsoft Windows NT and the Internet Information Server (IIS) need no introduction. Windows NT is becoming one of the major operating systems for application servers, and now Microsoft has integrated the Internet Information Server with the NT 4.0. With NT 4.0, IIS is a good choice for any corporate Intranet system. The IIS advantage comes from its features as well as its close integration with the NT monitoring, administration, and security systems.

In this chapter, you will learn about the following:

- Matrices for estimating an IIS system configuration
- Installing the IIS
- Testing the IIS installation
- Administration and security issues
- Integration with Windows NT

IIS Overview

On a top-level architecture, the Microsoft IIS (for trivia buffs, this product was known as "Gibraltar") extends Windows NT Server to the world of Intranets. It works closely with NT services, security, and monitoring. It adds World Wide Web Service, Gopher and FTP Service, Internet Service Manager, Internet Database Connector, and Secure Sockets Layer (SSL) to a Windows NT server. IIS 2.0 is a part of Windows NT 4.0. You can install IIS when you install Windows NT 4.0 or later, after installing Windows NT 4.0. We will cover the installation later in this chapter.

> **Note**
>
> You can download the IIS and the browsers free from Microsoft's WWW site. As an administrator of Intranets, it's a good practice to download the latest versions on a periodic basis. In addition to bug fixes, the upgrades in the Web site will include security patches, which are very important.

IIS provides full Intranet capability ranging, from publishing information, to complete access to data stored in various client/server databases. It supports the popular Common Gateway Interface (CGI). But CGI creates a separate process for every request, which could mean more server resources, including RAM. Microsoft's antidote to this is the Application Program Interface (API) called Internet Server Application Programming Interface (ISAPI). You can write ISAPI applications—as dynamic-link libraries—which will be loaded in the same address space of the HTTP server. One DLL can handle all the user forms, data, and so on. Another feature of the ISAPI is the ability to write HTTP filters to handle chosen events.

One of the most important, and possibly most useful, features for Intranets is the back-end database access and programming. IIS has IDC or Internet Database Connector, which connects to back-end ODBC databases. The IDC capabilities include insert, update, delete, and performing other SQL commands. We will introduce these areas in this book. Intranet interface to legacy and client/server databases is an essential part in the development of corporate information systems. So keep the intranet and database interface topic in the top five subjects to learn about!

The IIS is managed by using a graphical interface program called the Internet Service Manager. The Internet Service Manager uses the Windows NT DCE-compatible Remote Procedure Call (RPC) to securely administer the server and all the Web applications running on it. You can manage systems locally, over their LAN, and even over the Internet from a Windows NT Workstation.

Capacity Planning and Estimates

When you start budgeting for an IIS Intranet, questions like "How many servers do you need?" or, "How many users can you support?" or, "What is the estimated throughput?" or most importantly, "How long will our users have to wait to get to the information?" will be asked. These estimates are needed even after the successful implementation of an Intranet project.

It is almost impossible to estimate the capacity of an Intranet server. I have included this section to aid the Intranet practitioners in getting some idea about the throughputs, connections, interactive Web page performance, and so on. Hopefully, this section will give you a few performance measures and representative IIS ratings for those measures.

> **Note**
>
> More detailed and latest performance benchmarks for IIS are available at **http://www.microsoft.com/infoserv/docs/iisperf.htm**.

> **Note**
>
> The IIS ratings on the following performance measures are based on tests performed with the IIS 1.0 running on a 133 MHz HP server/32 MB RAM/ 2 X 1 GB Hard Disks/ DEC 10/100 Megabit Ethernet card. That looks like a good normal configuration for an IIS server. To run SQL server from the same computer, increase the memory to 64 MB.

Throughput

Throughput measures the maximum rate at which the Web server transfers data to its clients. Throughput is reported as megabits per second (Mbps). The IIS 1.0 rates at approximately 13 Mbps at 64 clients.

> **Note**
>
> When you compare the throughput numbers, remember that on corporate LANs with normal Ethernet, the maximum throughput is 10 Mbps while the newer fastEthernet clocks at a maximum of 100 Mbps; ISDN line has a maximum capacity of 64 Kbps for 1 channel or 128 Kbps for 2 channels combined.

Connections per Second

Connections per second represents the sum of successful interactions across all the clients. An interaction is successful when a connection is made from a client to a server, or data transfer was successfully done through the connection and the connection closed. The IIS 1.0 is capable of handling 250 such connections when handling only HTML data.

Average Response Time

Average response time measures the amount of time required to complete an operation once it is started. *Average response time* has two components: *connection response time* measures the time taken to establish a connection, and *transfer response time* measures the time to complete a data transfer once a connection has been established. A typical Web page is made up of several files, usually an HTML file, and several GIF/JPEG, or other graphics files. For IIS 1.0 the average response time ranged from 0.2 seconds per file (16 clients) to 0.5 seconds per file (128 clients). On small networks, the average time can be reduced to less than 0.1 seconds.

Dynamic Web Pages

Dynamic Web pages involve server-side programming using CGI scripts or ISAPI DLLs. CGI inherently is a slower approach. You should use the API native to a Web server, like the ISAPI, for faster web page processing. Table 4.1 shows the connection rate and throughput numbers for ISAPI and CGI programs.

Table 4.1 API Performance Estimates		
	100% ISAPI	**100% CGI**
Connections Per Second	90	20
Throughput (Megabits per second)	5	1

IIS Hardware/Software Requirements

As mentioned previously, IIS runs on the top of Windows NT 4.0 server. So the total IIS Intranet server requirements are Windows NT 4.0 requirements plus IIS requirements, as discussed next.

CPU and Memory

You will need a Pentium 120 or 133 MHz machine with 32 MB RAM for Windows NT Server and IIS. Add a minimum of 32 MB more memory for SQL server. For more than 25 users, I recommend about 80 MB RAM. Windows NT performance falls sharply when it exhausts the memory; it is not a gradual decay. This performance cutoff point can be extended by adding more memory. Servers with 128 MB memory are the norm today, so plan ahead.

Hard Disk

The recommended disk space is 4 to 8 GB. Again, this number will depend on the amount of data to be published. If you are also going to add SQL Server data, that should be taken into account.

Microsoft recommends that all IIS disks be formatted by using the NTFS format and enable auditing. This is recommended for security reasons as well as redundancy reasons.

If the Intranet server has mission-critical information, one or more of the following fault tolerance mechanisms should be considered. This strategy will affect the disk capacity required.

Disk Mirroring

In this case, two drives are connected to the same controller and all data on the first drive is duplicated on the second drive. Even though mirroring essentially duplicates one disk on another disk, NT does not require identical hard disks for mirroring. This is RAID Level 1.

RAID

RAID (Redundant Arrays of Inexpensive Disks) is a scheme to increase performance and reliability of disk storage using normal hard disks. The RAID levels range from 0 to 5. Windows NT server supports RAID 0, 1 and 5. The different RAID levels have different performance and reliability characteristics. The RAID level for a system depends on the requirement (for example, Mission critical systems need maximum reliability), type (for example, publishing systems with a lot of read only data can use a Level 5 RAID), and so on.

Disk Duplexing

Disk Duplexing is mirroring with two controllers, where the two drives are connected to two disk controllers. Duplexing improves performance (as parallel reads/writes result in faster I/O) and fault tolerance (as it protects against controller failures also).

Disk Striping with Parity

In this case, multiple partitions from different drives are combined to form logical drives. This is RAID level 5. The disk striping gives maximum performance, and the parity information gives the redundancy. This strategy is recommended over mirroring for applications that require redundancy and that are primarily read-oriented.

II

Setting Up Software

A CRT and Network Cards

Any normal VGA CRT is sufficient. Usually, when there are many servers, it is better to connect many computers to a master console and master mouse share device. This way, one CRT and mouse can be shared by many servers.

Now there are faster Ethernet cards (100 Mbps throughput, for example) that will give good performance in terms of raw throughput. To use one of these cards, your router or hub also should support the data rates and the cards. As you shall see later, there are also other components to be considered for a responsive Intranet site.

Internet Connection

An Internet connection is needed to publish on the Web. For small businesses, this will translate to getting the services of an Internet Service Provider (ISP). As a start, the URL **http://thelist.iworld.com/** gives a list of ISPs around the world, searchable in a variety of ways.

For corporate Intranets operating behind a fire wall, the organization is already on the Internet, and so you need to configure the TCP/IP protocol as discussed in the TCP/IP section below.

Windows NT Server 4.0

Windows NT Server 4.0 software from Microsoft includes the IIS 2.0 also.

TCP/IP

TCP/IP should be installed and configured as one of the network protocols and can be accessed from the network applet in the control panel. The typical Intranet server will be on a shared 10-100 MB network.

Figure 4.1 shows the IP Address configuration screen for the TCP/IP setup. To configure the TCP/IP, you need the server's Internet Protocol (IP) address, subnet mask, and the default gateway's IP address router addresses obtained from the network installation group. The default gateway is the computer through which your computer will route all Internet traffic.

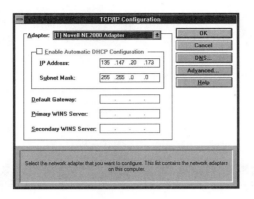

Fig. 4.1
NT configuration screen for the TCP/IP setup. In this property sheet you can enter the IP addresses.

You also will need to configure a Domain Name Service (DNS) like the Microsoft Windows Internet Name Server (WINS).

On Intranets, an alternative to WINS Servers is to use an LMHOSTS file, which contains the IP address and computer name.

> **Note**
>
> The WINS is a Windows NT Server computer running Microsoft TCP/IP and the Windows Internet Name Service (WINS). This server will be assigned a static IP address. The Windows Internet Name Server maintains a central database that maps the Intranet computer names to IP addresses. The TCP/IP driver will get the IP address of a computer from this server. In organizations where there are multiple WIN Servers, the directory database can be replicated among the different servers.

Pre-Installation Notes

The following are some points you should be aware of before installing the IIS on a Windows NT computer:

- IIS installation components depend on the OS. Installation on a computer running Windows NT Workstation will install only the administrator components. WWW, FTP, and Gopher services are not installed.

■ All user account creation, management, and File Access Controls are managed through the graphical Windows NT Server administration tools.

■ Uninstall all older versions, especially beta versions, of IIS. It is never a good practice to install released versions over beta versions, especially on production environments. This way, all outdated files are deleted and registry entries are removed/reset. Use the Remove All option in the IIS setup to remove the older installations.

Tip

After uninstalling older versions, it is a good practice to shutdown and restart the machine, because some files might be marked "remove during next reboot". If this is the case, a system reboot will delete all old files.

Note

Remember to back up or transfer HTML and other user files before the uninstall to a directory, because the uninstall procedure will delete all directories.

Installing IIS

While installing Windows NT 4.0, if the install program finds an earlier version of IIS, it will install IIS 2.0 automatically. Alternatively, on the desktop, an icon titled "Install Internet Information Server" will be created during the NT 4.0 installation. In this case, after Windows NT is installed and configured, log on to the NT domain with a user who has administrator privileges (the most common user is the "Administrator") and double-click the "Install Internet Information Server" icon to start the IIS installation process. Click OK to the Welcome screen.

Now the Options screen as shown in figure 4.2 appears. Usually, all the options are checked, and you can click OK to continue.

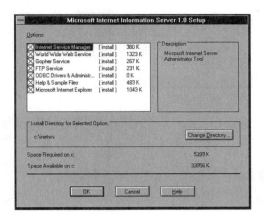

Fig. 4.2
IIS 1.0 Setup
Options screen.
You can select the
services to install
and the target
directory.

If you are re-installing some particular component or want to install a particular component, such as Internet Service Manager, for remote monitoring from a NT Workstation, this options choice comes in handy.

The next screen as shown in figure 4.3 is the publishing directories dialog box. This shows the root directories for the WWW, FTP, and Gopher services. The default directories are usually fine. Click the OK button to continue. The setup now continues.

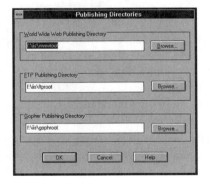

Fig. 4.3
IIS 1.0 Publishing
Directories screen.

As the setup progresses, the installation program will ask for confirmations to create directories, warning about services that are not available, and so on. Figure 4.4 is an example of a warning message. It is a security alert message which warns the installer about the GUEST account.

II

Setting Up Software

Fig. 4.4
Installation
Security Alert
message.

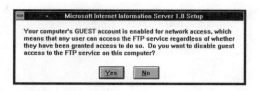

At this point, the message "IIS Successfully Completed" appears. It is always a good practice to reboot the machine after the installation.

Testing the IIS Installation

The default installation of the Microsoft Internet Information Server (IIS) contains sample files that can be used to test the functionality of your IIS WWW publication service.

To test a server connected to the Internet, follow these steps:

1. Ensure that your server has HTML files in the \Wwwroot directory.

2. Start Internet Explorer on a computer that has an active connection to the Internet. This computer can be the server you are testing, although using a different computer is recommended.

> **Tip**
>
> To test the Internet connection, try to access a well known site such as **http:/ /www.microsoft.com**. You should see the Microsoft home page.

3. Type in the Uniform Resource Locator (URL) for the home directory of your new server. The URL will be **http://** followed by the name of your server, followed by the path of the file you want to view. (Note the forward slash marks.) For example, if your server is registered in DNS as **www.company.com** and you want to view the file homepage.htm in the root of the home directory, in the Location box you would type **http://www.company.com/homepage.htm** and then press the Enter key.

To test a server on the Intranet, follow these steps:

1. Ensure that your computer has an active network connection and that the WINS service (or other name resolution method) is functioning.

2. Make sure the WWW service is started by opening Microsoft Internet Service Manager and verifying that State is "Running."

3. Start your favorite Web browser. (For most, it will probably be Internet Explorer or Netscape Navigator.)

4. Type in the Uniform Resource Location (URL) for the home directory of your new server.

The URL will be **http://** followed by the Windows Networking name of your server, followed by the path of the file you want to view. (Note the forward slash marks.) For example, if your server is registered with the WINS server as "Admin1" and you want to view the file "default.htm" in the root of the home directory, in the Location box you would type **http://admin1/ default.htm** and then press the Enter key. The home page as shown in figure 4.6 should appear on the screen.

> **Tip**
>
> You really do not need a URL to test the installation. From any computer connected to the company's Intranet or LAN, start a WWW browser like the Internet Explorer or Netscape Navigator and type in the IP address on the IIS server just installed. For example, **http://145.101.138.99/** and press the enter key. The IIS home page as shown in figure 4.6 will be displayed.

IIS Administration

Now that IIS is successfully installed and configured, you would think that your work is done. Well, now comes the problems, resolutions, and workarounds, which are a part of Web site administration. IIS administration is done using the Microsoft Internet Service Manager. Figure 4.5 shows the ISM window. The services and their status are displayed on the main window.

Fig. 4.5
Internet Service
Manager showing
the status of IIS
services.

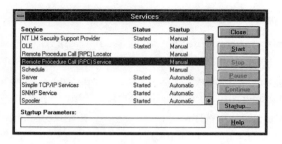

The properties for a service can be displayed by double-clicking a service. For
example, by double-clicking the WWW service, the property pages for that
service are displayed as shown in figure 4.6.

Fig. 4.6
WWW Service
property page
from the Internet
Service Manager.
This page shows
the logging
options.

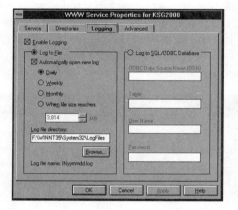

It is a good practice to log the activities for all the services and analyze the
logs periodically. After installation, check the logs directory and select a frequency (daily, weekly and so on). You can either use log analysis tools to analyze the logs, or log the activities to a SQL/ODBC database and do analysis by
writing a custom program.

> **Note**
>
> For the first few weeks, check the activities (of WWW, FTP, and Gopher services) on a
> daily basis, then move on to weekly or monthly basis.

To publish information via the World Wide Web, the HTML files should be copied to the directory specified in the directories property page, as shown in figure 4.7.

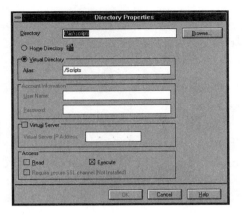

Fig. 4.7
WWW Service Directories property page from the Internet Service Manager. This page associates the directories where the HTML files for WWW publishing are stored with virtual servers,IP addresses, and so on.

IIS supports virtual servers to host multiple domain names on the same computer running Microsoft Internet Information Server. This is done, from the advanced TCP/IP configuration settings, by binding multiple IP addresses to the network adapter card connected to the Internet. This is done through the Network applet in Control Panel from the settings option in the start menu. The directories for the virtual servers are configured in the Directories property page as shown in figure 4.7.

IIS Security

Security is, and always will be, a major concern of Intranet practitioners and users. In general, the four most important characteristics of a secure system are as follows:

- Authentica6tion of the client and server. Assures the identity of the data sender and the data recipient. The client wants to authenticate the server and the server will authenticate the client.

- Access Control of resources. Assures that only users who have been given privileges to access resources can access those resources. This involves password, access control lists, and so on.

- Encryption of data. Assures that the data cannot be read by anyone other than the recipient.

- Integrity of data. Assures that the data being transferred has not been altered.

NT Security and Access Control

This section discusses the security issues related to the accounts created during installation. These discussions pertain mainly to the security from Windows NT server.

Password Authentication Options

The types available are Anonymous, Basic, and Challenge/Response. The screen is accessed from the Internet Service Manager Service property page.

1. Allow Anonymous. In case of the Web access through a browser, when this check box is checked, anonymous connections are processed with the username in the anonymous-logon group box. If this option is unchecked, all anonymous connections are rejected, and to access the web site the basic or NT authentication will be used where the user needs a user name and a password.

2. Basic. When this check box is checked, the Web service will process requests using basic authentication. This is also called "clear text." The user needs a user name and a password to access the web contents.

> **Caution**
>
> Basic authentication sends Windows NT user names and passwords across the network without encryption. Hackers using network packet sniffers can see the password as it is transmitted over the network. This check box is unchecked by default for security reasons.

3. Windows NT Challenge/Response. When this check box is checked, the user needs to enter a user name and a password. The user account information will be sent to the using the Windows NT Challenge/Response (NTLM) protocol. This protocol uses encryption for secure transmission of passwords. The NTLM authentication process is initiated automatically if an "access denied error" occurs on an anonymous client.

> **Note**
>
> If the client browser does not support the NTLM authentication, the users will get messages like "Access denied, Server does not specify the authentication method," or "Authentication required for this document," and so on. At that point, there are two alternatives: either disable challenge/response and enable basic, or get a client browser that supports the NTLM authentication scheme. Intranets inside a firewall can use the Basic method. If you are giving access to your sensitive data outside the firewall, you should consider secure communication alternatives, including digital signatures.

Suggested Best Practices

Microsoft suggests the following checks on the NT security system. Please follow them.

1. Review the IUSR_*computername* account's rights.
2. Choose difficult passwords.
3. Manage strict account policies.
4. Limit the membership of the Administrator's group.
5. Run only the services that you need.
6. Unbind unnecessary services from your Internet adapter cards.
7. Check permissions on network shares.

SSL support

The IIS 2.0 provides users with a secure communication channel through support for Secure Sockets Layer (SSL) and RSA encryption. This provides secure data communication through data encryption and decryption. SSL is a WWW feature that supports data encryption and server authentication. In the Open Systems Interconnect (OSI) model, SSL protocol layers between the TCP/IP transport/network layer and the application layer where HTTP operates. IIS 2.0 has a new program called Key Manager to manage SSL keys.

> **Portable Certificates and IDs?**
>
> Microsoft has proposed Personal Effects Exchange (PFX), which is titled "multi-browser, multi-platform, secure exchange interoperability standard for certificates, CRLs, private keys, and personal secrets." (Wow! It is an earful, isn't it?) Internet security is still a young field. A lot of work is being done to make security wallets and distributed security systems, like the public key/group based system proposed by Rivest and Lampson called SDSI, a Simple Distributed Security Infrastructure.

Enabling PCT/SSL security on a Microsoft Internet Information Server involves generating a key pair file and a request file, requesting a certificate from a Certification Authority, and then installing and activating SSL security.

> **Note**
>
> Digital certificates can be obtained from Verisign. More information is available from **http://www.verisign.com/microsoft/**. The IIS Installation and planning guide also has more information on the SSL implementation.

Integration with Windows NT Security System

All the IIS services rely on NT server user accounts, ACLs, and permissions. Every access to a resource (for example, a file, an HTML page, an Internet Server API (ISAPI) application, and so on) is done by the services on behalf of a Windows NT user. The service impersonates the user by supplying a username/password pair in the attempt to read/execute the resource for the client.

The Windows NT File System (NTFS) allows Access Control Lists (ACLs) to be assigned to files and directories. ACLs grant and/or deny access to the associated file or directory by specific Windows NT user accounts or groups of users. When an Internet service attempts to read or execute a file on behalf of a client request, the user account offered by the service must have permission, as determined by the ACL associated with the file, to read or execute the file, as appropriate. If the user account does not have permission to access the file, the request fails, and a response is returned, informing the client that access has been denied.

File and directory ACLs are configured by using the Windows NT File Manager, Security submenu. Remember, ACLS are supported in the NTFS partitions.

Customized Authentication

If you are publishing sensitive data and require a secure communication, the Internet Server API (ISAPI) Software Developer's Kit (SDK) can be used to develop filter DLLs that implement secure algorithms.

Performance Monitoring

Performance Monitor is a graphical tool in the Windows NT server that can be used for analyzing throughput, site traffic, and internal congestion measurements. It provides charting, alerting, and reporting capabilities that reflect current activity along with ongoing logging. One advantage is that the Performance Monitor program can function as a server data recorder when you log the counters to disk. You can then open log files at a later time for browsing and charting.

The monitoring should be an ongoing activity for an Intranet. A good plan is to log the counters and analyze them weekly.

The WWW server adds the HTTP Service, FTP Server, Gopher Service, and Internet Information Services Global performance counter objects to the existing list in the Windows NT Performance Monitor.

SNMP MIBS

SNMP MIBs: As with any network systems, management is an important part of IIS. The most commonly used protocol to gather information and manage network devices is the SNMP (Simple Network Management Protocol). The Windows NT SNMP service includes MIB II (based on RFC 1213). The SNMP and TCP/IP services use a set of objects known as the Management Information Base (MIB). Given the popularity of SNMP, it is not surprising that IIS supports the Performance Monitor objects as MIB objects for SNMP. These MIB objects are described in the IIS user's manual as well as at the Microsoft Web site **http://www.microsoft.com/ infoserv/samples/tour/mib.htm**.

Windows NT Registry: A Crash Course

Windows and DOS had config.sys, autoexec.bat, and a host of ini files. In Windows NT, configuration information is stored in the registry. If you are working with IIS, at some time you will need to edit the values in the registry.

The registry has a tree-like structure. There is one root and many branches. The major subtrees are HKEY_LOCAL_MACHINE, H_KEY_CLASSES_ROOT, HKEY_CURRENT_USER, and HKEY_USERS. (For IIS configuration and administration, we are mainly interested in the HKEY_LOCAL_MACHINE\System \CurrentControlSet\Services\InetInfo branch.) The leaf is an entry that appears as a string that consists of a name, data type, and a value. The name can be MemoryCachSize, Bandwidth, or something similar. The common data types we are interested in are REG_BINARY: Binary data in any form; REG_DWORD: a 32-bit number; REG_EXPAND_SZ: a null-terminated string that contains unexpanded references to environment variables (for example, %PATH%); REG_SZ: a null-terminated string. The value can be numbers or strings. The Registry preserves case as you type it for any entry, but ignores case in evaluating the data. The names are case insensitive. However, the data is defined by specific applications (or users), so it might be case sensitive, depending on how the program that uses it treats the data.

The registry is manipulated using the regedt32.exe program usually found in the winNT35\system32 subdirectory. You can start the program from the File Manager. I recommend creating a program icon for the regeditor in the Administrative Tools program group. Please refer to the help in the regedit32 program for more details like editing/adding/deleting an entry or key.

Caution

Be very careful when deleting a key entry because there is no Undo command. In general, exert caution when editing registry entries. A wrong or inadvertent mistake can result in a non-bootable system.

The Internet Information Server stores information in four registry keys. They are Internet Information Server (IIS), FTP, Gopher, and HTTP. These keys are independent of each other. ❖

CHAPTER 5

Installing and Configuring Netscape Enterprise Server and LiveWire

In this chapter, you are introduced to the Netscape Enterprise Server and LiveWire, and given step-by-step instructions to install and configure these two applications. This chapter will go through the basic steps needed to prepare windows NT for installation of the Enterprise Server, and then downloading, installing, and configuring the Enterprise Server and LiveWire.

The Netscape Enterprise 2.0 Web Server is a third-generation server from Netscape Communications, creators of the popular Netscape Navigator software. Due to the vast number of enhancements available on this server, it is impossible to detail the operations of each and every option. Instead, this chapter will outline basic installation, briefly describe each of the available options, and provide step-by-step instructions for configuring some of the more popular features.

LiveWire is an add-on to the Netscape Enterprise Server, compromised of three main components. The Site Manager and LiveWire compiler, the LiveWire server extension, and Netscape Navigator Gold. LiveWire serves two main purposes, to help manage a Web site, and to help create dynamic content. Even though this chapter is primarily geared toward installing the Enterprise Server and LiveWire on a computer running Windows NT, the downloading and configuration information presented can be used on most platforms (including UNIX) supported by the Server.

In this chapter, you will learn the following:

- How to obtain the Enterprise Server and LiveWire
- How to configure Windows NT to the install Enterprise Server
- How to install the Enterprise Server
- How to configure the Enterprise Server
- How to install and Configure LiveWire

Overview of the Enterprise 2.0 Server

Before considering installing the Netscape Enterprise Server, it is a good idea to check the supported configurations (see table 5.1) to see whether your current hardware and operating system are capable of running the Server.

Table 5.1 Supported Configurations			
Vendor	**Architecture**	**OS**	**Memory Requirements**
UNIX			
Digital	Alpha	OSF/1.3.2C	32 MB
HP	PA	HP-UX 9.x, 10.01	32 MB
IBM	RS/6000	AIX 3.2.5,4.1	32 MB
SGI	MIPS	IRIX 5.4, 6.2	32 MB
Sun	Sparc	SunOS 4.1.3, Solaris 2.4, 2.5	32 MB
Windows NT			
Digital	Alpha	NT 3.51, NT 4.0	32 MB
Intel	x486,Pentium	NT 3.51, NT 4.0	32 MB

Note

Netscape recommends 30 MB of free disk space for installation, as well as 30 MB free disk space for log files (for a server with approximately 300,000 accesses per day).

Enterprise 2.0 Features

The Netscape Enterprise 2.0 Server has all of the standard features available on most popular WWW server packages, as well as a few special enhancements that make it particularly well suited for Intranet use.

General Features

To make Web publishing easier and more convenient, the Enterprise Server can be used in conjunction with Navigator Gold, a WYSIWYG HTML editing and publishing tool. Using Enterprise's remote file manipulation feature,

Navigator Gold allows users to update Web files from any remote location that is networked to the Server. The familiar Web browser interface of Navigator Gold saves the user from having to learn to use other tools such as FTP and HTML. A revision control system allows multiple users to simultaneously work on documents without risking the integrity of the files on the Server.

A fully integrated, full-text search engine allows such features as full-text and field searches, incremental indexing, and add-on support for document types such as Portable Document Format (PDF) without having to revert to third-party software. An integrated cataloging system automatically generates catalogs of files on a site based on the creating author, the creation date, or through user-defined classifications. This catalog provides users with a quick overview of all the files available on the Server.

Administration

Administration of the Server has been simplified, and the interface has been made clear and logical. The new Administration Server has several new features, including new log analysis tools that create summaries on Web site statistics such as total hits, total number of unique hosts, and total traffic transferred. The new analysis tool also supports enhanced features such as identifying which clients are accessing the most number of pages and downloading the most information.

Support for multiple domains has been vastly improved over previous versions of the Netscape Server, enabling administrators to easily host multiple sites on a single machine. LiveWire, a standard component of the server, is a visual site management tool that allows administrators to view and restructure entire sites in a graphical form. To improve remote monitoring capabilities, the Enterprise Server now supports SNMP 1 and 2, allowing administrators to monitor their servers remotely using standard SNMP capable tools.

Security and Performance

To address security concerns, Netscape has upgraded its security with enhancements such as Secure Sockets Layer (SSL) 3.0 support, advanced access control, and client-side certificates. These components help to secure not only commerce but all communications that travel through the Server.

Netscape's second incarnation of its commercial Web Server software, the Enterprise 2.0 Server, combines new caching technology, platform-specific optimization, and multiprocessor support to create one of the best performing servers available on the market today.

II

Seting Up Software

Pre-Installation Requirements

The installation process of the Enterprise Server comes in several steps. First, it is necessary to configure Windows NT with the proper software and network settings so that the server can be installed. Next you need to obtain all of the software that you need to get the Enterprise 2.0 Server operating on your NT machine. Finally, you can customize your system to your needs by accessing the Administration Server.

Configuring Windows NT

The first step in preparing for the installation process is to make sure that Windows NT is properly configured. The following instructions assume that you already have Windows NT installed and running properly, and that you have already configured your network interface card.

> **Note**
>
> To install the Enterprise 2.0 Server, you must have the Windows NT 3.51 service pack #4 installed. You can find this service pack as well as other configuration tips for Windows NT Server at the NT server home page at **http://www.microsoft.com/ NTServer/**. Users of Windows NT 4.0 do not need to install any of the service packs.

To successfully operate an Enterprise Server, you must have the TCP/IP protocol installed on NT, and you must have a permanent IP address assigned to your Server. You will need to know your IP address to properly install your Server and for other people to be able to reach your Server.

> **Tip**
>
> To help users access your system, it is helpful to register a domain name in DNS for your permanent IP address. By doing so, users can access your server using the domain name (such as ian.digiknow.com) rather than a complicated IP address (192.147.147.142 would be the IP address associated to ian.digiknow.com).

Installing TCP/IP

Before installing TCP/IP on Windows NT, you will need to know the following information:

- The IP address(es) to be assigned to your computer
- The Host name(s) corresponding to the preceding addresses
- The IP addresses of the DNS servers you will use

■ The Domain name in which you will operate

1. Open the Network Control Panel and click on the Add Software button.

2. From the pull-down menu, highlight TCP/IP Protocol and Related Components and click on Continue.

3. Select the components you wish to install and click on Continue (At the very least you will want to install "Connectivity Utilities" and "Simple TCP/IP Services"). You will be prompted for the location of the NT software distribution disk.

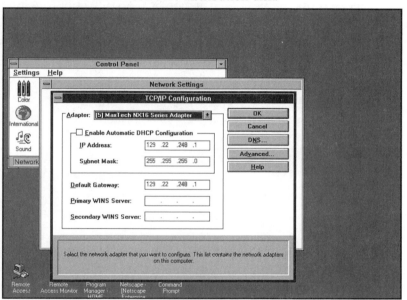

Fig. 5.1
The Network Control Panel allows you to add TCP/IP services and to configure them for use with the Enterprise 2.0 Server.

II

Seting Up Software

> **Note**
>
> If you want to use the Windows NT Performance Monitor to monitor TCP/IP statistics, you will have to install SNMP service. SNMP will also allow your computer to be administered remotely using remote management tools. If you choose to install SNMP, you will be prompted by the SNMP configuration dialog box. Unless you have particular needs for SNMP, you can simply select the OK button.

4. If you have installed RAS for dial-up access to the Internet (either via modem or ISDN), you will be prompted to configure RAS to support the TCP/IP. If you do, click OK.

> **Note**
>
> It is possible to use the Enterprise Server on a dial-up IP connection (either via modem or ISDN). For proper operation, you must have a static IP address defined, however. If you are using a dial-up connection to install the server, make sure the connection is live and running before installing the Enterprise Server.

5. Once the computer finishes adding TCP/IP services, click OK on the Network Settings Configuration Box. A TCP/IP Configuration box will appear allowing you to configure your network adapter.

6. From the Adapter pull-down menu, select the Adapter you wish to configure.

7. Under IP address, enter the IP address for your host.

8. Under Subnet Mask, enter the subnet mask for your host.

9. Under Default Gateway, enter the default gateway for your network.

10. If you are using DNS servers (if you are on the Internet, then you are), click DNS to bring up the DNS configuration dialog box.

11. Under Host Name, enter the host name of your server.

12. Under Domain Name, enter the domain in which your host is registered.

13. In the DNS Search Order box, enter the name(s) of the DNS servers you will be using for host lookups. Click OK to get back to the main configuration menu.

14. Now that you have TCP/IP properly configured on your NT Server, the last step is to reboot the machine to put the changes into effect. Click OK in the TCP/IP Configuration box and when prompted, restart the computer.

Configuring Security

The downside to the benefits that networking computers provides is that it also brings up several security issues. To meet this concern, Windows NT has several layers of security available to it, including user-account security and file system security using the Windows NT File System (NTFS).

Every operation that takes place under NT can be identified by the user name used to start the particular operation. The User Manager application allows you to set which resources a particular user is authorized to use on the computer, as well as which files they are allowed to access. To limit the level of access that the Enterprise Server has to your computer, it is recommended that you create a nonprivileged user account for the Server to run under. This account should be restricted to access only what is necessary to start up and operate the Enterprise Server software.

> **Note**
>
> By default, the Server uses the LocalSystem account under NT and the nobody account under UNIX. Under both systems, however, it is still recommended that administrators create a separate account for running the Server.

Installing the Enterprise Server

There are two ways to obtain the Enterprise server. The first (and the quickest) is to download the server from Netscape's home site at **http://www. netscape.com**.

> **Tip**
>
> Netscape allows a 60-day evaluation trial of all of their software packages, including Servers and browsers. If you want to have support, you can also purchase the server directly online and get 90 days of free technical support.

After you find the Server Download page, use the pull-down menus to select the files you wish to download. (You will need to specify the product you wish to download, the Operating System you are running, and the file type to download: .zip, .exe, or .gzip.) While you are at the Netscape site, you might also want to pick up a copy of the Navigator Gold software, which you will need to configure your Server if you do not have a Web browser installed yet. (It also allows for remote updates of Web files stored on the server.)

If you are not one for long downloads, for a negligible shipping and handing charge you can order an evaluation copy of the server on CD-ROM from Netscape's Web site at **http://www.netscape.com**. This CD will come with the Enterprise Server as well as the Navigator Gold Software.

> **Tip**
>
> You might want to install the Navigator Gold software before running the setup for the Server so that you will be able to jump right into the Administration Server after you are finished with the Enterprise Installation.

II

Seting Up Software

From the command prompt or from File Manager, run the executable file you have just downloaded (if you have the file on CD, run the setup.exe file).

> **Tip**
>
> Make sure that you shut down any other applications that are running before installing this software. If you are already running a WWW server, disable it in the Services Control Panel.

The setup program will first prompt you with the destination directory in which to install the Enterprise Server. If the directory you designate does not exist, don't worry; the setup program will create it for you. (Keep in mind, though, that you will need at least 30 MB of free space for the installation.)

> **Note**
>
> During setup, the server will come up with several queries. It is usually safe to use the default entries because you can change the values later using the Administration Server.

If you already have a Enterprise 1.1x server installed, the setup program will question whether you want to upgrade the server or if you want to install a new server. (You can run both concurrently, just not on the same port.) Either option will not write over your current 1.1x installation, however, and you can always reactivate it from the Services Control Panel.

Server Setup: Selecting Hostname

The Enterprise Server will automatically obtain the settings for your hostname as you entered them in your TCP/IP Configuration menu when you installed TCP/IP. If your server does not have a proper DNS entry set up, you should enter the IP address under which the server is running; otherwise, you will not be able to access your server properly.

Administration Server Setup: Choosing Administration Access Username

The administration access username is the name and password you will use to connect to and administer your Enterprise Server. Because the Enterprise

Administration Server can be reached via the Netscape Navigator browser from any site on the Internet, it is crucial to set this feature for security purposes.

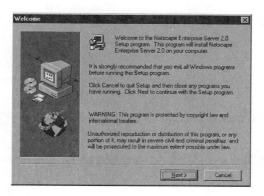

Fig. 5.2
If a host name does not automatically come up, it means that you have not yet properly configured TCP/IP. Without a proper hostname, you will not be able to access your server once it is installed.

Administration Server Setup: Choosing Administration Port Number

The Administration port is the port number on which you wish to operate your Administration Server (for example: **http://www.myserver. com:8888**). The installation process will randomly select a default port from the available ports on the system. You will need to remember this port so you can later be able to access your Administration Server and make changes in your Enterprise Server configuration.

> **Caution**
>
> Netscape randomly chooses a port for the Administration Server for security purposes. Because this is the gateway into your Server configuration, it would be unwise to run it on a port that could be easily identified by others (even though it does prompt you for a password).

Administration Server Setup: Choosing Administration User

This name is the name of the user under which the Administration Server (as well as the Enterprise Server) will be run. At this time, you can leave this option as is because you will be able to make changes later within the Administrative Server.

II

Seting Up Software

Fig. 5.3
By default, the administration server runs as LocalSystem. For security purposes, you might wish to change the name under which the Administrative Server runs.

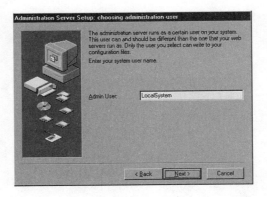

Web Server Setup: Choosing Document Root

The document root is the highest level directory visible to the Enterprise Server. You have to specify the full path to the location where your Web documents will reside. If the directory does not exist, it will be created for you.

> **Caution**
>
> This setting is vital because a large portion of Web security is based on the premise that the server cannot access files outside of this directory tree. Make sure that the server root directory tree does not contain any files that should not be accessible by the guests to the system.

Click finish to complete the installation and to start up your Server. If you have already installed the Navigator Gold browser, it will start itself up and display the new default home page on the Enterprise Server.

> **Tip**
>
> If at this time, the Server does not start up, you can use the Event Viewer in the Administrative Tools folder of Windows NT to see what caused the Server to fail.

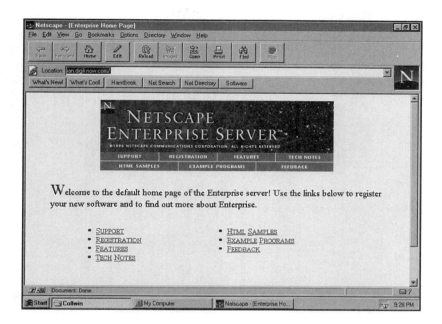

Fig. 5.4
If the installation is complete, and TCP/IP is configured properly on your system, the Enterprise Server Home Page should appear within Navigator Gold.

Configuring Enterprise Server

To start configuring your new Enterprise Server, open your Web browser to the following URL:

```
http://www.yourmachine.com:<admin port>
```

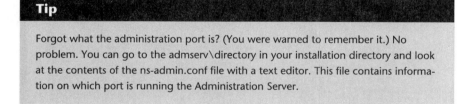

Tip

Forgot what the administration port is? (You were warned to remember it.) No problem. You can go to the admserv\directory in your installation directory and look at the contents of the ns-admin.conf file with a text editor. This file contains information on which port is running the Administration Server.

When you first connect to the Administration Server, you will be prompted for the login name and the password for your Administration Server. After you enter these, you will be welcomed by the Enterprise 2.0 configuration page.

To view and/or change the configuration of your server, click the server name. Doing so will bring up two menu bars in the Server Configuration page. The bar across the top has the main headings for configuration. The tool bar in the left frame shows the individual settings available under each main heading.

II

Seting Up Software

Fig. 5.5
When you are entering the Administation Server you will be prompted for the user name and password which you entered during installation.

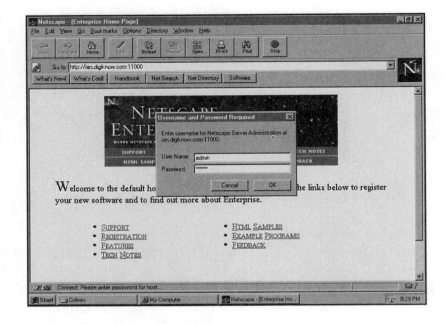

Fig. 5.6
Once you successfully enter the Administrative user name and password, you will see the Enterprise 2.0 Configuration Page. From here you will be able to administer all the servers installed on your system.

There are too many options available on the Server Configuration page to outline them all in this chapter. Instead, you will be provided with a general overview of what each "section" of configuration options does, and how it can be utilized in an Intranet setting.

System Settings

The system's settings are the critical configuration options that determine how your Server operates. Settings include turning your server on and off, setting default values for server configurations (see table 5.2). At any time, you can use the restore configuration to restore previous settings of your server. (A great feature when you first start experimenting with the configuration files and all of a sudden, everything stops working.) By default, the Server will store the last 10 changes. To increase this number, click Configure Backups and enter the number of backups to store in the Number of backups field.

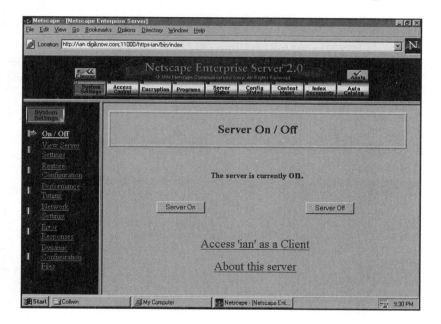

Fig. 5.7
Once you select a Server from the Configuration screen, you will be given a variety of options for modifying settings on a particular Server. View Server Settings.

This option provides a quick overview of the following Server variables:

Setting	Default Value	What It Does
Server Root		This is the directory in which your server files will be installed.
Hostname	Name of your computer	This is the name by which your server can be reached by others.

(continues)

(continued)

Setting	Default Value	What It Does
Port	80	This is the default HTTP Port under which your server can be accessed.
Error Log	ROOT\logs\errors	This is the file that stores the errors that the Enterprise Server detects.
DNS	off	This determines whether or not the server will execute a domain name lookup on hosts accessing the server.
Security	off	This determines whether your server is capable of secure transactions.
Additional ns-icons Documents mc-icons Directory		These are directory trees outside of the document root that can be accessed by the server.
Primary Document Directory		This is the main document tree that is accessible to the server and houses HTML files.
Index Filenames	index.html home.html	These are the files the server will look for if user does not specify a file in a directory.
Default MIME type	text/plain	This defines the default method that files are sent by the server if the server can't determine the proper type for the document.
Directory indexing	fancy	This option sets how the server responds if it cannot find one of the default file types in a directory.
Access log	ROOT/logs/access	This is the location where the Server stores a record of the hosts accessing files on the Server.

Note

Making changes in fields is a two-step process. The first step is to enter the changes and click OK. Next, you will be given the option to Undo the changes you have just made or to Save and Apply the changes. Clicking Save and Apply will make the changes and will restart your server to put the changes into effect.

Performance Tuning

This option allows you to configure the DNS settings for the Server. Turning DNS on will cause the Enterprise Server to look up the domain name of every computer that accesses files on the site. While this does improve security and tracking capabilities, it also causes a heavy load penalty on high-traffic systems. To help alleviate some of this load, the Server has a new feature that allows you to cache DNS entries. After performing an initial lookup, the Server then stores the results so that subsequent accesses by the same host do not have to be looked up.

You can specify the size of the cache as well as the amount of time before an entry is expired. By default, the Server will cache 1024 entries and expire them after 1200 seconds (20 minutes). You can specify between 32 to 32768 entries, and set an expiration time between 1 second and 1 year (specified in seconds).

Caution

While disabling DNS can lead to performance gains on busy systems, it disables hostname restrictions, and hostnames will not appear in the log files. Log files will contain IP addresses instead, and host-based access restrictions have to be based on IP numbers rather than domain names.

Network Settings

This option allows you to set the name of the user under which you wish to run the Enterprise Server. To change the user name, you will need to enter the new name under which you wish to run the Server, as well as the password set for this user. Without the proper password, your Server will be unable to restart properly. If you ever change the hostname of your server, or if you set up an alias for the server, you would register this change in the Server Name field. The Server Port field sets the port that the server listens to for incoming requests. By default, the HTTP port is 80, and the standard HTTPS port is 443. Technically, the port number can be any port from 1 to 65535. Bind To Address: shows you the current IP address that the server is responding to.

II

Seting Up Software

> **Note**
>
> Changing to a nonstandard port means that users will be required to add the port number to the URL they use to access your site. For example, if you use port 8080 for your server, your URL is http://www.yourhost.com:8080.

Error Responses

This option allows you to customize the message that the Server displays to a client when it encounters an error. The new error message can be either a file on the Server or a CGI script. You can set customized error messages for the following:

- Unauthorized Access
- Forbidden Access
- File Not Found
- Server Error

> **Note**
>
> For several settings, Error Responses being one of them, the Enterprise server allows you to select which files are affected by the modifications that you make.
>
> **Choose Entire Server** applies your changes to every document that the server maintains.
>
> **Browse files** allows you to specify files or directories to which you want to apply or deny the changes.
>
> **Choose Wildcard Patterns** lets you apply your changes to files or directories you specify with wildcard patterns. This is an easy way to specify a large number of files in separate directories (such as *.html) or files in specific subdirectories (such as /image/*).

Dynamic Configuration Files

Even though Web Server Content is often maintained by several people, for security purposes it is ill-advised to give every user access to the Administration Server. At the same time, a Webmaster could easily get innundated with requests if he has to make every small configuration change on a Server for all of the users. The Dynamic Configuration Files option allows a Webmaster to give users access to a subset of configuration options, so that they can control only those elements which they need to.

Individual users can use a configuration file called .nsconfig in their personal directories to set a number of parameters, including custom error messages, defining file types or encoding, as well as activating access control.

Access Control

Access Control serves two major purposes: managing user databases, and controlling access to directories and files on the Server. Information on individual users or groups is stored in the Servers' built-in user databases. This information can be used in a variety of ways, the most important of which is user authentication.

Since Access Control allows you to set both read and write permissions on specific directories and files, it can be used in two separate ways. The first is to restrict individuals not found in the database from accessing information on the site. (Alternatively you can also deny access to particular hosts or domains.) Since Access Control also sets write access, it can also be used to select which users are able to use Navigator Gold to remotely create or update files on the server.

Encryption

The basic concept that allows the Internet to exist, the free passing of information from one computer to another over public networks, is also its key drawback. Since information being sent from one host to another is passing over public networks, it is possible that the information could be intercepted by others. What is worse is that due to the basic fundamentals of Internet Networking, it will always be possible for users to intercept data in transit.

Does this mean that you are exposing yourself to all sorts of risks? Thankfully, no. Consider most network communications to be as safe as voice communications over the phone or sending a letter via the mail. If, however, you do have information that is sensitive to prying eyes, encryption is the solution. *Encryption*, similar to encryption on your PC, disguises information before it is sent over the Internet, making it meaningless if someone intercepts it.

To address the security issue, Netscape products use the Secure Sockets Layer (SSL). SSL guarantees that information sent over a network can not be deciphered even if it is intercepted. It also ensures the integrity of information, not allowing users to intercept, change, and resend pieces of information. Finally, it can also be used to authenticate that a piece of information was actually created by the party claiming to have created it.

II

Setting Up Software

Using SSL

The basic operation of SSL is simple. The Enterprise Server has a "privacy key" attached to it. One part of this key is public, the other is private. When a browser wants to send encrypted information to a server, it reads in the public part of the Server's key. It then encrypts the message with the public side of the key and sends the encrypted message to the Server. Since only the private side of this particular key can decrypt the message, the Server is the only place where the message can be decrypted. Setting up SSL on the Enterprise Server takes several steps and involves a few different parties.

1. First, generate a Key using the "Generate Key" option. This part is the public key and will be used to create your private key.

   > **Caution**
   >
   > If you forget your password, you will have to generate a new key-pair file and obtain another certificate (leading to additional costs). This will lead to your secure server being down until you receive the new certificate, and you will be unable to read already encrypted messages.

2. Next, request a Certificate from a Certification Authority (CA) by filling in the request form and completing the appropriate paperwork. (There is a setup fee and an ongoing fee for Server Certificates. Rates vary among Certification Authorities.)

   Obtaining a certificate can take anywhere from two days to two months so plan ahead!

3. Once the Certificate comes back from the CA, you can install it on the server and activate security.

   Since it is possible to have multiple certificates, and since certificates run out every year, the certificate management option becomes important to ensure that all the right certificates are installed and activated.

Programs

The Enterprise Server is capable of much more than just serving up HTML, text, and graphics files. It is possible to run programs either on the client or on the Server that allow for any type of interaction you can imagine. You might allow users to use a search program on your server to find information that they need; a user might use a custom group-scheduling program to schedule a meeting; or a user might be logging her timesheets trough a Java application.

The Enterprise Server currently supports three types of programs: CGI, Java, and JavaScript. CGI (Common Gateway Interface) programs can be written in any number of languages such as Perl, C, and C++. The common feature between CGI programs is that they have a standard method in which they accept and return information. Java is a full-featured programming language that was created by Sun Microsystems for use on the Internet. JavaScript is a simpler scripting language based on Java, especially useful for creating simpler Web applications.

CGI

CGI scripts can be run on the Server in one of two ways. The first is to set the server up with a cgi file type (with a .exe or .cgi extenstion), so that CGI scripts can be run from anywhere on the server. The other option is to specify on directory as the cgi directory and only allow files within that particular directory tree to be executed. To set up a cgi directory:

1. Under URL Prefix, enter the trailing part of the URL that indicates you are accessing a CGI script (this is usually *cgi-bin).*

2. Under CGI Directory, enter the full path to your CGI directory (such as c:\Server\cgi-bin).

> **Caution**
>
> You can use both the CGI Directory and the CGI extension settings concurrently. For security purposes and due to the nature of CGI scripts, however, it is recommended that you keep all of the CGI scripts in one directory and that you not let inexperienced users install their own CGI scripts.

Java and Javascript

This option allows you to activate the Server's Java interpreter and to specify the Java applet directory. Similar to the CGI directory, this allows you to specify a directory on the server where all Java applets will be stored.

> **Note**
>
> No, this feature does not turn your computer into a coffee grinder. Java is a new programming language based on C++ that was designed to run as an interpreted language. Rather than have users download precompiled applications, by using Java a client can download a section of source code, interpret it, and run it on the client machine. Java applets can be used to generate on-the-fly graphic reports, query databases, conduct interactive training and provide continuous updating information.

Server Status

The most important aspects of running a server are to be able to identify which files are being accessed and how many people are accessing those files. The Access Log stores information on traffic to the server that can later be analyzed using built-in features. The Enterprise Server also allows you to monitor the Servers' usage so that you can keep it operating at its highest efficiency.

View Error Logs

Viewing the Error log allows you to keep track of any errors that the Enterprise Server encounters. If CGI scripts are failing, the error log will often tell you at which point a script might be failing. The error log will also point out when files are requested that do not exist. Often this is due to links becoming outdated or being misspelled. Correcting errors such as these will help avoid aggravating users with a "File Not Found" error message.

Monitor Current Activity

This option displays the current output of the server as well as the number of active processes the server is handling. If you are running a high-traffic server, this monitor will help determine where bottlenecks in the system might lie, and what can be done to enhance performance. (It could show that your system needs more memory to run more processes, or that the system is running faster than the Ethernet card can handle.)

Log Preferences

This option allows you to customize the location of your log files as well as the format to use. By default, the Enterprise Server uses the common log file format. You can also set whether the server will register hosts based on their domain name or IP address (if you have DNS turned off, it will always register them under their IP address). Additional logging features include the following:

- **Referer Headers**: This will log the last page that a user visited before coming to your Web site. This will show what part of your site they were visiting that led them to another area. (Shows cause and effect.)

- **User-Agent Headers:** This will log the type of browser that users are using to access your server. When making decisions on what enhancements (advanced HTML, Java, plugins, ActiveX) to use, knowing what the browser base is will help to make decisions that will benefit the largest numbers of users.

- **Query string of the URI:** This will log the entries after the question mark in a URI. Typically, this is the query string used in searches, allowing you to see what terms people used to find your information.

Generate Log

Rather than having to decipher a list of thousands of individual entries of visitors to a site, this option creates a summary of the log file entries that actually makes sense. Summary results can be displayed on-screen or saved to a file for future reference and comparison.

This option allows you to create a summary of your log file entries that actually makes sense (rather than a list of thousands of entries). By default, the summary results will be displayed to the screen but can be configured to save to a file (in HTML or text format).

> **Tip**
>
> Log files are often overlooked as not being vital. The log files, however, are a direct evaluation of your Web server, showing what areas are popular and what areas are not. They also give vital statistics on the number of hosts connecting to the server, as well as the amount of traffic that different areas of the server receives.

After generating a summary report of your Access Log, you might wonder what the numbers mean. Here is a summary of some of the important figures:

- **Total hits:** This count tells you how many pieces of information were downloaded from your Server. A single page accessed by a client containing 20 small graphics would be registered as 21 hits. Because of the way the counter works, this number has little value, other than it sounds nice being able to claim that your server gets 100,000 hits a day.

- **Total unique client hosts:** This count gives the closest estimate of the number of individuals that are accessing servers. The true meaning of this number is a count of the number of individual IP addresses that are accessing your system. However, it is possible that more than one person might be using the same IP address, so the number of total users lies somewhere above the number of unique hosts.

- **Total kilobytes transferred**: This count shows how much outgoing traffic is leaving your server. This might be a vital number if you are paying for bandwidth on a usage basis.

- **Top X periods:** This shows the times of the day that your server is the busiest.

- **Most commonly accessed URLs:** This shows the individual directories and files that are accessed most often.

Configuration Styles

Configuration styles are a quick and simple way to apply a set of configuration options to specific files or directories on your Server. You could for example set up a configuration style that configures how to handle access logging, how to handle errors, and where to look for cgi scripts. The style can then be applied to files or entire directories, saving the time of having to individually set options for files and directories.

Content Management

Because it is likely that your computer will be used for purposes other than as a Web Server, you probably want to be able to limit the areas that the Web Server can access. The Enterprise Server allows you to configure which areas of your server are accessible to the public, as well as which files are sent by default to a client.

The Primary Document Directory is the highest level which is readable by the web Server. Optionally, however, you can set Additional Document Directories which map to other directories outside of the Server document tree. You could, for example, have the directory /images/ point to d:\images, even though the server root is c:\Server\docs. This option is especially helpful if you are running short on drive space and want to move high disk volume directory trees to another drive or partition.

Remote File Manipulation

One of the most convenient features of the Netscape Enterprise Server is that it allows users to update files remotely via the Navigator Gold software. Using the familiar Navigator interface, combined with a simple WYSIWYG HTML editor, updating files on the Server has become quick and easy.

> **Caution**
>
> If you turn on Remote File Manipulation, you should use Access Control (as mentioned in "Configuring Netscape Server" and "Access Control") to restrict the users that are allowed to write to particular files or directories. Otherwise, anybody will be able to edit your files.

Document Preference

This option allows you to set the files that the Server looks for when a user enters an URL that ends in a directory name. By default, it will look for a file called index.html and then a file called home.html in a directory. To change or add to this list of files, under Index Filenames: enter the names (in order) of the files that you want the Enterprise Server to look for. (Use commas to separate file names.)

If one of the default files is not found, by default the Server will show a directory listing of the files available in the directory, along with graphics to depict the type of each link (directory, file, sound, image, and so on). To turn off graphics, set directory indexing to simple. To turn off directory listings all together, set directory indexing to None.

Note

Turning off directory indexing is often a good way to protect your files. If you have a directory containing only images, a user could easily back into this directory and get a full listing of all your graphics. While theoretically they have access to each of them through the separate Web pages that incorporate these images, there is no reason to make it easy for someone to grab all of your graphics.

In certain situations, you will want your home page to be something other than one of the default file names, or a file other than one in the root directory. If so, click home page and enter the name of the file you want to set as your default home page.

URL Forwarding

As Websites develop, files are bound to move around the server, often onto another server. URL Forwarding allows you to set up automatic fowarding for particular files and directories which have been moved elsewhere.

Virtual Servers

A common need is to have one computer act as if it is hosting multiple web sites. Both Hardware Virtual Servers and Software Virtual Servers allow you to create the appearance that you are running multiple Servers. (See the section "Virtual Hosts" for more details.)

Document Footer

This option allows you to specify the text for a generic footer to add to the selected files. This is especially handy when you want to install navigation bars in the bottom of pages that may change in the future. (With the footers, you have to edit only one file to make changes on all the pages, rather than having to edit all the affected files.)

Version Control

Enabling Version Control prevents two users from editing a single file simultaneously. If Version Control is activated, users can "check-out" documents, preventing others from editing the file. (Other people can still see the document, they just cannot modify it.) Only once a person "checks-in" a document will it be available for others to edit again.

Index Documents

Up until now, searches on Web sites required the installation of third-party search software packages such as Glimpse and WAIS or CGI scripts to do simple searching. The Enterprise Server comes with a built-in, full-text search engine that can quickly be configured to offer your users a quick and easy overview of files on your Server. The search engine allows you to create "collections" of pages and directories, which can then be searched for key words.

Collections are easy to create, and once created can be automatically re-created at specified intervals, or can be edited manually at any time. To create a new searchable collection:

1. Under Collection Name:, enter the name of the collection.
2. Under Description:, enter a brief description of the collection.
3. Under directory to index:, enter the full path of the files to be indexed in this database.
4. Specify whether you want to include subdirectories.
5. Specify the file types to index.

Auto Catalog

Often, a search engine by itself does not provide users with the information they are looking for, nor does it supply them with other relevant information. To address this need, the Enterprise Server comes with a Cataloging system that catalogs files on the server based on modification date, title, author, and a user-defined classification. This allows users to quickly access all files created by a certain author or to view all the files that have been updated or created in the last few days.

Similar to the searchable collections, Catalogs are easy to create, and once created can be updated automatically at specified intervals or can be updated manually at any time.

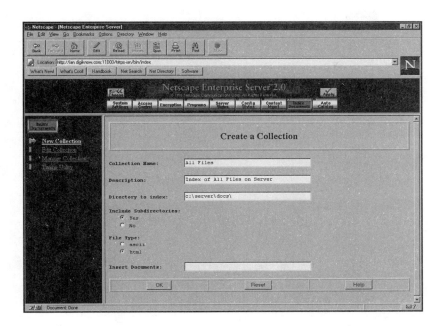

Fig. 5.8
Creating a new collection is as simple as naming it and entering the path of the files to be included in the database.

Installing and Configuring LiveWire

LiveWire is an add-on for the Netscape Enterprise Server which allows administrators to create client-server applications that run over the Internet. Using JavaScript, a variety of programs can be written to create dynamic HTML pages that process user input and maintain data both in files and relational databases. Applications could include in-house on-line training sessions with Interactive tests, Intranet publishing, order tracking, or even something as simple as timesheets.

LiveWire comes in three parts, the Site Manager and the LiveWire complier, the LiveWire server extension, and Netscape Navigator Gold. LiveWire Pro, which comes bundled with an Enterprise Server 2.0 purchase, also comes with a Structured Query Language (SQL) database and report generator.

Installing LiveWire

At this point, you should already have installed the Netscape Enterprise Server, as well as Netscape Navigator Gold.

1. Open the Services Control Panel and highlight your Netscape Enterprise Server. Click the Stop button to halt the Server.

2. Run the LiveWire executable file which you have downloaded.

3. When prompted to Select HTTP Servers to Configure, select the Servers for which you wish to configure LiveWire. (In most cases you will only be running one server.)

4. When prompted to Enter Information, enter the host name under which your server is operating.

5. When prompted to Enter Information for a second time, leave the option blank and click "next."

6. Go back to the Services Control Panel, highlight your Web server and click "start."

Fig. 5.9
The LiveWire application manager is the key to creating Dynamic Web pages.

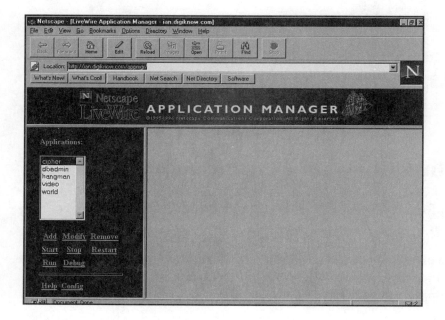

Configuring Enterprise Server for LiveWire

1. Connect to your Netscape Administrative Server through Navigator Gold.

2. Within the Server configuration, click Programs.

3. Under Programs select LiveWire.

4. Toggle "Activate the LiveWire application environment" to yes and click OK.

5. Click "Save and Apply" changes to activate LiveWire.

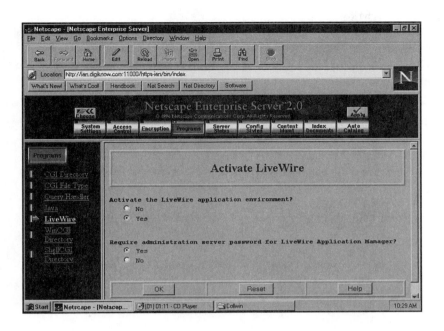

Fig. 5.10
Once LiveWire is installed, it has to be activated from within the Enterprise 2.0 Configuration menu.

Using LiveWire

Once LiveWire is installed, it can be used in one of several ways to help enhance a site. For the Web Site novice, the Site Manager is an easy way to get started building a Web Site. Using a few standard queries, Site Manager will create an entire website based on one of the many templates included with the software. These sites can then be customized to better suit the user.

The most exciting (though most difficult to master) feature of LiveWire is that it helps users develop client-server applications. These applications can serve any number of purposes, from simple mathematical calculations to complete database management.

Virtual Hosts

One of the new integrated features in the Enterprise Server is that it allows you to run multiple Web sites on the same machine. This might be helpful when one department wants to have a Server accounting.company.com, while another wants to have a Server legal.company.com. Rather than purchase two separate Web Servers (which would get expensive if you have many departments), it is possible to run multiple Servers on a single computer.

II

Seting Up Software

The Enterprise Server allows two ways of running additional Servers. The first option is to install a new Server and to run it on a different port. The other option is to run multiple Servers on the same port, 80. Because port 80 is the standard port, the second option is the preferable way of accomplishing this.

There are two ways to run multiple Servers under port 80. The first is to run hardware Virtual Servers; the second is to run software virtual servers.

Installing a Hardware Virtual Server

Before making any changes to the Server, you will need to load additional IP addresses that your NT server will respond to. Under NT, follow these steps:

1. Open the Network Control Panel and double-click TCP/IP protocol in the Installed Network Software box. This will bring up the TCP/IP Configuration   box.

2. Click Advanced to bring up the Advanced Microsoft TCP/IP Configuration box.

Fig. 5.11
NT's Advanced TCP/IP Configuration.

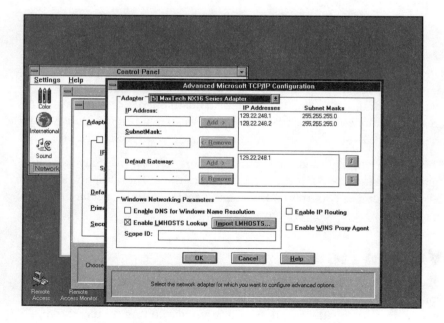

3. To add an IP address to your computer, enter the IP address and the corresponding Subnet Mask in the appropriate fields and click Add.

4. Click OK to return to the TCP/IP Configuration menu, then click OK again to return to the Network Settings menu.

5. To put your changes into effect, click OK in the Network Settings box and restart NT when prompted to do so.

> **Note**
>
> By using this method, you can add only five IP addresses to your NT server, even though the Enterprise server is capable of supporting up to 16 addresses. If you wish to add additional IP addresses, you will have to edit the Windows NT system registry directly. This is an option recommended only to experienced users, as mistakes in editing the registry can cause your system to fail. (Still have that rescue disk handy?) For more information on the subject, see **http://www.lancomp.com/MultipleDomains/**.

6. Under Content Mgmt, go to the Hardware Virtual Servers Setting.

7. In the IP Address field, insert the IP address you just added.

8. In the document root field, insert the document root for the new Server you are installing.

9. Click OK, and then click Save and Apply to make the changes and restart the Server. Now try to open your browser to the new Server you have just created.

Installing a Software Virtual Server

Software virtual servers behave slightly differently than hardware virtual servers in that they do not require a separate IP address. Rather, software virtual servers look at the domain name asked for on the incoming request and will serve up a file appropriately. To install a software virtual server, follow these steps:

1. Under Content Mgmt, go to the Software Virtual Server setting.

2. In the URL Host field, enter the host name to which you want the Server to reply.

3. In the Home Page field, enter the path to the home page to use for the virtual server. (Typing a full path will use the specific document; typing a partial path will be interpreted as being relative to the document root set in the Primary Documents Directory setting.)

> **Note**
>
> For software virtual servers to work, the host name specified in the URL Host field has to have a DNS entry pointing it to the IP address of the server.

II

Seting Up Software

4. Click OK, and then click Save and Apply to make the changes and restart the Server. Now try to open your browser to the new Server you have just created.

Netscape FastTrack Server

The only drawback at this time of the Enterprise Server is the high costs associated with the server. For the business that does not need all of the features that are offered with the Enterprise Server, Netscape offers the FastTrack Server. Smaller, quicker, and easier to install, the FastTrack Server is ideal for businesses setting up their first Web Server.

FastTrack still allows users to update files remotely via Navigator Gold, supports SSL security, and comes bundled with LiveWire. Features that are lacking from the Enterprise Server include the integrated text search, revision control, the Cataloging system, SNMP support and the LiveWire Pro Database.

Troubleshooting

If nothing seems to want to work properly, don't worry. There are several options available for help when you are having trouble with your new Enterprise Server installation. NT itself comes with two management tools—the Event Viewer and the Performance Monitor—that can help to detect errors and optimize a system.

Detecting Problems with Event Viewer

Event Viewer, an application in the Administrative Tools program group, keeps a record of critical events and system errors that might give clues as to why certain operations might be failing. (For example, it would show that the Enterprise Server ran out of memory if you tried to run it on a system with only 16 MB of RAM). If you run into a situation where the server is not loading properly and the Server's Error Log does not offer an explanation, it is highly likely that the Event Viewer will have a detailed description of why the Server failed to work.

Monitoring with Performance Monitor

The Performance Monitor, also in the Administrative Tools program group, allows you to measure a handful of different performance elements. You can measure memory load, CPU load, as well as I/O information to determine where possible bottlenecks on the server might lie. If you installed SNMP when you configured your TCP/IP settings, you will also be able to monitor several TCP/IP elements.

Fig. 5.12
The Windows NT Event Viewer can help lend clues as to why a Server might be failing.

Online Help

If you have tried everything, even having gone so far as to read the manuals and on-line help that come with the Server (which, by the way, are extremely helpful), don't give up yet. There are a number of online resources that can be extremely beneficial in solving problems.

Usenet Newsgroups are a great source of information on any problems you might be having. Following are some related groups:

- **comp.infosystems.www.servers.unix** is a great source of information on UNIX servers.

- **comp.infosystems.www.servers.ms-windows** is a great source for information on Windows 95 and Windows NT-based servers.

- **comp.os.ms-windows.*** offers several groups on various Windows-related issues.

Netscape Communications Corporation has several Server-related help areas available on its home site at http://www.netscape.com. Netscape NUGgies, or Netscape User Groups, are a group of dedicated, secure newsgroups run by Netscape. Discussion groups range from Browser discussion groups to the all-important (for you) Netscape Server User Group. NUGgies can be reached at **http://www.netscape.com/commun/netscape_user_groups.html**.

II

Seting Up Software

The Netscape Server Support page at **http://www.netscape.com/assist/support/server** has links to a wealth of server-related information, including a FAQ, an online installation guide, Technical Notes, Patches, and, if all else fails, a Help Request Form to the friendly techies at Netscape.

No matter what happens, don't give up! Web technology is still fairly new and is evolving every day. New techniques and services are constantly being added, with the result that actual documentation is often hard to find. Most importantly, don't be afraid to ask for help when you need it. There are plenty of friendly WebMasters out there that remember what it was like when they first started administering a Web site. ❖

CHAPTER 6

Installing and Configuring Novell Netware Web Server

Novell Netware is based on the concept of using software modules, called Netware Loadable Modules (NLMs), to extend the functionality of Netware. The use of these modules helps make installations and upgrades faster and easier with less down time when upgrades are being performed.

Novell's Netware Web Server is a high performance Web server capable of providing superior data through-put while offering the ease of installation and configuration features Novell products are known for.

The Netware Web Server is a set of Netware NLMs that run on a Netware 4.x server and responds to requests for documents from other computers, using HyperText Transfer Protocol (HTTP). A request identifies the document by Uniform Resource Locator (URL). The most commonly requested documents are HyperText Markup Language (HTML) documents, but the server can handle requests for any type of file. These documents, referred to as Web pages, can contain any type of information and usually consist of text and graphics. Web pages can also contain sound and movie files as well as other multimedia elements.

In this chapter, you will learn about the following:

- Pre-installation, before you begin, notes
- Installing the Web server
- Configuring and starting the Web server
- Testing the Web server

Module Definitions

The different modules required for the Web Server vary depending on the release, but for the current release, v2.0, the following basic modules are present:

pinstall.nlm	This nlm provides the product installation screen during initial installation.
pconfig.nlm	This nlm provides the product configuration screen during initial installation.
docupd.nlm	This nlm is the installation utility.
webinst.nlm	This is the Web server initialization utility used to start, and restart, the Web server.
uninstal.nlm	This allows for the product to be removed from the Netware server.
pwgen.nlm	This nlm generates the password for the Web server. The password is created in the Web Manager utility.
netdb.nlm	This nlm provides access to the network database.
http.nlm	This is the actual Web server nlm. By default this server listens for requests on TCP port 8000. The server has an information screen that provides directory information, number of requests made to the server, amount of information sent by the server, as well as errors logged and a description of the past nine errors.
basic.nlm	This nlm is the Basic Script Server. By default this server listens for requests on TCP port 8001.
perl.nlm	This nlm is the Perl Script Server. By default this server listens for requests on TCP port 8002.
perlglob.nlm	This nlm is used in conjunction with the perl.nlm.
libgcc.nlm	This allows GCC floating point math glue routines to be performed by the HTTP server.

Before Installing the Web Server

Before installing the Netware Web Server there are a few important items to point out that will help you with installing and using the Web Server.

Set the Maximum Receive Buffers

By default, Netware 4.1 sets the maximum number of packet receive buffers to 100. This number is not sufficient for the Netware Web Server to run reliably, and the Netware server is very likely to abend. Abend errors on Netware servers are critical software processing errors, and for the most part prevent the server from processing any requests until the system has been restarted. Before you install the product, increase the maximum number of packet receive buffers to 1000. You should add the following command to the SYS:\SYSTEM\AUTOEXEC.NCF file:

```
set maximum receive buffers=1000
```

If You Ever Need To Reinstall the Web Server

If you reinstall the Web server, the installation will overwrite the configuration files in the \WEB\CONFIG directory. If you want to keep your existing configuration, you will have to save the configuration files with different file names, and then restore the files after the software installation.

Web Server Language Support

By default the Netware Web Server supports only the English language. When installing the Web server on a Netware server with the Netware server's LANGUAGE set to either German, Spanish, Italian, or French the Web server installation module will load displaying prompts and instructions in English, and not the language the Netware server is set to use. You do not need to change the LANGUAGE parameter value to English.

Configure TCP/IP

TCP/IP must be configured and loaded before proceding with the Netware Web Server installation.

Installing the Netware Web Server Software

II

Setting Up Software

Note

If you are installing the Netware Web Server on a Netware 4.1 SMP Server, the Web Server installation utility will automatically install a SMP version of the WebNLM (HTTPSMP.NLM) to the SYS:SYSTEM directory. If you are using Netware 4.1 SMP, you will need to manually unload the Web server (HTTP.NLM). The HTTP.NLM is for

(continues)

(continued)

the single-processor version of Netware. You will then need to load HTTPSMP.NLM.
To do this, type the following commands at the server console prompt:

```
unload http <enter>
load httpsmp <enter>
```

You will then need to edit the SYS:\SYSTEM\UNISTART.NCF file to load
HTTPSMP.NLM and SYS:\SYSTEM\UNISTOP.NCF file to unload HTTPSMP.NLM.

Installation of the Netware Web Server is very simple. The experienced
Netware administrater should be able to install and configure the software in
10 to 15 minutes.

To install the Web server insert the Netware Web Server CD-ROM into the
server's CD-ROM drive. At the server console prompt type the following commands:

```
LOAD CDROM <ENTER>
CD MOUNT WEB: <ENTER>
LOAD INSTALL <ENTER>
```

In the Installation Options menu make the following selections:

PRODUCT OPTIONS

INSTALL A PRODUCT NOT LISTED

When prompted press the F3 function key to select a source other than drive
A:. Type in the following path:

```
WEB:\DISK1\ <ENTER>
```

The installation utility will start and the message that there is a README.TXT
file to read over will appear. Press the ESC key to continue. You will want to
view the README.TXT file before continuing. When you are finished with
the README.TXT file you will be brought back to this same screen after
pressing the ESC key. Select NO to continue with the installation.

If your server does not have a HOSTS file in the SYS:\ETC directory, you will
be prompted to enter a host name. If your server does have a host file and
there is a name entered in the file, you can just press <ENTER> to continue.

During the copy process you will be asked if you want to install the online
documentation. The Web Server online documentation does not contain any
information to assist you with configuring the Web server software, but it
does contain useful information to assist you with developing Web pages.

> **Note**
>
> If you have a HOSTS file, and you do not remember the host name, you will need to get the host name before continuing. The easiest way to get the needed information is from a work station connected to the Netware server. Use a text editor in Windows or OS/2, or from DOS you can use EDIT or the TYPE command.

You will then be prompted for a password for the Web server. Anytime you make changes in the Netware Web Server Administration Utility you will be prompted for this password before you can successfully save the changes.

> **Note**
>
> We have noticed that if the incorrect password is entered when trying to save changes to the Server Administration Utility a General Protection Fault will likely occur. If this happens, it is best to exit then restart Windows.

When the installation is completed you can press the ESC key four times to exit back to the server console prompt.

Configuring the Netware Web Server

Now you are ready to configure the Netware Web Server. When prepairing to configure the server you will need to perform the following tasks:

- Set up name resolution files, which allow the server to log host names in the ACCESS.LOG file.
- Set up and start the Netware Web Server Administration Utility. This will allow you to configure the Web server parameters to your needs. Settings in the Administration Utility are used to control access of users and other servers on the Intranet.

Setting Up Name Resolution

When a browser makes a request to the Web server the request is logged to the ACCESS.LOG file. The ACCESS.LOG file is in the SYS:\WEB\LOGS directory. Normally the server records the entries with IP addresses. If you want the server to record host names, you will need to set up the name resolution for the server.

You can configure your name resolution as follows:

- If your Netware server is using a DNS server, you will need to verify that your SYS:\ETC\RESOLV.CFG file has the proper entries. If the server does not have a RESOLV.CFG file, you can create one. The following syntax is recommended:

```
domain domain_name nameserver ip_address
```

In this example domain_name is the DNS domain that the Netware server belongs to. The IP_address is the IP address asigned to the DNS name server for the domain. The Web server will automatically try to query the DNS name servers listed in the RESOV.CFG file. If DNS is not used on your network, or the DNS name server is down, or the RESOLV.CFG file has incorrect entry syntax formats, you will notice delays in response times from the Web server.

- If your Netware 4.x server is not using a DNS server, you will need to add IP address-to-host name mappings for each of your client (user) systems to the SYS:\ETC\HOSTS file. Or if you are using a DNS server off site from another server, you will need to include that server's IP address-to-host name mapping. An example follows:

```
127.0.0.1 loopback lb localhost local
IP_address domain_name
IP_address domain_name_offsite_DNS
IP_address router
IP_address dialin_banks
```

Running the Netware Web Server Administration Utility

Before starting the Netware Web Server administration utility you will need to map a drive for the Web server. The mapped drive needs to be on the SYS: volume on the Netware server that contains the Web server software. You can map the drive from either DOS or Windows. The system administrator can setup a permanent mapping in his login script or in Windows if so desired. If the drive was mapped in DOS, start Windows. Once Windows has started you can create a new program item for the Web server administration utility either on your desktop or in the Netware Tools group.

Note

The Server Administration Utility runs in Windows, and there is not a DOS based version available.

The command line on your mapped drive is:

```
\PUBLIC\WEBMGR.EXE
```

The working directory on your mapped drive is:

```
\WEB
```

> **Note**
>
> If the incorrect password is entered when trying to save changes to the Server Administration Utility, a General Protection Fault will likely occur. If this happens, it is best to exit then restart Windows.

Selecting the Web Server to Configure or Modify

Start the Web Server Administration Utility (see figure 6.1). Select the \WEB directory on the Netware Web Server's mapped drive, and click OK. The first page that is displayed is the Server tab page.

Fig. 6.1
The Select Web Server Window.

Now that a server is selected you can procede with configuring the Web Server for use. The Administration Utility can also be used to modify the servers settings to add new users, Web page directories, or add access privilages to other network systems.

The Administration Utility is composed of five seperate configuration pages. Each page is assigned to a specific area of the server's configuration. Each of the configuration pages is assigned a heading tab. The headings are as follows:

- Server. The Server Page configures the server's name, which TCP port is used, the Administrater's e-mail address, the HTML documents directory name, the name of the directory for storing the log files, and whether the server will store and use user documents.

- Directory. The Directory Page configures which existing directories the server will allow outside access to, and what type of documents, features, and indexing options will be used.

■ User Access. The User Access Page configures which users on this
Netware server are allowed access to documents on this server. This
page contains entry fields for the user's name, authentication method,
and a list of allowed users.

■ System Access. The System Access Page is basically the same as the User
Access Page. It is used to allow specific systems on the Intranet access to
pages on this server.

> **Note**
>
> The Netware Web Server has a default configuration that allows all users and
> all systems to access documents published on the server.

■ Logs. The Logs Page configures the maximum number and size of the
log files. Options are also set for how many old log files are saved, and
whether a debug log file should be kept.

Server Tab Page

Fig. 6.2
The Netware Web
Server Utility
screen with the
selected Web
Server's server
configuration tab
page shown.

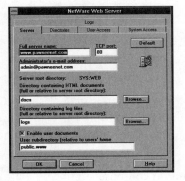

Full Server Name

The majority of Web servers on the Internet, and on Intranets, use their host
names rather then just their IP addresses, if the Netware server uses a DNS
server. Type the fully qualified DNS name for this server in the full server
name field. If your site does not have its own DNS server, leave your IP address in this field. You will then need to verify that the HOSTS and
RESOLV.CFG files are properly setup. We will get to those later.

TCP Port

By default the Web server will listen for HTTP requests on port 80. This is the standard setting for HTTP servers. If the server should listen for requests on a port other than port 80, type the port number in this field.

Administrator's E-mail Address

This field is used for the system administrator's e-mail address. This can be used for users to report problems with the Web server to the administrator.

> **Note**
>
> System administrators can also setup e-mail accounts for problem reports using the Web site's e-mail server.

HTML Documents Directory

This field contains the entry for the default directory name that contains your HTML documents. This field can contain the full or relative path to the Web server's root directory. The default entry is DOCS.

Logs Directory

This field contains the entry for the default directory name that contains your log files. This directory contains your access.log, error.log, debug.log, etc. files. This field can contain the full or relative path to the Web server's root directory. The default entry is LOGS.

Enable User Documents

To allow users of your system to publish their own Web documents from their home directories leave the "x" in the ENABLE USER DOCUMENTS box. If you leave this option enabled, you can leave the user subdirectory set to PUBLIC.WWW or change the name of the directory they publish their documents from. This directory is relative to the user's home directory.

Directory Tab Page

The following tasks can be performed from the Directory tab page, which is shown in figure 6.3:

- Set up or remove a directory from the Netware Web Servers Index
- Set up automatic directory indexing
- Enable server-side includes

Fig. 6.3

The Directory tab page.

Note

You can add a new directory to the document tree by creating a new directory under the document root in DOS or in File Manager. The documents and images stored in the directory will be accessible by Web clients immediately. The new directory inherits the directory options and access control settings from the parent directory. To change the directory options and access control settings start the Web server administrator utility and select the directory on this tab page.

Existing Directories

This field contains the list of directories in the document tree. The document tree is the directory structure of the Web server's file system that has been setup to store documents for the Web. Web browsers can only access documents that are in the document tree, and can't access other directories on the Netware server.

Directory Path

This field displays the path for the directory selected in the Existing Directories Field. It can also display the directory you are adding to or deleting from the document tree.

Contains

This field has a drop-down list to select the contents of the selected directory. You must fill in the Contains Field when adding a new directory to the document tree. You can choose from documents, images, or scripts.

Features Box

Contains check boxes for enabling automatic directory indexing and server-side includes for the selected directory.

Automatic Directory Indexing enables the Web server to generate an index automatically when a browser sends an URL that contains a request on a directory instead of a file. Automatic Directory Indexing can be useful if a directory contains many files or the documents in the directory are changed often and there is not an INDEX.HTM file in the directory.

Server-Side Includes (SSIs) are contained inside the HTML documents. SSIs allow the Web server to modify documents that have a .SSI file extension to enhance capabilities of Web documents. One of the features of using SSIs is to allow a document to request another document inside the calling document.

Index Options Box

This field contains check box options for enabling automatic directory indexing options. These options are only available if automatic directory indexing is enabled for the selected directory.

- Fancy indexing. An automatic directory indexing feature that enables the Web server to generate index entries that show icons, file size information, and file descriptions in addition to filenames. This is useful for directories that contain lists of files and sub-directories and is most commonly used when supplying files for clients to download from your site.

- Icons are links. An automatic directory indexing feature that enables the Web server to create index entries in which the icons that display along with a filename are active links to the document. This is useful for providing a thumbnail of an image file to be downloaded.

- Scan titles. An automatic directory indexing feature enabling the Web server to generate a description for documents in the directory by scanning the HTML documents for titles. Although this feature is useful it should be used sparingly. This feature requires a significant amount of server processing resources and can affect the performance of the system.

User Access Tab Page

The User Access tab page is used to restrict directory access to only authorized users (see figure 6.4). This feature is useful for allowing access only to qualified users.

Fig. 6.4
The User Access tab page is used to restrict directory access to authorized users.

> **Note**
>
> Useful for allowing departments to share information on projects that are in a need to know phase.

Directory Field

This field contains a drop-down list of all the directories that you have access to for authorizing access to.

Authentication Method Field

Describes the type of authentication used to restrict users. A drop-down list is available to choose an authentication method from. You can use Netware Directory Services (NDS) authentication or you can make your own text-based username/password file services.

Network Users List

This is a list of all the users you can allow to access the selected directory using the selected authentication method. The users that are selected for a particular directory will be the only users allowed access to the directory.

Authorized Users List

Contains all the users who have access to the selected directory. Users can be added to this list by selecting a user entry from the Network Users List and clicking the Add to Authorized Users list button. Users can be removed from this list by selecting the entry you want to remove and clicking the Remove button.

System Access Tab Page

The System Access tab page is used to restrict directory access to authorized systems. This feature is useful for allowing access only to qualified systems.

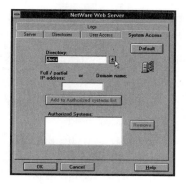

Fig. 6.5
The System Access tab page.

Directory Field

This field contains a drop-down list of all directories for which you can set up access control.

Full/Partial IP Address or Domain Name Field

This field identifies the systems you want to allow directory access to. This field requires either the full or partial IP address or the fully qualified DNS domain name or hostname of the systems you want to be able to access the selected directory.

When access is restricted to authorized systems, the Web server checks the Web client's IP address or DNS domain name before fulfilling a document request. Access can be restricted to authorized systems by the following methods:

- By full IP address. Restrict directory access to 123.12.1.1. Only the system with that IP address will be able to access documents in the directory.

- By partial IP address. Restrict directory access to 123.12.1. Only the systems in the 123.12.1.0 subnet will be able to access documents in the directory.

- By DNS domain name. Restrict directory access to the company_name. com domain. Only systems in that domain will be able to access documents in the directory.

II

Setting Up Software

Authorized Systems List Field

Contains the list that lists all IP addresses or domains that currently have access to the selected directory. Entries can be added to this list by typing an IP address or domain name in the appropriate field and then clicking the Add to Authorized systems list button. Entries can be removed by selecting the entry you want to remove and clicking the Remove button.

Restrict directory access to authorized systems with this procedure:

1. Select the directory to control access from the Directory drop-down list.

2. Enter the full or partial IP address or the fully qualified DNS domain name or hostname in the address field.

3. Click the Add to Authorized systems list button.

4. If you need to restrict access to more directories or systems repeat preceding steps for each authorized system or group of systems.

5. Click OK.

6. Click Save and Restart.

7. Enter your Web server password then click OK.

Logs Tab Page

This page is used to manage the logging files.

Fig. 6.6
The Logs tab page.

Log File Handling Field

This field contains option buttons that specify whether or not the Web server starts a new log file when a log file reaches a set maximum size.

When the ACCESS.LOG file reaches its maximum size, the server saves the file to ACCESS.1. Then a new ACCESS.LOG file is opened. If the option not to roll the log files is selected, the server keeps adding to the log files until the logs are manually cleared.

Server Debug Log Field

This field contains option buttons that specify whether or not the Web server generates a Debug Log. If the option to generate a Debug Log is selected, a log file will be created to assist in troubleshooting if any problems occur while using the Web server. To view the Debug Log in the Netware Web server administration utility select the LOG menu and click on Open Debug.

Maximum Log Size Field

This field specifies the maximum size of the log files in kilobytes. The values of this field can be set if the Log File Handling field is set up to roll the log files. The server will close the log file when it reaches the maximum size specified, and then continue logging with a new file.

Maximum Number of Old Logs Field

This field specifies the number of old log files the server will save. The value of this field can be set if the Log File Handling field is set up to roll logs. When the /LOGS directory contains the maximum number of old log files specified the server will delete the oldest log file, and then open a new file.

Running the Netware Web Server

When the Web server is installed the Netware Configuration Files (NCF), unistart.ncf and unistop.ncf, are automatically updated or created.

The following is an example unistart.ncf file.

```
load netdir
load rpcbstub
load tcp_nd
load local_nd
load tirpc
load netdb
load dispatch
load nisbind
load nisserv
load unixlib
load hostg
load nisswdd
load http.nlm -d sys:Web
load basic.nlm -d sys:Web
load perl.nlm
```

The following is an example unistop.ncf file.

```
unload netdir
unload rpcbstub
unload tcp_nd
unload local_nd
unload tirpc
```

```
unload netdb
unload dispatch
unload nisbind
unload nisserv
unload unixlib
unload hostg
unload nisswdd
unload http.nlm -d sys:Web
unload basic.nlm -d sys:Web
unload perl.nlm
```

The unistart.ncf file is automatically added to the Autoexec.ncf file. This allows the necessary files needed to start the Web server to be loaded during system startup.

If your server has a SYS:ETC\RESOLV.CFG file you should make sure that:

■ Entries in the resolv.cfg file use the correct syntax.

■ If DNS name servers listed in the file verify they are up and running.

The following is an example RESOLV.CFG file.

```
domain company_name.com
nameserver 167.95.7.2
nameserver 167.95.2.3
nameserver 127.0.0.1
```

Set the rights to the \CONFIG directory (SYS:WEB\CONFIG by default) so that the people responsible for administering the Web server are the only people with rights to this directory.

Set the rights to the scripts directories (SYS:WEB\SCRIPTS, SYS:WEB\ SCRIPTS\PERL and any other script directories you create) so that only people responsible for writing, managing, or editing the scripts have rights to these directories.

Once the Web server has started you can test the connection to the server by logging in on a workstation and running an internet Web browser. With the browser running enter the location of your Web server, http://company _name.com/. If this does not work, then try entering the ip address of your server, http://ip_address/.

Note

If your Netware server is not using extended file names, you can save all your HTML documents with the extension .HTM. If your server is using the extended file names, then you can save your files with the .HTML extension.

The Netware Web Server comes with sample .htm files, and has a prewritten INDEX.HTM file so you can easily test the server. There are also sample Pearl and script files included with the server. They are kept in the PEARL and SCRIPT directories. A few images are also included, but they are very basic images.

> **Note**
>
> If you update the Web Server software, run UNISTOP to unload the Web server and its supporting modules. Install the updated software, and then restart the Netware server. To verify the update is running correctly it is recommended to use CONLOG or a DEBUG log file.

Occasionally the Netware Web Server will have problems running. If the Web server itself has an error, it will halt the Netware Server with an abend error, which means the server will need to be downed and restarted.

If errors continue, verify the error you are receiving when the abend occurs. You can also use the DEBUG log file feature in the Administration Utility application to see if errors are being logged by the Web server. If the debug log file does not show any problems, you can use the CONLOG. A conlog file will keep track of the all the messages the Netware server reports. This is very usefull for verifing the server's startup procedure since many modules are loaded, and rarely will you have time to properly note the error condition before it scrolls off the screen. A conlog is started by adding the following line to the start of the Autoexec.ncf file:

LOAD CONLOG

The conlog file can be read from the server or from a workstation that has administrative access.

Additional information about the Netware Web Server can be accessed on the Internet at Novell's site. The address to Novell's Home Page is **http:// www.novell.com**. ❖

II

Setting Up Software

## CHAPTER 7

Installing and Configuring the Lotus Notes Web Publishing Products

Good management is the key to a successful Web site. The most visually stimulating, graphically intense, professionally designed pages on a Web site only have effect on the very first visit. After that, you need to keep people coming back. For electronic commerce, you need to provide visitors with new information, presented in new ways. On a company Intranet, you need to keep your information current. This is accomplished through constant creation and updating of content, directories, templates, forms, and information. The Lotus Web publishing products, either separately or in tandem, can streamline the management of your Web site, and harness the powerful synergy that exists between Lotus Notes and Web technology.

Interactivity is the future of the Web. Most Web sites now only publish static information and maybe permit browsers to submit responses or requests in the form of e-mail. This is only the beginning of what Web technology can do for us. These Lotus products make Notes interactive applications available to Web users. They provide today what most products can only promise in the future.

In this chapter, we will introduce you to the two Lotus Notes Web publishing products, InterNotes Web Publisher and Domino Web Server. If you already have Lotus Notes in your organization, this will be very useful information to you. If you're not yet familiar with Notes, read the section on Lotus Notes in chapter 18, "Groupware Applications." There, we have described Notes and its various Internet connectivity tools.

In this chapter, you will learn the following:

- How Lotus Notes Internet publishing products can affect your Intranet and Notes installations
- How to install, configure, and run the InterNotes Web Publisher
- How to install, configure, and run the Domino Web Server
- How to apply Web publishing technology to your Lotus Notes applications

The Lotus Notes Web Publishing Products

The InterNotes Web Publisher is a set of tools that permits the periodic conversion of views, forms, and documents in Lotus Notes databases into HTML formatted files stored on an HTTP server.

The Domino Web Server is a Lotus Notes server process that incorporates the HTTP and HTML protocols into Notes, effectively making Notes a combination Notes server and Web server, all rolled up into one product.

The products are similar in intent and effect. Both products are add-ons to the basic Notes server. Both products make it possible for you to publish the contents of Notes databases to the company Intranet as HTML documents for viewing with a Web browser.

The InterNotes Web Publisher permits you to convert the contents of any Notes database into a series of linked HTML documents. It also permits a person browsing through those documents to enter search requests and fill in forms. The Notes server will execute any search request and return the results as a linked list of HTML pages. Forms filled in on the Web are converted to Notes documents in the original Notes database. You can republish these new documents as HTML pages. And the arrival of a filled-in form in the Notes database can trigger all sorts of automated workflows. For example, if the submitted form was an enrollment in a training session, its arrival in the database might cause Notes to send an e-mail to the enrollee's manager requesting approval for the enrollment.

There are two key points here. First, InterNotes Web Publisher will publish Notes databases and, as they change, republish the changes. In this process, Notes automatically maintains document links for you. Second, InterNotes Web Publisher accepts queries and form submissions from a Web browser. This permits non-Notes users to participate in Notes workflow applications.

The Domino Web Server does everything InterNotes Web Publisher does, as described previously. However, it works differently than InterNotes Web Publisher. To use InterNotes Web Publisher you have to marry your InterNotes server (the Notes server running InterNotes Web Publisher) to a third-party HTTP server. InterNotes Web Publisher publishes Notes databases by dumping HTML pages into one or more of the HTTP server's directories of HTML documents, and then updating those documents periodically.

The Domino Web Server, on the other hand, does away with the third-party HTTP server and the periodic, scheduled updating of HTML documents under that server's control. Rather, Domino turns your Notes server into a combination Notes/HTTP server. Domino effectively incorporates HTTP and HTML into your Notes server, so that they are now native Notes protocols. As a result, your Web browser can now work directly with your Notes server and participate directly in Notes workflow applications. To put it another way, it makes Notes the world's first Internet application server.

Say you're surfing around with your Web browser. You want to browse a Notes database on a Domino server called (forgive us) DomiNotes. The server appears to you as simply another HTTP server. Its host name, to you, is dominotes.companyname.com. You send your query. DomiNotes replies directly, sending you a list of available databases, or views in a database, or a document, depending on how it is configured and on what you asked for in your query. You sent your query via HTTP. Notes replied in HTTP, converting its database views or documents to HTML on the fly.

At this point, you might ask why are there two products. Well, Domino is really the successor to InterNotes Web Publisher. We suspect that it will eventually replace InterNotes Web Publisher entirely.

But InterNotes Web Publisher is a mature product. Domino is not. Lotus first released InterNotes Web Publisher in May 1995. They upgraded it in November 1995, and again in March 1996.

In December 1995, Lotus announced its intention to eventually incorporate HTTP, HTML, and other Internet protocols into Notes. Domino, initially released in July 1996, is the first fruit of that initiative. It is in release 1. It will be a while before it matures. In the meantime, you may prefer to stay with InterNotes Web Publisher, especially if you already have third-party Web servers in place.

For the time being, each product can do things that the other cannot. Your needs and goals will determine which tool is better for you. You may decide to use one, the other, or both.

Notes and Your Intranet

Notes and InterNotes Web Publisher or Notes and the Domino Web Server can make your company Intranet a truly powerful management tool. To understand how, it might help to step back and look at the current and future benefits of your company Intranet. In this case, we're interested in the HTTP/HTML portion of your Intranet, your "Company Wide Web."

The original and still primary benefit of Web technology is the elegant and inexpensive way it provides for disseminating information far and wide. Management can use it to publish all sorts of important information to its employees. For example, suppose your company training department wants to publish its course offerings and class schedules to the rest of the company. They could distribute it on paper and post it on non-computerized bulletin boards. They could flood the network with e-mail. Or they could publish it on the Company Wide Web, making it widely and conveniently available to anyone with a connection to the network and a Web browser.

The mere publishing of the course schedule solves only one of many problems for the training department. Employees still need to call the training department to enroll in class, find out more about class content, or request an approval form for their manager to sign. A really effective Company Wide Web would allow for interactivity—with online registration, automatic notification of enrollment acceptance, automatic mailing of approval forms, and up-to-the-minute details of class enrollment. A *really* useful Web application would publish information stored in back-end databases to the Web, and would receive information entered in the Web browser back into the back-end databases for further processing.

While it's possible to marry Web technology to other programs in this way, it's no trivial undertaking. It requires some pretty long-haired programming in one or more database languages as well as one or more scripting languages such as CGI, SSI, and PERL.

Furthermore, while cheap and widely available Web browsers make retrieving information on the Internet/Intranet wonderfully easy, publishing that information and managing a Web site full of interconnected pages is a major undertaking. Someone has to create all those HTML documents. Someone has to maintain all the links between those documents. Doing these things by hand quickly approaches impossibility as a Web site grows beyond a couple dozen pages.

There are many tools available to help you code links to back-end databases, to automate the creation of HTML documents, and to manage a Web site full of interlinked documents. Some tools are described elsewhere in this book. Some are cheap and adequate. Others are expensive and elegant. Most require that you have some degree of expertise in HTML, CGI, and maybe other scripting languages. Lotus Notes does the whole job for you, and it does it elegantly, at low cost, and without CGI programming on your part.

The InterNotes Web Publisher

The InterNotes Web Publisher will automatically convert Notes databases into a series of HTML documents, then place those documents into one or more directories under the control of a Web server, so that they are accessible to Web browsers. The InterNotes Web Publisher is designed to make Web publishing less expensive and easier than ever before. InterNotes Web Publisher manages your Web site, taking care of the complex creation, maintenance and linking of documents.

System Requirements

There are two versions of InterNotes Web Publisher:

- InterNotes Web Publisher 2.1 runs on a Notes 3.x server
- InterNotes Web Publisher 4.0 runs on a Notes 4.x server

InterNotes Web Publisher 2.1 runs on the following Notes platforms:

- OS/2
- Windows NT Server

InterNotes Web Publisher 4.0 runs on the following Notes platforms:

- OS/2
- Windows NT Server
- Sun Solaris
- IBM AIX

The InterNotes Web Publisher resides on the same server as Lotus Notes, the system requirements are the same as for Lotus Notes, except that extra memory is required. Lotus may release InterNotes Web Publisher for other platforms after we write this. You can get the most up-to-date information from Lotus' Web site (**www.lotus.com**).

Hardware

InterNotes Web Publisher runs on whatever hardware platform its underlying operating system runs on, which may include an Intel® 80486 or greater microprocessor (33MHz or higher) or a RISC-based processor. In addition to the basic memory requirements of the underlying Notes server, Lotus recommends the following additional server memory to accommodate InterNotes Web Publisher:

- OS/2 and Windows NT: 32 megabytes
- Solaris and AIX: 64 megabytes

Also, you should reserve, say, 100 megabytes of hard disk space for Notes program and basic data files and InterNotes Web Publisher files. Add to that whatever disk space your HTTP server requires and lots of disk space for Notes databases (which are not compact) and your HTML file system. Lotus recommends at least 1 gigabyte of disk space for a basic InterNotes Web Publisher installation.

Network Requirements

Notes operates in virtually any local area network environment. It works with all of the common network protocols including TCP/IP, IPX/SPX, NetBEUI, NetBIOS, Banyan Vines, and AppleTalk. However, InterNotes Web Publisher must be able to communicate with at least one HTTP server. Therefore, the Notes server on which InterNotes Web Publisher resides must use the TCP/IP protocol. Notes can work with the following implementations of TCP/IP:

- OS/2 Notes server: IBM TCP/IP 2.0
- Windows NT server: Windows NT TCP/IP
- Sun Solaris 2.4 UNIX server: Sun Solaris TCP/IP
- IBM AIX 4.1.3 UNIX server: IBM AIX TCP/IP

Software

InterNotes Web Publisher 2.1 (for Lotus Notes 3.x) requires Windows NT Advanced Server version 3.1 or later, and Lotus Notes server for Windows NT version 3.2 or later. It requires OS/2 version 3.0 or later, and Notes Server for OS/2 version 3.31 or later.

For this book, we ran on an NEC PowerMate V100 with a 100mHz Pentium processor, 80 megabytes of RAM, and a 1 gigabyte hard disk drive. We ran InterNotes Web Publisher version 4.0, first with Lotus Notes 4.0, later with Lotus Notes 4.1, both on Windows NT 3.51 (Service Pack 3). We ran it with both the Microsoft Internet Information Server release 1.0 (which is a combined HTTP, FTP, and Gopher server) and the beta 2 release of the Netscape FastTrack HTTP server.

We had difficulty getting the HTTP servers to run properly until we removed Novell's NetWare Directory Service client from the computer. We also had difficulty configuring the InterNotes Web Publisher to work properly with the Microsoft Internet Information Server, and had to seek help on the Lotus InterNotes Web site to solve our problems. Considering how many HTTP servers there are in the world, it is understandable that Lotus could not document the details of running InterNotes Web Publisher with every one of them. Be prepared to seek help on the Lotus Web site (www.lotus.com) if you cannot get InterNotes Web Publisher to work with your HTTP server. Lotus hosts a discussion there in which you can seek answers to your questions about InterNotes Web Publisher.

> **Tip**
>
> To get InterNotes Web Publisher 4.0 to work with the Microsoft Internet Information Server 1.0 under Windows NT 3.51, set the following variable in the Windows Registry:
>
> In HKEY_LOCAL_MACHINE under the subkey:
>
> > \SYSTEM
> > \CurrentControlSet
> > \Services
> > \W3SVC
> > \Parameters
>
> Add the following value:
>
> | Value Name: | CreateProcessAsUser |
> | Data Type: | REG_DWORD |
> | Value: | 0 |

Configuring Your Site

To set up Lotus InterNotes Web Publisher, you must have both a Lotus Notes server and an HTTP server. You can run both servers on the same computer or on separate computers. These two computers must be able to communicate with each other on a TCP/IP network.

You lose the interactivity features (form inputs and full text searches) if both servers are not on the same computer. Therefore, we recommend that you run your Notes server, InterNotes Web Publisher, and your HTTP server all on one computer, as illustrated in figure 7.1.

Fig. 7.1

This diagram illustrates two possible InterNotes Web Publisher site configurations, using either two computers or one.

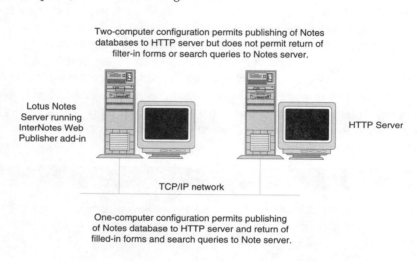

Two-computer configuration permits publishing of Notes databases to HTTP server but does not permit return of filter-in forms or search queries to Notes server.

Lotus Notes Server running InterNotes Web Publisher add-in

HTTP Server

TCP/IP network

One-computer configuration permits publishing of Notes database to HTTP server and return of filled-in forms and search queries to Note server.

HTTP Server and Lotus Notes Server running InterNotes Web Publisher add-in, all running on one computer

TCP/IP network

The Lotus Notes server is actually a group of programs that share memory space on the computer and work cooperatively with one another. The mix of programs that constitute a given Notes server varies according to the tasks it must perform. For example, one Notes server may act as a gateway to other mail systems and so would run mail gateway software that other Notes servers would have no need to run. The other Notes servers, when they have mail to deliver outside Notes' mail system, would simply deliver it to the gateway server.

A Lotus InterNotes server is itself a gateway server. It transfers information back and forth between the Notes domain and the Web server with which it is paired. The InterNotes Web Publisher program runs on the Notes server as a Notes server add-in program. InterNotes Web Publisher consists of a publishing module, an interactivity module, a CGI script, a configuration database, a log database, a help database, and miscellaneous supporting files and databases.

The two modules are executable programs. Along with the CGI script, they do the actual work of converting and passing information back and forth between Notes and HTTP servers. They refer to documents in the configuration database to determine precisely how to do their jobs. And all of their activities are recorded in the log database.

The publishing and interactivity modules reside on disk in the Notes program directory and in memory with the other Notes server modules. The CGI script resides in the HTTP server's designated CGI script directory, and the HTTP server pulls it into memory as needed. The actual filenames of these files vary to conform with the underlying operating system.

The publishing module is the main server add-in program that actually converts Notes databases to HTML files and puts them in the HTTP server's output directory. The interactivity module works with the CGI script to convert information entered into search fields and forms by Web surfers into queries of and documents in Notes databases. (See figure 7.2.)

Fig. 7.2
Webpub converts Notes data to HTML and delivers it to the HTTP server. The HTTP server uses the inotes CGI script to deliver user input to the Notes server, where inotes converts it back into Notes format.

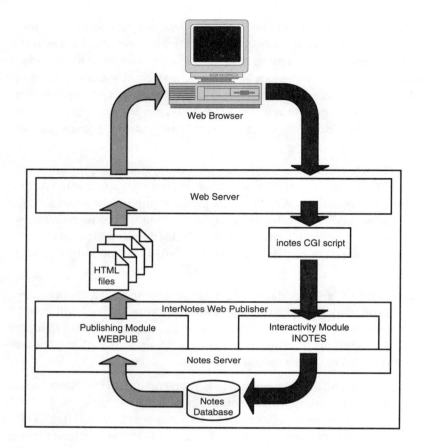

You configure these programs in a Notes database called the Web Publisher Configuration database. One of the documents in this database is the WebMaster Options document. Here, you set global variables that affect all of your published databases. For each published database, there is also a Database Publishing Record document that defines the "local" variables of the publication of that database.

Installing InterNotes Web Publisher

The precise details of installing InterNotes Web Publisher vary depending on the underlying operating system. Lotus provides detailed installation instructions with the software. In all cases, you will accomplish the following steps:

1. Run the install program, which may prompt you for information and will install the InterNotes Web Publisher program files and CGI script in the Notes program directory and the InterNotes Web Publisher databases in the Notes data directory. You may have to tell the install program the names of these directories.

2. If the HTTP server resides on the same computer as the Notes server, copy the InterNotes CGI script from the Notes program directory to your HTTP server's designated script directory. The Windows install process will do this for you. On the other platforms you will have to do this yourself.

3. Add the InterNotes Web Publisher databases to the workspaces of the Notes clients from which you will administer the Notes server.

Starting InterNotes Web Publisher

To start InterNotes Web Publisher manually, enter commands at the Notes server console. To start the publishing module, type **load webpub**. To start the interactivity module, type **load inotes**.

To cause InterNotes Web Publisher to start automatically whenever you start the Notes server, edit the SERVERTASKS variable in the Notes initialization file, NOTES.INI. You can either edit the file directly or use the SET CONFIGURATION command at the Notes server console. In either case, you want to add the variables *webpub* and *inotes* to the list of variables already there. For example, if the line currently reads:

```
SERVERTASKS=Replica,Router,Update,Stats,Amgr,Adminp
```

you will edit it to read:

```
SERVERTASKS=Replica,Router,Update,Stats,Amgr,Adminp,Webpub,Inotes
```

You may want to load multiple instances of the interactivity module into memory. Each instance of it can handle only one request at a time. If you anticipate heavy usage of the search or form fill-in features of InterNotes Web Publisher, loading multiple copies of the interactivity module in memory will allow your site to process multiple requests simultaneously. To load multiple copies manually, just enter the *load inotes* command once for each instance of it. To set up Notes to load multiple instances automatically whenever the server starts up, edit the SERVERTASKS variable so that it looks something like this:

```
SERVERTASKS=Replica,Router,Update,Stats,Amgr,Adminp,Webpub,Inotes,Inotes,Inotes
```

Each instance of the interactivity module occupies about 2.5 megabytes of RAM.

When the publishing module starts, it looks in the root Notes data directory for the Web Publisher Configuration database. It looks for it under the default filename of *webcfg.nsf*. If you want to store the file in another data directory or you want to give it a different filename, you must add a variable to the NOTES.INI file, such as follows:

```
webpubcfg=path\filename
```

where *path* is the partial path, starting at the root Notes data directory, to the subdirectory in which the database will reside, and *filename* is the alternate filename of the Web Publisher Configuration database.

Stopping InterNotes Web Publisher

To stop InterNotes Web Publisher manually, enter commands at the server console. To stop the publishing module:

```
tell webpub quit
```

To stop the interactivity module:

```
tell inotes quit
```

> **Note**
>
> One instance of the *tell inotes quit* command will stop all instances of the interactivity module currently in memory.

To stop InterNotes Web Publisher from starting automatically when the Notes server starts, remove the variables *webpub* and *inotes* from the SERVERTASKS variable in NOTES.INI.

You can also disable publishing of databases without stopping InterNotes Web Publisher. To disable publishing of all databases, set the Publishing Enabled field to *Disabled* in the WebMaster Options document in the Web Publisher Configuration database. To disable publishing of any one database, set the Publishing Status field to *Disable* in the Database Publishing Record for that database in the Web Publisher Configuration database.

Understanding HTML Output Directories

Notes doesn't do all of your Web site management for you. You still get to use some of the skills you learned elsewhere in this book. For example, if you publish multiple Notes databases, you have to link them to one another manually. Also, if you want to integrate Notes-published pages into a preexisting Web site, already occupied by non-Notes-generated pages, you have to take measures to ensure that the Notes-generated pages don't overwrite the non-Notes pages, especially the site home page. You also need to link your non-Notes home page to your Notes database home pages.

When you configure your Web server, you typically specify a directory as the root directory of your Web site. Depending on which brand of Web server you are running, this may be called \HTTP or \WWWROOT. Your site home page resides here, and has a file name that your Web server will look for whenever anyone requests your site home page. The file may be called INDEX.HTM or DEFAULT.HTM or something equally as clever and original. Your site home page will have links embedded in it that will lead eventually to every other publicly available page in your site, as well as to pages at other sites. And the pages on your site will typically reside in subdirectories of the site root directory. Thus, the structure of your site might look something like what's shown in figure 7.3.

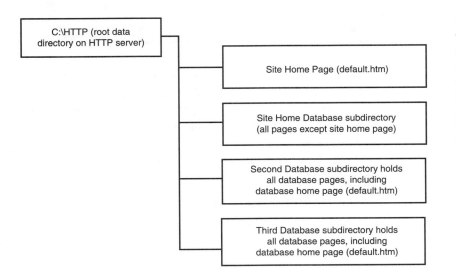

Data directory structure of HTTP server in which all
HTML pages are derived from Lotus Notes databases.

Fig. 7.3
This diagram illustrates the data directory structure of an HTTP server in which all HTML pages are derived from Lotus Notes databases.

II

Setting Up Software

When you configure your InterNotes server, you have to go through the same exercise. That is, you have to specify an output directory for the HTML files that Notes will generate. You have to specify a filename for your Notes home pages, that is, for each published Notes database's home page. You do these things in Notes, in the WebMaster Options document in the Web Publisher Configuration database (see figure 7.4).

Fig. 7.4
The WebMaster Options document tells Notes where to put its HTML output, how to name its HTML output files, and where to look for the inotes CGI script.

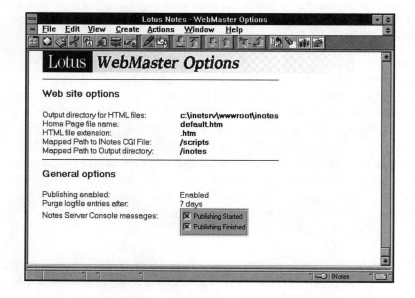

When you publish each Notes database, you have the opportunity to designate it as the "Home Page Database". You may designate the home page of any one Notes-published database as either the site home page, from which all public documents on the site can be reached, or as the home page from which all other *Notes* home pages can be reached. If you only generate pages with InterNotes Web Publisher, your site directory structure will look something like figure 7.3.

Alternately, if you're adding Notes-generated pages to an established Web site, your site directory structure might look like figure 7.5.

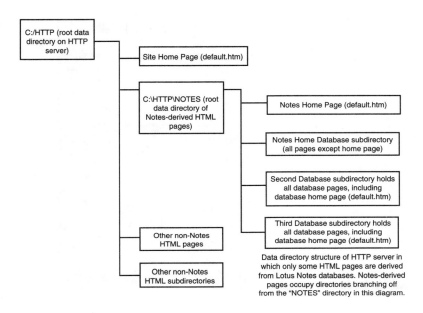

Fig. 7.5
Here, only some HTML pages are derived from Lotus Notes databases. In this diagram, Notes-derived pages occupy directories branching off from the "NOTES" directory.

To set this up, you would configure your Web and InterNotes servers to recognize a subdirectory of your site root directory as the output directory for your Notes HTML pages. You would designate one Notes database (and *only* one Notes database) as the Home Page Database. When InterNotes publishes the database, InterNotes creates a subdirectory for each database beneath the InterNotes output directory. Then, with one exception, it publishes all pages for each database into that database's designated subdirectory. The one exception is the home page for the Home Page Database; *it alone* would reside in the main Notes output directory.

You would have to craft a pointer from your site home page to the home page of the Notes Home Page Database. And you would have to create pointers from the Notes Home Page Database's home page to the home pages of all your other Notes home pages. (Beam us home, Scotty!)

You can insert links by hand in Notes documents or Notes forms in several ways, all of them illustrated in figures 7.6 and 7.7.

Setting Up Software

Fig. 7.6

This figure shows a form in Notes in design mode. It includes four examples of the same URL: a DocLink, a text URL, a graphic URL, and a hotspot link URL.

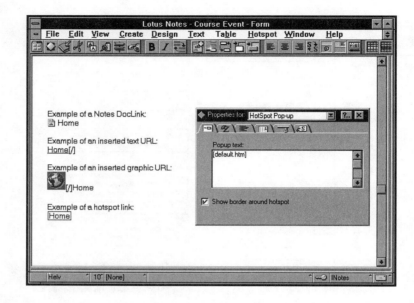

All the examples in figure 7.6 include the word "Home," which is descriptive, intended to tell the reader what document this URL will return. The notation "[/]" is the URL; it points to the home page of the current Web server. The Properties Infobox shows the URL for the hotspot link. Figure 7.7 shows how each of these references appears from within a Web browser.

Fig. 7.7

This figure shows how the examples in figure 7.6 appear in a Web browser.

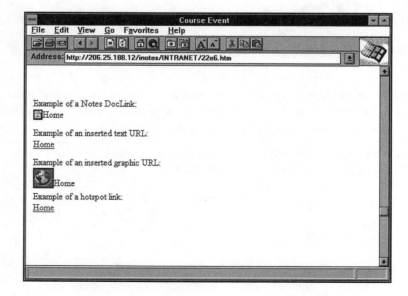

First, you can insert standard Notes DocLinks. In Notes Release 3, you can only link Notes *documents* to one another this way. Beginning in Release 4, you can link Notes documents to other Notes documents, Notes views, or other Notes databases. Notes 4 also allows you to insert hotspots, which act like DocLinks but look like highlighted text, a graphic image, or maybe a button.

Second, you can insert URL references into Notes documents. These can link to any page in your site, to a Notes view, or to another Web site. You can do this either as a text link or a graphic link. To create a text link, underline a block of text, then insert the URL reference, enclosed in square brackets, immediately following the underlined text. To create a graphic link, embed a graphic image in your Notes document, followed by the URL reference enclosed in square brackets. Figure 7.6 shows how text links and graphic links appear in a Notes form in design mode. Figure 7.7 shows how they appear in a Web browser.

Third, in Notes 4.x, you can create a hotspot link in a Notes document or form. In a form in design mode, or in a rich text field of a document in edit mode, enter a block of text and select it. Then, in the menu, choose Create, Hotspot, Text Popup. A box appears around the selected text and an Infobox appears, called Properties for hotspot Pop-up. On the first tabbed page of the Infobox, in the Popup text field, enter the URL surrounded by square brackets (refer to figure 7.6).

An Example Notes Application

Using the example of our training department, we're going to walk you through a typical Notes application. Once we explain the application and how it works in Notes, we'll show you what happens when we publish that application through the InterNotes Web Publisher to our Company Wide Web.

Our training department maintains its class schedule in a Notes database (see figure 7.8). When an employee telephones the department to inquire about a class, the training department employee looks up the information in a Notes database.

Fig. 7.8
The Training Department database, as seen in Notes, with a list of views on the left and a view of available classes on the right.

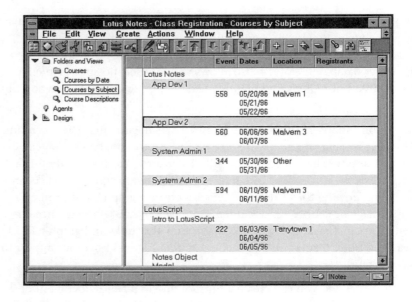

If the caller then decides to enroll in the class, the training department employee fills in a Notes form and stores it in the Notes database (see figure 7.9).

Fig. 7.9
Lotus Notes displays the database enrollment form in edit mode. Corner brackets surround fields where the user enters data. No brackets surround fields completed automatically by Notes.

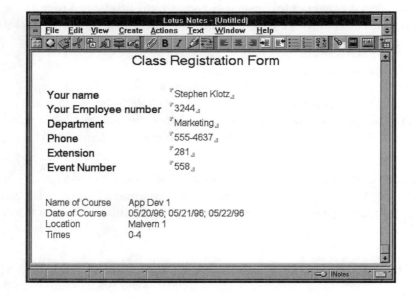

Upon completion of the enrollment form, the training department employee can see the enrollee listed in the Notes view (see figure 7.10).

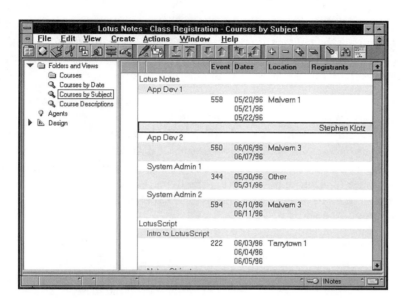

Fig. 7.10
Lotus Notes now displays the name of the new enrollee in the Application Development class.

Notes provides *views* for seeing collections of documents. Notes views look like tables you see in a relational database. Each document constitutes one row of the view. Each column conveys specific information about the document, culled from one or more of the fields. A given database usually has multiple views. In our example, we can view classes by course date, by event, or by course description.

Our example training department application works well, is efficient, and takes little time to learn to navigate. But there's a catch. Any person in our organization who needs to see or retrieve information from our Notes database must have Lotus Notes installed. Or we must Web-enable the database.

Publishing Our Notes Application

How can we benefit from the publication of this database to our Company Wide Web? Well, employees can see the class schedule without having to telephone our training department. Employees can enroll themselves into a class. The database might even be configured to mail a reminder to the employee two days before the class. InterNotes Web Publisher expands our Lotus Notes applications to our employees without our needing to install Notes Desktop licenses.

How would this work? Both Lotus Notes and the World Wide Web consist of server computers and client computers. In both systems, the servers store documents in a particular format and deliver them on request, via a particular delivery system, to the clients. Web servers store files in HTML format and deliver them via the delivery system known as HTTP, which depends on TCP/IP as its underlying LAN protocol. Notes stores documents in Notes databases and delivers them on request via the underlying LAN protocols.

In both cases, the client programs then display those documents as formatted text with various objects embedded in them, such as files, graphic images, sound clips, and video clips. The authors of HTML documents and the managers of the servers upon which they are stored can link the documents together, using hypertext links. Doing so allows readers to jump easily from one document to another by activating the hypertext links. Notes documents can also be linked to one another and to external objects, using a series of tools built into Notes.

You can publish Notes databases to the Web in one of two ways: the quick and dirty way, or the "embellished" way. With the quick and dirty way, you publish a database "as is." You need only to create a Database Publishing Record document in the Web Publisher Configuration database, as shown in figure 7.11. This document instructs Notes to publish the database and defines such details as how and when the HTML version will be refreshed from the Notes version, and which parts of the database will be published.

Fig. 7.11

The InterNotes Web Publisher Database Publishing Record, displayed here by Lotus Notes Release 4, governs how and when a Notes database is published to the Web.

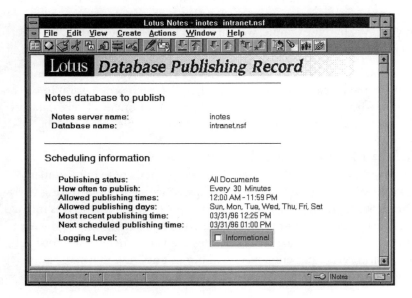

When you save the Database Publishing Record, the Web publisher program creates a series of linked HTML pages from the views and documents in the database. It then copies those pages to the designated subdirectory on the Web server. The "About[database name]" document will (unless you changed the defaults) become the home page, and links to the published views will be embedded in it. The views will become lists of documents, with links to each document associated with its name in the list. Each listed document will become a separate HTML page, and any Notes hypertext links (known as *DocLinks*) will become HTML-style hypertext links.

Let's look again at our Training Department application. This time, we'll look with a Web browser on our Company Wide Web. As employees open their browser, they are greeted with the company home page shown in figure 7.12.

Every database that you publish with the InterNotes Web Publisher has a home page. By default, the home page is a list of all the views in the database, with links to each view. The home page automatically supports navigation of published files through Web browsers.

Fig. 7.12
The Company Wide Web home page is displayed here in Microsoft Internet Explorer, a Web browser. This page originated as the "About [database name]" document in a Lotus Notes database.

You'll want a home page for your entire site. On this site home page, you can add links to the database home page document of every database you publish. You can tell the InterNotes Web Publisher which of your home pages is the home page for the entire site. (Got that? Beam us home, Scotty!)

From the site database home page, we navigate to the Training Department home page (see figure 7.13).

> **Tip**
>
> Since HTML does not support alignment settings, everything in your document will be left aligned by default. To have items appear side-by-side in the published version of your document, enter the items in a Notes table. HTML will preserve alignments in tables.

Fig. 7.13
The Training Department home page is displayed here in a Web browser.

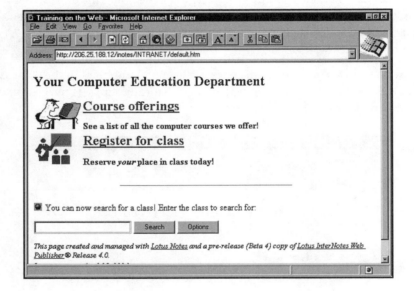

We used an image map in our database home page. Here are the steps we took:

1. Create a graphic and save it as a bitmap.
2. Copy it to the clipboard.
3. Open your database, and choose Create, Design, Navigator.
4. Paste the graphic by Create, Graphic Background.
5. Define hotspots by selecting Create, Hotspot (rectangle or polygon).

6. Click a Run option in the design pane and assign the action for each hotspot.

7. Close and Save the navigator.

8. Create a Notes form that will contain your navigator.

9. Add the navigator to the Notes form as a field named $$ImageMapBody. Choose text as the field type.

10. On the Options tab, enter the name of the navigator in the Help description box.

11. Close and save the form.

12. Publish your database and view it through a Web navigator.

You may want to add some other fields to your home page, as listed in Table 7.1.

Table 7.1 Additional Fields for Home Page	
$$AboutDatabase	Instructs the Web Publisher to include the contents of your database About Database document on the home page
$$ViewList	Instructs the Web Publisher to include a list of all of the database views on the home page, and create links from each view name to the corresponding view
$$ViewBody	Instructs the Web Publisher to include a specific database view on the home page, and create a link from each document name in the view to the corresponding document
$$ImageMapBody	Instructs the Web Publisher to include a specific image map on the page

Because our page incorporates a search bar, it originated as a Notes form designed specifically to be published on the Web. If we did not need the search bar, we could have simply used a standard Notes document, the "About Class Registration" document, of the "Class Registration" Notes database.

Now we can take a look at the course offerings by clicking the hypertext, "Course Offerings" (see figure 7.14). This hypertext was created with a Notes Hotspot.

Fig. 7.14

The course listing is displayed in a Web browser. This page originated as a view in the Training Department's "Class Registration" Notes database.

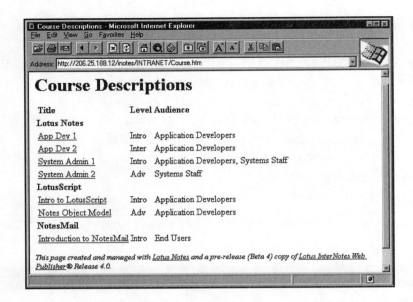

We are interested in App Dev 1. Clicking its URL takes us to a document that describes the course in detail (see figure 7.15).

This page originated as a document in the Training Department's "Class Registration" Notes database. If we want to enroll, we can click the "See Schedule" URL to find out when the course is scheduled.

Fig. 7.15

A document describing a course is displayed in the Web browser.

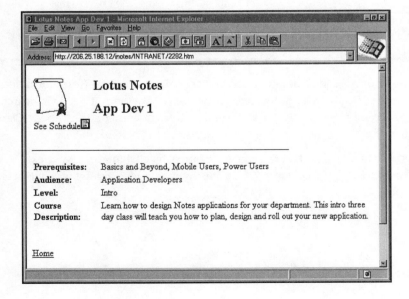

If we want to enroll in the course, we can click the "See Schedule" icon. A list of courses and their scheduled times appears as shown in figure 7.16.

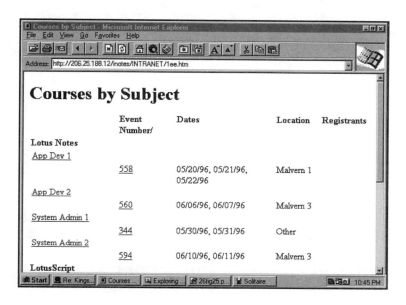

Fig. 7.16
This list shows the dates, times, and locations of the offered courses.

If we click the URL for one of the scheduled dates, the Class Registration Form appears (see figure 7.17).

This form originated as a form in the Training Department's "Class Registration" Notes database. When the enrollee submits the form, it will generate a document in the Notes database. If we desire, it can also be published back to the Web.

As you can see, our Notes databases look very much like they did when we viewed them in Notes, and Notes doesn't care which Web browser you use.

II

Setting Up Software

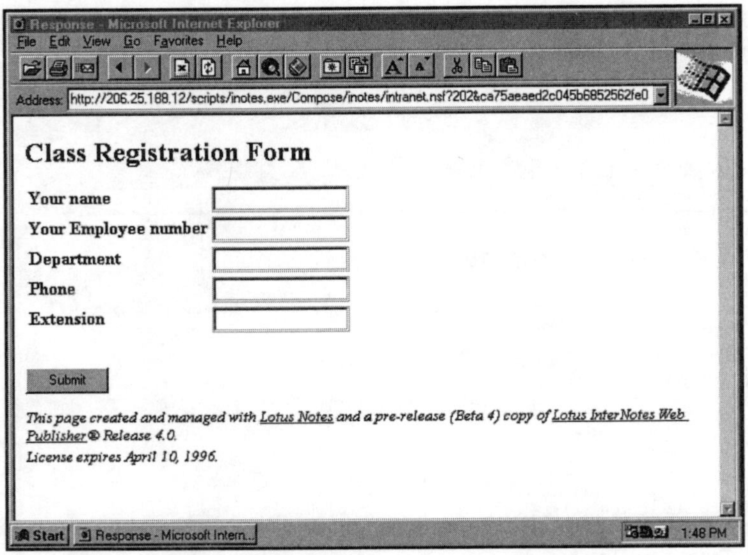

Fig. 7.17
The Class
Registration Form
is displayed here.

A Snapshot of Publishing with InterNotes

In the preceding example, when the database was published, InterNotes did the following:

- Published the About Database document from our Training database (TRAINING.NSF) and made it the home page for the database

- Listed our database views as hypertext links on the home page

- Converted each Notes document into an HTML file

- Converted our Notes forms into HTML forms

- Converted our Notes DocLinks into hypertext links

- Converted our Notes tables into HTML tables

- Converted bitmaps in our Notes documents into online GIF files

- Preserved the full text index so users can search the database and view the search results in their browser

- Preserved attachments to Notes documents so users can download them from the Web with a browser

Searching Notes Databases from Within a Web Browser

Lotus Notes, being a repository of information, naturally comes with a lot of tools intended to make it easy to find the information you need. One of the most powerful is its full text search engine. To enable it, you have to create a full text index of the database to be searched. You create the index by selecting options in the Notes menu or, in Notes Release 4, by selecting an option when you create the database. After you have created the index, you can use Boolean search terms ("x and y", "x or y", and so on) to search for any text string that appears anywhere in any document in the indexed database.

InterNotes Web Publisher extends this powerful tool out to the Web. You can insert a search bar into a Notes-generated home page or view page. A user who brings up the page in his or her browser can enter a search string into the text field in the search bar, then click the Search button (see figure 7.18).

InterNotes Web Publisher conveys the search string to the Notes server, which performs the search. InterNotes Web Publisher takes the search results and displays them to the user as a linked list of HTML documents. Those having the most "hits" appear at the top of the list. Click the link for any document to display it in the usual fashion.

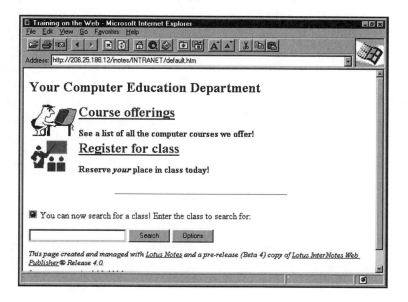

Fig. 7.18
This is the Training Department home page, as seen in a Web browser. Note the search input field.

II

Setting Up Software

This search bar was embedded in our Notes form by adding a field to a form call $$ViewSearchBar, as shown in figure 7.19. The Notes Help Description of this field is the name of the Notes view we wish to search.

Fig. 7.19
This is a Notes document in design mode, displaying the search bar field ($$ViewSearchBar), which becomes the search input field illustrated in figure 7.18.

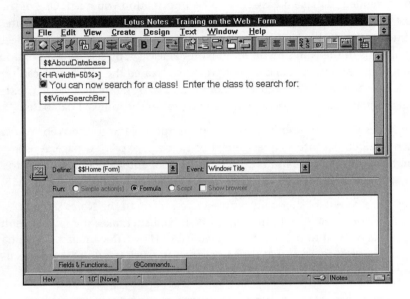

Building Interactive Web Applications with Notes Forms

As you can see, Notes users use Notes forms as templates to create new documents. InterNotes Web Publisher permits the WebMaster to publish Notes forms as HTML forms that people can fill out in their browsers. When a user clicks the Submit button on the form, InterNotes Web Publisher submits the form to the Notes server, which then stores the form in a Notes database as a standard Notes document. If you don't create a Submit button on the form, InterNotes Web Publisher automatically creates it for you.

What Notes does with that document next is solely up to the Notes database designer. The document might be republished as yet another HTML document, now available for anyone to view in their browser. Or it might be internally processed by Notes and become part of a workflow in the everyday business of the company. Either way, the WebMaster has just extended Notes functionality to non-Notes users, either in the form of a Web-based discussion database, or as a Notes workflow application.

WebYou can also capture information from Web users by adding CGI environment variables to Notes response form fields. When the user submits the form, INOTES.EXE populates the fields with the appropriate information, which can then be used by Notes to process the response.

Adding HTML Code

You might have existing HTML files that you want to display on your Intranet, or you may want to apply HTML attributes and formats that are not available in Notes. To do so, you have two choices:

- Store existing HTML pages in a Notes database
- Include HTML code within a Notes document or form

To store HTML pages in your Notes document, you can paste them into a special field, a rich text field which you have named "html." When the Web Publisher publishes the document, it creates a separate HTML file containing the output of the HTML code. This page will display as a separate page on your Web.

To include HTML code in a Notes document, you can enter the HTML instructions on the form or in a rich text field in a document. You can also create and apply a paragraph style named HTML. Either way, the syntax for HTML code is:

```
<html code>
```

where *html code* is the HTML instruction you want to include. For example:

```
<center>
```

Some Notes formatting is not converted or supported by HTML. Table 7.2 lists some of those features.

Table 7.2 Notes Formatting Features Not Supported by Nor Converted to HTML

Text Size	Use Paragraph Styles in Notes or map fonts through fields in the Database Publishing Record
Alignment	HTML displays all text and graphics left aligned, unless placed in a table
Borders	The top left cell of the table determines if the table will have cell borders. If the top left cell has no border, the entire table will have no border. If the top left cell has a border, the entire table will have a border

(continues)

Table 7.2 Continued	
Column Widths	Column widths will be sized to the column's widest entry
Font and style	Rich test attributes are not supported, except attributes **bold** and *italics*
Buttons	The Web Publisher will not translate buttons

The Lotus Domino Web Server

In July 1996, Lotus released the Domino Web Server, which is a Notes server task that effectively makes the Notes server an HTTP server or, in Lotus's words, an Internet application server. It incorporates six Internet protocols right into the Notes server: HTTP, HTML, URL syntax, CGI, MIME encoding for the Web, and SSL. It also supports Java and Javascript. Lotus promises to support future Internet protocols as they emerge, including fast CGI, ISAPI, and NSAPI.

System Requirements

Unlike InterNotes Web Publisher, Domino only works with Notes Release 4. If you are still using Notes Release 3, you can only use InterNotes Web Publisher.

The initial release of Domino runs only on the Windows NT platform. Lotus is actively developing it for Solaris, AIX, and HP/UX as well.

The system requirements for Domino are the same as for the Lotus Notes server, except that Lotus recommends more RAM than the Notes server would otherwise require. Lotus normally recommends 48 megabytes of RAM under Windows NT, but recommends 64 megabytes of RAM when running Domino.

Also, the server must be running the TCP/IP suite.

Domino, like InterNotes Web Publisher, runs on the Notes server as a Notes server add-in program. It consists of a server add-in task, nhttp.exe, plus a series of supporting DLL programs

Installing the Lotus Domino Web Server

Domino I, released in July 1996, is an add-in server process downloadable from the Lotus Web site free of charge that must be installed manually. Domino II, a fully integrated Notes/HTTP server announced by Lotus for release in the fall of 1996, will probably automate the install process. The process includes the following steps:

1. Download the Domino files from the Lotus Web site, www.lotus.com. You actually want to perform at least two downloads. One is the Domino program files. The second is the Domino User's Guide, which is a Notes database covering all aspects of Domino setup, configuration, and use. Optionally, you may want to download whatever sample databases may be currently available, either to adopt them to your own use or to examine for programming ideas.

2. Shut down the Notes server and client if they are running.

3. Run the install program, DOMINO.EXE, which is the only file that you receive in the download from Lotus. The InstallShield Wizard prompts you for the locations of the Notes program and data directories, and for the name of the Windows Program Manager group in which it will create program icons. Then, it creates several subdirectories and places executable files and DLLs in the Notes program directory, some databases and templates in the Notes data directory, and some support files in the created subdirectories.

4. Update the Notes public address book by adding a subform and a field to it. In this step, you actually copy and paste the subform and field from a database template, HTTPCNF.NTF, that comes with Domino, to PUBNAMES.NTF, the template for the Notes public address book. The subform will later show up in the Domino server's server document as a new section called HTTP Server, which includes all the fields necessary to configure the HTTP side of the Notes server. The new field is the HTTP Password field, which will later appear in every Person document. You might want to make backup copies of the public address book and its template before you perform this step.

5. Refresh the design of the public address book to complete step 3. In step 3, you updated the server and person forms in PUBNAMES.NTF, the template on which the public address book is based. In this step, you update the same forms in NAMES.NSF, the public address book itself.

Configuring and Starting the Lotus Domino Web Server

After you install the Domino Web Server on your Notes server and update, you have to confirm the settings in the HTTP Server section of the server document, then confirm that everything is working properly by starting the server.

The HTTP Server Section of the Server Document

The HTTP Server section of the server document controls the behavior of the HTTP side of the Domino server. It includes default settings for the TCP/IP port number, Home URL, SSL port number and key file, several directories and their mappings, and various other server settings. You may not need to change any settings, but you should review them to make sure. The HTTP Server section of the server document, with its default settings, appears in figure 7.20.

Fig. 7.20
The HTTP Server section of the server document, shown here with its default settings, controls the behavior of the HTTP side of the Domino Server.

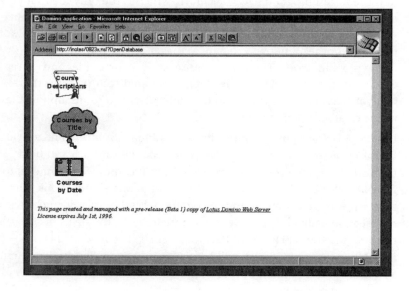

Settings that you might especially want to change include the Host Name, DNS Lookup, Home URL, and the Logging fields. The Host Name field starts out blank, which means that your server will answer to whatever name appears in its TCP/IP stack. Alternately, you could enter the host name or an alias name that is registered with the computer's Domain Name Server, or its IP address. If Web browsers cannot find this server after you start it up, you may need to change the entry in this field.

Use the DNS Lookup field to tell your server whether or not to look up the host names of requesting Web clients. By default, DNS Lookup is disabled. Enabling will slightly slow down the server's performance.

The Home URL is set by default to /?Open. This means that when a Web user accesses the server by site name only, without specifying a directory or file name, your server will return a list of available Notes databases. The Web user could then click a database name to open it and see its available views, then click a document name to see a document. First impressions are all important on the Web, however, and you may want to present something a little catchier than a list of databases when a Web user comes calling. If you prefer, therefore, to have Domino return the site home page, you could either enter its name (which by default is /default.htm) or leave this field blank.

The server logging fields, by default, are blank, and therefore the server will *not* maintain an activity log. If you want to maintain a log, enter log file pathnames in the Access log and/or Error log fields. You can also enter user names in the Log filter field to specify those users whose activities you do *not* want to log.

Starting and Testing the Domino Web Server

Restart your Notes server. Start Domino by entering the following command at the server console prompt:

```
load http
```

A copyright notice should appear on the console, followed by the message "HTTP started." Congratulations! It's running. Now try to access the server with any Web browser. Enter its URL or IP address in the browser and press Enter. If you did not change Home URL field in the server document, your browser should now be displaying a list of Notes databases stored in the data directories of the Notes/Domino server. If you did change the Home URL field, you should be seeing the server's home page.

Finishing Domino Web Server Setup

If, from now on, you want HTTP Services for Lotus Notes to start automatically along with the Notes server, you can edit the NOTES.INI file, adding *HTTP* to the SERVERTASKS variable. When edited properly, SERVERTASKS will look something like this:

```
SERVERTASKS=Replica,Router,Update,Stats,Amgr,Adminp,HTTP
```

This statement will cause HTTP Services for Lotus Notes to start up along with all the other Notes server tasks listed, when you start the Notes server.

If you ever need to start the HTTP server task manually, enter the following command at the server console:

```
load http
```

If you ever have to stop the HTTP server task manually, enter the following command at the server console:

```
tell http quit
```

Notes Security

At this point, with the HTTP server task running and the Notes server connected to the Internet or Intranet, any Web user can access your databases. Since you probably don't want just any net surfer browsing around in our Notes databases and perhaps making changes in them, you may now want to invoke Notes security features to limit database access.

Notes has very strong security features. To gain access to databases on a standard (non-HTTP) Notes server, a Notes user has to first *authenticate* with the server, then survive the server's access list, then get past a series of access lists in each database. In the authentication process, both the user and the server have to prove to each other that they are members of *trusted* organizations and they have to prove their identities. This involves a series of encryptions and decryptions of information using public and private keys. Once the server has authenticated the user, the server may still refuse the user access to the server if the user is in a *Not Access Server* field or is *not* in an *Access Server* field in the Server's server document.

If the user gets past this checkpoint, the server will consider any user request to access a database. The server will consult the database's Access Control List, where the user may be listed, either individually or as a member of a group, as having *Manager* access, *Designer* access, *Editor* access, *Author* access, *Reader* access, *Depositor* access, or *No* access. Or the user may not be listed at all, in which case the user will be granted the *Default* level of access, which could be any of the listed levels. The rights that each access level grants are in Table 7.3.

Table 7.3 Lotus Notes Database Access Rights	
Access Level	**Activities Allowed**
Manager	The database manager can do anything in a database, including change the Access Control List
Designer	Database designers can do anything in a database, including making changes in the database design, but excluding making changes in the Access Control List
Editor	Database editors can add data documents to a database and can make changes in any data document in the database, regardless of the document's authorship. Editors *cannot* change database design or the Access Control List
Author	Database authors can create new data documents and they can edit documents they originally created. With certain exceptions, they cannot edit documents not authored by themselves. Nor can they make changes in the database design or Access Control List
Reader	Database readers can read data documents and views but cannot make changes of any kind in the database
Depositor	Database depositors can create and save new data documents but cannot read any document, including their own after they close it, nor make changes of any kind in the database
No Access	Users with no access will not be allowed to open a database at all

Assuming a user has some degree of access that allows him to at least read documents, the user may further be restricted by:

- View access lists, which forbid the use of a particular view to see what documents are in the database
- Form access lists, which forbid the use of a particular form when creating, editing, or reading documents
- Readers fields and $Readers fields, which may forbid the viewing of a particular document
- Authors fields, which may forbid the editing of a particular document
- Section access lists, which may forbid the reading or editing of a section of a document
- Encrypted fields, which may forbid the reading of those fields in a document

II

Setting Up Software

In Notes Release 4, you may relax Notes security by allowing unauthenticated users to access a given server and its databases. An unauthenticated user is one whose identity the server has not ascertained and who, therefore, is essentially *anonymous* to the server. You permit anonymous access by setting the *Allow anonymous connections* field in the server document in the public address book to "yes." You can control the degree of access such users have to given databases by adding *Anonymous* to each database's access control list and specifying the degree of access that *Anonymous* shall have. If you don't add *Anonymous* to a database Access Control List, anonymous users are granted *Default* access.

Notes Security and the Domino Web Server

When you install Domino on a Notes server and load the HTTP server task into the server's memory, you permit unauthenticated users to access your server and its databases *even though you didn't expressly do so* in the *Allow anonymous connections* field. As a result, whether you like it or not, Web users now have access to your databases. They have *Anonymous* access to any database in which *Anonymous* appears in the database's Access Control List. They have *Default* access to all other databases.

You can tighten up the security of the databases on your Domino server in several ways. First, you can review the Access Control List of every database on the server and ensure either that there is an entry in it for *Anonymous*, with the appropriate degree of access assigned, or that the degree of access assigned to *Default* is appropriate for unauthenticated Web users. Second, you can deny anonymous access to a given database, then require Web users who want access to it to register with you. This is known as "basic authentication," is a standard Web authentication technique, and gives a Web user *individualized*, that is, no longer anonymous access. Third, you can activate Secure Sockets Layer (SSL) security for Web-based transactions.

You can give a Web user *individualized* database access if you create a Person document for that user entering data in two fields. First, you must enter the user's name in the User Name field. This must be a *non-distinguished* name. That is, it must consist of a first name, optional middle initial, and a last name, and nothing more. Second, you must enter a password into the HTTP Password field. The password will be encrypted as soon as you save the Person document.

You can also give your registered Notes users access to the server via Web browser by making two changes in their Person documents. First, you have to change the User Name field so that it includes a non-distinguished version of their name as the first entry in that field. For example, that ace salesman for Acme Corporation, Bob Dobbs, is a Notes user whose fully distinguished name, as it appears in his Person document, is *Bob Dobbs/Sales/AcmeCorp*. You can insert his *common name*, Bob Dobbs, at the beginning of the field, separated from his fully distinguished name by a carriage return. The resulting entry in the field will look like this:

```
User name:     Bob Dobbs
               Bob Dobbs/Sales/AcmeCorp
```

Second, you have to enter a password in the HTTP Password field of the user's Person document. Thereafter, your Notes users will be able to access the Notes server using either their Notes client or Web browser.

Tip

If you don't feel like personally creating a Person document for every Web user who wants access to restricted databases (you lazy person, you!), you can set up a Notes registration application that will allow Web users to register themselves. Lotus provides a sample registration application at domino.lotus.com. Download it, use it as is, customize it, or pirate pieces of it and create your own registration application.

Domino and the SSL Protocol

The Domino Web Server supports the Secure Sockets Layer (SSL) security protocol. SSL is a public/private key encryption system that supports encryption of data transferred between the Domino server and Web clients, validation that messages were not tampered with en route, and digital signatures. This, in turn, permits you to establish true user/server authentication between Web users and your Domino Web server.

The SSL system works like other public/private key systems, such as Notes' own security system. That is, each user and server generates both a private key and a public key. The user or server then makes the public key available to the world and keeps the private key to him/her/itself.

The private key can decrypt data that was encrypted with the public key. The public key can decrypt data that was encrypted with the private key. If I want to encrypt a message to you, I do so with your public key. Only you have possession of your private key, so only you can decrypt the message. If I want to assure you that the message is really from me and not some impostor, I can sign the message with my private key. If you can decrypt the signature with my public key, you can assume it came from me, since (presumably) nobody but me has access to my private key.

The weakness of public/private key encryption systems is that anyone could send you a public key and tell you it is from me. How do you verify that it really is from me? Either you have to get the public key from me personally, establishing positive identification of me at that time, or you have to get someone whom you trust, a Certification Authority (CA) in SSL parlance, to vouch for me and the public key I am offering you. And, of course, I have to establish trust of your public key the same way. SSL, as implemented by Domino, permits you to establish trust either way. Either you can self-certify or you can involve a CA.

The way it works with a CA is that you and I both get the same CA to vouch for us (sort of like a mutual friend). The CA does it by issuing each of us a certificate, which we store in a file called a *keyring* file. My certificate states that I am who I claim to be. The CA signs the certificate and includes its own public key. When you and I initiate a conversation, we exchange certificates. Each of us trusts the certificate presented by the other because it is signed by the same CA who signed our own certificate. Therefore, we can safely assume that the public key presented by each other is genuinely the other's own public key.

When you set up a Notes/Domino server, if you want to set up secure transactions within your own Intranet, you can set yourself up as the company CA. Your office will issue the certificates to your Domino server and to all of the secured users. If you want to set up secure transactions outside your company, say, on the Internet, you could fall back on a commercial CA, such as VeriSign (www.verisign.com).

Domino comes with a Notes application, Domino SSL Administration, that automates the establishment of SSL security. It guides you through the process of either self-certifying or submitting a request for a certificate to either your own internal CA or VeriSign. It also guides you through the process of merging the resulting certificate into your keyring. Finally, if you want to become a CA yourself, it guides you through that process as well as the process of issuing certificates to others.

Publishing Our Notes Application

We wanted to take immediate advantage of the Domino. But some of the techniques we used for publishing our database with InterNotes Web Publisher would not work well with Domino, as indicated in Table 7.4.

Table 7.4 InterNotes Web Publisher Features Not Supported in Domino			
$$ViewList	$$ViewBody	$$ImageMapBody	$$Response
$$ViewSearchBar	$$AboutDatabase	$$Views	

On the other hand, Domino supports certain Notes features that InterNotes Web Publisher does not support, such as navigators created with background bitmaps and hotspots. So we copied our database and made the following changes:

- We created a default Navigator, complete with hotspots as shown in figure 7.21.

- In design mode for all of our views, we added column properties to show "twisties" to support collapsible views, as shown in figure 7.23.

- We deleted our submit button and replaced it with a bitmap hotspot on our class description form (see figure 7.24), which uses the @Command([Compose];formname]).

Searching Notes Databases from Within a Web Browser

To open a Notes database from within your Web browser, enter its URL. Notes equates the server's name with its Internet domain name, so you do not have to know the Notes server name. If you know the path and file name of the Notes database, enter its URL in the following format:

```
http://server.domain.etc/path/filename.nsf
```

If you do not know a Notes database's filename, there is a URL which will prompt the Notes server to send you a list of available Notes databases, in which you can locate the database you want and then double-click its URL to download its default view. To receive a list of Notes databases, enter a URL in the following format:

```
http://server.domain.etc/?Open
```

II

Setting Up Software

Everything up to the question mark is the *Notes object path*, that is, the actual URL itself. The question mark is a delimiter. And the word *Open* is an *implicit action*, that is, a directive to Notes to open an object for you—in this case, to send you a list of available databases.

Figure 7.21 is a look at our application as published by our Domino server. First, we see our Navigators on the Web. This is an unfinished page—we were anxious to see the Navigators print.

Fig. 7.21
Domino will
publish Notes
Navigators.

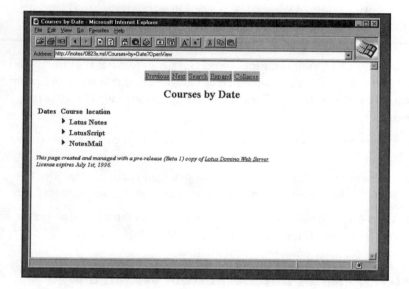

Our Web navigator has three Notes hotspots, one pointing to each of our views. We move to see courses by date by clicking the hotspot. This view shows all courses collapsed in the view. Notice the options across the top of the page. These options, expand, search, and so on, were built by Domino. We did not have to create them. (See figure 7.22.)

Each of the triangle bullets, called "twisties" in Notes parlance, represents a collapsible section of a Notes view. This is a Notes Version 4 feature and it published well to our Web site. Clicking once on the category "Lotus Notes," we can see an offering of Notes classes by class title. Clicking once on the class title, the view expands to show dates and locations of the classes. (See figure 7.23.)

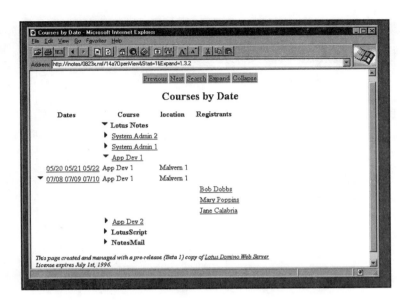

Fig. 7.22
Collapsible Notes views published by our Domino server. Note the hypertext for Search, Expand, and so on. These were created by Domino.

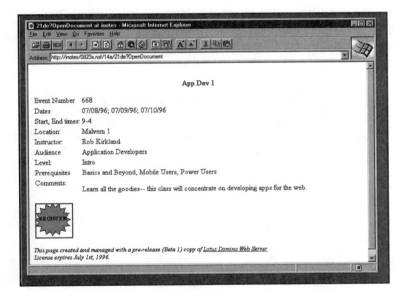

Fig. 7.23
Expanded view of collapsible sections from a Notes view. All of the view features designed in Notes (collapse, and so on). publish to our Web site.

Clicking the hypertext which indicates the date for the scheduled class, we move to the event description to see more detail about this class. (See figure 7.24.)

Fig. 7.24
This is a view of our Notes form, called Event. No HTML code was included in the Notes form itself.

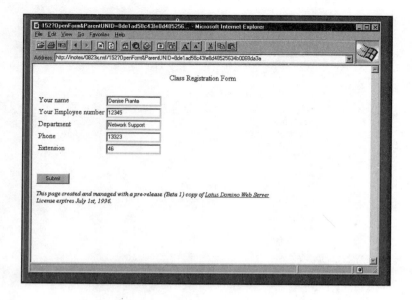

Deciding that we want to register for the class, we click the Register hotspot. This opens the registration page. When we complete our registration, and click the submit button, our registration becomes a Notes document, available to our Notes users with proper access immediately. (See figure 7.25.)

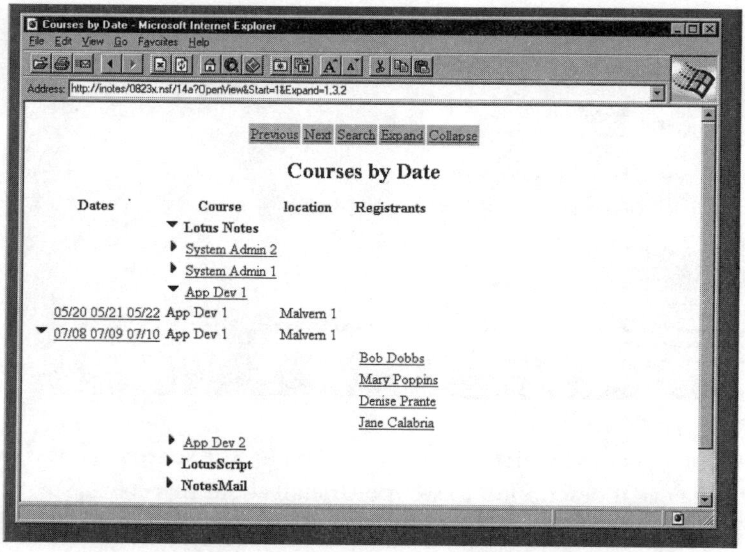

Fig. 7.25
The Notes registration form as designed in Notes. No HTML code was created on this page in Notes. The submit button uses @Commands to save the file and exit the window.

CHAPTER 8

Installing and Configuring Browser Software

One of the most visible choices you will make when designing your Intranet is the browser. This is the software that all the users will use everyday.

Once you choose a browser you need to set it up and also set up the networking software. In addition to this you may also need to set up helper applications, these are programs that work with the browser to display files.

In this chapter, you will learn the following:

- What are MIME types
- How to configure an external viewer
- What is an IP stack
- What to look for in a browser
- How to fix common browser problems

Introduction to Browsers

Setting up a Web server is only a part of setting up an Intranet. You must also configure and install a WWW browser. This browser is what the users see and therefore must be chosen carefully. This chapter covers how browsers work, what software is available, and what features to look for.

Web browsers talk to servers using the HTTP. Once the browser gets the document it must decide how to view or save it.

This is done by comparing the documents mime-type with a list of supported MIME types. MIME stands for Multipurpose Internet Mail Extensions, MIME types are a way of telling software, such as mailers, what type of data a file contains. Some MIME types such as text/html can be displayed directly in the browser. Other types may need to use an external viewer. MIME types are discussed later in this chapter.

Documents may contain more than one file type. A good example of a document that has more then one mime-type would be a document with inlined images. When the browser downloads the file, it sees the inlined images and also requests those from the server. The page is actually one mime-type but the entire document consists of multiple MIME types.

Some browsers, such as Netscape's Navigator, display the text before downloading the images; so users can start reading the page without having to wait for all the images to download. Other browsers such as lynx, don't download the images at all. This is also true if your browser has an option to delay image loading.

Certain images can be partially viewed as they are being downloaded. These include interlaced gifs and progressive jpeg files. These images may start out blurry looking and gradually get clearer and clearer until they are in focus, or they might start displaying at the top of the screen and fill in as they are downloaded. It's also possible to have animated gif files, in which simple movement can occur within the image.

MIME Types

MIME types are used to tell programs what type of data is stored in a file. When a server sends a page, it also sends the mime-type with it.

When the browser receives a document it looks at the mime-type to decide how to display the document. Some MIME types can be handled by the browser, such as text/plain or text/html. Other MIME types need to launch an external program.

When a browser needs to start an external viewer it looks at the mailcap file to see what program to use and what arguments it needs. The MIME types and mailcap files may be stored in a number of places depending on the browser. Some broswers allow you to edit the MIME types and mailcap files in the browser. Check your browser documentation for more details.

The MIME types file normally consists of lines containing:

```
mime-type    ext1, ext2
```

The mailcap file consists of lines of the form:

```
mime-type  ;  program [args]
```

The args section can contain %s. This is replaced with the filename the browser is using to reference the file. For example, to have a program called docview get started with the filename as the only argument, when it receives a file type of application/doc, add:

```
application/doc    ; docview %s
```

to your mailcap file. If it needs other arguments, for example a view option, you could add it to the line as well. This changes the line to:

```
application/doc    ; docview -view %s
```

Using the MIME types and mailcap files in an Intranet facilitates storage and retrieval of company specific files from a central repository. If your company makes foo programs that can be viewed with the bar viewer. You can add an entry to the client and servers MIME types files and an entry to the client mailcap file to have the browser automatically start the bar program when the user clicks on a foo file.

Caution

It's also possible to setup the MIME types and mailcap files to automatically start program interpreters, such as command.com or /bin/sh. Though this can make it much easier to make changes to software, it opens up many security holes. This is because any document with the right mime-type will be interpreted as a command. This includes documents malicious crackers or users may setup on the Internet.

External Viewers

External viewers are separate programs that the browser knows how to use. The browser saves the file in a temporary area and calls the external viewer to look at it. The viewer is displayed in a separate window and may have a different look and feel than the browser.

There are many different types of viewers some of the more popular ones enable you to view:

- FrameMaker documents. Adobe enables users to download and use the FrameViewer free of charge. FrameViewer runs on UNIX machines, and Windows machines (**http://www.adobe.com**).

- Adobe Acrobat files. Adobe has also made a free viewer that allows users to view and print PDF (Portable Document Format) files. PDF files are used to be sure a document will be formatted a specific way regardless of the client's machine.

- Microsoft Word documents. Microsoft has made a document viewer and printer available for free. Unfortunately, there isn't one available for UNIX systems. Microsoft's home page is **http://www.microsoft.com**.

- Graphics images . Lview enables the viewing of many different types of graphic images. Lview is shareware, it can be downloaded from **ftp://oak.oakland.edu/SimTel**. Lview runs on Microsoft Windows platforms. XV is a shareware program for UNIX platforms. It can be downloaded from **ftp://ftp.cis.upenn.edu/pub/xv**.

- Sounds. Microsoft bundles sound players in with Microsoft Windows 3.1 and newer. It requires the presence of a sound card. Some UNIX machines have audio players built in. Check your system's documentation.

- Mpeg Video. Microsoft has a program called Amovie that runs on Windows 5 machines. It allows windows users to view MPEG files using the media player. It is available on the Microsoft Web site, **http://www.microsoft.com/**.

- Mpeg Video. Unix users can download mpeg_play for their systems. It is available from **ftp://mm-ftp.cs.berkeley.edu/pub/mpeg/play**.

External viewers start up in another window. The next set of programs we will look at are called plug-ins. They are Netscape specific, at this time. Plug-ins are third party add-ons to the browser that extend its use.

Plug-ins

Starting with Navigator 2.0, it's possible for software companies to easily build add-on utilities into the Netscape browser. These utilities are built to extend the Netscape browsers. Unlike viewers, they are integrated into the browser and look like a part of it.

The following plug-ins are on the CD located on the back cover of this book.

- ShockWave. This is used to integrate Macromedia Director files to be viewed in the Netscape browser. The presentation can be used as an imagemap, or a standalone application.

- RealAudio. This can be used to transfer real-time audio to the browser.

- Amber. This is a pdf viewer plug-in from Adobe. Instead of having to download the entire file, pdf files can be viewed a page at a time. Embedded links in the pdf file can point to other Web pages instead of just to other pdf files. Many Web designers use PDF files because it allows them to be certain of how a document will be viewed regardless of the client's platform.

- Keyview from FTP software. This is a plug-in for Microsoft Windows systems only. It facilitates the viewing of more than 200 file types, including Microsoft Excel, and Word files. It can also view EPS files, and many types of graphic files.

- DWG/DXF. This is from SoftSource and is made for the viewing of DXF or DWG files. These formats are used by AutoCAD and other CAD programs. With this plug-in you can pan, zoom, or hide certain layers. SoftSource also sells a plug-in for viewing Simple Vector Format (SVF) files. Both plug-ins cost $50.00 for commercial use.

- Look@Me. This plug-in from Farralon, enables you to view another Look@Me users screen. This can be used to help assist users, go over presentations or to view documents.

- PointCast. The PointCast Network is a free service that lets the user receive up-to-the-minute news, weather, and other information. This plugin enables users to view the latest information from within the browser. If the user clicks on an ad, they are instantly taken to the advertisers Web site.

- PointPlus. This plug-in enables users to view PowerPoint presentations over the Net.

Plug-ins are available for many different applications, from sounds, to graphics, to 3D. There is even a text to speech plug-in available for Macintosh, called Talker, that reads the Web page to you.

TCP/IP Software

Because the Intranet is IP-based, it's necessary to setup IP networking software on the clients and servers. IP networking can be run in addition to other networking protocols such as IPX.

IP was designed to link many different types of machines together. It can be used on a UNIX machine to talk to a Macintosh, or on a VMS machine to talk to a Windows machine.

IP is a layered protocol, so it can run on many different media types, and networking topologies. IP, for instance, can run over 10Base-2 Ethernet, or Token Ring using unshielded twisted pair.

IP stacks, or TCP/IP stacks as they are commonly referred to, may also include applications, such as telnet, ftp, sendmail, and a web browser. These applications together make up a TCP/IP suite.

II

Setting Up Software

Built-in stacks

TCP/IP is such a popular protocol many companies have incorporated it into their operating systems. Microsoft now includes a built in TCP/IP stack into their Windows 95 software, as well as their NT operating system. You can also download a TCP/IP stack for Windows for Workgroups from Microsoft's Web server, **http://www.microsoft.com/**.

There are also shareware and commercial TCP/IP stacks available for Windows machines. These include:

- Trumpet Winsock. Trumpet is a shareware package written by Peter Trattam. It is available from **ftp://ftp.trumpet.com/pub/winsock**. If you decide after 30 days that it fits your needs, then you can register it for $25.00.

- NetManage's Chameleon Desktop. This includes a TCP/IP stack and many applications, including mail software, FTP, Telnet and a Web browser. You can contact NetManage at **sales@netmanage.com or http://www.netmanage.com/**.

- FTP Software's OnNet. Like Chameleon this suite of applications comes with a TCP/IP stack and many applications. More information is available at **http://www.ftp.com/**.

- Frontier Technologies Corporation's SuperTCP package. This includes a TCP/IP stack, many applications and an X windows display. More information is available by contacting **SuperTCP@frontiertech.com** or **http://www.frontiertech.com/**.

Unix vendors have had TCP/IP built in to their systems for quite a long time, and it would be hard to find a UNIX vendor that didn't ship TCP/IP with a new OS. Some UNIX versions may have the IP software unbundled but it should be available from the vendor or a third party source.

Macintosh systems also have TCP/IP software built into the newer releases of system software.

Configuring TCP/IP

There are many different versions of TCP/IP stacks, some UNIX versions have many different files that need to be edited, others have a graphical interface. Window machines, Macintoshes and OS/2 machines also have graphical interfaces.

No matter what type of machine you are on or what type of operating system there will be a few things that needs to get filled in. These are:

- IP address. This is the local machine's IP address in dotted quad notation. This is also referred to as an octet. Example 123.123.123.123

- Netmask. This is the number of bits that is used for the network portion. Networks are commonly split into three main classes A, B and C. A networks have one octet for the network number, and three for the host. B networks have 2 octets for the host, and 2 for the machine and class C networks have three octets for the network, and 1 for the host. For a Class C network you would have a netmask of 255.255.255.0; the first three octets are used for the netmask. A class A network on the other hand would have a netmask of 255.0.0.0 and three octets for the host portion. A class B network would have 2 octets for the network and 2 octets for the host portion. A class B netmask is 255.255.0.0

- Domainname. This is the domain name of the local host. For example, if the FQDN of your machine is machine.company.com, the domainname would be company.com.

- Name server. This is a list of name servers to query when doing IP address to name translations. You can have more than one for redundancy.

- Default Gateway. This is where packets not destined for the local network should be relayed. The local network is determined by looking at the netmask. If you don't need to talk to anyone outside of your local network you can leave this blank.

Where and how you fill this information in will depend on which machine and operating system you are running. Consult your documentation.

Choosing the Browser Software

After the TCP/IP software has been chosen, you need to decide on a browser. Since this is the part of the Intranet the users see, this is the most important part. This is also the hardest part to change later so careful planning is necessary when choosing a browser.

Standardizing on a browser is one of the benefits of an Intranet. If everyone is using the same interface it can make developing documents much easier because the developer knows which features will work.

Normally, a developer must try to work with the least common platform. This either requires pages that do not take advantage of the latest specification, or writing pages that can handle both newer platforms, as well as the older ones. This is often done by using CGI scripts.

Having one browser type in use also makes it easier on users. They can sit down at any machine and be comfortable using the Web browser. If you have multiple types of machines, such as UNIX and Windows, it might make sense to choose a browser that runs on both platforms. Some browsers, such as Netscape or Mosaic, can run on OS/2, 16 bit windows, 32 bit windows, UNIX, and Macintosh. This makes it easy if a user ever needs to switch hardware since they will be familiar with the Web browser.

If possible, setup your browser on the network, rather then on each users machine. This makes it much easier when the time to upgrade comes. UNIX versions of Netscape and Mosaic allow multiple users to use a single executable. If this is not possible, you can create a script that the users can run to upgrade their software from the network. Using a script to upgrade the network can save much time and allow the IS staff time to do other things.

> **Note**
>
> There are some packages that can be used to automatically load new software on everyone's machine. These packages can save hundreds of hours of administrator time and are generally well worth the money. One of these packages is ManageWise from Novell (**http://www.novell.com**) and SMS (Systems Management Server) from Microsoft (**http://www.microsoft.com**).

Integration with Mail and Usenet

Most Intranets are going to be built using e-mail and Usenet, as well as Web servers. E-mail has been used for years and is probably already in place at your company. If you choose a browser that allows reading and sending of e-mail and Usenet articles you can eliminate the need to have two additional clients on the desktop.

Some features to look for include reading and posting e-mail and reading and posting usenet articles. Some browsers may allow reading usenet and posting e-mail but not reading e-mail and writing articles. Currently, Netscape and Internet Explorer are the only two that integrate both reading and writing of e-mail and usenet. Figure 8.1 shows a user reading e-mail with the Netscape browser.

Browsers should also let users reference hyperlinks that are embedded in the mail message or article. This will allow users to click on a hyperlink in a mail message and have a browser open up displaying the link. This makes it much easier on users since they don't need to type in URLs by hand.

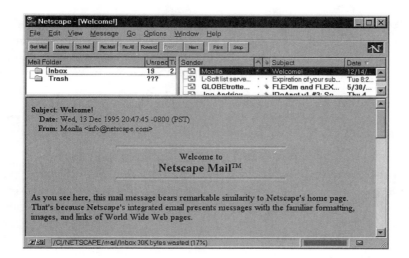

Fig. 8.1
Reading e-mail from the Netscape browser.

Frames

Frames are currently supported on the Netscape and Microsoft browsers, though more browsers will be supporting them in upcoming releases. Frames enable the client's browser view to be separated into multiple windows so that multiple screens of information can be displayed side-by-side. For example, an index page can appear on part of the screen and the information on another. Frames have many uses in an Intranet, some places where the use of frames make sense include:

- A user needs to look up a parts list for a product. Each part also consists of other parts, one frame shows the part, broken down by sub-part, and another frame shows the sub-part.

- An employee handbook with a table of contents in one frame can have links, which when followed show up in another frame.

- A print queue monitor can show a list of printers in one frame. When a printer is selected, the queue entries show up in a separate frame.

- An employee list can appear in one frame. When the user is selected another frame is brought up showing the employee's picture, phone number, and e-mail list.

Frames are a very useful feature if used with some common sense. Many sites have too many frames on one screen, instead of making it easier to navigate, this actually makes it more confusing. It's best to limit users to two or three frames per screen. Any more than three frames and they can get to be too small and confusing.

Customization

You may want to customize your browser to make it more "Intranet aware." Some browsers such as Microsft Explorer and Netscape have administration kits. These kits allow you to customize the look of a browser.

Such customizations may include changing the Netscape icon to the company logo or changing the URL that loads when the users select Help. These customizations might also allow you to add buttons or additional menus.

The administration kit for Explorer is available from **http://www. microsoft.com/ie/ieak**. The Netscape administration kit is available from **http://partner.netscape.com/comprod/products/navigator/ version_3.0/index.html**.

Java

Java is Sun Microsystems's hot new programming language. It uses a virtual machine, the Java VM, to enable code compiled on any machine to run on any machine that supports the Java VM. This can help to reduce development time and can allow programmers to focus on new projects, not porting to new platforms.

Java enables developers to develop executable content, which ranges from something as simple as an animated icon to something as fancy as a 3 dimensional viewer. Java programs can be downloaded over the Internet or Intranet. This enables developers to easily upgrade existing applications. Currently Netscape, Microsoft and Sun have Java enabled browsers. Java programs that can be embedded in an HTML page are called applets.

Java programs can be developed to run on the client rather then the server. This is important for CPU intensive programs because the server won't get bogged down running the application. This client processing enables developers to create true distributed applications. This can also help reduce network traffic since the data doesn't have to travel to the server to be processed.

Some Intranet uses for Java include:

- Client-side form checking. Normally, when a form is processed, it gets sent to the server, where it is checked to make sure all the fields have been filled out properly. Using Java, the client can verify the fields before sending them.

- Database searching. Instead of sending database queries to the server for submission to the database engine, the client can talk directly to the database server. This reduces the load on the Web server.

■ Client-side processing. Some applications need to total data or perform other processing on it to get a useful result. This could be used for data viewing, the client could download a Java applet and some data and perform translations on how the data is viewed, without having to query the server for a different view. For example, if the browser downloads a list sorted alphabetically starting with A and wanted to start with Z. With Java the applet could resort it, without java the client would have to request and download the new view from the server.

As Java becomes even more popular, developers might want to convert from their existing programs to Java programs. This would enable the company to move from client-server applications to distributed applications. A good example of this would be a data entry program that interprets the data that is being entered, performs calculations, and then submits the data to multiple databases.

Note

Current Java uses are geared more towards "cool tricks." Intranets shouldn't be based on coolness but rather on usefulness. Don't use Java just because it is the "in thing." If you don't have a need for it, don't use it.

Java is covered in Chapter 13, "Java and JavaScript."

Forms

Forms are supported by almost all current browsers. They enable users to enter data and submit it back to the server for processing.

Forms are built using HTML tags, which are tags that build buttons, menus, select lists, and text areas. Figure 8.2 shows a page using forms. Forms are also covered in more detail in the next chapter.

Forms have many uses in an Intranet. They can be used in place of paper-based forms to facilitate easy submissions and updates.

Electronic submission is particularly well suited for forms that need to go to multiple departments at once. Each form can be processed and sent to the appropriate groups at submission time. This eliminates the need for copies of the same paper form.

It is often possible to automatically handle a form submission by creating a script that acts on the form data. An example of this would be a scheduling page. This page could have projects deadlines and scheduling delays. If an employee realized a deadline would be missed they could fill out a form to automatically update the global schedule.

Fig. 8.2
Forms can contain different elements.

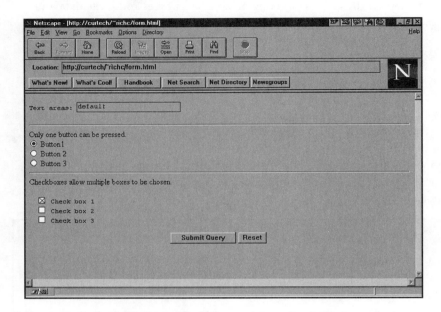

Electronic forms can be used to request new equipment, vacation time, new accounts, as well as network or phone changes.

In addition forms can be used to enable users to submit data to other programs, such as:

- Search engines. Sophisticated search engines can be developed, which search on multiple requisites.

- Database queries. Users might want to check the status of a request, or check to see if a particular software bug has been fixed.

- Online surveys. IS Departments should always try to get feedback from other departments to help them focus on technology that is needed.

Users could fill out a form saying what applications they use and don't use.

Forms can be used to submit many types of data. This makes them very powerful. Forms have many uses in an Intranet, they are limited only by the developers creativity.

Forms are covered in Chapter 11, "HTML Forms."

Tables

Tables are a new feature to HTML so some browsers may not include support for them yet. Netscape Navigator and Microsoft Internet Explorer are two browsers that can display tables. Tables enable the developer to set up rows and columns. Figure 8.3 shows an example of a table.

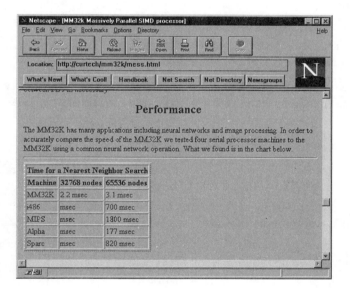

Fig. 8.3
Tables make data easier to read.

Standard HTML didn't allow precise control of horizontal layout so it was hard to make columns line up properly. Most developers resorted to using the <pre> (preformatted) tag to handle this. The <pre> tag tells the browser the text is already formatted correctly and not to perform any other formatting on it. The <pre> tag however didn't work very well if the browser windows were too small.

Tables can specify the number of columns across a page. For example, you could tell your browser to have four columns. It would automatically size the table to fit four columns of equal size on the screen.

Tables can set up to use a certain percentage of the screen per column so you can set up a defined number of columns, regardless of how wide the screen is. For example, you could say each column is to use 25 percent of the width, to get four columns. If the screen were 600 pixels across each column would be 150 pixels. If the screen were resized to 400 pixels each column would shrink to 100 pixels. You could also use three columns one could be set to use 25 percent of the width, one could use 50 percent and the last could use 25 percent. This allows variable sized columns.

Tables can also have captions defined. This is text that describes what the table is showing the reader. This can be be placed above or below the table. Table headers can also be setup for each column.

Tables are as useful on the Web as they are in paper-based documents. They allow easy reading of numbers, and summary of data.

Tables are used mostly in static documents to emphasize a point. They can also be used dynamically to organize information retrieved from a database. However the tables are generated they are very useful in an Intranet.

Some common uses for a table in an Intranet include:

- Test results. Test results are often easier to understand if they are in a tabular format.
- Accounting or budgetary figures. Numbers are often displayed in tables to make them easier to read and understand.
- Available equipment lists. This might be used to show the amount of capital equipment and where it is being used.
- Schedules. Since tables allow more precise formatting, schedules can be made using tables.
- Anywhere more precise formatting is required. Tables are often used to produce effects that standard HTML cannot handle, such as lining up lists in a different way than DL (Description Lists), or UL (Unordered Lists) allow.

Multiple Platforms

Tables, forms, frames, and Java are all very useful features but it's more important to make sure the browser works on the platforms in use at your company. Many companies have different platforms; engineering may have high-performance UNIX machines. Marketing might have Macintoshes and accounting might have ASCII terminals.

While it is important to standardize on a browser, it may not be feasible for the entire company to use a single type of browser. For example, if one group of people are using dumb terminals, it doesn't mean everyone should use lynx. You should try to limit the number of different browser types in use. For example, all graphics terminals might run Netscape and anyone with an ASCII terminal might run lynx. This would enable the users that can view graphics to take advantage of them, while those that can't, still have access to the data.

Troubleshooting

Configurations differ from browser to browser, though they all work basically the same way. If you are using a browser as an e-mail client you will need to define a mailhost or SMTP gateway. This is the machine that actually sends and receives mail.

If you are using it to read news, you need to define an NNTP server. You must also enter the real name of the user, the organization, and an optional signature file.

Once the browser is up and running, it doesn't need to be changed often. Sometimes things go wrong, however, and some troubleshooting will be needed.

By understanding how a client and a server communicate you can test certain parts of the process and narrow down what is causing the problem. By testing the process in pieces you can narrow down the problem to the client, server, or the network in between.

In the next few sections, we will look at some common problems and some techniques that are useful in troubleshooting.

Connection Problems

One of the more common problems relates to communications. These normally are caused by network errors. Error messages that should indicate a communications problem would be:

- Unknown host or DNS failure.
- Connection refused
- Destination unreachable

II

Setting Up Software

> **Note**
>
> The actual error message you receive may be worded differently than these. If the error messages you are getting look similar to the ones above then you may have a connection problem. For example your browser may report "host unknown" instead of "unknown host."

Unknown Host

Unknown host means the browser couldn't figure out what IP address to use to get to the host in the URL. This may be a permanent problem or a temporary one.

When a browser tries to resolve a name it does one of three things. It checks the local host file, checks the name server, or checks the NIS server. Which action it takes depends on your network setup.

If there is a problem trying to reach the DNS or NIS servers, this might be caused by an overloaded network. If the problem goes away after a few minutes, then network congestion is more then likely the culprit. You can also try using the ping program to reach the IP address of the DNS or NIS servers. If you can't get an answer from the server using ping you have a network problem that needs to be solved first. This can also mean the machine is crashed or turned off.

If the servers answer, check to make sure they are running the correct processes to resolve names. If you are administering the server, you can check this by trying to resolve a name on the server, using nslookup. If this doesn't work then they may be having problems reaching the root servers, try to ping one of the root servers. If you aren't sure what this means, check your documentation on DNS resolution.

If you are running NIS and can resolve fully qualified names properly on the server, you may need to check the flags on the ypserv program. Ypserv needs to be told to check the DNS if it can't resolve the name by itself. For most versions this is the -d option.

You can usually get around resolution problems by using the IP address of the machine in the URL.

Connection Refused

This error message usually means that the Web server is not running or is running on a different port than the one your are telling it to use. This can also be a temporary problem caused by too many users trying to connect to the server at one time.

The best way to check this is to login to the server, if possible, and try to connect to the server from there. If you can't then the server is probably not running. Restart it and try again.

If you can connect locally but not remotely, then you may have a network problem. On the client, ping the server, verify that the IP address is the correct one. It is possible that the client is resolving the name incorrectly and is connecting to the wrong host.

Destination Unreachable

Destination unreachable can be caused by a number of network problems. You may also get port unreachable or host unreachable. All three point to the same issue.

This condition is usually caused by a Router or gateway being down or misconfigured. The best programs to use for finding the problem is traceroute, or Iptrace. Some TCP/IP suites have this program included. It tests the network between two machines, much like ping, but it also shows all the gateways that it goes through to get there.

Traceroute tells you how far it gets through the network before it is refused.

Viewing Problems

Sometimes a connection works and the browser gets documents but doesn't display them correctly. This may not give an error message but will show garbled output or nothing at all in the browser.

Some browsers may interpret HTML slightly different than others. Standardizing on a browser will help alleviate this problem.

Documents Look Funny

If the document shows up in the viewer but doesn't look right, the server is probably sending an incorrect mime-type. If you maintain the server, you can check the MIME types file on the server. Check Chapter 1, "The WWW and the Intranet," for more information on MIME types.

If you do not maintain the server, for example, if it is a remote server, you may be able to get around the problem by downloading the document to a file. Name the file with the correct extension to assign the correct mime-type to it. Most browsers allow you to download a file to disk. Once the file is downloaded you can use the Open local file option to read the file. You should also notify the server administrator so they can correct the problem.

Viewers Don't Start

If your viewer can't display a document, it tries to start an external viewer for it. Occasionally the external viewer won't start. It may give an error message or it may silently fail. Either way it signifies a problem in the mailcap file.

> **Note**
>
> Some browsers don't have a mailcap file. They use an internal table or a different configuration to define external viewers. Check your browsers documentation to see how to define external viewers.

The first step in troubleshooting is to download the file to local disk. Save it with the correct extension since some programs require certain extensions. Next, check to make sure your viewer can handle the file. Start the viewer and try to open the file. If it works correctly, then you might have a problem with the mailcap. If it doesn't display correctly, you may have a corrupted file.

If it displays correctly when you run the viewer by hand, check the syntax in the mailcap file. Make sure you are using the right arguments and passing the correct filename. %s is usually replaced with the name of the file the browser is using for temporary storage.

If everything looks right, you might need to set your path. If the viewer is not in your path you need to add it and restart your browser.

If the viewer still doesn't work, it's possible the server is sending the wrong mime-type. Check the server to be sure it is correctly identifying the file. If you don't have access to the server, you can use a LAN analyzer or network sniffer to see the packets sent to the client. ❖

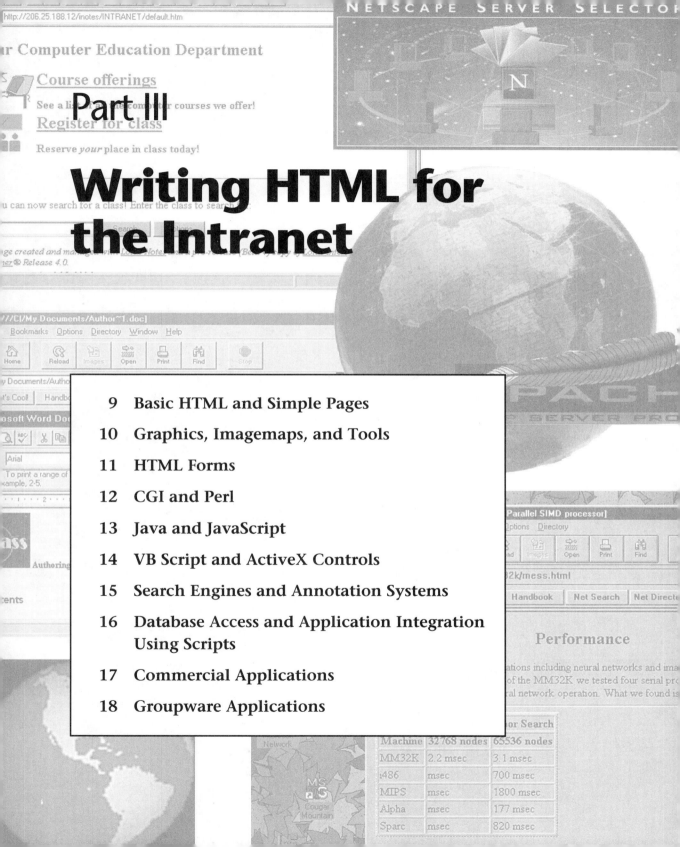

Part III

Writing HTML for the Intranet

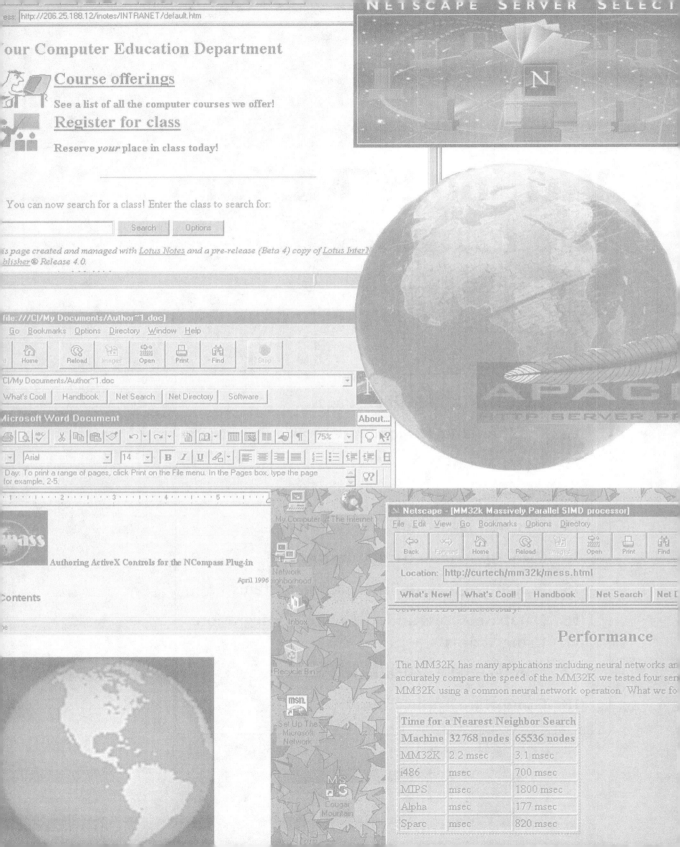

our Computer Education Department

Course offerings

See a list of all the computer courses we offer!

Register for class

Reserve *your* place in class today!

You can now search for a class! Enter the class to search for:

[Search]   [Options]

is page created and managed with *Lotus Notes* and a pre-release (Beta 4) copy of *Lotus InterN*
blisher ® Release 4.0.

NETSCAPE SERVER SELECT

---

file:///Cl/My Documents/Author~1.doc]

Go Bookmarks Options Directory Window Help

Home | Reload | Images | Open | Print | Find | Stop

Cl/My Documents/Author~1.doc

What's Cool! | Handbook | Net Search | Net Directory | Software

icrosoft Word Document   About...

Arial   14   B I U   75%

Day: To print a range of pages, click Print on the File menu. In the Pages box, type the page
for example, 2-5.

Authoring ActiveX Controls for the NCompass Plug-in

April 1996

Contents

Netscape - [MM32k Massively Parallel SIMD processor]

File Edit View Go Bookmarks Options Directory

Back | Forward | Home | Reload | Images | Open | Print | Find

Location: http://curtech/mm32k/mess.html

What's New! | What's Cool! | Handbook | Net Search | Net D

Performance

The MM32K has many applications including neural networks an
accurately compare the speed of the MM32K we tested four ser
MM32K using a common neural network operation. What we fo

Time for a Nearest Neighbor Search		
Machine	32768 nodes	65536 nodes
MM32K	2.2 msec	3.1 msec
i486	msec	700 msec
MIPS	msec	1800 msec
Alpha	msec	177 msec
Sparc	msec	820 msec

CHAPTER 9

Basic HTML and Simple Pages

HTML is one of the building blocks of any Intranet. HTML allows the document writer to be assured that a document will look reasonably good on any screen, from a large, high-resolution screen to a dumb ASCII terminal. Though this book doesn't get into intricate detail on HTML we do cover HTML basics.

After reading this chapter, you will know the following:

- How to create simple and complex HTML pages
- How to create Tables and Frames in your HTML documents
- How to convert from various formats
- How to use some of the popular HTML editors

Introduction to HTML

Chapter 2 discussed HTTP, the language Web browsers and servers use to communicate. This chapter covers the *HyperText Markup Language*, commonly called *HTML*. HTML allows browsers to display information in a display-independent way. This is done by describing how the document is laid out, not how it should look.

HTML 1.0 is a basic language with support for preformatted text, headers, and different type styles such as Bold or Italic. HTML 2.0 adds to these formatting tags and allows for more advanced controls; the latest specification HTML 3.0 allows text to flow around images, tables, and many other features.

> **Note**
>
> This book is not a tutorial on HTML. We will quickly cover the basics of HTML, but if you want to learn HTML, you should read Que's *Special Edition Using HTML, 2nd Edition*.

Content versus Style

Because HTML describes a document layout rather then how a document should look, the content of a document is more important than the style it is written in. Normally when creating a document, the user must decide which font style to use, which size font, and many different formatting options.

HTML however takes these decisions away from the developer and automatically handles the formatting details. This allows HTML to be viewed on dumb terminals as well as high resolution monitors.

> **Note**
>
> There have been "advancements" in HTML that some browsers take advantage of. These advancements include defining the colors, font sizes, and other features of how the document looks. These are discussed in the section "Advanced HTML."

About HTML

HTML documents are standard text documents that have special markup "tags" embedded in them. These tags are character or characters surrounded by < and >. These tags tell the browser what the text is and how to display it.

> **Note**
>
> Tags can either describe a *logical* or a *physical* style. The logical tag tells the browser what a piece of text is; for example, a major heading. Physical tags, on the other hand, tell a browser how to display something, such as italics.

There are three main rules to HTML:

- **White space is ignored in an HTML document.** White space such as " ", tabs, and carriage returns are ignored when parsing HTML. This means to insert a carriage return, you need to specify an HTML tag. This also means you can't simply line up columns by putting in multiple spaces. This does allow the designer to make the HTML source look cleaner, though.

- **Tags are not case sensitive.** `<Pre>` and `<PRE>` are exactly the same. Most designers make tags all uppercase to make them easier to spot in a document, but this is not a requirement.

- **Most tags occur in pairs.** Tags usually have a start tag and an end tag. End tags have a slash / in front of the tag. For example, `<B>` will start the bold text, and `</B>` ends it.

HTML documents are made up of three parts: the *declaration*, the *header*, and the *body*.

The declaration is simply a tag that defines where the HTML document starts and ends. The tag to use is `<HTML>`, and the closing tag is `</HTML>`. This goes at the beginning and end of all HTML documents.

The header part contains information about the document. This includes at least the `<TITLE>` and `<BASE>` tags. The `<TITLE>` tag is usually displayed at the top of the browser and should be something that will allow the user to understand what the document contains. The `<BASE>` tag defines where relative URLs are referenced from. The header is enclosed by `<HEAD>` and `</HEAD>`.

The body document is contained between the `<BODY>` and `</BODY>` tags. This is where the document content is stored along with the tags that describe it.

Basic HTML Tags

The earliest version of HTML contained only a handful of tags. These few tags allow documents to be viewed on many different types of machines in a format that mimics the way the document is laid out.

The HTML specification requires that tags be surrounded by greater than and less than signs < and >. Some tags may be embedded in other tags. To end a tag, you precede it with a frontslash /. For example, for preformatted text you would start with `<pre>` and put your text in, then end the preformatted section with `</pre>`.

> **Note**
>
> HTML tags aren't case sensitive. `<PRE>` is the same as `<pre>` and `<Pre>`. The tags can also be ended with tags using different capitalization, so `<PRE>` can be ended with `</pRe>`.

III

Writing HTML

The most common tags available include the following:

- **TITLE.** This tags defines the title of the document. This tag should always give the viewers a descriptive title because they may jump to that document and not work their way to it through your site. Using a title like "Example 1" is not a real good idea.

- **BASE.** This is used to define where relative URLs are referenced from.

- **HEAD.** This tag is used to separate the body section of the document from the head section.

- **BODY.** This helps to separate the head section of a document from the body section of the document.

- **HTML.** This is used to tell the viewer what is HTML and what is not HTML.

- **H1, H2, H3, H4, H5.** These stand for headings. H1 is for major headings, H2 is for minor headings, H3 for major subheadings and so on.

- **PRE.** This is used for preformatted text. This tells the browser that the text is already formatted. It can be used to set up tables or to allow extra spacing around words.

- **I.** This stands for Italics. It can be used to tell the browser that the text between the opening and closing tag should be displayed in italics.

- **B.** This tag stands for Bold. It can be used like the italics tags.

- **DL.** This stands for Definition List, a list of items with definitions.

- **DT.** These are used to identify the Definition Text in a Definition List.

- **UL.** This starts an Unordered List. You can also have an Ordered List (OL). These require each list item to begin with the LI tag.

- **LI.** This is used inside the UL and OL tags. It surrounds the different List Items.

- **HR.** This stands for Horizontal Rule. It inserts a line at this point. For dumb terminals, it uses the underscore for a horizontal line.

- **BR.** This tag inserts a line break.

- **P.** This tag signifies the beginning of a paragraph.

- **IMG.** This allows inlined images to be inserted. If the browser couldn't display images, there would be an ALT option that would display text instead.

- **HREF.** This stands for Hypertext REFerence. This is used to link in other documents.

- **ISINDEX.** This can be used to submit information to a script. This is often used to allow searches.

These are just some of the HTML 1.0 tags. By using these simple tags, you can create very usable documents that can be viewed on any screen. You can also link documents to other documents and have images embedded in with the text. It does not allow you to define the screen color, font size, or other attributes to define how a document will look; rather, it allows you to define how it is written.

Here is a simple HTML document:

```
<HTML>
<HEAD>
<TITLE> Test Document </TITLE>
</HEAD>
<BODY>
This is line 1.
This is line 2. Note there are no line breaks unless we specify
them.<BR>
Like we just did.
<P>
<UL>
<LI> This is item1</LI>
<LI> This is item2</LI>
</UL>
<HR>
</BODY>
</HTML>
```

This page is shown in figure 9.1.

Converting Static Documents

Many companies start their Intranets by putting existing documents on-line. This has many advantages over paper based documents. These advantages include the following:

- **Easy distribution.** Because the documents are available electronically, it isn't necessary to hand deliver them to everyone. When someone needs to see them, they can start a browser.

- **Cheaper to print.** Users can only print the document out if they need to. They can also just print the sections they are interested in. This allows the company to save on paper costs.

- **Easy to change.** Electronic documents can be changed by using a standard text editor or word processor.

- **Centrally stored.** All the company's documents can be centrally stored and accessed from one place.

Fig. 9.1
A Test HTML page.

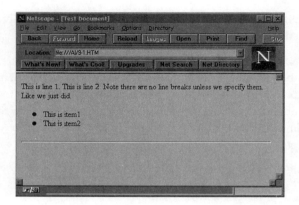

■ **Universally accessible.** Because electronic documents are transmitted over the network, users anywhere in the world can have instant access to them.

■ **Easy to search.** Electronic documents can be indexed and quickly searched for a particular word or phrase.

With all these benefits, it's no wonder that so many companies are starting to build Intranets.

Most companies have many static documents, which can include employee handbooks, newsletters, specifications, phone lists, policies or job postings.

These can all be easily converted to electronic documents and placed on the company Intranet server. Because the documents are fairly static, they can easily be added without having to learn CGI programming or advanced HTML topics.

Saving as ASCII

The quickest way to get your Intranet started is to store all your documents in an area of your Web server. They can be saved as regular text and viewed in a WWW browser. Most word processor programs allow the user to save as text or ASCII. Browsers usually have a Find option available which makes searching a file easy.

> **Note**
>
> It is possible to view documents without having a Web server running. Simply save all the documents in a central directory and use the Open Local option that most browsers have.

This is a quick way to get started, and for some companies or departments, this may be all that is needed. Other companies might want to go a step further and convert their documents to HTML. This would allow them to take advantage of the hyperlinking and embedding of documents.

Saving as HTML

In the past year or so, most of the large word processors have come out with updates that allow documents to be saved as HTML. Some of these word processors actually can be used as HTML editors by adding a template or style sheet.

Microsoft Word, Adobe's FrameMaker, and WordPerfect all have new versions that allow you to save a document as HTML.

> **Note**
>
> Because HTML is an evolving specification, some features may not be available using these applications. It may be necessary to save the document as HTML and then edit it with a text editor to add some HTML features.

Let's look at a few word processor add-ons that can make saving as HTML easier.

CU_HTML

CU_HTML is a Microsoft Word 2.0 or 6.0 template that allows easy creation of HTML files. It is available from **http://www.cuhk.hk/csc/cu_html/cu_html/htm**.

After you get the .zip file and uncompress it, you can install it by following the instructions in cu_html.htm or cu_html.doc. After it is installed and the template is selected, you will have an additional pull-down menu and another toolbar. These allow you to insert links, images, and tagging options. There is also an option to write html. This is used to save an HTML file. Figure 9.2 shows Word after loading in the CU_HTML template.

III

Writing HTML

Fig. 9.2
Word with the
CU_HTML
template loaded.

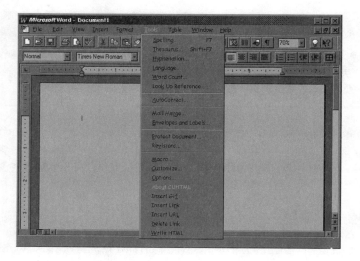

After you create the text, you can simply highlight it and select the style you want to apply. This is just like the normal Word tools; the only difference is the style names in the list. Some of the styles you can apply include bold, italics, underline, Header 1-6, addresses, preformatted text, ordered lists, unordered lists, and horizontal rule.

Internet Assistant

Internet Assistant (IA) is a free add-on for Word that allows editing and browsing of WWW documents. It is available from Microsoft's Web site (**http://www.microsft.com/msoffice/freestuff/msword/download/ia/default.htm**), or you can order a disk from Microsoft for $5.00. To order a disk, call 1-800-426-9400.

When you install the package, you will have the option of setting Internet Assistant up as the default viewer. If you do this, then every time you start Word the Internet Assistant will also be loaded. Figure 9.3 shows Internet Assistant.

To start editing, you need to select the HTML.DOT template, or opening an existing HTML document (with an .htm extension) will automatically load the HTML template. Loading the template adds many new features to the pull-down menus and also adds new toolbars.

Using Internet Assistant is almost the same as using standard Word with a few more styles. Some of these styles are bold, italics, and underline. IA also allows you to add special symbols and correctly converts them to the HTML equivalent.

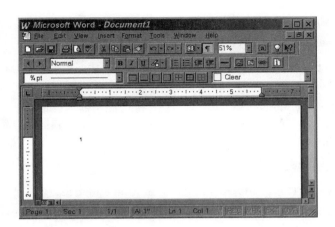

Fig. 9.3
Microsoft's
Internet Assistant
loaded in Word.

The Internet Assistant also has a forms generator. This is similar to the forms tool built into Excel. It allows you to select checkboxes, submit and restart buttons, pull-down lists, text areas, and radio buttons. IA prompts you for the correct information to finish making the form.

Converters

Having a word processor save documents as HTML is a good way to add existing documents or to convert a few documents to HTML. If you have many files, though, it can be time consuming to have to start the word processor, open the document, make any changes, and save the file as a different name.

If you have many documents, you really need a converter. Converters allow you to automate the conversions by using a script or batch file. There are many converters available on the Internet. We will cover converters that will allow us to convert FrameMaker documents, Microsoft Word documents and WordPerfect documents.

Using MIFtran

MIFtran is a program that converts FrameMaker documents that were saved in the Maker Interchange Format to HTML files. MIFtran is a C program that was written by Jim McBeath. It is available from `ftp://ftp.alumni.caltech.edu/pub/mcbeath/web/miftran`. It has been compiled and run on many versions of UNIX and should on most machines with a C compiler.

After you download the file and unpack it, you should have a number of files.You should read the file README and follow these instructions to get miftran working.

1. Edit Makefile and make changes if necessary.

2. Type **make** to build miftran.

Once miftran is built you can test it by changing to the html directory and running make there.

To use miftran, you need an "RC file." This file controls everything about miftran. See the Chap3.html file for details on the rc file. You may be able to use miftran.rc in the mtinc directory.

The command line options for miftran are

- **-version.** This prints the version of miftran and exits.
- **-rc *filename*.** This defines the rc file to use. If left out, miftran defaults to the file called "miftran.rc" in the current directory. This can also be defined by the environment variable.
- **-I *directory*.** This tells miftran where to search for include files.
- **filename.** Any filename after these options is considered the input file. The input file can also be defined in the rc file.

A sample miftran run would be

```
miftran -rc miftest.rc test.mif
```

Using rtftohtml

rtftohtml is a filter that can translate Rich Text Format (RTF) documents to HTML. Many word processors can save files in RTF format, so rtftohtml can be used to turn almost any word processor into an HTML editor.

Rtftohtml is available in binary form from **ftp://ftp.skypoint.com/pub/ members/s/spimis/latest/binaries/**. You can also get the source code for compiling on UNIX machines from **ftp://ftp.skypoint.com/pub/ members/s/spimis/latest/src/unix.tar.Z**.

Rtftohtml binaries are available for Macintosh, SunOS, Solaris, DOS and OS/2.

We are going to take a look at using rtftohtml to convert an rtf file. In this example, we are using rtftohtml version 2.7.5a for DOS.

Rtftohtml uses the html-trans file to decide how to convert the rtf code to html. If you add a new RTF style, you will need to understand this file. There are basically four parts to this file. They are the .PTag, .TTag, .Tmatch, and .Pmatch. These sections are used to define paragraph styles, text styles, text matching, and paragraph matching.

> **Tip**
>
> The html-trans file is complicated. If you need to add a style, read the instructions found in the Users Guide (guide.htm).

The command line options for rtftohtml are

- **-i.** Imbedded graphics should be linked into the document using IMG rather then an HREF tag.
- **-V.** Prints the version number.
- **-o.** Output filename.
- **-P.** extension to use for graphic files. Default is "gif"
- **-T.** Do NOT generate a table of contents.
- **-G.** Do NOT write graphics files. The links are still created for the graphics though.
- "file." this is the input filename. Default is stdin.

Therefore, the following command will convert doc.rtf to doc.html without a table of contents, and all images will be linked using an HREF.

```
rtftohtm -T doc.rtf
```

To convert doc.rtf to test.html without re-creating graphics and with links to ".jpg" files instead of ".gif" files, you would use

```
rtftohtm -o test -G -P jpg doc.rtf
```

Using wp2html

wp2html is a shareware program written by Andy Scriven. You can download the evaluation copy from many sources; one of them is **http://www.res.bbsrc.ac.uk/wp2html**. If you decide you like the program, you need to register it. Registration costs five English pounds, or around seven U.S. dollars.

Wp2html handles WP tables and converts them to HTML tables. It also can handle graphics by either linking in a gif or jpeg version or by creating a description of the image, usually the name and size of the image.

III

Writing HTML

> **Note**
>
> When you get the software, there will be one file called README.1ST and another called WPTOHTML.EXE. Run the WPTOHTML.EXE program, this is a self extracting file that will unpack itself and create several files. WP2HTMl can be installed by following the instructions in README.1ST.
>
> This section discusses the DOS version. There is also a UNIX version available. The instruction will vary depending on which version you get.

wp2html can be run with just a filename. If you run it this way, it will create a new file with an .htm extension. For example, if you run wp2html junk.wp, it will create a junk.htm file.

You can also use one of four flags:

- **i.** This is the input filename.
- **o.** This is the output filename.
- **c.** This defines the configuration file to use.
- **s.** This defines the style file to use.

To use the configuration file called test.cfg, a style file called wp.sty and using input.wp as the input file you would run:

```
wp2html -c test.cfg -s wp.sty -i imput.wp
```

HTML Editors

HTML editors are a very good way for people to create basic HTML documents without having to learn the language. They allow you to see the document the way it will look in a browser.

> **Caution**
>
> Not all browsers support all tags the same way. Users can also change the way a tag is displayed. The term WYSIWYG (What You See Is What You Get) is not always true with HTML.

HTML editors are available for Windows platforms, Macintosh, and UNIX platforms. Most newer editors are WYSIWYG editors and allow the designers to simply grab the styles they want to use and apply them. It is also easy to add in hyperlinks by typing in the URL.

> **Note**
>
> Because HTML changes so quickly, most HTML editors can't be used to incorporate all the latest functions. It is often required to tweak HTML files after they come off the editor. This is especially true if you use Server Side Includes to set the look and feel of the site.

There are many editors on the market; most of them are for the Windows platform, though, so UNIX users have fewer choices. Two common UNIX editors are HoTMetal Pro and Netscape Gold. These editors are also available for the Microsoft Windows platforms. FrontPage from Microsoft and HotDog from Sausage Software are two also very nice HTML editors.

HoTMetaL Pro

HoTMetaL is developed by SoftQuad. They develop both a free version and the professional version. The free version is available for ftp from **ftp:// papa.indstate.edu/mirror/SoftQuad/hmfree2.exe**.

> **Note**
>
> HoTMetaL Free is for use for noncommercial use only. If you are developing Intranet pages, this is considered commercial use, and you will need to purchase the Pro edition.

To run HoTMetal under Windows, you will need Windows 3.1 or higher running on a 486/33 or better, and at least 8 MB of RAM. SoftQuad also makes a version of HoTMetaL for UNIX machines.

Once you have downloaded the hmfree2.exe executable, you will want to save it to a temporary directory. This allows you to remove the installation files after the installation is complete.

In your temporary directory, run the hmfr22.exe program. This will extract the distribution files. In Windows, run the setup.exe program you just extracted. Once setup finishes you can remove the files in your temporary area. HoTMetaL has a very good help system and allows most of the current tags. It has a nice table editor and will warn you if you try to save a document that has invalid syntax in it. Figure 9.4 shows HoTMetal free in action.

III

Writing HTML

Fig. 9.4
HoTMetaL Free is
a very nice editor.

Netscape Navigator Gold

Netscape's top-of-the-line browser package called Netscape Navigator Gold is actually a browser and editor combined. This allows you to edit documents and view them in the same software package. The Gold version costs 79 dollars and is available from the Netscape site (**http://home.netscape.com**).

To edit a document with Navigator Gold, you can simply view an HTML document and then switch to edit mode. This will add three toolbars. The toolbars each have a different function.

- The top toolbar is mostly for font styles.
- The middle toolbar is for file and editing controls.
- The bottom toolbar includes options that allow the formatting of text.

One of the nicest features of Navigator Gold is the Drag and Drop feature. This allows you to quickly move images, links, and horizontal rules by dragging them on the screen. Figure 9.5 shows a page in edit mode of Navigator Gold.

Microsoft FrontPage

FrontPage, available from Microsoft (**http://www.microsoft.com/fp**), is one of the more advanced HTML tools. It is actually much more than just an editor, it is a site development package. In addition to allowing you to create HTML you can also graphically view your site, test for broken links and use server robots.

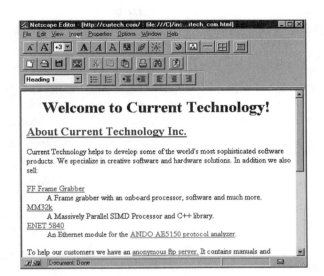

Fig. 9.5
Navigator Gold
edit window.

FrontPage requires you to add server extensions if you want to use the server robots. There are server extensions for Netscape servers, O'Reilly's WebSite and IIS. More server extensions are being created to be able to use robots with even more servers.

FrontPage has all the features of a WYSIWYG editor plus the ability to develop an entire site using wizards. These wizards guide you through creating different types of web sites. These include corporate home pages, workgroup servers and discussion areas.

FrontPage also has a screen where you can graphically view your site and see where your links go. You can also verify your links and check to make sure they actually all point somewhere.

HotDog Pro

HotDog Pro from Sausage Software is another WYSIWYG editor. It can be downloaded from **http://www.sausage.com**.

HotDog Pro allows you to add styles, images and links easily using a graphical interface. HotDog Pro also has an HTML validator, spell checker and a real time viewer. This viewer eliminates the need to have a browser open and constantly hitting reload to see your new changes. You might still want to check your work in the standard browser you have chosen for your Intranet.

III

Writing HTML

Advanced HTML

As more and more people started using HTML for more things, it became evident that the specification needed to be expanded if it was to be used for more than simple documents. Netscape decided to add extensions to the HTML specification to make it more useful for users of the Navigator software. These extensions are called the Netscape Extensions or "Netscapisms."

Note

When Netscape first introduced these extensions, many people were upset that Netscape didn't wait until the HTML working group approved them and added them to the new specification; however, now most browsers support at least some of these extensions.

Netscape, however, always seems to be pushing the envelope and adding new extensions before the HTML working group gets them added. Whether this is bad or not is still very controversial.

The HTML specification has also been expanded, and version 3.2 is now being worked on. Version 3.2 adds many features over the original specification. Some of the more useful features for an Intranet include Forms, Tables, Frames, different font sizes, and image dimensions.

Forms are used to submit data to a script. They are covered in Chapter 11, "HTML Forms." Tables are used to display data in a more organized fashion. Frames are useful for allowing the user to see more than one screen at once. Different font sizing is useful for making things look better, and image dimensioning is helpful in making an image always fit in a browser window.

Tables

Tables are used to display information that needs to be displayed in rows and columns. HTML doesn't allow the writer to force extra spaces between words, so using tables is the best way to format how a document will look.

Note

It is possible to use the <PRE> tag to get multiple spaces in to force a document to line up properly.

Table Tags

The tags that are needed when working with tables are:

- **table.** This is used to signal the start and the end of a table.
- **tr.** This tag is used to delimit the rows in the table.
- **th.** This tag is used for table headers. It can be in any row, not just the top row.
- **td.** This is the table data.

The table tag can also be changed by adding other options. These include:

- **height.** This can be either a number or a percentage. If it is a percentage, then it is the percent of the window screen that is being displayed.
- **width.** Like height, this can be either a number of pixels or a percentage of screen.
- **border.** This is the number of pixels to use for a border around the table.

The td tag can also have options such as:

- **Align.** This can be used to align the text horizontally to the left, right, or center.
- **valign.** This is used for vertical alignment. It can be either top, middle, bottom, or baseline.

Cells can also be setup to span either rows or columns using the th tags and one of the following:

- **colspan.** This is the number of columns to span across.
- **rowspan.** This is the number of rows to span up and down.

Using these tags, you can generate very interesting tables. It is also possible to embed other html elements inside a table to get special formatting.

Table Example

This is a sample table to show how a table is structured. This is not a complete html document; rather, it is a snippet that contains the table code. It would need to be placed in the body portion of an HTML document.

```
<TABLE border=3>
<TR>
<TH colspan=3>                Time for a Nearest Neighbor Search</
TH><P>

<TR><TH>Machine  </TH><TH>  32768 nodes  </TH><TH>  65536 nodes  </
TH><P>
```

III

Writing HTML

```
<TR><TD>MM32K      </TD><TD>2.2 msec      </TD><TD>3.1  msec<BR></
TD></TR>
<TR><TD>i486       </TD><TD>350 msec      </TD><TD>700  msec<BR></
TD></TR>
<TR><TD>MIPS       </TD><TD>970 msec      </TD><TD>1800 msec<BR></
TD></TR>
<TR><TD>Alpha      </TD><TD>81  msec      </TD><TD>177  msec<BR></
TD></TR>
<TR><TD>Sparc      </TD><TD>410 msec      </TD><TD>820  msec<BR></
TD></TR>
</TABLE>
```

This would generate a table that looks like the one shown in figure 9.6.

Fig. 9.6

A sample table.

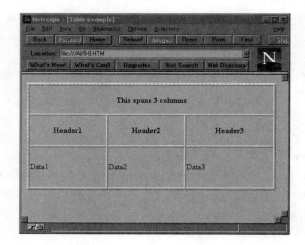

Frames

Frames aren't part of the HTML specification, but they can be very useful in an Intranet. They are used and supported by Netscape browsers and compatible browsers.

Frames are used to allow multiple HTML documents to be displayed in a single browser window. Frames can be used in such a way to make multiple screens easier to use, but they can also make a screen too complicated.

The most popular applications for frames in an Intranet are the following:

■ **Navigational links.** Allow the user to always have the buttons to take them to the home page, up a layer, to the print queue, to the phone list or whatever links are commonly used.

- **Table of contents.** It is nice when viewing a large document, such as an employee handbook, to be able to have the table of contents in view so you can jump from section to section more easily.

- **Indexes.** These are useful when converting a book or other large documents.

- **Nested menus.** Frames can be used to migrate current multilevel menu systems to an HTML interface. For example, a bill of materials system that allows the user to probe down in a part to look at subparts might have a frame listing parts and another frame listing subparts.

Frame Tags

There are three basic Frame tags:

- **Frameset.** This declares a new group of frames. They can be in columns or rows.

- **Frame SRC.** This is the document to be displayed in this frame.

- **NOFRAME.** This is what browsers that can't handle frames will see. Frames-capable browsers will ignore what is in here.

When building frames, there is more than one file used. The first file simply sets up the placement of the frames and allows a noframes section for non-frames-aware browsers to see. Then each separate frame will call a new document to be displayed in the frame.

For example, look at a simple frames document:

```
<FRAMESET COLS="50%,50%">
<FRAME SRC="frame1.html">
<FRAME SRC="frame2.html">
</FRAMESET>
```

The first line tells the browser to have two frames side by side, each using 50 percent of the browser. The next two lines tell which HTML document to place in each frame. The last line ends the frameset.

The frameset tag describes how the document is laid out, either horizontally or vertically. It can also be used to specify the size of the frame. The size can be a percent, as in our example, a size in pixels, or an asterisk *. An * means divide the remaining space evenly between the remaining frames. The default is *. Framesets can also be nested to allow frames to be set up both horizontally and vertically.

The Frames tag also has attributes that can be used to define a frame. These include the following:

III

Writing HTML

- **SRC.** This is the document to load in the frame. This was used in our example.

- **NAME.** This is used to assign a name to a frame. This name is used in the TARGET tag, which is discussed later.

- **MARGINWIDTH, MARGINHEIGHT.** This is used to define the margin between the frames and the edge of the screen.

- **SCROLLING.** This is defined to be either yes, no, or auto. Yes allows the frame to be scrolled, no disallows scrolling. The default is auto.

- **NORESIZE.** If this tag is used, the user can't resize the window.

The Target tag was mentioned earlier when discussing assigning a name to a frame. The Target tag tells the browser which frame the action should be applied to. This action may be a new link or a form action.

Note

Target tags can be used anywhere an HREF tag is used plus anywhere an ACTION tag is used.

Target tags are used in links such as:

```
<a href="home.html" target="target_name">Hyperlink</a>
```

Targets can also be used as a base case. A base is defined as the default target. Base defaults to the same frame. An example of the use of Base is

```
<base target="frame2">
```

There are also some reserved target names. These names are:

- **"_blank."** This is used to load the link in a new window.

- **"_self."** This is used to tell the browser to load the link in the same frame it is called from. This overrides the Base tag.

- **"_parent."** This is used to load the link in the parent frame. This is used in nesting frames.

- **"_top."** This is used to end the frame grouping. It loads the link in the entire browser.

Frames Example

Frames are very useful both for navigational links and for a reference such as a table of contents. You will learn how to develop a frame using two columns. One small one on the left for an index and one larger one on the right for the page.

This could be used for the employee handbook or for newsletters or any large document.

First, you need to create the frameset:

```
<html>
<head>
<title>Frames example</title>
</head>
<body>
<frameset cols="10%,90%">
<frame SRC="index.html" NAME="index">
<frame SRC="page1.html" NAME="page">
</frameset>
</body>
</html>
```

This will create the frameset with two frames side by side. The one on the left will take 10 percent of the space, and the right one will use the rest.

The frame on the left will be called index and will contain the contents of the "index.html" file. The one on the right will contain the contents of "page.html" and will have the name "page."

In an Intranet, you want all of your browsers to be able to handle frames, but since that isn't always possible, you would want to add a NOFRAMES section to your frameset. This would go in the body of the document but not in the frameset:

```
<NOFRAME>
This page is designed for use for frames browsers.
Since you don't have a frames browser you may want to
jump to <A href="page.html"the first page in this document"</a>
to get started.
</NOFRAME>
```

Now in the index.html page, add hrefs for each entry. Update the entries in the page frame, so you can set a base tag equal to page:

```
<html>
<body>
<base target="page">
<ul>
<li><a href="page1.html">Page1 </a></li>
<li><a href="page2.html">Page2 </a></li>
<li><a href="page3.html">Page3 </a></li>
<li><a href="page4.html">Page4 </a></li>
</ul>
</body>
</html>
```

This sets the base to be page. This tells any links in this frame to display in the page frame. The next lines simply set up an unordered list of pages that

III

Writing HTML

the user can jump to. These lines can be any valid HTML. As long as the href doesn't have a target set, it will show up in the page frame.

All the page*.html documents are valid HTML. They don't have anything special with them, though it might be desirable to include a NOFRAMES section. This might have links to go back a page, forward a page, and back to the index. This would make it easier for people who don't have frames-capable browsers.

Figure 9.7 shows the frames example in the Netscape browser.

Fig. 9.7
The frames example.

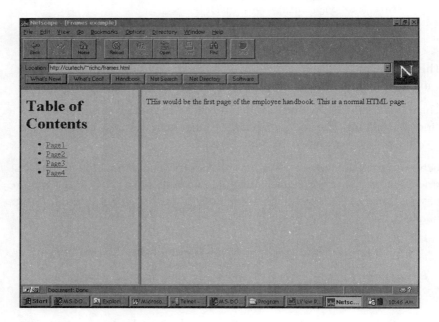

Using HTML to display information makes alot of sense and with newer features being added such as tables and frames there is almost nothing that can't be displayed. ❖

## CHAPTER 10

Graphics, Imagemaps, and Tools

If it weren't for the ability to embed graphics into an HTML page, the WWW probably never would have been as popular as it now is. Graphics can explain complicated ideas easily and can also make a page more interesting.

Imagemaps allow a user to graphically choose a direction. This can be used to show a geographic map and allow the user to choose a site. Intranets might use imagemaps to show a floorplan of a building.

In this chapter, you will learn:

- What type of image formats are available
- What imagemaps are
- The difference between client-side and server-side imagemaps
- How to reduce graphic size to make downloading easier
- How to use dome graphics tools

Graphics

One of the popular features of the early Web browsers was the capability to display images in the text of a document. This is one of the advantages the WWW had over other information systems such as Gopher.

Using inlined images makes a document much more interesting than just plain text. Adding images to a page, however, makes it take longer to download. This time can be substantial over slower modem links, especially with larger images. However, loading over a network like Ethernet or Token Ring makes images load much faster than they would over a modem line.

Images can also be used as a map, called an *imagemap*. Imagemaps allow the Web designer to define certain areas called "hotspots," which, when activated, link to certain pages.

Many sites use imagemaps as a way to navigate the site. Although this is often nicer to look at than a list of links, it often takes much more time to download. Imagemaps do have some uses in an Intranet and the "Imagemaps" section will cover these. The "Imagemaps" section will also discuss server-side and client-side imagemaps.

Graphics Formats

There are many different graphics formats. Some are *pixel-based*, and some are *vector-based*. Pixel-based graphics record each dot in an image, and they are often larger than vector-based images. Vector-based formats record the lines, or vectors, that are drawn.

There are also *lossy* or *lossless* formats. Lossy formats may look different than the original when they are viewed. This is because they have lost information. Lossless formats will not lose data and will look the same as the original.

Fortunately, the Web uses only two major formats: GIF and JPEG. *GIF* stands for the *Graphic Interchange Format,* which was developed by CompuServe. *JPEG* stands for the *Joint Pictures Experts Group*. Each format has its strengths and weaknesses. Let's take a look at these formats in more detail.

GIF

GIF, or Graphics Interchange Format, is a lossless 8-bit pixel-based format that allows for up to 256 colors per pixel. The latest release of GIF is called GIF89a. It was released by CompuServe in 1990.

GIF files use LZW compression on data to make it smaller to store and faster to download. LZW compression works very well on simple images, but complex images may compress at a ratio of only 2:1. For complex images, a better format to use is JPEG, because it compresses better.

GIF files are stored as a series of blocks and sub-blocks that are used to accurately reproduce the graphic. These blocks contain data and descriptions of the data, which allows different types of GIFs to be created.

Normal GIF images store the image block by block, and are displayed that way. The GIF image is read in, in one pass. During this pass, each block is read and placed in the image where it belongs. This can take some time to get the whole image downloaded and placed. GIF files can also be stored as interlaced images.

Interlaced images start with a blurry picture and gradually fill in the details of the image as they are downloaded. This is done by storing the data in a different order in the file. The GIF decoder is first given the incomplete image, and then more detail is added later. This allows the user to get a good idea of what the image is before having to download the entire image.

GIF images can also be used as transparent images. These images define one color to be invisible. When the decoder sees this invisible color, it replaces it with whatever color the background is. This gives the appearance of being able to look through the image. This is a very nice feature for having odd-shaped images, such as circular buttons.

GIF89a also supports animated GIFs. These are GIF files that have multiple images stored in them. As the decoder displays these images over each other, it appears to cause animation. This can be used to have an icon "morph" into something different or to have a simple animation on the screen.

Caution

Not all browsers can handle animated GIFs. These browsers will commonly display only the last image in the animation.

GIF was the first adopted graphics format for the Web and is supported on the widest number of browsers. JPEG is also a very popular format, but some older browsers don't support JPEG files.

JPEG

JPEG format is a set of standards for compressing a full-color or grayscale image. JPEG allows for 16.7 million colors (24 bits per pixel). This makes it much better for photographs, art, or other images where many colors are needed than the GIF standard, which can use only 256 colors.

JPEG is a lossy format. This means that the image may look different than the original when it is decompressed. This is not too bad since the JPEG compression loses colors in the higher frequency colors. These colors are not as noticeable to the human eye, and the image still looks OK.

One big advantage JPEG has over GIF, besides having so many more colors, is the compression. GIF images are compressed at a ratio of 2:1 to 4:1. JPEG images can achieve 10:1 to 20:1 with little loss in picture quality. This can make images download much faster. You can also compress JPEG images more than this, but it will affect the quality of the picture.

III

Writing HTML

One of the good things about GIF images is the interlaced GIF images. This gives the user the fading-in effect when downloading the images. The JPEG format called *p-JPEG*, for *progressive JPEG*, can be used to give the same sort of effect. There is one difference between the GIF and JPEG versions, though. The GIF version takes only one pass through to load the interlaced image; the JPEG version requires multiple passes, and each pass requires as much time as the first. Normally on faster processors, the fact that JPEG takes more time than the GIF to decode is not as noticeable because JPEG takes less time to download.

JPEG files can be read and displayed by most current browsers such as Netscape, Mosaic, and Microsoft Internet Explorer. Older browsers, though, may not be able to handle JPEG images.

Design Considerations

The two formats, GIF and JPEG, are the ones used on the World Wide Web today. Each format has its strengths and weaknesses. Knowing when to use each one is important. This section discusses when to use GIF over JPEG, and vice versa.

JPEG files are required for any image that needs to display more than 256 colors. Some Intranets might be PC-based and have systems that can't display more than 256 colors, so this would not be an issue. Newer systems or higher-end systems, though, usually can display all 16.7 million colors. If your image requires this many colors, then JPEG is the way to go.

JPEG files also compress much better than GIF files. This is very important for slow links, such as most Internet links. LANs have much higher speeds and often the extra size for a GIF is not as noticeable. Still, trying to reduce the load on the network is a very important task. If there is no reason to use extra bandwidth, then you shouldn't use it.

If your Intranet is using browsers that don't support the JPEG format, then obviously the choice of which to use would be GIF. You would also want to use GIFs for simple animations or if you need transparency. GIF images are also better for images that have a few sharp colors or for black-and-white images.

Image Tools

Most internal Web site developers will not have access to a graphics design house to create images for them. Instead, they will have to learn how to create graphics on their own. There are many different graphics tools available. This section discussed four of the more popular ones. One of these is for UNIX-based systems, and three are for Windows systems.

XV

XV is a shareware utility that can be used for most versions of UNIX. It is available from **ftp://ftp.cis.upenn.edu/pub/xv**. The licensing information is available under the About XV button. Basically, commercial users need to buy a license for $25. The printed manual can also be purchased for $15. XV is written by John Bradley.

XV can handle many different image formats, such as the following:

- GIF
- JPEG
- TIFF
- PostScript (save only)
- PBM/PGM/PPM either ASCII or raw
- X11 bitmap
- BMP. Windows BitMap file
- Sun Raster File

XV has many features, including the following:

- Rotate 90 degrees either direction; also flip horizontally or vertically
- Image resizing
- Grab images from the screen
- Automatically crop the images
- Smooth, blur, brighten, dim, sharpen, and dull the image

When you start XV, you will see the title screen if you don't give it an image to view. Otherwise, the image will appear in a window. This window is shown in figure 10.1.

Fig. 10.1
The XV control
window.

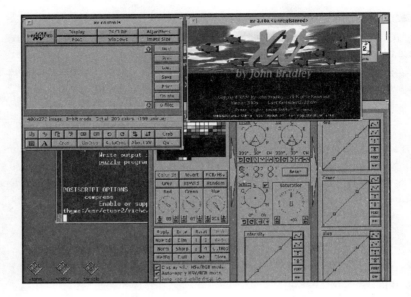

The top toolbar consists of six pull-down menus. These menus consist of the
following:

- **Display.** This menu changes how the colors are viewed and the algorithm that the viewer uses to display the image.

- **24/8 Bit.** This allows you to display how many bits are used and the
  algorithm used to convert between 24- and 8-bit colors.

- **Algorithms.** This allows you to perform some image conversions such
  as blur, sharpen, or despeckle.

- **Root.** XV allows you to display the image in the root window in different styles, as well as in a separate window.

- **Windows.** This allows you to open other XV windows, such as the
  Visual Schnauzer, Color Editor, or Image info.

- **Image size.** This menu has commands for resizing the image.

XV also has a row of buttons down the right side. These allow for quick
access to the file commands, such as Load, Save, and Print.

The row across the bottom has buttons to flip the image, rotate it, shrink or
enlarge the image, grab an image from the screen, and crop the image.

XV allows you to change an image's characteristics and to convert between many different formats. It has many image manipulation features. XV cannot be used to create images, though; to do that requires a drawing package such as Microsoft Paint.

Lview PRO

Lview PRO is another neat little image manipulator like XV. Lview PRO is available for the Windows systems. There is both a 16-bit and a 32-bit version for Windows 3.x and Windows 95. Lview PRO is available from **http:// www.std.com/~mmedia/lviewp.html**.

Lview supports the following formats:

- GIF
- JPEG
- BMP
- DIB
- Targa
- TIFF
- PPM/PGM/PBM

When Lview comes up, you will see a window like the one shown in figure 10.2.

Fig. 10.2
Lview PRO window.

Along the top of the windows, you will see five pull-down menus. They include the following:

- **File.** This menu allows you to perform the usual file functions: Load, Save, Print, and Exit.

- **Edit.** This menu allows you to cut, copy, and paste from the images. It also allows most editing functions such as flip, rotate, crop, and resize the image.

- **Retouch.** This allows you to manipulate the image. Some of the functions under this menu allow you to adjust contrast, color, brightness, and luminance. There are also many image filters such as blur, sharpen, and dull.

- **Options.** This allows you to define some things about the user interface, force GIFs to be saved as interlaced images, and to set the JPEG compression.

- **Help.** Lview PRO includes a windows Help file. This makes it easy to get help on-line.

Lview also has a toolbar along the right side of the image that allows most of these functions to be activated with just a click. This allows the user to get at functions without having to select from the menus.

Note

Lview, like XV, is an image manipulation program. It is not used to create the images. To create images requires a drawing program such as Paint Shop Pro.

Paint Shop Pro

Paint Shop Pro is a shareware graphics tool. It allows editing, screen capture, and simple image manipulation. It does not allow the fine tweaking of the image that Lview does, but it can be used as a drawing package. Paint Shop Pro is available from **ftp://ftp.the.net/mirrors/ftp.winsite.com/pc/win95/desktop/psp311.zip**. There is a $69 license fee if used for more than evaluation purposes.

Once Paint Shop Pro is installed and run, you will see a screen similar to the one in figure 9.12. The following pull-down menus appear across the top bar:

- **File.** This handles file operations such as Open, Close, Save, and Print. Paint Shop Pro can also do batch conversions of files from one format to another.
- **Edit.** This has the options for editing the images such as cut, copy, and paste.
- **View.** This allows you to zoom in and out. You can also customize the toolbar by using the options selection.
- **Image.** This menu has image utilities. These include the capability to flip the image, rotate the image, and create a mirror image. You can also add noise, enhance colors, brighten, darken, blur, sharpen, and soften the image.
- **Colors.** This menu has utilities dealing with color manipulation. Some of these options allow you to adjust brightness, gamma correction, convert to grayscale, create a negative, and load new color palettes. There is also an option under this menu to increase or decrease color depth. This can be useful when trying to decrease image size.
- **Capture.** This menu allows you to capture the entire screen, an entire window, or the client portion of a window, as well as a part of the screen. You can also choose whether the mouse pointer will show up or not.
- **Window.** This menu allows you to cascade and tile windows as well as duplicate images.
- **Help.** This accesses the on-line help system.

Paint Shop Pro also has a toolbar that allows you to perform common actions. These include opening and saving files, printing the image, cutting, copying, and pasting. Paint Shop Pro can also be used to read images in from a scanner.

Paint Shop Pro has three panels. These panels include the zoom tool, select tool, and paint tool. These tools allow quick access to common actions. Paint Shop Pro is shown in figure 10.3.

III

Writing HTML

Fig. 10.3
Paint Shop Pro has
menus, toolbars,
and panels.

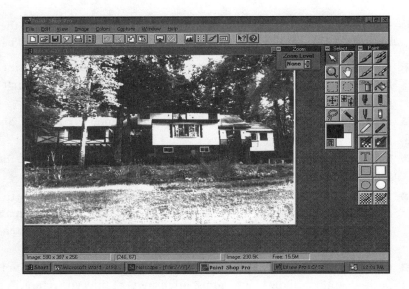

Paint Shop Pro can load and save in many different formats. These formats include the following:

- GIF
- JPEG
- PCX
- PBM
- PCX
- CorelDRAW! (Load only)
- Micrografx (Load only)
- Ventura (Load only)

Imagemaps

Imagemaps are graphics images that contain "hotspots" in them. When you click the hotspot, you are taken to a new page or document. This can be used instead of normal text links to create a more natural effect.

> **Note**
>
> On a slow network, such as accessing the Internet with a modem, imagemaps may take a long time to download. If an imagemap takes too long to download, it detracts from the page rather than enhancing it.
>
> You should always have an alternate way for people to access a link because not all browsers can support imagemaps. If your company has standardized on a browser that supports imagemaps and no one will be using a different browser, you may be able to get away with not having a text alternative.

About Imagemaps

There are two different types of imagemaps: *client-side* imagemaps and *server-side* imagemaps. Client-side imagemaps are processed by the browser but are supported only by the newest browsers. Server-side imagemaps are processed by the server, but not all servers support them.

Both types of imagemaps will appear the same to a user because the browser and servers handle the processing. When designing imagemaps, make sure it is clear where the hotspots are defined. This can be done by outlining the hotspot or by using a specific color. Imagemaps also usually have a default region. This is anywhere that is not a hotspot and can be specified to go to a specific URL.

When creating an image to use as an imagemap, you should note the coordinates of the hotspots. Write down the vertices of the shapes for later reference. For the following shapes, you will need the following coordinates:

- **Rectangle.** The upper-left and lower-right corners.
- **Polygon.** The coordinates of each vertex.
- **Circle.** The coordinates of the center and an edge point.

You will need these coordinates later when you create the map file.

Let's take a look at the different imagemap formats, both client-side and server-side, to see how they work.

III

Writing HTML

Server-Side Imagemaps

Server-side imagemaps are images that the browser is told are imagemaps. This is done by using the ISMAP tag inside the IMG tag. This would be a server-side imagemap:

```
<IMG SRC="imagemap.gif" ALT="Imagemap" ISMAP>
```

When the browser gets an image that is defined as an imagemap, it sends back the X and Y coordinates of the mouse pointer when it is clicked. In other words, when you click an area of the map, the X and Y coordinates are sent back to the server. The server then decides which URL to send back to you.

Server-side includes usually require some configuration on the server end. You will also need to create a map file. This map file is used to tell the server which URL to send back for the coordinates the users selected. A map file is usually of the following form:

```
RECT <URL> Upper_Left(x,y) Lower_Right(x,y)
CIRCLE <URL> center(x,y) Edge_Point(x,y)
POLY <URL> vertex1(x,y) vertex2(x,y) vertex3(x,y)...
DEFAULT <URL>
```

As you can see, there are three shapes that can be defined: a rectangle, circle, and polygon. There is also a line that sets the default URL if the user clicks an undefined region. These shapes are not case sensitive; RECT, rect, and ReCt are all the same, like HTML tags, though most designers use all uppercase to make it easier to read.

A sample map file might look like this:

```
RECT http://www.server.com/offices/office1   10,10 20,20
RECT http://www.server.com/offices/office2   20,10 30,20
RECT http://www.server.com/offices/office3   10,20 20,30
RECT http://www.server.com/offices/office4   20,20 30,30
DEFAULT http://www.server.com/offices/list
```

Note

Some servers may use the words "RECTANGLE," "CIRCLE," and "POLYGON" instead. Check your server documentation if you are having problems.

Most servers also have an imagemap.conf file. This file tells the server which imagemap file goes with each imagemap image. The syntax for this file is

```
image_name  :  physical path
```

> **Note**
>
> The path to the map file is the physical path, not the URL to the map file.

A sample imagemap.conf file may look like this:

```
officemap  :  /imagemaps/office.map
product1   :  /imagemaps/prod1.map
buttonbar  :  /images/button.map
```

When adding an imagemap to a document, you need to reference the map file that is to be used. This is normally done by passing the map file as the argument to an HREF tag. For example:

```
<A HREF="officemap">
<IMG SRC="offices.gif" ISMAP>
</A>
```

This will use the imagemap map file for officemap to decide which URL to go to when the user clicks a point in the offices.gif file. This assumes your server can automatically handle imagemaps. If your server needs to call a separate CGI program, then you would use something like

```
<A HREF="/cgi-bin/imagemap/officemap">
<IMG SRC="offices.gif" ISMAP>
</A>
```

Client-Side Imagemaps

Having the server process the imagemaps can lead to performance problems if your server is already heavily loaded. Client-side imagemaps cause the client to process the coordinates and to request the correct link.

Documents that contain client-side imagemaps have the map file included in the document. There are currently two ways to handle this. One way is by using the MAP and AREA tags, and the other uses the FIG tag.

III

Writing HTML

The MAP and AREA tags are used to define the coordinates that were previously stored on the server in the map file. Once you have defined a map region, you also give it a name in the HTML file. The IMG tag has also been changed to add a USEMAP tag. This is used to define where the map regions are defined. A sample application follows:

```
<MAP NAME="offices">
<AREA SHAPE="RECT" COORDS="10,10,20,20" HREF="http://
➥www.server.com/offices/office1">
<AREA SHAPE="RECT" COORDS="20,10,30,20" HREF="http://
➥www.server.com/offices/office2">
<AREA SHAPE="RECT" COORDS="10,20,20,30" HREF="http://
➥www.server.com/offices/office3">
<AREA SHAPE="RECT" COORDS="20,20,30,30" HREF="http://
➥www.server.com/offices/office4">
</MAP>
```

The first line names this map region "offices"; this is used by the USEMAP attribute to define which region to use. The AREA tags define the shapes, coordinates, and HREF that were used in the server's map file. The last line simply ends the map region.

When the imagemap is placed, either in this file or in another file, the USEMAP points to this area. For example, if the USEMAP were in the same file as the map region:

```
<IMG SRC="offices.gif" USEMAP="#offices">
```

Or if they were in different files:

```
<IMG SRC="offices.gif" USEMAP="file.html#offices">
```

The MAP and AREA tags were developed by Spyglass while they were developing a version of Mosaic that could handle imagemaps without the use of a server.

The other alternative uses the FIG tag instead of the MAP and AREA tags. The FIG tag defines a figure that is to be used as an imagemap. The text between the <FIG> and </FIG> is shown to browsers that can't handle imagemaps. It is also used as the map coordinates.

This is done by adding to the HREF tag a SHAPE. The SHAPE consists of the shape name and the coordinates. An example of a client-side imagemap using the FIG tags is

```
<FIG SRC="offices.gif">
<B>Select an office to view</B>
<UL>
<LI> <A HREF="http://www.server.com/offices/office1" SHAPE="RECT
```

```
➥10,10,20,20">Office number 1
<LI> <A HREF="http://www.server.com/offices/office2" SHAPE="RECT
➥20,10,30,20">Office number 2
<LI> <A HREF="http://www.server.com/offices/office3" SHAPE="RECT
➥10,20,20,30">Office number 3
<LI> <A HREF="http://www.server.com/offices/office4" SHAPE="RECT
➥20,20,30,30">Office number 4
</UL>
</FIG>
```

One of the nice things about the FIG tag is that browsers that can't do client-side imagemaps will get the text between the <FIG> and </FIG>. By making this a nice list, any browser can view this page and navigate from it.

Intranet Uses

Imagemaps have normally been abused on the Internet. Companies may have a 70K imagemap leading to three or four links with no alternative navigation for users who don't have graphical browsers or choose to not load images. This has caused imagemaps to get a bad reputation.

Imagemaps can be useful in both the Internet and Intranets if they are used properly. There are a few rules to follow when using imagemaps.

- Use the smallest size image possible. If your image can use only a few colors rather than 16.7 million, use the smallest amount of colors. This will greatly reduce the size of your graphics and make them load faster. Even on Intranets where the network speed is much faster, image size should be kept as small as possible.

- Always have an alternate menu. Not all browsers support imagemaps and not all users load images. Some users may prefer the look of a text menu rather than the sometimes distorted images displayed on poorer monitors.

- If you don't need an imagemap, don't use one. You should never try to use an imagemap or other tag. You should simply use the tool that is right for the job. Some companies actually create a GIF image that contains nothing but text just so they can use an imagemap.

Those rules aside, imagemaps do have some very beneficial uses in an Intranet. They are very useful for explaining an image, for example. Imagemaps are also useful in places where geography is important in deciding which URL to follow. Following are a few examples of where an imagemap would fit into an Intranet setting:

- **Office maps.** In a networking environment, it is common to have network maps showing the network drop numbers and phone extensions. These maps are very useful when tracking down problems. Having an imagemap with this information, stored in a separate URL for each office, can make it easier for technicians to quickly tell which drop they are working on by clicking the office they are in.

- **Product diagrams.** When introducing or describing a product, it is often easier to explain with a picture than with words. An imagemap drawing of a product with hotspots defining major components can help employees and customers get a better understanding of how everything will look and work.

- **Technical diagrams.** If your company has a helpdesk, then they know how it is to try to explain where the printer cable gets plugged into the back of a computer. An imagemap of the back of a machine with hotspots defining the different ports can make it easier on the helpdesk and the employees. This is also true of phones, fax machines, and any equipment that often needs to be explained.

- **Geographic decisions.** Any choice that is geographic in nature can benefit from an imagemap. This could be a campus of buildings with hotspots defined as each building. This could get linked to a page describing the building, who is in it, and what they do.

Imagemap Tools

Creating imagemaps requires drawing the image, figuring out the hotspots' shapes and coordinates, and writing the map file or document. Fortunately, there are tools that can be used to map the image for you. These tools will also generate a server-side or client-side map file. Most tools can handle either GIF or JPEG files and can write server- or client-side map files.

Map THIS!

Map THIS! is a freeware Imagemap tool. It was created by Todd C. Wilson and can run on 32-bit Windows machines such as Windows 95 or Windows NT. It can handle GIF or JPEG image formats. Map THIS! can also create either server-side or client-side imagemaps.

> **Note**
>
> Map THIS! is available from **http://www.ecaetc.ohio-state.edu/tc**.

When you start Map THIS!, you will see a screen with menus across the top and two toolbars. Most of the features can be used from the toolbar. This includes the circle, rectangle, and polygon tools. Figure 10.4 shows MapTHIS! in action.

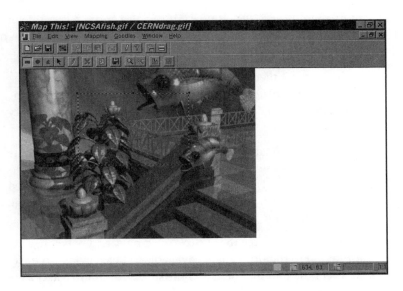

Fig. 10.4
MapTHIS can be used to create client-side or server-side images.

You can use any of these tools to outline the hotspots. Once a hotspot is defined, you need to go into mapping and define a URL for it to use. The tools allow you to start at a vertex, or an edge for the circle, and drag away to the other side or another vertex to define a spot.

When defining many hotspots, it is easy to get confused and forget which ones you have already defined. Map THIS! allows you to turn on shading. This will automatically shade in the hotspots that have been defined. You can also enable the area list. This will tell you which shapes have been defined and where they will link to.

You can also work with multiple images with Map THIS! You can choose to cascade or tile the windows. You can also zoom in or out with this tool.

When saving the map file, you will be asked if you are saving a client-side or server-side imagemap. If you choose server-side, you will be asked if it is NCSA or CERN style. If you choose client-side, it will ask you for a file to store the HTML in.

III

Writing HTML

Map Edit

Map Edit is a shareware imagemap tool. It is available from **http://www. boutell.com/mapedit**. It can be used for evaluation for 30 days. After this time, you need to license it and pay the $25 licensing fee.

Map Edit can handle GIF and JPEG formats. It can also create server-side or client-side imagemap map files. The server-side files can be in either NCSA or CERN style.

Map Edit consists of three menus: File, Tools, and Help. File allows you to save, open, and use other file options. It also contains the Default URL option. This is used to define a default action in case the user clicks an empty region.

When you open a file, Map Edit will ask if this is for a server-side or client-side imagemap. If you choose server-side, you will be prompted for the format, either NCSA or CERN. If you choose client-side, you will be prompted for the file to write the HTML code in. You also need to tell it which image to use for the imagemap.

The Tools menu consists of three tools: circle, rectangle, and polygon. These, of course, correspond to the three shapes available to imagemaps. To trace out an image, select the tool that describes the shape you want. Select a corner, or the center (for the circle tool) and click the left button. For circles, you can drag out the circle until you get to the edge, then click the right button to define the region. For the rectangle, you still drag out until the outline covers the area you want defined, then click the right button. Clicking the right button defines the outlined region as a hotspot.

Polygons will need to be defined by going to each vertex in succession and clicking the left button. When you get to the last one, click the right button. This will define the region. If you decide to cancel the trace before you finish it, you can simply press the Esc key.

Once a region has been defined, a prompt box will pop up and ask you for the URL to link to. You can also enter a comment or description. You can continue adding regions until you are done. Then you can choose the Save option under the File menu.

Web Hotspots

Web Hotspots is another shareware imagemap tool available to Windows users. To register, it costs $49 plus $5 shipping and handling. You can download the evaluation copy from **http://www.cris.com/~automata/ hotspots.shtml**. Web Hotspots was written by Keith Doty from 1Automata.

Hotspots supports GIF and JPEG images and can write both server-side and client-side map formats.

Web Hotspots has a series of buttons down the left side. These buttons allow you to quickly choose the tool you need. These include the usual circle, rectangle, and polygon. It also includes a free form tool. This allows you to draw a region freehand. This region is then automatically converted to a polygon by the software.

As you define a region, it is automatically shaded to let you see at a glance which regions have already been defined. After you define a region, you can simply add the URL to the URL line at the bottom of the screen.

Web Hotspots also allows you to rescale the image and rotate the image without having to save it, and start a drawing package to perform this. This makes Web Hotspots much more user-friendly.

Web Hotspots can also be used to move a region to the front of the map file. This is useful if you have regions that overlap, because the first region that a coordinate pair matches is used. ❖

III

Writing HTML

CHAPTER 11

HTML Forms

The most commonly used container for structured data is the paper form. Forms permeate our lives as social beings, from a birth certificate to school report cards, from 1040 forms and mortgage applications to requests for social security.

Small wonder, then, that forms are the bedrock of user interaction on an Intranet. The ease with which HTML forms—sometimes called *fill-in forms*—can be created is one of the technology's big benefits, for users and developers alike.

HTML forms provide a rich set of data input features that emulate those found on common paper forms. For instance, a form can be used to capture manually-entered information to a database. A related application is the use of forms to input free text, such as a discussion forum message.

Web-based forms do have an important limitation, though: You have to submit them to validate their data. This compares unfavorably with client/sever applications developed using PowerBuilder or Visual Basic, which can do on-the-fly validation based on built-in business logic.

Fortunately, scripting languages such as JavaScript are beginning to make it possible to build Web pages that do everything a client/server application can do. The downside is that such pages are no longer simple to develop and maintain, sacrificing much of what makes an Intranet attractive in the first place.

Later chapters cover the use of CGI scripts to process forms and connect them to legacy applications.

In this chapter, you learn:

■ How to design and build forms using HTML

■ What you can do with forms on an Intranet

■ How online forms can replace paper flows

■ Where Web-based forms don't fit

Forms Tags

Forms elements make up a significant part of HyperText Markup Language. This section covers the use of HTML tags to create forms. Also discussed are the methods available for submitting forms to a server for interpretation and processing.

The set of tags useful for designing forms is listed in Table 11.1.

Table 11.1 HTML Tags for Building Forms	
Tag	**Brief Description**
<FORM>...</FORM>	Begins and ends an HTML form within a Web page.
<INPUT>	Inserts a variable field such as a button, checkbox; or text box.
<SELECT>...<SELECT>	Creates a scrolling list box of options for user selection.
<OPTION>	Specifies values for a list box created with <SELECT>.
<TEXTAREA>...</TEXTAREA>	Creates a scrolling box where users can enter free text, such as comments.

Figure 11.1 shows a simple form composed of these elements.

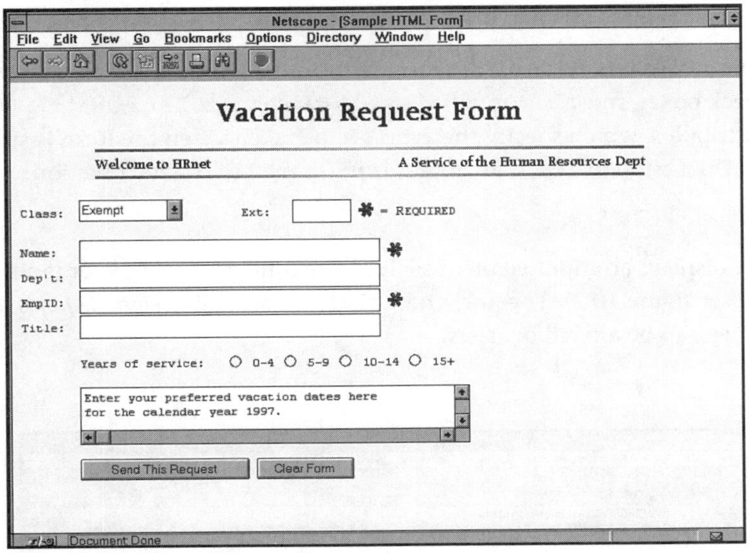

Fig. 11.1
Sample Intranet form showing how INPUT, SELECT/OPTION and TEXTAREA tags display in Netscape Navigator.

Using the Forms Elements

> **Note**
>
> NCSA's primer on HTML forms support is one of several handy online guides. You'll find it at **http://www.ncsa.uiuc.edu/SDG/Software/Mosaic/Docs/fill-out-forms/overview.html**.

This section walks you through the form tags, giving a short code example of each to show how it's done. The examples are on the accompanying CD-ROM. Feel free to use them as a springboard for your own HTML forms.

> **Note**
>
> The sample code is typical in that much of the HTML serves a cosmetic purpose. Users are accustomed to paper forms with neatly aligned fields; it's a good idea to mimic this online. Two techniques can help.
>
> The technique used here is to set off the form code in a <PRE></PRE> tag pair. This causes the browser to display text, tabs and spaces in a fixed-width font. Designers can use the uniform length of such features to line up the elements in a form.
>
> Another technique is to place form elements in the cells of an HTML table. Table layouts are more complex than preformatting, but provide greater design versatility.

III

Writing HTML

Element: <FORM>...</FORM>

This pair of tags sets off an HTML form. Other elements, such as text areas and check boxes, must be contained in a FORM tag pair. The FORM tag takes three attributes, which specify the action to be taken when the form is submitted. Discussion of FORM attributes is postponed to the next section.

Element: <INPUT>

This tag displays an input element such as a text field, checkbox, or radio button (see figure 10.2). Together these elements are called *editable fields*, because they can be altered by users.

Fig. 11.2
Web form showing various types of INPUT: checkbox, radio button, password, text, submit, and reset. The HTML code is given below.

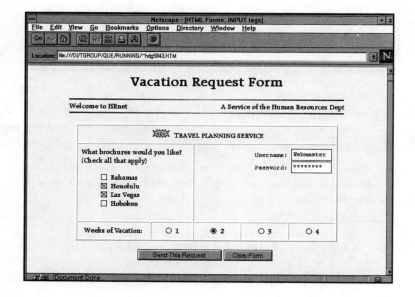

The syntax for INPUT is illustrated in the code for figure 11.2, shown below in Listing 11.1.

**Listing 11.1   HTML code for implementing the form shown
in figure 11.2**

```
<FORM METHOD="POST" ACTION="/cgi-bin/vform">
<CENTER>
<TABLE WIDTH=75% CELLPADDING=8 BORDER=2>
<TR>
     <TD ALIGN="center" COLSPAN=5><IMG HSPACE=6 SRC="pix/y2_new.gif"
➥ALT="New!">
     <FONT SIZE=+1>T</FONT>RAVEL PLANNING SERVICE</TD>
</TR>
<TR>
     <TD ALIGN="left" COLSPAN=2>
     What brochures would you like?<BR>
     (Check all that apply)
     <BLOCKQUOTE>
       <INPUT NAME="VacLoc" TYPE="CHECKBOX" VALUE="Bahamas"> Bahamas<BR>
       <INPUT NAME="VacLoc" TYPE="CHECKBOX" VALUE="Honolulu">
➥Honolulu<BR>
       <INPUT NAME="VacLoc" TYPE="CHECKBOX" VALUE="Las Vegas"> Las
➥Vegas<BR>
       <INPUT NAME="VacLoc" TYPE="CHECKBOX" VALUE="Hoboken"> Hoboken<BR>
     </BLOCKQUOTE>
     </TD>
     <TD VALIGN="top" ALIGN="right" COLSPAN=3>
     <PRE>
     Username: <INPUT NAME="Username" TYPE="TEXT" ROWS=1 MAXLENGTH=10
➥SIZE="10">
     Password: <INPUT NAME="Password" TYPE="PASSWORD" ROWS=1
➥MAXLENGTH=10 SIZE="10">
     </PRE>
     </TD>
</TR>
<TR ALIGN="center"><!-- Bottom Line -->
     <TD WIDTH=28%>Weeks of Vacation:</TD>
     <TD WIDTH=18%><INPUT NAME="VacWks" TYPE="RADIO" VALUE="1"> 1</TD>
     <TD WIDTH=18%><INPUT NAME="VacWks" TYPE="RADIO" VALUE="2"> 2</TD>
     <TD WIDTH=18%><INPUT NAME="VacWks" TYPE="RADIO" VALUE="3"> 3</TD>
     <TD WIDTH=18%><INPUT NAME="VacWks" TYPE="RADIO" VALUE="4"> 4</TD>
</TR>
</TABLE>
<INPUT TYPE="submit" VALUE="Send This Request"> <INPUT TYPE="reset"
➥VALUE="Clear Form">
</CENTER>
</FORM>
```

III

Writing HTML

Each INPUT statement has a *name* and a *type* attribute. The name is the variable name associated with input data, which in turn is captured as the *value* in a name/value pair.

Type must be one of following:

Input type	Description
checkbox	This multiple choice element behaves much as its paper equivalent. Checkboxes are off by default, but the CHECKED attribute can be used to turn them on. When a checkbox is on, the associated name/value pair is submitted with the form. Multiple checkboxes with the same NAME can be used to select several values at once. For example:

Hobbies (check all that apply):

```
<INPUT TYPE="checkbox" NAME="hobby" VALUE="computers">
<INPUT TYPE="checkbox" NAME="hobby" VALUE="movies">
<INPUT TYPE="checkbox" NAME="hobby" VALUE="reading">
<INPUT TYPE="checkbox" NAME="hobby" VALUE="sports">
```

Input type	Description
radio	Radio buttons, like checkboxes, are a multiple choice input element, but radio choices are mutually exclusive. The buttons in a group must have the same NAME. Turning one button in a group *on* turns the other buttons *off*. The following example assigns the value of the selected button to the variable *EmpYrs*:

```
<INPUT TYPE="RADIO" NAME="EmpYrs" VALUE="0" CHECKED> 0-4
<INPUT TYPE="RADIO" NAME="EmpYrs" VALUE="5"> 5-9
<INPUT TYPE="RADIO" NAME="EmpYrs" VALUE="10"> 10-14
<INPUT TYPE="RADIO" NAME="EmpYrs" VALUE="15"> 15+
```

Input type	Description
text	A line of text. The width of the displayed input field can be set by the SIZE element. Text fields take an optional attribute, MAXLENGTH, which specifies the size in bytes of the input buffer. Without MAXLENGTH the buffer is unlimited. Example:

```
<INPUT TYPE="text" SIZE=36 MAXLENGTH=128 >
```

Input type	Description
hidden	This tag prevents an INPUT element from being displayed. Any VALUE information is still submitted with the form. The reason for using *hidden* is to keep track of the *state* of an interaction. HTTP is normally stateless, meaning it has no memory of prior exchanges during a session. Hidden fields can be used in a script-generated form to convey the state of a transaction. For instance, to give a user three tries in a guessing game, you might use a hidden field to keep track of past tries:

Input type	Description
`<INPUT TYPE="hidden" NAME="try" VALUE="2">`	
password	This INPUT type is identical to *text*, except that characters typed into the field are echoed password-style, as asterisks or whitespace. Note that this protects the user's password at the client only, since all form data (including INPUT TYPE="password") is sent over the Web as plain text.
reset	This INPUT tag places a button on the form which, when pressed, clears all values entered by the user and restores the defaults. Like *submit*, the button can be labeled using the VALUE attribute:
`<INPUT TYPE="reset" VALUE="Clear Form">`	
submit	This INPUT tag places a button on the form which, when pressed, sends all form data as name/value pairs to the URL specified by the FORM action tag. Like *reset*, the button can be labeled using the VALUE attribute. Example:
`<INPUT TYPE="submit" VALUE="Send Form">`	

Element: <SELECT>...<SELECT>

Element: <OPTION>

This tag pair can contain a set of options presented to the user as a scrolling list from which one or more items can be selected. Each item is specified by an <OPTION> element. Figure 11.3 shows a typical use of the SELECT statement to implement a user survey.

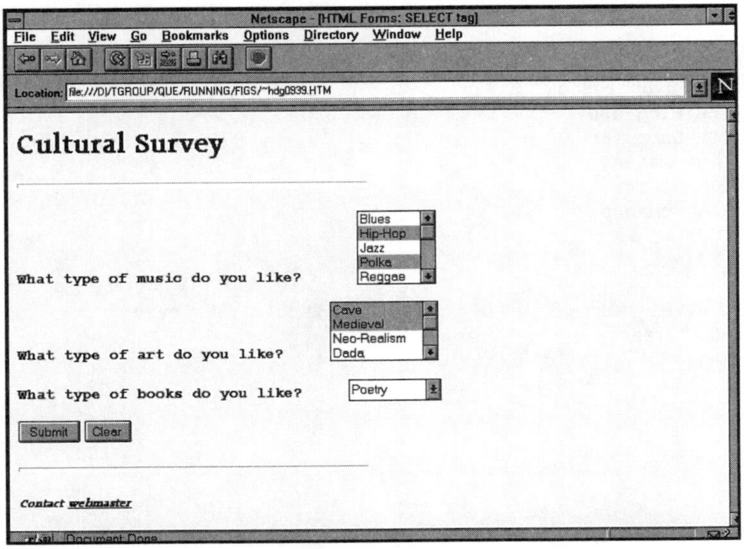

Fig. 11.3
Web form showing variations of the SELECT/OPTION tag pair. The HTML code is shown in Listing 11.2.

III

Writing HTML

Listing 11.2 HTML code for implementing the form shown in figure 11.3

```
<HTML>
<HEAD>
    <TITLE>HTML Forms: SELECT tag</TITLE>
    <!-- To see what this code looks like, refer to
    Figure 10.3 in *Running a Perfect Intranet* -->
</HEAD>

<BODY>
<H1>Cultural Survey</H1>
<HR WIDTH=50% ALIGN="left" SIZE=4>
<BASEFONT SIZE=4>

<!-- Note: HTML Form Begins Here-->
<FORM METHOD="POST" ACTION="/cgi-bin/vform">
<PRE>
<B>What type of music do you like?</B>              <SELECT
➥NAME="FavoriteMusic" SIZE=5 MULTIPLE>
<OPTION>Blues
<OPTION>Hip-Hop
<OPTION>Jazz
<OPTION>Polka
<OPTION>Reggae
<OPTION>Waltz
</SELECT>

<B>What type of art do you like?      </B>  <SELECT NAME="FavoriteArt"
➥SIZE=4 MULTIPLE>
<OPTION>Cave
<OPTION>Medieval
<OPTION>Neo-Realism
<OPTION>Dada
<OPTION>Cubism
</SELECT>

<B>What type of books do you like?</B>              <SELECT
➥NAME="FavoriteBook" SIZE=1>
<OPTION>Biography
<OPTION>Computer
<OPTION>Mystery
<OPTION>Poetry
<OPTION>Romance
<OPTION>Sci-Fi
</SELECT>
</PRE>
<INPUT TYPE="submit" VALUE="Submit"> <INPUT TYPE="reset"
➥VALUE="Clear">
</FORM>
```

```
<HR WIDTH=50% ALIGN="left" SIZE=4>
<H5><I>Contact <A HREF="mailto:gbenett@shore.net">webmaster</A></I></
➥H5>
</BODY>
</HTML>
```

SELECT takes three attributes:

Attribute	What it does...
MULTIPLE	Enables users to select more than one item from a SELECT list, usually by holding down a key while selecting. Absent MULTIPLE, only one item can be selected. In the example of figure 11.3, the music and art lists use MULTIPLE, while the book list does not.
NAME(required)	Specifies the variable name assigned to the submitted value.
SIZE	Specifies the number of text lines displayed in the SELECT list, which typically appears as a scrollbox. In figure 11.3 the music and art lists are scrollboxes with SIZE > 1, while the book list is a pull-down menu of SIZE=1.

Element: TEXTAREA...</TEXTAREA>

TEXTAREA creates a scrolling box where users can enter free text. Any text placed between the opening and closing tags appears in the TEXTAREA as an initial value. In the Vacation Request Form example of figure 11.1, a TEXTAREA is used to get employees' date preferences.

TEXTAREA takes three attributes (which *must* be present):

Attribute	What it does...
COLS	Specifies the width of the text entry area in columns.
NAME	Specifies the variable name assigned to submitted text.
ROWS	Specifies the height of the text entry area in rows.

HTTP Methods for Submitting Data

Note

For a technical discussion of the client/server exchange kicked off when you submit a Web form, see the tutorial hosted by the University of Kansas at **http://kuhttp.cc.ukans.edu/info/forms/formsintro.html**.

The few simple elements presented in the last section account for all the power of HTML forms. They enable you to create powerful data entry (or query) screens with only a few lines of code.

Form data is processed on a Web server. To send the filled-out form from her browser to the server, a user clicks the form's SUBMIT button—an INPUT element of TYPE="submit".

Earlier in the chapter we noted that the FORM element takes three attributes. These determine where, and by what HTTP method, the form is shipped for processing. The attributes of FORM are given below.

Attribute	What it does...
ACTION(required)	Specifies the URL to which FORM content is to be sent for processing. This is usually the address of a script or mailto target. Example:

```
<FORM ACTION="mailto:g.benett@ieee.org">
```

METHOD	HTTP provides several methods for clients to request service: GET, POST, PUT, HEAD. By far the most prevalent in GET, which gets an object from the server, and POST, which posts data to an object on the server. As a rule of thumb, use POST when passing form data to a program, and GET when making a request or performing a search. Examples:

```
<FORM ACTION="http://www.que.com/cgi-bin/readform" METHOD=POST>
<FORM ACTION="http://www.que.com/cgi-bin/locate?G+Benett"
➥METHOD=GET>
```

ENCTYPE	If present, this optional attribute specifies the MIME type used to encode data exchanged with the POST method. At present only one value is allowed (URL-encoding):

```
application/x-www-form-urlencoded
```

Protocols for writing forms-processing scripts are well-established. We discuss them in the next chapter. The remainder of this chapter focuses on the use of forms on an Intranet.

Forms for Intranet Applications

> **Note**
>
> The tutorial *How to do Forms*, at **www2.ncsu.edu/bae/people/faculty/walker/ hotlist/forms.html**, features many examples of scripts you can adapt to process your own forms.

The Vacation Request Form used as an example earlier in the chapter represents one way forms can add value on an Intranet. Rather than sending a paper form to employees via interoffice mail, a Human Resources department might develop an HTML form such as the one in figure 11.1. Such a form would have a shorter turnaround time than paper, eliminating a round-trip mailing. Moreover, an electronic form can feed database applications directly, without error-prone rekeying.

This type of forms-based application replaces one or more paper forms. Another class of application for HTML forms is collaborative. Forms make a convenient front-end to discussion forums, a text-based medium useful for engaging in dialogue at a distance. Workgroups and departments can often reduce time spent traveling to meetings by exchanging ideas on the Intranet.

Additional uses for HTML forms are described later in the book.

Replacing Paper Flows

Any business process that relies on the exchange of paper forms is a candidate for improvement via an internal Web. One of the first successful projects in this area was the Enterprisewide-information Viewing Environment (EVE), developed in 1995 at Sandia National Labs, Albuquerque, New Mexico.

EVE is a forms-based suite of productivity applications that includes:

- Conference-Room Scheduling. Employees can search for room features such as whiteboards or handicap access, then reserve the room online.

III

Writing HTML

- Project-Management Query. Using EVE, Sandia managers now enjoy access to project data formerly available only through custom mainframe queries.

- Official Airline Guide. This application delivers airline, car rental, and, hotel information for domestic travel. If the Labs realize the goal of adding foreigntravel authorization to EVE, it will trim a process that today involves routing paperwork to six different people.

- SAND Reports. In addition to paper versions of the Lab's research articles housed in the corporate library, EVE now puts abstracts searchable by key words on the internal Web.

What features do these applications share that make them suitable for implementation on an Intranet? For one thing, they enable queries against corporate databases to take place from the desktop. For another, applications like SAND Reports shift the traditional "push model" of disseminating documents everywhere to a more effective "pull model" in which only interested parties receive data. EVE applications share a common foundation in TCP/IP and HTTP, as well—the hallmark of an Intranet.

Distributing interactive documents using a Web lends itself naturally to *workflow automation*. This class of applications unites e-mail, forms processing, and security tools such as digital signatures to streamline paper-driven business processes.

Formerly the province of vertical application suites or proprietary groupware such as Notes, workflow software is enjoying new popularity on corporate Intranets. Web browsers with integrated SMTP mail and digital certificates make a familiar, cost-effective front end for the software. If today's Web server technology lacks strength as a workflow engine, products like Livelink Intranet from Open Text Corporation are filling this gap. Figure 11.4 shows a screen from a workflow demonstration on the Open Text Web site.

Note

For more information on *Livelink Intranet*, visit Open Text's Web site at **http://www.opentext.com/**.

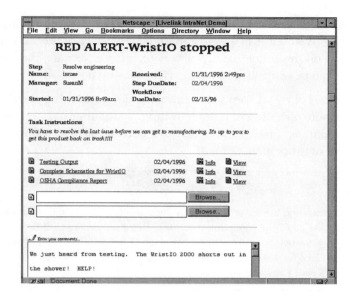

Fig. 11.4
Sample workflow automation screen using Livelink Intranet. Note the integration of forms and tabular information to show project status. (Courtesy: Open Text Corp.)

Forms for Collaboration and Control

One of the straightforward uses for forms on an Intranet is as a standardized means of data entry. HTML forms designed to mimic their paper counterparts fall in this category. Forms can also be used to carry on written dialogues between users. While this is similar to an e-mail exchange, it has unique features that may be advantageous for some communications. Messages appear in a public forum, for instance, visible to all users or a special-interest workgroup. The precise sequence of original messages and replies is concisely displayed. And the dialogues are captured for posterity in a format easily tapped as a knowledge base.

In addition, forms can be used to extend the forum concept in novel ways. One example is to let users create their own Web pages. This amounts to allowing HTML tags to be entered in forum messages. Besides opening the medium of exchange to include images and hypertext, this can be a handy technique for updating the content of standard Web pages. Webmasters and users alike can benefit from this distribution of tasks. Users might enter new material on forms provided expressly for that purpose. The target script would validate the content and, perhaps, install it in the appropriate place on a Web page.

III

Writing HTML

Forms can also be used for *control*. Numerical data can be processed and exported by the Web server in a form appropriate to device or process control. For instance, on the Edime™ family of Web Servers for Netware, the server's serial ports can be controlled by special HTML instructions.

Interesting uses of HTML forms for control include positioning surveillance cameras, remote operation of HVAC (Heating, Ventilating and Air Conditioning) equipment, fax-on-demand of digitized documents, text-to-speech conversion, and network management.

> **Note**
>
> If you're considering the use of HTML forms for control, keep in mind that Intranet messaging, like all TCP/IP communications, uses statistical media access techniques. You can't know whether a control action will execute in one second or one minute. Web forms can offer real benefits where timing isn't critical, but for real-time process control, stick with a deterministic system.

Much as happened with PC's, character-based user interfaces will give way to graphical controls as applet technology matures. Libraries of JavaScript and ActiveX "widgets"—autonomous graphic control elements—have already begun to appear for the Web. A year from now, expect to turn a dial rather than enter a numerical temperature to control your Web-based thermostat.

Limitations of HTML Forms

If Web-based forms are so powerful, won't they eventually replace other types of software interface, such as graphical screens created with PowerBuilder and Visual Basic? Eventually, maybe, but not any time soon.

HTTP transactions have some key drawbacks that guarantee stand-alone GUI applications a future. These drawbacks issue from two aspects of the protocol:

- HTTP connections are stateless
- Each HTTP connection transfers at most one item from the server to the client (browser)

The fact that HTTP transactions don't keep track of state means that each current activity is unaware of prior transactions. Put simply, Web work has no memory. This makes it difficult to keep track of a user's path through a Web site, for instance.

Various artifices exist to get around the Web's inherent statelessness. Forms can be generated on-the-fly, for instance, recording state in "hidden" INPUT tags. Netscape developed another technique called "cookies" (now supported by Microsoft as well) in which state information is written to the client's disk. This has an advantage over form-embedded state, in that it can survive the session. Using cookies, a server can resume a state-specific dialogue several hours, or days, later. A disadvantage of cookies is that any process that surreptitiously writes to the client's disk poses a security hazard.

In any case, the absence of state memory from native HTTP limits the technology's use for robust transaction processing.

The other limiting factor is the single-item nature of HTTP connections. This accounts, among other things, for the confusing disparity between hits and visits in server logs. Each file component of a Web page is transferred (and logged) in a separate connection. A more serious consequence of single-item transfers, at least from the standpoint of forms, is the fact that Web connections are opened and closed for each transfer.

This means that a Web server remains unaware of any dialogue with a client until the client submits the form. Many niceties of the modern graphical interface are lost as a consequence. For instance, the server has no knowledge of, and therefore can't validate, data entered by the user. Compared to a typical GUI application, in which later fields are automatically prefilled as the user completes earlier ones, Web forms are quaint in this regard. The ritual of submitting only complete forms, only to have them rejected when the server finds an error, recalls the days of programs submitted whole on keypunch cards to a data center. Applications that enable incremental data transfers by leaving the client/server connection open have a clear advantage in this regard.

The ultimate workaround for both statelessness and single-item connections is to bring HTTP up to the level of other client/server protocols. This might happen in a couple of ways. HTTP might itself be extended as an Internet standard. Another, superior protocol (possibly proprietary) might replace HTTP altogether. Or, modular extensions to HTTP might appear that provide the missing functionality.

In fact this third option corresponds to the rise of scripting subsystems such as JavaScript and VBScript, and of server-side Java applets as well. These innovations fill many gaps in early Web functionality. They are discussed in the next chapter. It may be worth remarking that much of an Intranet's initial appeal comes from its simplicity and cost-effectiveness. Extending the technology with complex object-oriented languages may, or may not, preserve these attractive benefits. If nothing else, it makes deciding between a pure Web-based solution and a hybrid of Web and non-Web client/server applications much more interesting. ❖

CHAPTER 12
CGI and Perl

Up to this point, we have focused on those aspects of Intranet design that involve presenting data and documents to users. HTML forms, discussed in the last chapter, move us into the realm of interactive Web pages. In the next several chapters, we turn our attention to Intranet programming.

Programs can run in one of two places on an Intranet: on the server, or on the client. The trend is toward client-side execution, which gives better performance and allows local events, such as data entry or a mouse click, to directly influence execution. The chief problem with client-side techniques is lack of standards. The technology is being pioneered by individual vendors, each with a proprietary language of its own.

Examples include Netscape JavaScript and Microsoft VBScript, interpreted languages that run, respectively, within the Navigator client (2.0 or later) and Internet Explorer client (3.0 or later). Java applets are platform-independent programs that execute on a special type of client (called a virtual machine) within the Web browser. And from Microsoft we have ActiveX controls, software components similar to Java applets that can move between client and server to perform application functions.

In this chapter the emphasis is on server applications, particularly those written in Perl, a popular scripting language available on almost every platform. After reading this chapter, you'll know:

- What the Common Gateway Interface (CGI) standard is
- Basic commands of the Perl language, and where to learn more
- How to write Perl scripts that process HTML forms
- How to generate Web pages "on-the-fly"

- What server-side includes (SSI) are, and when to use them
- How Perl scripts can compromise security and what you can do about it

CGI Programming

Right away, our intention to run programs on the server runs into a snag. Web servers are tailored to provide HTTP services, not to perform complex processing of client data. To accomplish such tasks, the server must hand off the job to an external program called a gateway program. The standard protocol governing this exchange is called the Common Gateway Interface (CGI).

> **Note**
>
> The CGI standard is documented online at **http://hoohoo.ncsa.uiuc.edu/cgi/intro.html**.

Gateway programs are called from within a browser just as any other Web resource: by URL. For example:

http://www.innergy.com/myscript.pl

When the server receives the URL of a gateway program, such as myscript.pl above (the .pl extension typically indicates a Perl script), the server runs the program, using CGI to pass parameters forwarded by the client, if any. The program likewise uses CGI to return result data to the server, which forwards it, using the appropriate MIME content type, to the requesting client.

What kind of programs can the server run? Theoretically, any program that performs, reads, and writes in conformance with the CGI standard. This includes compiled executables, such as C programs or Windows DLLs, as well as interpreted scripts written in any of the Unix shells, in Perl, or, on the Macintosh, in AppleScript.

The focus here is on scripts, but the same principles govern the design and execution of binary programs. As long as the program is designed to accept input and return output in accordance with the gateway interface standard, it can cooperate with a Web server to get your work done.

Understanding the Common Gateway Interface

CGI is a standard specified and maintained by the National Center for Supercomputing Applications (NCSA). The current version, CGI/1.1, designates four distinct methods by which Web servers and gateway programs can communicate:

CGI method	Brief Description
Environment Variables	Set when the server executes a gateway program, these can be read by most scripts using native commands or operating system calls.
Command line	Search queries are the only type of request conveyed to a gateway program via the command line.
Standard input <STDIN>	Forms and other requests that pass data to a gateway program do so via standard input.
Standard output <STDOUT>	Gateway programs write results to the server's standard output. This might be a document or image generated on-the-fly by the program, or instructions to the server to access another URL.

Three of these methods specify input; the last, output. Any program that runs on the Web server can serve as a gateway program, provided it conforms to the following output rules:

- It directs all output to <STDOUT>.
- It precedes the first line of output with a header specifying content-type, location, or status, followed by an empty line.

Content-type headers are used to return data to the browser. You'll see more of them in the section, "Generating HTML on-the-Fly." Location headers direct the browser to another Web resource once the gateway routine exits. This might be a page of HTML, such as a thank-you-for-completing-our-form message. Status headers, the rarest of the bunch, are used to return a particular HTTP status code to the calling browser. The following line is an example that tells the browser not to do anything, useful for unallocated regions in imagemaps, for instance:

```
Status: 204 No Response
```

Input can be passed to a gateway program via the environment, the command line or <STDIN>. Command-line exchanges are used exclusively for non-form queries, not discussed in this book. (The method is less important now that forms-capable browsers are everywhere.)

Forms submitted with the HTTP POST method make their data available to scripts on standard input. This process is described in the section, "Form-Processing scripts."

The set of standard CGI environment variables is listed for reference in the next section.

III

Writing HTML

> **Note**
>
> Depending on whose Web server you use, you may have access to several non-standard CGI variables in addition to those shown here. Refer to your server documentation for details.

Environmental Variables

Environment variables are a general feature of most operating systems, widely supported by programming languages. They therefore represent a flexible and broadly available means of data exchange. The CGI standard specifies a set of variables supported by all Web servers, in the following list:

Variable: SERVER_SOFTWARE

Description: Name and version of the server software making the CGI call.

Example: SERVER_SOFTWARE = NCSA/1.3

Variable: SERVER_NAME

Description: The server's hostname, DNS alias, or IP address.

Example: SERVER_NAME = que.mcp.com

Variable: GATEWAY_INTERFACE

Description: Version of the CGI specification.

Example: GATEWAY_INTERFACE = CGI/1.1

Variable: SERVER_PROTOCOL

Description: Name and revision of the protocol the CGI request was issued under. For Web servers, the protocol will be HTTP; but CGI works on other server types as well (such as Gopher).

Example: SERVER_PROTOCOL = HTTP/1.0

Variable: SERVER_PORT

Description: Port number to which CGI request was sent, often 80 for HTTP.

Example: SERVER_PORT = 80

Variable: REQUEST_METHOD

Description: HTTP method used to make the CGI request, either GET, HEAD, or POST.

Example: REQUEST_METHOD = POST

Variable: PATH_INFO

Description: Extra path information appended to the calling URL by the client.

Example: A client calls the gateway program *foo* with the URL **http:// www.innergy.com/cgi-bin/foo/whitepaper/may15**. The server treats everything after the program name as extra path info. Thus:

PATH_INFO = /whitepaper/may15

Variable: PATH_TRANSLATED

Description: Servers often use aliases or relative addressing to shorten pathnames. PATH_TRANSLATED gives the absolute location on the server file system of the path specified by PATH_INFO.

Example: If a gateway program is called with URL **http:// www.innergy.com/cgi-bin/foo/whitepaper/may15**, and the server root has an absolute path */bin/httpd/docs*, the translated path would be:

PATH_TRANSLATED = /bin/httpd/docs/whitepaper/may15

Variable: SCRIPT_NAME

Description: Path to the script being executed as it would be specified in an URL.

Example: /cgi-bin/foo

Variable: QUERY_STRING

Description: Information following a question mark ("?") in the calling URL. Empty if no such data is passed, or if an HTTP method other than GET is used.

Example: Say a gateway program is called with URL **http:// www.innergy.com/cgi-bin/foo?gordon+susan**. Then:

QUERY_STRING = gordon+susan

Variable: REMOTE_HOST

Description: The hostname making the request. If the server does not have this information, it should set REMOTE_ADDR and leave this unset.

Example: REMOTE_HOST = slip-08.shore.net

Variable: REMOTE_ADDR

Description: IP address of the remote host making the request.

Example: 192.233.85.130

Variable: AUTH_TYPE

Description: The protocol-specific authentication method used to validate the user. Empty unless the server supports user authentication, and the called program requires it.

Example: AUTH_TYPE = Basic

Variable: REMOTE_USER

Description: The authenticated username. Empty unless the server supports user authentication, and the called program requires it.

Example: REMOTE_USER = aeinstein

Variable: REMOTE_IDENT

Description: Set to the remote user name retrieved. Empty unless the HTTP server supports RFC 1413 identification (*identd*, Unix only).

Example: REMOTE_IDENT =

6193, 23 : USERID : UNIX : stjohns

Variable: CONTENT_TYPE

Description: The MIME content type of data forwarded by the requesting client, if any. Blank unless HTTP methods POST or PUT are being used. (Actual data is available on standard input.)

Example: text/html

Variable: CONTENT_LENGTH

Description: The length of the data message forwarded by the requesting client, if any. Blank unless HTTP methods POST or PUT are being used.

Example: CONTENT_LENGTH = 23

> **Note**
>
> The foregoing environment variables are server-specific. In addition, all HTTP header information received from the client is placed into the environment, in a set of variables named with prefix HTTP_ followed by the header field name. Examples follow.

Variable: HTTP_ACCEPT

Description: Comma-separated list of MIME types acceptable to the client, as indicated by the client's *Accept* HTTP headers.

Format: type/subtype, type/subtype

Example: HTTP_ACCEPT = image/gif, image/x-xbitmap, image/jpeg

Variable: HTTP_REFERER

Description: URL of the document from which the request originated.

Example: HTTP_REFERER = http://que.mcp.com/newbooks.htm

Variable: HTTP_USER_AGENT

Description: Browser the client is using to send the request.

Example (for a client using Netscape Navigator 2.0 for Windows 3.1):

HTTP_USER_AGENT = Mozilla/2.0 (Win16)

The best way to understand the way CGI works is to see how it's used in scripts. The most popular language for processing HTML forms is Perl. Let's see how it's done.

Introducing Perl

Great computer languages are rarely the work of committees. More often than not, they spring fully clad from the brow of a great thinker or two. Nikolaus Wirth was solely responsible for Pascal, for instance. Dennis Ritchie and James Kernighan of Bell Labs wrote C, and (in C) much of Unix. The power of Unix owes much to its rich, evolving toolset, contributed over two decades by software inventors like Richard Bourne and Aho, Weinberg and Kernighan.

Perl is a tool in this tradition. It was created by Larry Wall, a systems programmer at the Jet Propulsion Laboratory, as "a language for easily manipulating text, files, and processes"[1] (*Camel*). Legend has it that Perl stands for *Practical Extraction and Report Language*—though reputable sources refer to it as a *Pathologically Eclectic Rubbish Lister* (*Camel & Llama*). You can choose for yourself once you've experienced Perl firsthand.

> [1] *Quotes in this chapter are marked either "Camel" to denote Programming perl, by Larry Wall and Randal L. Schwartz (O'Reilly & Associates, 1991), or "Llama," to denote Learning Perl, by Randal L. Schwartz (O'Reilly & Associates, 1993).*

Many UNIX systems already have Perl installed. To find out if the one you're working on does, enter:

```
which perl
```

If Perl is available, you'll get a response like /USR/LOCAL/BIN/PERL. If not, you'll need to download and install it. The sidebar "Getting Perl" covers the basics.

Getting Perl

The latest version of Perl (5.003 at this writing) can be downloaded from The Perl Language Web site, at **http://www.perl.com/perl/info/software.html**.

Perl is distributed as source code that compiles for virtually all flavors of UNIX (its native environment), VMS and OS/2. The site has links to a wide variety of what it calls "alien ports": from Atari, to MVS, to NetWare.

The definitive Perl for Windows NT is available from Hip Communications Inc. Binaries for NT on Intel, Alpha, and PowerPC can be acquired at **http://www.perl.hip.com/**.

If you are installing Perl on a Windows platform, refer to the Perl for Win32 FAQ, at **http://www.perl.hip.com/PerlFaq.htm**.

One thing about which there can be no contention: Perl is powerful. As an example, consider the following Unix command line, which replaces all occurrences of the string QUE.COM with QUE.MCP.COM inside every HTML file in the current directory:

```
perl -pi.0 -e 's#que\.com#que\.mcp\.com#g' *.htm
```

The command also backs up each original file by appending the extension .0 to its name (INDEX.HTM becomes INDEX.HTM.0). If a single instruction can do this, you can imagine what longer Perl scripts can do.

The price for this economy of expression is complexity. It's not that the programming constructs in Perl are especially tricky. Like any procedural language, Perl has variables, arrays and operators, commands for manipulating files and controling program flow, and many of the syntactic niceties of C (such as '++' for auto-incrementation). Perl adds to these primitives many of its own, notably associative arrays (also called "hashes"), a type of list structure optimized for table lookups. Like almost every Perl construct these take some getting used to, but quickly become intuitive.

Newcomers to Unix will find the going tougher when it comes to Perl's extensive use of *regular expressions*. A regexp is a pattern to be matched against a string. Sophisticated pattern matching is a basic feature of Unix tools like *grep*. Perl uses this feature to enable sophisticated file editing on-the-fly. Pattern matching thus plays a big role in CGI routines and HTML form processing.

Unfortunately, learning regexp syntax is more an exercise in memorization than logic. The peculiar string of symbols in the previous example is a simple regexp. Here's another:

```
$var =~ s/%([a-fA-F0-9][a-fA-F0-9])/pack("C", hex($1))/eg;
```

The strings between the slash marks are regular expressions. This line, which comes from a working CGI script, cleans up URL-encoded input by replacing characters of type "%xx" (where xx is a pair of hexadecimal digits) with an ASCII equivalent.

The good news is that this translation, like other routine CGI processing steps, has been enshrined in one or more library scripts, available free of charge on the Internet. This won't eliminate the need for you to learn regexp's, but at least you'll have expert examples to study.

Writing CGI Scripts in Perl

Let's look at a very short Perl script:

Listing 12.1. The classic program 'Hello, World' in Perl

```
1.    #!/usr/local/bin/perl
2.    # My 1st Perl script
3.
4.    print "Hello, World!\n";
```
---

1. Any line that begins with the "#"-sign is a comment—unless it's the very first line of a script. The first line starts with the characters '#!' followed by the absolute pathname of the perl interpreter on your server.

2. A comment, ignored by Perl.

3. A blank line, ignored by Perl.

4. A command that writes the string "Hello, World!" followed by a newline character to <STDOUT>. Executable Perl statements must end with a semicolon.

The print statement is the most important output command from the standpoint of CGI scripting. It writes to <STDOUT> by default, but can be directed to any open filehandle as follows:

```
print FILEHANDLE "Your string here";
```

If you run Listing 10.1 off the CD-ROM, you should see the result "Hello, World!" on your screen.

Note

To run Perl scripts from the command line, enter:

```
perl script_name
```

The script file must be executable. Under Unix, you can make a file executable by all users with the following command:

```
chmod 755 script_name
```

To run CGI programs (Perl or otherwise) from a web browser, enter the program's URL. For instance, to launch a script name *my_1st_perl* in directory **http://xyz.com/cgi-bin**, enter:

```
http://xyz.com/cgi-bin/my_1st_perl
```

The script's permissions must allow execution by all users.

But is this a CGI script? It can't be, since it doesn't preface printed output with HTTP header information. We can fix that in a jiffy, though:

Listing 12.2. 'Hello, World' as a CGI script.

```
1.     #!/usr/local/bin/perl
2.     # My 1st Perl script
3.     print "Content-type: text/html\n\n";
4.     print "Hello, World!\n";
```

Here the MIME content type TEXT/HTML is sent to the browser before any displayable data. Note the double newline ('\n\n') terminating the header; this provides the blank line required by the CGI standard. The browser interprets any output received following a content-type header as content of that type—HTML in this case.

Here's another example:

Listing 12.3 On-the-fly Web page generation.

```
1.    #!/usr/local/bin/perl
2.    # My 1st Perl script
3.    print "Content-type: text/html\n\n";
4.    print "<html><head><title>My 1st Perl Script</title></
      ➥head>\n";
5.    print "<body><h1>The Message You've Been Waiting For:</h1>\n";
6.    print "<h3>Hello, World!</h3>\n";
7.    print "<pre>\n\n\n\n\n<center>\n";
8.    print "-- This space intentionally left blank --\n";
9.    print "\n\n\n\n\n</pre>\n
10.    print "<hr>Your webmaster, <address>tgroup@innergy.com</
      ➥address>
11.    print "</body></html>\n";
```

When called from a browser, this script returns a bona fide Web page, shown in figure 12.1.

That's really all there is to it. Of course, Perl can do a few tricks besides printing strings to standard output. Let's take a short survey of the language, then use some of its features to work more CGI magic.

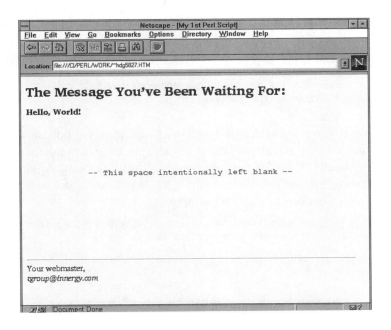

Fig. 12.1
HTML response generated by the Perl script of Example 3.

A Perl Primer

What's the best way to get your arms around a new computer language? Here we follow a divide-and-conquer strategy, breaking Perl into its essential elements. These include:

- Native data types and operators
- Control structures
- File operations
- Built-in functions or commands

Note

Looking for an online reference? You're in luck: Carnegie-Mellon University maintains a hypertext version of the Perl 4 manual at **http://www-cgi.cs.cmu.edu/cgi-bin/perl-man**.

Once you know how Perl handles these basic constructs, you'll be poised to start reading scripts you find on the Web and customizing them to do your bidding. Then, with a little practice (okay, a *lot* of practice), you'll be writing Perl scripts of your own.

Data and Operators in Perl

Perl distinguishes three types of data: scalars, arrays, and associative arrays. *Scalar data*, the simplest kind, includes numbers and strings. Perl scalars begin with a dollar sign:

```
$numeric_var = 4;
$big_number = 4000000;
$tiny_number = 3.14E-12;      # 0.00000000000314
$string = "Bartelby the Scrivner";
$char = 'c';
```

The difference between single- and double-quoted strings is important in Perl. Single quotes are stronger; almost any character appearing between them is to be taken literally. There are two exceptions. To indicate a single-quote mark in a string, preceed it with a backslash: \'. To indicate a backslash, preceed *it* with a backslash: '\\'. For example:

```
$single = 'this_so-called \'string\' contains_a_single_quote';
$backslash = 'this string contains a backslash: \\';
```

Double quotes can contain special *control characters*, similar to those in the C language:

Construct	Meaning
\n	newline
\r	carriage return
\t	tab
\b	backspace

Construct	Meaning
\cZ	control character (here, ^Z)
\\	backslash
\"	double-quote mark
\l	lowercase next letter
\L	lowercase letters until \E
\u	uppercase next letter
\U	uppercase letters until \E
\E	end \L or \U

In addition, double-quoted strings are *variable interpolated*— variable names are replaced with their current values when the strings are used. For instance:

```
$x = 4;
$y = 'eva';
$z = "Love you $x$y";
```

assigns "Love you 4eva" to variable $z.

Scalar operators in Perl include numeric arithmetic (+, –, *, /), exponentiation (**) and a modulus operator (%). The obvious numeric comparisons are available (<, <=, ==, >=, >, !=). In addition, Perl has the friendly autoincrement (++) and autodecrement (––) operators from C. For example:

```
$i = 9; $j = 0;
$i + $j;      # equals 9
$i ** 3;      # is nine cubed, or 81
$i + ++$j;     # equals 10, since $j is prefix autoincremented
$i % 5;       # equals 4, the remainder of 9/5
```

In the first line variable $i and $j are assigned values. Line two shows addition, line three exponentiation. In line four, variable $j is incremented before adding it to $i. Line five shows the modulus operator in action.

String operators include *concatenation*, signified by a dot:

```
"World" . "Wide" . "Web"    # equals "WorldWideWeb"
```

and *repetition*, signified by a lowercase 'x':

```
"Magic" x 4    # is "MagicMagicMagicMagic"
```

Arrays are ordered lists of scalars. Array literals are enclosed in parenentheses, while array variables begin with an at-sign ('@'):

```
@mylist = (1, 2, 3);    # assigns three elements to variable
➥@mylist
@yourlist = @mylist;     # copies three elements to @yourlist
$mylist[1];              # is scalar 2 (indexing starts at zero)
```

III

Writing HTML

The first line assigns three scalar elements to the array @MYLIST. The second line copies these elements to another array variable, @YOURLIST. The third line shows how elements in an array can be referenced by index. The first element of a Perl array has index "0"; hence, the second element has index "1".

One of Perl's conveniences is that array variables can be used without declaration or initialization; they can shrink to zero or grow to the size of available memory as items are removed or added.

By convention, the index of the last element of array @LIST is given by the scalar $#LIST. Perl offers a number of useful array operators as well. To use an array like a stack, adding and deleting elements as needed, there are the LIFO operators *push()* and *pop()*. Conversely, to manipulate an array like a queue, use the FIFO operators *shift()* and *unshift()*.

A third major data type is a special class of array called an *associative array* (or *hash*). What makes hashes special is their indexing scheme. Instead of a numeric value counting a certain number of elements into the array, associative indexes are *strings* (called *keys*) mapped one-to-one to the elements (called *values*). The effect is a data store optimized for lookups.

Perl provides two useful operators for associative arrays. The *keys()* operator returns a list of keys, while *values()* returns the elements.

> **Note**
>
> In Perl, the variables $var, @var and %var are not only of different types, but are completely unrelated. This expands the namespace at some risk of confusion, but the meaning is always clear from the notation.

Hash variables begin with a percent sign (%), and are indexed with curly braces rather than square brackets. Here are some examples:

```
%java = ("strong", "kona", "medium", "kenya", "light", "carib");
$java{ "medium" };     # equals "kenya"
$java{ "extra" } = "sumatra";     # creates new key "extra" with
value "sumatra"
@strength = keys( %java );     # assigns list ("extra", "strong",
➥..., "light") to @strength
$strength = "extra"; print $java{ $strength };     # prints
➥"sumatra"
print $java{ $strength[0] };     # also prints "sumatra", since 1st
element of @strength is "extra"
```

The first line defines a hash, %JAVA, that associates a list of adjectives (strong, medium, light) with a list of coffee types (kona, kenya, carib). The second line shows how values are referenced; the keyword "medium" selects the value "kenya", for instance. In the third line, a new value, "sumatra", is added to the array simply by associating it with the keyword "extra". Perl allocates the required memory on its own.

The fourth line of the example shows how the Perl function KEYS() operates on hash %JAVA to create a regular array, @STRENGTH, containing the hash's keys. The fifth and sixth lines show different ways of referencing the same value. Note that the variable $STRENGTH[0] is the first element of the (regular) array @STRENGTH, which in line four of the example was made equal to "extra".

Control Structures in Perl

In its control notation, Perl borrows even more heavily from C than elsewhere. Those familiar with C can, therefore, forge ahead with confidence (excepting the *switch{}* statement, which Perl lacks). Others familiar with structured programming, but not with C per se, should find the material intuitive.

Structured programming is enabled by blocks, conditionals, and loops. Let's look at how Perl implements each of these in turn.

Any group of Perl statements enclosed in curly braces becomes a *statement block*, which can play the role of a single statement. The standard conditional is the *if-then-else* construct. Conditions must be enclosed in parentheses, and blocks require curly braces. Another conditional is *unless*, which behaves inversely to *if*. The following example illustrates these concepts:

Listing 12.4 Using Perl conditionals.

```
if ($name eq "Microsoft") {
    print "Welcome to Big Green!\n";
    $ms++;
} elsif ($name eq "IBM") {        # elsif is a Perlism for 'else
if'print "Welcome to Big Blue!\n";
    $ib++;
} else {
    print "Welcome to Burger King!\n";
    $bk++;             # count visitors
}
print "Total visits:\n";
print "Microsoft\t$ms\n";
print "IBM\t\t$ib\n";
print "Burger King\t$bk\n";
```

III

Writing HTML

Listing 12.5 The UNLESS statement.

```
unless ($x < 0) {
    print "$x is non-negative\n";
    $x--;      # decrease by 1
}
```

Few programs execute linearly from start to finish without some sort of iteration, or looping. Perl has several looping constructs, summarized below.

The *while* statement repeats a block as long as a given condition remains true. The condition is tested by evaluating an expression once per loop. It's used as follows:

```
LABEL: while (EXPR) {
   # code to repeat goes here
}
```

The optional LABEL facilitates control of nested loops.

A similar loop construct, *until*, repeats as long as a given expression is false.

```
LABEL: until (EXPR) {
   # code to repeat goes here
}
```

Note that for both *while* and *until*, the truth value of the expression EXPR is tested before the first iteration. To execute the loop once before testing, use the *do* command:

```
do {
   # code to repeat goes here
} until (EXPR);
```

The following examples show how these constructs are used.

Listing 12.6 The Camel Countdown using *while.*

```
#!/usr/local/bin/perl
$countdown = 10;
while ($countdown > 0) {
    print "T minus $countdown seconds and counting ...\n";
    sleep 1;         # Perl command that causes program to pause for
➥1 second
    --$countdown;   # decrement count by one
}
print "BLAST OFF!\n";
```

Listing 12.7 The Camel Countdown using *until.*

```
#!/usr/local/bin/perl
$countup = 0;
until ($countup == 10) {
     # In this example we use a variant of the print command, printf,
     # which can print the results of expressions
     printf ("T minus, %d seconds and counting ...\n", 10-$countup);
     sleep 1;        # Perl command that causes program to pause for
➥1 second
     ++$countup;     # increment count by one
}
print "BLAST OFF!\n";
```

Listing 12.8 The Camel Countdown using *do.*

```
#!/usr/local/bin/perl
$countdown = 10;
do {
     print "T minus $countdown seconds and counting ...\n";
     sleep 1;        # Perl command that causes program to pause for
➥1 second
} until (--$countdown == 0);
print "BLAST OFF!\n";
```

Another looping construct, the *for* statement, has the form:

```
for (EXPR1; EXPR2; EXPR3) {
   # code to repeat goes here
}
```

Here, the loop is executed while EXPR2 is true. EXPR1 can be used to initial-ize a counter (e.g., $i = 0), while EXPR3 performs an operation (e.g., $i++). Together they look like this:

Listing 12.9 The Camel Countdown using *for.*

```
#!/usr/local/bin/perl
I
for ( $i=10; $i>0; $i-- ) {   #repeats ten times, with $i=10..1
print "T minus $i seconds and counting ...\n";
     sleep 1;                 # Perl command that causes program to
pause for 1 second
}
```

III

Writing HTML

print "BLAST OFF!\n";A somewhat different tool for iterating code is *foreach*, which has the following syntax:

```
foreach VAR (ARRAY) {
    # code to repeat goes here
}
```

This construct iterates once for each element in ARRAY. VAR takes the value of the current element. No condition is tested.

foreach is useful for printing out associative arrays, as shown here:

```
print "If you like your java ...\n";
foreach $strength (keys %java) {
    print "$strength, try $java{ $strength }\n";
}
```

Recall that the keys of hash %JAVA are adjectives like "medium", and that the values are types of coffee, like "kenya". This example uses the Perl function KEYS() to assign each key in turn to the scalar $STRENGTH, which is used iteratively to print output until the hash is run through.

Loops are often used in combination with input and output operations, discussed next.

Simple File Operations in Perl

How does a Perl script read from standard input? Very simply, it turns out. Every Perl process comes with pre-defined filehandles STDIN, STDOUT, and STDERR. To read from STDIN, use the following syntax:

```
$line = <STDIN>;      # reads one line of input
```

Alternatively, you can read a sequential set of lines by assigning <STDIN> to an array:

```
@lines = <STDIN>;      # reads all lines up to EOF (CTRL-Z)
```

Perl is craftier than these simple assignments imply. Consider the following widely-used loop:

```
while (<STDIN>) {       # iterate until no more input
    chop;          # chops terminating newline off input buffer
    ⋮                  # other commands
}
```

In this example, the *while* statement is used to repeat a sequence of commands as long as more input is available. The loop terminates when STDIN receives EOF.

Perl stores the lines it reads from input in a special, built-in variable, *$_*. By default, functions operate on $_ unless another variable is explicitly specified.

For instance, the CHOP() function in the example removes the last character of the data passed to it; here, it is used to remove the trailing newline (\n) on the line of input to be processed. To chop the end off a different variable—say, $OneByteTooLong—you would write

```
chop( $OneByteTooLong );
```

Often, of course, you will need to work with files other than standard I/O. Use the Perl *open* command to open an arbitrary file. The syntax is:

```
open( FILEHANDLE,EXPR )
```

where EXPR specifies the filename, associated after opening with FILEHANDLE. EXPR can be a literal filename, such as /HOME/WEB/SPARKY/FAQ.HTML or an expression that resolves to a filename.

```
open(HOSTS, ">hostfilename");     # opens file for writing
open(LOG, ">>logfile");     # opens file for appending
```

There is also a *close* command, but because Perl cleans up after itself, few programmers make use of it.

Perl Built-in Functions

Perl comes with a large set of functions that can be referenced without explicit operating system calls. Besides the savings in overhead this entails, Perl's built-in functions are highly optimized and sometimes outperform the equivalent system ones. (A good example is *grep*, the Unix pattern searching tool.)

By far the most important functions in Perl's arsenal are those related to pattern matching. Two, in particular, stand out: *Match* and *Substitute*.

The Match function, shown below, searches a string for the specified regular expression.

```
/REGEXP/;     # match function
m!REGEXP!;     # alternate form; any pair of delimiters permitted
```

What string is searched? By default, the string stored in Perl's magic placeholder, *$_*. The following example shows how to search a set of input lines for HTML comments -- lines that begin with "<!--" and end in "-->":

```
while (<STDIN>) {     # iterate until no more input
    chop; # chops terminating newline off input buffer
    if (/<!--\s*(.+)\s*-->/) {     # find HTML comments
        print "Comment: $1\n";
    }
}
```

The *Substitute* function, which extends Match to Match-and-replace, looks like this:

```
s/REGEXP/REPLACEMENT/;       # string is searched for REGEXP, which,
if found, is replaced
```

Like *Match*, *Substitute* operates by default on the magic variable $_. As an example, say you wanted to precede all the HTML comments in a web page with a set of author's initials, *gb*. You could use the substitute function as follows:

```
while (<STDIN>) {             # iterate until no more input
   chop;   # chops terminating newline off input buffer
   s/(<!--\s*)(.+)(s*-->)/\1 gb: \2\3/;
}
```

This example illustrates another powerful feature of Perl pattern matching: *backreference*. Enclosing parts of a pattern to be matched causes Perl to memorize those parts under the labels \1, \2, ... , up to \9. In the example above, "<!--" is found and memorized as \1; the comment text, represented by the regular expression ".+", is found and stored as \2; and the trailing "-->" is found and memorized as \3. These references are then used in the replacement expression to insert the initials *gb*.

What if you need to apply the match or substitute functions to a variable other than $_? You could set $_ equal to the target variable, but Perl has an easier way. The symbol "=~", called the *pattern binding operator*, applies a Perl pattern-matching function to any variable. Here's how it's used:

```
$url =~ s/(que)(\.com)/\1\.mcp\2/;     # uses regexp backreference
```

This example finds occurences of the string "que.com" in the variable $URL and replaces them with "que.mcp.com" using backreference.

That's just scratching the surface of this rich langauge. Besides pattern-matching functions, Perl offers a respectable set of commands including mathematical, string manipulating, I/O, system interaction, and networking functions. Systems having DBM (a Unix database engine) can take advantage of Perl's data manipulation functions as well.

Perl CGI Scripts Revisited

At this point, you have the basics of Perl and CGI scripting under your belt. That means you're ready to appreciate the gory details of real-world gateway programs written in Perl.

In this section, you'll learn to process forms and generate Web pages on-the-fly using Perl.

Form-Processing Scripts

The aim of HTML form processing is to recover the name/value pairs entered at the browser and submitted to a script, and to process this data appropriately.

The first step toward recovering the name/value pairs is decoding the input stream. This is necessary because a form sends data not in plain text, but in a format called *URL encoding*, required to ensure all characters transfer properly over the network. (Without encoding, certain message characters might masquerade as network control characters, garbling the transfer.)

> **Note**
>
> You can see the URL-encoded output of a form by changing the form's ACTION attribute to a mailto URL that points to your e-mail address. On submitting the form, you'll be sent a mail message like this:
>
> ```
> ThisForm=Survey&Name=Max+Headroom&Age=None
> ```

Here are the rules for URL-encoding a form's name/value pairs:

- A name field is separated from its corresponding value by an equal sign (=)
- Multiple name/value pairs are separated by ampersands (&)
- Characters above ASCII 7Fh are encoded as a hexadecimal number prefixed by a percent sign (%)
- Spaces are encoded as plus signs (+)

Decoding form input amounts to reversing these steps. Perl regular expressions make short work of such manipulations—if you remember how to use them. Fortunately, script libraries exist on the Web to solve this and other routine problems. One good library for HTML form processing is CGI-LIB.PL.

> **Note**
>
> CGI-LIB.PL. is Copyright 1994 by Steven E. Brenner. You'll find additional info at **http://www.bio.cam.ac.uk/web/form.html** or **http://www.seas. upenn.edu/~mengwong/forms**.

To include foreign code such as a sub-routine library in your Perl script, use the *Require* statement. Add a line at the top of your script (but below any leading comments) as follows:

```
require 'cgi-lib.pl';
```

The package contains several subroutines, the most important of which is the *&ReadParse* routine. According to the library code:

```
# ReadParse
# Reads in GET or POST data, converts it to unescaped text, and
➥puts
# one key=value in each member of the list "@in"
# Also creates key/value pairs in %in, using '\0' to separate
➥multiple
# selections
```

In other words, *&ReadParse* handles form data transmitted with either the GET or POST method, takes care of URL decoding, and parses the form's name/value pairs into a Perl associative array (%in). Once *&ReadParse* is called, therefore, field names from the form can be used as keys to look up the corresponding content.

Other CGI-LIB.PL routines determine whether GET or POST is being used, insert a TEXT/HTML content-type header, perform CGI error handling, and print out a listing of name/value pairs retrieved from the form.

There are some remarkably accomplished Perl scripts on the Web, most available cost-free. Look to the following URLs for valuable routines and a glimpse at the power of expert Perl.

URL Site	Scripts Offered
http://www.perl.com/perl/ index.html	The closest thing to an official Perl Web site. You'll find the Comprehensive Perl Archive Network (CPAN) here, plus FAQs, USENET links, and all known ports of Perl itself.
http://www-genome.wi.mit.edu/ ftp/pub/software/WWW/	Lincoln Stein's superb collection of Perl 5 modules for CGI processing.
http://worldwidemart.com/ scripts/	Matt's Script Archive offers simple, configurable back-ends for mailing form results, keeping a GuestBook, and hosting on-line discussion forums.

Generating HTML on-the-Fly

In Listing 12.3, you saw a brief Web page generated by a CGI script. Creating more complex pages is really no different, but you need to be aware of a few Perlisms.

Suppose you want to embellish the page shown in Figure 12.1 with a graphic or two. The HTML to do this is straightforward (assuming you know the URLs of the desired elements). But wait. The tag for placing an in-line image contains double-quote marks, as follows:

```
<IMG SRC="image_file" ALT="image_description">
```

What do you think happens if we generate this line with the Perl code shown below?

```
print "<img src="pix/goldline.gif" alt="golden line">\n";
```

What happens is that Perl chokes on excess quote marks. The interpreter can't distinguish between those to be printed and those that specify the print list.

To include quote marks or other characters special to Perl in output generated on-the-fly, you must *escape* each offending character by preceding it with a backslash ("\"). Characters requiring escape within a Perl PRINT statement include double- and single-quote marks, the dollar sign ("$"), percent sign ("%"), at-sign ("@"), square brackets ("[]"), and the backslash character itself. A CGI script that prints such characters might look like this:

Listing 12.10 CGI script that returns HTML containing characters special to Perl.

```
1.     #!/usr/local/bin/perl
2.     # Yet Another Perl script
3.     require 'cgi-lib.pl';
4.
5.     &PrintHeader;     # inserts appropriate content type
6.     print "<html><head><title>Perl Example 4: On-the-Fly Web
Page</title></head>\n";
7.     print "<body><h1>The Message You've Been Waiting For:</h1>\n";
# Escaped quote marks in next line:
8.     print "<h3 align=\"center\">Hello, World!</h3>\n";
9.     print "<pre>\n\n\n\n\n<center>\n";
# Escaped quote marks in next line:
10.    print "<img src=\"pix/goldline.gif\" alt=\"gold line\">\n";
10.    print "<img src=\"pix/westhemi.gif\" alt=\"World (western
hemishphere)\">\n";
10.    print "<img src=\"pix/goldline.gif\" alt=\"gold line\">\n";
11.    print "\n\n\n\n\n</center></pre>\n";
# Escaped at-sign in next line:
```

(continues)

III

Writing HTML

Listing 12.10   Continued

```
12.     print <hr>Your webmaster,
<address>gbenett\@innergy.com</address>\n;
13.     print "</body></html>\n";
```

Figure 12.2 shows how Netscape Navigator displays the resulting page.

Fig. 12.2
HTML page generated
on the fly by Perl
Example 4.

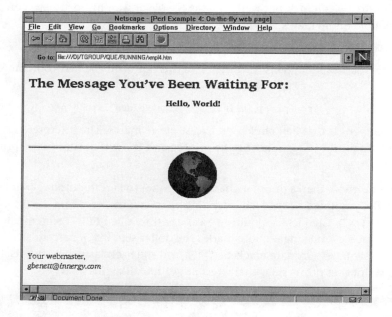

Server-Side Includes

An *include* is a bit of code or text inserted in the body of a document as it is being processed. Programmers have been using includes for decades to modularize their code. *Server-side includes* are an extension to HTTP that enables HTML authors to embed executable commands in their Web pages. SSI commands execute on the server.

> **Note**
>
> The essential reference for SSI is at NCSA's Web site **http://hoohoo.ncsa. uiuc.edu/docs/tutorials/includes.html**.

SSI is the simplest form of interaction with a Web server. It makes possible, with single lines of self-explanatory code, effects much trickier to achieve with CGI scripts. For instance, the following code snippet causes the current date/time to be displayed on a Web page:

```
<p>
It's <!--#echo="DATE_LOCAL"--> in server land.
</p>
```

Those familiar with HTML will recognize what looks like a comment (any-thing set off with <!--comment here-->) in the middle of the text. That's all there is to SSI. Insert one of the six allowable commands from the SSI specifi-cation, preceded by '#', into an HTML comment field. Moreover, you can reference the full set of CGI environment variables, plus an extended SSI environment, which includes DATE_LOCAL and other convenient system data. The complete list of environment options, with descriptions, is posted on NCSA's Web site.

This seems like a pretty good way to identify a visitor's IP address, report the current time, or check for a certain browser version. And it is. But as with all neat tricks, there's a catch.

Two catches, actually. SSI loads the Web server fiercely. It requires the server to scan each document for SSI code before transporting it. On top of that, it's the least secure of all the interactive modes. SSI in effect enables users to run embedded code on the server without restriction.

To mitigate these risks, servers like NCSA HTTP provide SSI-specific configura-tion options for administrators. One such option makes it possible to disable the most dangerous SSI command, "exec". (This is the one that lets users run loose.) Administrators can also enable SSI in some directories and not others, permitting only trusted users to create Web pages with executable code in-cluded. (SSI code in an unauthorized Web page is ignored.) Finally, to alleviate the parsing burden on the server, a configuration option exists to define which files should be scanned for SSI code. The following line, for example, tells the Web server to parse only files ending in *.SHTML:

```
AddType text/x-server-parsed-html .shtml
```

The NCSA documentation contains additional details.

Script Security

CGI scripting and the easy programming interface it provides are among the most attractive features of an intranet. Unfortunately, they're also the great-est contributors of security risk in a Web-based network.

The problem lies not with the Common Gateway Interface itself, but with the power it gives to CGI script authors and, potentially, to users. The burden of establishing secure CGI guidelines falls on the server administrator. This sec-tion tells you what to look out for.

III

Writing HTML

> **Tip**
>
> Remove shells and interpreters from the server that you don't intend to use. For example, if you don't run Perl-based CGI scripts, remove the Perl interpreter.

There are two types of risks associated with scripts. One is the inadvertent disclosure of server information, such as password or registry files, that could be used to further subvert security measures. The other is the potential that users can spoof the script into doing something perverse, like executing system commands.

You can take several precautions to lower the risk of running CGI scripts on your Web server:

1. Keep all CGI scripts in a single directory (e.g., /cgi-bin) that only the Web administrator can write to.

2. If possible, use compiled executables rather than Perl scripts, and avoid shell scripts altogether for CGI processing. (This includes *.BAT programs on NT-based servers.)

3. Never trust input data. Variables populated from a web form can contain strings that break unwary scripts, causing them to execute unauthorized operations. In Perl, data of unknown pedigree is called "tainted." If the variable $SCARY contains tainted data, for instance, the following routine can be used to create an "untainted" copy in the variable $COOL:

```
$SCARY =~ /^([\w.]*)$/;        # matches only alphanumeric
characters ➡and dots
$COOL =~ $1;                    # use $COOL for remainder of
➡program
```

4. If you must allow non-alphanumeric characters, here's a filter to escape potential metacharacters:

```
s/([;<>\*\|'&\$!#\(\)\[\]\{\}:'"])/\\$1/g
```

> **Tip**
>
> If you're using Perl 5, test your scripts using perl -T to invoke the "taint" checking option.

5. You may wish to investigate *safecgiperl*, a modified interpreter being developed by Malcolm Beattie to enable secure Perl execution. Visit **http://users.ox.ac.uk/~mbeattie/perl.html** to learn more.

6. Check out the following Web sites for additional details on safe scripting:

Document Title	URL
The WWW Security FAQ	**<http://www-genome.wi.mit.edu/WWW/faqs/www-security-faq.html>**
Safe CGI Programming	**<http://www.cerf.net/~paulp/cgi-security/safe-cgi.txt>**
CGI Security Tutorial	**<http://csclub.uwaterloo.ca/u/mlvanbie/cgisec/>**

III

Writing HTML

CHAPTER 13

Java and JavaScript

One of the advances the Netscape corporation added to its second generation Web servers, Enterprise Server and FastTrack Server, was the ability to uniquely utilize the Java and JavaScript languages for server side work. This integration is designed to help you, more easily, perform the tasks which were previously accomplished through CGI scripts.

In this chapter, you will learn:

- What Java and JavaScript are
- How to configure the Enterprise and FastTrack Servers for Java
- How to write a Java application
- How to enable the LiveWire options on the Enterprise and FastTrack Servers
- How to use JavaScript with LiveWire

What this chapter will not cover:

This chapter is not designed to teach you how to write Java or JavaScript. Both of those subjects are far too large for a single chapter. If you would like to learn Java it would be a good idea to pick up another QUE book, *Special Edition Using Java*; for JavaScript get *Special Edition Using JavaScript*.

Java and JavaScript Defined

Before you start to learn about Java and JavaScript, it is important to first establish what they are. You see, it's important to establish that Java and JavaScript are at best very distant cousins. Despite what the names might suggest JavaScript is not Java 'lite' or 'Java for Beginners.' The two technologies have very diverse histories, and are quite different.

JavaScript is a language that was developed by Netscape Communications. Originally, JavaScript was developed under the name LiveScript. In November 1995, when Sun Microsystems and Netscape realized that Java was fast becoming the most hyped technology of the year, LiveScript was renamed JavaScript. Both languages are very well suited to creating dynamic Web pages. These pages can save your users time, and add a level of interaction, which was not possible before.

Java Defined

The programming language, Java was developed by Sun Microsystems. Java is roughly based on another popular programming language called C++. Actually, Sun borrowed from a great number of languages. Java has many advantages over traditional languages such as C++. The most significant of which, is that Java is not tied to one type of computer platform.

Sun's official definition for Java is:

"Java is a simple, object-oriented, distributed, interpreted, robust, secure, architecture neutral, portable, high-performance, multithreaded, dynamic language."

That definition is more than Sun's attempt to use every buzz word they could think of. Each of the terms in the definition have a specific meaning to the language. If this book were about Java, it would be important to look at how each one of these terms relates to Java uniquely; however, that's a bit too detailed for a single chapter. For now, let's look at the two portions of this definition which are of particular interest to Web masters.

Java Is Architecture Neutral

Architecture Neutral is a complicated way to say that a Java program can run on any computer, or platform. Architecture neutrality is also known as platform independence. This is one of the main reasons why Java is the best solution for many problems on the Internet or an Intranet. Because Java is platform independent, once a Java application is created, that same application can be run without any modifications, on any computer. Well, that's not entirely true. In order for a computer to support Java, it must have support for what is known as the Java Virtual Machine (VM). Currently, there are dozens of machines which support the VM, with more on the way.

One way to visualize the power of architecture neutrality is to consider what would happen if your favorite word processor were written in Java. If that application were written in Java, the same application could be installed on a Windows 95 machine, on a Macintosh, a UNIX machine, or a Dec VAX. So, you're saying to yourself, but I do. I have Microsoft Word for Windows and

Microsoft Word for Macintosh, isn't that the same thing? The answer is no. You actually have two separate and distinct programs there. If the program were written in Java, the exact same disks could be placed in both your Macintosh and your Windows machine and execute the same code.

Platform independence may or may not be important to you for server-side interaction. If you are writing a program which will run on your server, and are not planning on using it on any other system, being architecture neutral doesn't mean much. On the other hand, the odds are that if you take the time to write a server application, you will want to use it on more Web servers than your own, or even sell it. In that case, you will appreciate Java's ability to run on any UNIX machine and Windows NT. In fact, one of the reasons that Perl has become the de facto standard for CGI on the Web is that Perl's scripting language is also fairly architecture neutral.

Java Is Secure

Java was designed from the very beginning to be a secure language. What Sun meant by secure was that they did not want a programmer to be able to write a Java applet, which could harm your computer. Just imagine the havoc that could be caused by a virus written in Java which could run on any computer! Fortunately, because Sun had the foresight to see this, such attacks are not possible with Java.

Java's security is actually of more benefit to the people who view your Web pages than you as a Web master. Java's security model means that the Java applications, which are placed on the Web, can't do malicious things to your machine when it is downloaded. In a world, which is constantly fighting the computer flu (virus), it was extremely important for Sun to minimize the threat that Java applets could be used as a means to distribute such attacks. Sun also limited the applets' ability to access the local file system. This means that a Java applet can't be used to steal the information on your local hard drive.

The security model, however, does not extend to Java-based applications. This means that the Java applications that you use on your server are able to violate some of the holds on the security model. For instance, Java applications can access your local disk drive, both for reading and writing. If they could not do this, they would be of little use to you for CGI applications, but installing someone else's server-based Java application is as dangerous as any other type of CGI. The one benefit that Java's security model does still afford you, though, is that the applications are still not allowed to access the computers memory pool. They are restrained to their own working set of memory; this eliminates the ability to corrupt other running programs.

JavaScript Defined

JavaScript is a scripting language, and is actually embedded into an HTML file. Where with Java, a reference to the Java applet is added to the HTML file, with JavaScript the whole program is actually contained inside of the HTML file.

JavaScript was designed to be a complimentary language to Java and to act as middleware between Java and Plug-ins. Though there are several distinctions between the two, the syntax of JavaScript does vaguely resemble that of Java; this is primarily due to the fact that both Java and JavaScript are derived from the same source C language.

JavaScript was designed to be an easy language to learn and use. In fact, JavaScript was designed for the majority of Web designers who, understand-ably would rather deal with the aesthetic appearances of their Web pages than the technical details of programming. Nevertheless, to program compli-cated applications in JavaScript requires a bit of programming skill.

Java versus JavaScript

There are a great number of differences between Java and JavaScript beyond syntax. These differences have their pluses and their minuses.

JavaScript Is Contained in the HTML File

The source code, for a JavaScript program, is contained within the HTML file along with the other text, which is interpreted by the browser.

In the case of JavaScript, which is interpreted by the server, this embedding in HTML can be very helpful. You can, for instance, write an HTML file in much the same way as you ordinarily would, and only change the part of the page that you want to be dynamic.

JavaScript Is Interpreted

For server-side pages, Netscape extended the byte-code technology of Java to JavaScript and so the interpretation doesn't really affect purely server-side pages. These pages must pass through a special compiler which Netscape ships with their LiveWire product.

For standard Web pages, however, JavaScript is interpreted so there is no need to compile the script before it is available for use. Java, on the other hand, re-quires an initial compilation to occur before it can be utilized. On the flip side, this compilation does make Java a faster language.

At this point, you might be saying to yourself, "but I have heard that Java is both compiled and interpreted, how does JavaScript differ?" The answer to this question lies in the level at which Java is interpreted.

Every computer has what is known as a machine language. This language is made up entirely of ones and zeroes, and essentially turns transistors on and off. Machine language is a very complicated beast, and as such, the only people who program in it are the true gurus of this world. A very close cousin to machine language is assembly language. Assembly language converts the machine language to letters, which are more easily remembered by humans. Now, how this applies to Java is that Java has a unique pseudo-assembly language of its own. This assembly language is not a real language for a real computer; it is an abstract language for Java. When Java is compiled, it generates, more or less, to this pseudo-assembly language. When your computer downloads a Java class file, it must then convert the pseudo-assembly language to the actual assembly language of your machine. This translation is a relatively simple one. This is the level where Java's interpretation originates—interpreting the virtual machine's assembly language into the native assembly language of your computer. In addition, the interpreter also performs some work, called object-linking.

Now let's look at a typical JavaScript which might be included in standard HTML. With JavaScript, your browser downloads something that looks like listing 13.1

Listing 13.1

```
<HTML>
<HEAD>
<SCRIPT>
document.write("<H1>This is a simple JavaScript demo">);
</SCRIPT>
</HEAD>
<BODY>
</BODY>
</HTML>
```

There is a lot there, but to be fair, the JavaScript interpreter has to only look at one line:

```
document.write("<H1>This is a simple JavaScript demo">);
```

This is a very simple line of code, but to a computer it doesn't mean anything. The JavaScript interpreter must first translate the *document, write,* and then figure out how to use it. With Java, much less translation is required, since most of it was done when the class file was created.

III

Writing HTML

Why Use Java for Server-Side Applications

So why would you want to use Java to perform server-side interaction? Well, first, for developers, who are already working in the Java programming language and who want to take advantage of the rapid development cycles afforded by Java, server-side Java is a natural extension. Second, it's often advantageous to utilize the efforts that are put into a client-side Java applet and utilize them on the server. One prime example of where this can be extremely helpful, is with programs that serve dual purposes. Java can be used not only on the Web, but also on desktops. As a result of the unique platform independence Java provides, it is being used to develop in many situations where the medium of delivery is both CD-ROM and Internet. With Java, it is possible to deliver exactly the same application in both forms, and take advantage of the unique abilities that each medium provides. When many of these applications hit the Internet though, they suffer badly because of bandwidth restrictions. With a CD-ROM, it is menial to place and search large amounts of data, since all the data is right there on the disc. Transferring all the data across the Internet is very problematic. As a result, it would be nice to limit the data set. By extracting the search portion the applet for the server (without any other code changes), this limitation is simple and very cost effective.

In addition to these benefits, with server-side applets, there is a great power that can be derived by utilizing the client-server abilities of Java. By interacting with a client-side Java applet, a server-side applet can share the load with the client. When this situation is put into effect, you can produce the best fit solution for your environment and limit the amount of calculations performed by the server, thereby reducing your load, and at the same time limiting the amount of bandwidth which is required by the client.

Server-side Java can be done in three ways. First, using standard CGI, the program, written in Java, must actually comply with the application specification for Java, and can't become an applet. Using Java to perform standard CGI is similar to doing CGI with Perl or C. However, there is one major disadvantage to this mechanism. In order for a Java applet or application to run, a "supporting" program, known as the Java Virtual Machine, must first be loaded and run. The virtual machine actually runs the Java applet or application. The time involved for the Virtual Machine to load, while not long, is prohibitive for CGI applications where short response times are critical.

The second mechanism for running a server-side Java application is through the Netscape Server-java directory with Netscape Enterprise or LiveWire servers. These servers eliminate the need for the Virtual Machine to load by keeping it in memory at all times. In addition, Netscape has built an API, which allows server-side applets to obtain information about various states of the network in an almost rudimentary way.

The third option for doing server-side Java is through a brand new API which Sun Microsystems has announced it will be releasing. Under the new API Java, objects known as servlets, can be loaded dynamically by a Java-based server. These servlets can actually be linked into the server and extend the capabilities of the server. The server is actually able to, quickly and efficiently, interact with the power of Java.

Enabling Java on the Enterprise or FastTrack Server

In order for you to take advantage of the Java serving capabilities of the Enterprise or FastTrack servers, you must first enable these options on the server.

The controls for the Java Virtual Machine are located in the server controls. Netscape's new integrated server management system includes many controls for your server, each of these is placed under different headings. To get to the Java controls, the first thing you need to do is select the *PROGRAMS* file in the main window. Next, you need to select the *JAVA* controls in the side frame. Finally, to have the server utilize the Java Virtual machine, you must select YES and select OK.

Once you select OK, the server prompts you to confirm the changes, and to restart the server. If all goes as planned, the server should notify you that it has been restarted (as seen in figure 13.1). If not, you may need to manually stop and restart your server for these changes to take effect.

Fig. 13.1
The Server should confirm that it has restarted.

III

Writing HTML

With the Netscape 2.0 servers, the directory /server-java has been set aside in much the same way that /cgi-bin has been used on first generation HTTP servers. Now that you have enabled Java on your Web server, you can confirm that it is working by utilizing some of the Java applications that are included with the Enterprise and FastTrack Servers.

> **Note**
>
> In order for you to utilize the demonstration classes, which are shipped with the Enterprise and FastTrack servers, you need to make sure you have entered the correct directory in the 'Java Applet Directory' during your server configuration. By default, this directory is **/usr/ns-home/plugins/java/applets.**
>
> Change the /usr/ns-home to the directory which is appropriate for your installation.

To test the Java implementation with your server, you can now open the URL /server-java/BrowserDataApplet in your browser. This should cause the server to run the BrowserDataApplet and return information about your browser as shown in figure 13.2.

Fig. 13.2
The BrowserDataApplet reveals information about your browser.

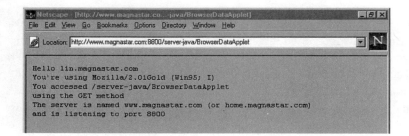

Notice that the information that is shown about the browser is the information the browser provides to the server. There is no magic bullet here, the server must rely on what/who the Browser claims to be. As a result, if you use the information, you should be aware that a browser can provide information that may not seem to be correct. Some browsers, such as Microsoft Internet Explorer, show themselves as being Mozilla for compatibility with Netscape as shown in figure 13.3.

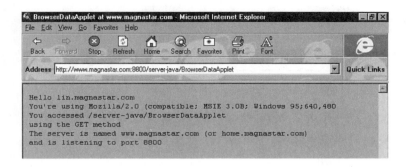

Fig. 13.3
Microsoft Internet
Explorer claims to
be Mozilla.

So where does this information come from? First, take a look at the directory:

/Netscape-server-directory/plugins/java/applets

Make sure you substitute /Netscape-server-directory for the directory in which
your Netscape 2.0 server resides. In that directory, there are several files, one
of which is called BrowserDataApplet.class. If you are already a Java programmer, you will recognize this as a Java class file, which is Java's equivalent to
an .exe file.

When you accessed the directory /server-applets, the Enterprise server went
out and loaded the BrowserDataApplet class into its interpreter and the results were sent to your browser, just like a CGI program.

Begin Developing a Java Applet

There is not enough space in this book to truly cover Java. In addition, this
chapter only talks about using Java to create Server-Applets. It should be
pointed out that Java can, just as easily, be used to create applications that
run on local machines, or for applets that can be distributed as easily as GIF
files to your Web clients.

Before you can create a Java applet, it is necessary to first download the Java
Developers Kit (JDK) and install it. The JDK includes tools to compile the Java
source code into Java class files, which can then be run. You can obtain the
JDK from Sun Microsystems at:

http://java.sun.com/devcorner.html

III

Writing HTML

> **Note**
>
> In Java, what JavaScript and many other languages call functions are called methods.

HelloWorld Java Application for a Server Applet

Before we dive into our own version of the BrowserDataApplet, let's take a look at how to do something a bit simpler. In almost every language since Kernie and Richie invented C, the first program is traditionally one that says "Hello World." Java is a unique language in that it has a number of different "Hello World" implementations depending on how it is being used. In the current situation, you want to have the server send a document which simply says "Hello World" to the browser.

Listing 13.2 shows the source code for the server-side applet Hello World program.

Listing 13.2   Hello World for Server Side Java Application

```
/*  Import the required classes from other packages  */
import netscape.server.applet.HttpApplet;
import java.io.PrintStream;

/*  The class which is created is called HelloWorld  */
public class HelloWorld extends HttpApplet{

  public void run() throws Exception {
     PrintStream out = getOutputStream();
     out.println ("HelloWorld");
  }

  }
```

Understanding the Source Code for the HelloWorld Application

In order to understand the source code for the HelloWorld application, let's take it line by line. The first two lines of the code import two classes. The first class is provided by Netscape and the second is included with the Java library provided with Sun's Java Developer Kit:

```
/*  Import the required classes from other packages  */
```

```
import netscape.server.applet.HttpApplet;
import java.io.PrintStream;
```

netscape.server.applet.HttpApplet is probably the most important class included with the API from Netscape. The server expects all the programs that it loads to be HttpApplet. As you will see in the next line of code, you can make the HelloWorld class into an HttpApplet by extending, or inheriting, the characteristics of HttpApplet.

The next line of code is what is known as the class declaration. In the declaration you need to declare the properties which the HelloWorld class will have. In order to be usable as a server-applet, all classes must be declared to be public (so the server can read them) and to extend HttpApplet.

```
/*  The class which is created is called HelloWorld  */
public class HelloWorld extends HttpApplet{
```

All server applets need to overload the method run(). The run method is the method that the Server will run when a user attempts to access the URL where the HelloWorld applet is located. In a certain sense, you can think of the run() method as the cousin of the main() function in C or C++.

```
public void run() throws Exception {
```

The next two lines perform the actual work of the class. In this case, you want to write the text "Hello World" out to the browser. In order to do this, the first thing that you need is a place to write the text. This may seem obvious, but remember the class doesn't know what you want to do. Fortunately, Netscape has included a method called getOutputStream(), which provides us a means to get to the stream of data going back to the client.

```
PrintStream out = getOutputStream();
```

Finally, now that you have access to the stream handler you can place the text "Hello World" on the browser screen. To do this, use the println() method provided in the PrintStream class.

```
out.println ("HelloWorld");
```

The last two lines can also be written as:

```
getOutputStream.out.println("Hello World");
```

if you prefer. If you are used to the syntax System.out.println(), this may make more sense to you.

III

Writing HTML

Creating and Compiling the HelloWorld Application

To create this application, copy the contents of listing 13.3 into your favorite text editor. Then compile them using the javac program supplied with Sun's JDK.

Note

In order to compile a Java application, you need to obtain a copy of the Java Developers Kit (JDK) supplied by Sun Microsystems. Among other things, this kit contains a compiler that can take the source code, such as that in Listing 13.1, and convert it into a Java class file. You can obtain the JDK at **http://www.javasoft.com/ java.sun.com/products/JDK/index.html.**

Including the Netscape Package in the Classpath

The Syntax for compiling the HelloWorld Application is not quite as simple as for most Java code. The reason for this is that we need to import a class from the Netscape package. As a result, it is necessary to include the file that contains the package in the classpath.

Before you can include the file though, it's necessary to determine where the file is located. What you will be looking for is a file called serv2_0.zip. By default this file is located at:

```
/usr/ns-home/plugins/java/classes/serv2_0.zip
```

You need to substitute the /usr/ns-home directory with the correct directory for your Enterprise or FastTrack server. As with the rest of this chapter, the location that is used for the installation is /optl/ent-home so the actual path is:

```
/optl/ent-home/plugins/java/classes/serv2_0.zip
```

but your installation is likely to be different. To obtain the proper file name, substitute /optl/ent-home for the directory in which you have installed the FastTrack or Enterprise server.

Caution

In addition to the serv2_0.zip, you may need to know the location of the classes.zip file included with the JDK. This file is located in the /java/lib directory. For the purposes of this chapter, the file is located at /optl/java/lib/classes.zip.

As with the location of the serv2_0.zip file, you need to substitute the actual directory in which you have installed the JDK.

If you obtain an error, such as

```
class java.io.PrintStream not found on import
```

the odds are that you need to also add the classes.zip file to your classpath.

Once you have located the classes.zip and serv2_0.zip files, there are two ways to add them to the class path. The first and simplest way is to do so on the command line. To compile the HelloWorld file, include the netscape package in the class path as shown in the following command line:

```
javac -classpath /optl/ent-home/plugins/java/classes/serv2_0.zip
HelloWorld.java
```

This should produce a file, called HelloWorld.class, in the directory you have the HelloWorld.java file in.

If you are like most people, you don't really want to have to type out 81 characters every time you want to compile the HelloWorld program. To eliminate the need to always specify the *-classpath* option, you can set an environment variable called *CLASSPATH* to point to the serv2_0.zip file. Once the CLASSPATH has been set, you can compile a program in much the same way you would any other Java application.

To set the CLASSPATH variable using CSH, type **CLASSPATH=/optl/ent-home/plugins/java/classes/serv2_0.zip export CLASSPATH.**

Tip

Windows NT users, note that the examples given here are for UNIX machines. When using an NT machine, the directories should use the backslash (\) instead of the forward slash (/). To set an environment variable, you need to use the set command.

```
set classpath=\ns-home\plugins\java\classes\serv2_0.zip
```

Once you have set the CLASSPATH variable, you can compile the HelloWorld application by typing **javac HelloWorld.java.**

III

Writing HTML

Viewing the HelloWorld Application

To be able to run the HelloWorld application, copy the HelloWorld.class file, which the compiler produced, into the directory you specified when you configured the Enterprise, or FastTrack server to enable the Java Interpreter. If you placed the HelloWorld.java file in this directory, and compiled it there, there is no need to move anything. It will already be in the correct location.

To test out the HelloWorld application, open the URL /server-java/ HelloWorld in any browser. It does not need to be a Java-enabled browser such as Netscape Navigator. Figure 13.4 shows the page you should see.

Fig. 13.4
The HelloWorld application should generate a simple page in your browser.

As you can see from figure 13.4, the application that you wrote produced something, which, to your browser, looked exactly as it were coming from a HTML file. Of course, this was a lot of work to produce a simple line of text, but before you learn to surf the big waves, it is generally a good idea to learn to swim first.

A Bigger Greeting Example

Now, let's take a look at a more advanced Java application, which shows some information about the incoming browser. Listing 13.3 shows the source code for the new application.

Listing 13.3   Greetings Java Source Code, a Server Side Applet that Displays Browser Information

```
import netscape.server.applet.HttpApplet;

import java.io.PrintStream;
import java.net.Socket;
import java.net.InetAddress;

public class Greetings extends HttpApplet {

public void run() throws Exception {
```

```
        //Check to find out if browser can accept normal text output
        if (returnNormalResponse("text/plain")) {
            //Get the output stream to send data to client
            PrintStream out = getOutputStream();

            //get the socket the browser is connected to
            Socket client = getClientSocket();

            //find the hostname of the socket
            String clientAddress = client.getInetAddress().getHostName();

            //Check to see if it's my IP address
            if (clientAddress.compareTo ("206.31.43.250")==0)
                    out.println("Greetings great and wonderful master!");
            else
                    out.println("Nice to meet other netezins");

            //Find out what browser the client is using
            String browser = getHeader ("user-agent");
            if (browser != null){
                    if (browser.startsWith ("Mozilla"))
                            out.println ("Your using Netscape... Hey this
    is a Netscape Server too!");
                    else
                            out.println("You're using the" + browser+"
    browser");
            }
            else
                    out.println("Hey, your browser didn't identify
    itself.");

        }
    }

} //end class Greetings
```

Notice that just like our HelloWorld example, the very first thing that you
need to write is:

```
    import netscape.server.applet.HttpApplet;
```

This includes the class from the Netscape library into the Java environment.
Netscape actually provides four classes to assist the construction of server side
applications. These four are:

- netscape.server.applet.Server
- netscape.server.applet.ServerApplet
- netscape.server.applet.HttpApplet
- netscape.server.applet.URIUtil

III

Writing HTML

Each of these classes provides a means to access data about the server or the client in order to make writing server applications easier.

Each different class contains various methods to place or get information about the environment. In the HelloWorld example, the only method which we used was getOutputStream(). The Greetings shows the use of several more of methods in HttpApplet.

The first line in the Greetings class shows an example of one such method. Before you blindly write to the browser (like you did with the HelloWorld application), it is better to first check to make sure that the browser is willing to accept text output. If not, you may have to respond differently, so the first line of the Greetings application checks to see if the browser has a standard "text/plain" response.

```
if (returnNormalResponse("text/plain")) {
```

After you have verified the browser response, the application opens the output stream, just as it did in the HelloWorld application. Once the connection has been established to the browser, the program proceeds to send data, the same way that it did for HelloWorld.

Now, it's often convenient to know who is accessing your server. Based on who it is, you might want to give a different response to the user, so let us retrieve some information about the client accessing the Greetings app.

The next line of code defines a Socket variable that points to where the client has attached. If you're familiar with Java programming, this socket can be used just as it would in any other Java application.

Once you have a pointer to the client socket, you can use it to determine the address the client browser is coming from, using the getInetAddress() method. Once, you have the client's IP address, you can use it to determine if the client is a valid host, or someone else. In this example, I choose to simply have the application greet my computer differently than other people on the net.

```
        //get the socket the browser is connected to
        Socket client = getClientSocket();

        //find the hostname of the socket
        String clientAddress =
client.getInetAddress().getHostName();

        //Check to see if it's my IP address
        if (clientAddress.compareTo ("206.31.43.250")==0)
                out.println("Greetings great and wonderful mas-
ter!");
        else
                out.println("Nice to meet other netezins");
```

Note

For experienced Java programmers, it might be interesting to note that the getClientSocket() method is not one from HttpApplet, but rather from its parent ServerApplet.

The getInetAddress() and getHostName() methods are not part of the Netscape package at all, but rather part of members of the java.net package.

Another useful piece of information to use is what type of browsers are accessing your pages? If they are not Netscape-compliant, you may actually want to give them a completely different Web page. The next several lines of the Greetings application deal with doing just that. First, the type of browser is obtained using the getHeader method. This method can be used to retrieve a variety of information about the standard HTTP header. The HTTP header contains a lot of information about the browser, but the one we're interested in is the agent (or browser) that the incoming request is coming from. This information is contained in the user-agent portion of the header. To retreive the various other pieces of information contained in the header, the string user-agent should be substituted with the appropriate title.

```
//Find out what browser the client is using
String browser = getHeader ("user-agent");
```

You may initially wonder about the next line of the code, which reads:

```
if (browser != null){
```

It's important to make sure that you actually received a string from the getHeader request, because unfortunately, it is not always the case that information obtained using the various methods will actually return data. For instance, some browsers do not return information about who they are. If this is the case, the method will return null, and unless you check for this, you will run into problems using the string.

I decided that if the browser that was coming in was a Netscape Navigator browser (or any browser claiming to be Netscape), I would give the user a friendly hello. To do this, you need to compare the browser name with Mozilla. In fact, all you really care about is, does the browser's name start with Mozilla. And, if not, you will simply give them another message.

Using JavaScript on the Server

In addition to providing the ability to include Java applications on the server, Netscape also extended its JavaScript technology for server side use. This technology was placed into what Netscape calls the LiveWire program. With LiveWire JavaScript, pages, which produce data on the server side, can be written. Because the pages are processed on the server side, these pages can be viewed by any browser, not just the ones from Netscape that support JavaScript.

Enabling LiveWire on the Server

In order to utilize the LiveWire applications, it is first necessary to activate LiveWire on your server. To do this, go to the Server Control center page, and select the programs menu. Now, select the LiveWire sub-menu and activate LiveWire for your server as shown in figure 13.5.

Fig. 13.5
Enable LiveWire on the Enterprise or FastTrack Servers.

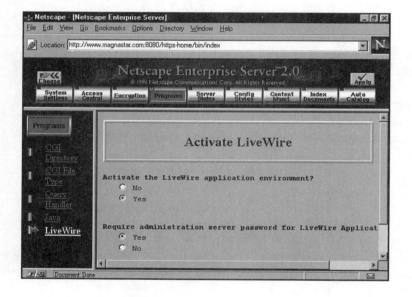

Once you have enabled LiveWire for your server, you can then go to the LiveWire Application manager. To access the manager, open the URL /appmgr in your browser. The appmgr is located at the URL of your standard Web page, NOT on the administration port. The Application Manager is shown in figure 13.6.

Now, don't go looking for the *appmgr* directory in your *docs* directory. The Application Manager and all other LiveWire applications are symbolically linked into the server.

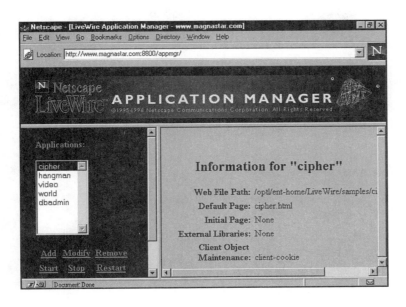

Fig. 13.6
The LiveWire Application Manager is where you control LiveWire applications.

Running Some LiveScript Applications

Now that you have the Application Manager up and running, it's possible to run some of the sample applications that come with the server. To test a typical LiveWire application, select the application from the Applications list box. For instance, select Hangman and then press the *run* hyperlink as shown in figure 13.7. You should see the Hangman page come up as shown in figure 13.8.

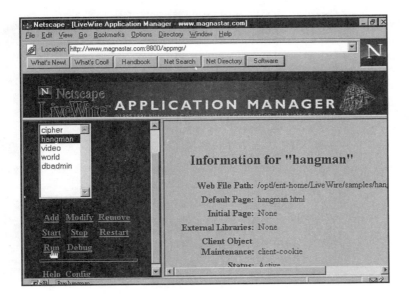

Fig. 13.7
Select Hangman and click the run hyperlink.

III

Writing HTML

Fig. 13.8
The Hangman
applications.

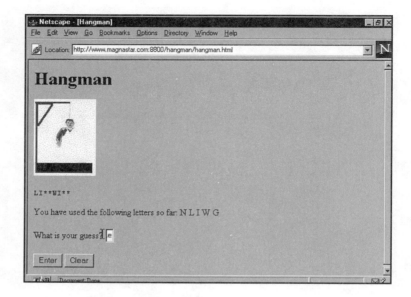

Writing LiveScript Pages

The Hangman application is a bit complicated for this chapter, so let's take a look at a simpler application. The application we will be looking at (used in the previous Java section) is the HelloWorld example.

Listing 13.4 shows the source code for the HelloWorld application, also available in the demo applications List Box.

Listing 13.4   The HelloWorld Application as Written Using JavaScript for LiveWire

```
<html>
<head>
<title> Hi There </title>

</head>
<body>
<h1> Hi There </h1>
<server>write("<P>The last time you where here you entered " +
client.oldtext + ".");</server>
<P>But this time you entered <server>write(request.newtext);</server>

<server>client.oldtext = request.newtext; </server>

<p>Your IP address this time is <server>write(request.ip);</server>
<br>The last person to access this page was
<server>write(project.lastAccess);</server>.
```

```
<server>
project.lock();     // Initialize or increment total number of ac-
cesses.
    project.lastAccess = request.ip;
project.unlock();


  if (client.count == null)
    client.count = 0;
  else
    client.count = parseInt(client.count,10) + 1;

</server>

<p>Oh, by the way, you have been here <server>write(client.count);</
server> times before.

<h1> Enter some text below </h1>
<form method="post" action="hi2.html">
<input type="text" name="newtext" size="20">
<br>
<p><input type="submit" value="Submit">
</form>


</body>
</html>
```

Notice that much of the code looks very similar to standard HTML. This is, in fact, the great benefit of using JavaScript/LiveWire to write programs you might otherwise have written in Perl or some other language. Since JavaScript utilizes the standard HTML format, you can first create a page to look like you would want it to under normal circumstances, and then enhance it using JavaScript.

To understand the JavaScript page, let's once again break it down line by line, as we did for the Java applications.

JavaScript Pages Start with HTML

Each JavaScript program is built around a standard HTML page; so, as with regular HTML pages, these pages must begin with <HTML>, <HEAD> and <BODY> tags.

```
<html>
<head>
<title> Hi There </title>

</head>
<body>
```

The most basic page could actually end with the next line, which, just like standard HTML, creates a level one header and writes Hello World.

```
<h1> Hi There </h1>
```

Including JavaScript in LiveWire pages

Starting with the next line, the HelloWorld script becomes different. Notice the <SERVER> and </SERVER> tags? These tags tell the server to perform some action with this part of the text.

There are two ways to include JavaScript information in a LiveWire page. The first is to include JavaScript execution instructions between the <SCRIPT> and </SCRIPT> tags. The second way to include JavaScript in a LiveWire page is to include JavaScript variables between back quotes ('). But you can only include variables between back quotes, not instructions.

In the previous line of code, you are introduced to the write() function. This function tells the LiveScript server to write text in this location. The write function is one of the most important ones of LiveWire because it lets you add text to an existing document.

The text that you directed LiveScript to write comes from the *request* objects IP. That is the IP of the client accessing the page. There are four basic objects in the LiveWire set. These are:

- request: contains data about the current request. Each time a client accesses a page the request data changes.
- client: contains data about the individual client. Each client who accesses a page has a unique client object. When you install an application to the Application Manager, the maintenance method determines how this data is stored.
- project: contains data about the entire project. This object is initialized when the application is started, and is the same for each application. To share data between same applications, the project object should be used.
- server: contains data about the entire server. This object is initialized when the server is started, and is the same for all applications. To share data between multiple applications the server object should be used.

Displaying Text from the Client-Cookie

The next line of code demonstrates the use of the client object. This object is specified by default by the client-cookie. If you reload this page, the client object will be the same for that browser. Notice that you can add and remove variables from the client object at will.

```
<server>write("<P>The last time you where here you entered " +
client.oldtext + ".");</server>
```

Next, the program displays the value of the newtext variable. This value comes from the form data you will see later, when we cover the form at the bottom of the page.

```
<P>But this time you entered <server>write(request.newtext);</
server>
```

Saving Data to the Client Object

The next task is to put the newtext value somewhere so that the next time you load in the page, you can tell the user what they had typed this time. The place to store this is the client.oldtext variable we saw just two paragraphs ago. The client object, since it is a client cookie, is stored for each different client separately.

```
<server>client.oldtext = request.newtext; </server>
```

Displaying the Client's IP Address

As you did with the Java example, let's print out the IP address from which the client is connecting. To do this, you will need to access the request.ip value, which stores this information.

```
<p>Your IP address this time is <server>write(request.ip);</server>
```

I thought it might be interesting to also tell the user who/where the last user came from. To do this, I have stored the IP address of the last access in a variable called project.lastAccess.

```
<br>The last person to access this page was
<server>write(project.lastAccess);</server>.
```

Storing a Value to the Project Object

Actually, storing the project.last access value is the function of the next three lines. The project object is shared between all instances of the Hi.html page, and since we want each page to be able to tell us who the last person was, the page must use the *project* object that is shared between all applications.

What happens, though, when multiple pages are accessed at the same time? If two programs tried to read lastAccess in at the same time, and then update it, the odds are that only one of the changes would actually take place. To prevent this kind of activity, LiveWire allows you to lock an object. Once the variable is locked, no other page can access or change the information in that object, until it has been unlocked. So the file continues, by first locking the project object, updating it, and then unlocking it so that other pages can read in the values.

```
project.lock();     // Initialize or increment total number of
accesses.
    project.lastAccess = request.ip;
project.unlock();
```

In addition to name information, the HelloWorld page also keeps and displays some statistical information about the use of the Web page. The information about the total number of accesses by this client will be stored in the variable client.number.

The first time through the page for a unique client, the Web page initializes the number of accesses to 0. You can determine if the number value has ever been initialized before by finding out if it is null. The Hi There page uses the if...else construct to first determine this (if the value is null) and then increment or initialize the value of client.number depending on the result.

```
if (client.count == null)
    client.count = 0;
  else
    client.count = parseInt(client.count,10) + 1;
```

Finally, the updated values of the client.number are written to the client.

```
<p>Oh, by the way, you have been here
<server>write(client.count);</server> times before.
```

The Input Form

In the next several lines, the program returns to what you should be familiar with under standard HTML. Notice that the form data is written exactly as it would be for regular HTML.

```
<h1> Enter some text below </h1>
<form method="post" action="hi2.html">
<input type="text" name="newtext" size="20">
<br>
<p><input type="submit" value="Submit">
</form>
```

Compiling JavaScript Pages

The first task in creating the HelloWorld application is to copy the contents of listing 13.4 into a file called Hello.html using a standard editor such as nedit or vi. Once you have a file containing the code, the next step is to compile this page into a LiveWire document or .web file.

There are two ways to compile JavaScript applications. The first is with the command line compiler; the second is using the Application Manager. The second method has been promised by Netscape, but at the time of this writing is unavailable, so we will only cover the command line compiler.

The compiler included with LiveWire is the program *lwcomp*. The lwcomp program should install in your LiveWire/bin directory, and you may wish to include this in your path.

Now, to compile your HelloWorld example, all you need to do is type:

```
lwcomp hi.html
```

If you look in the directory where the hello.html file is located, you should now find two additional files: build and hello.web. *Lwcomp* has many other options which enable you to link multiple html files in, but they are beyond the scope of this chapter.

Now that you have built your application, you need to add it to the Application Manager so that it can access your new page. To do this, select *add* from the Applications Manager.

The side window should now switch to the Add function, as shown in figure 13.9. You need to specify the name of the application. This name also appears in the directory that is accessed from your Web browser. In this case, that means that you access it as **http://www.yourcompany.com/Hi/.** The Web File Path is the actual full name of the Hi.web file that you created using *lwcomp*. This directory need not reside within your server directory, as demonstrated in this example. Finally, include the default file name that you wish to have the server send. This file is probably the name of the HTML file you used to create the .web file. The file name for the default page is relative to the .web file, so you need not include the entire path.

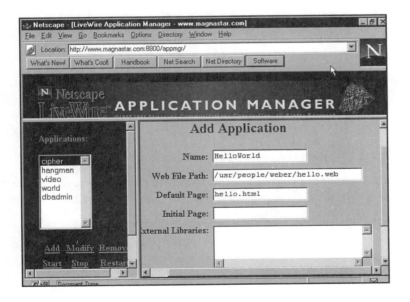

Fig. 13.9
Add the Application to the Application Manager.

> **Note**
>
> You should not use an Application name that is the same as any directory in your Web servers *docs* directory. The LiveWire application overrides this directory and you won't be able to access the contents of the actual directory in docs.

Testing the LiveScript Page

You can access the HelloWorld Web page to test it in one of two ways. First, after you add the Application to the manager, you can click the *run* hyper link and it will automatically launch another browser and take you to your new Web page.

Alternatively, you can access the Web page by opening the directory that has the same name as the application.

Java and JavaScript Resources

There are a number of locations on the Web that specialize exclusively in indexes on Java and JavaScript applications.

Example Applets and JavaScript Pages

One of the largest directories currently available is Gamelan:

> **http://www.gamelan.com**

JARS or the Java Applet Review System is another great site which rates applets on a top 1%, 5% and 25% basis:

> **http://www.jars.com**

Apple Flavored Java is a site dedicated to Java on the Macintosh:

> **http://www.seas.upenn.edu/~mcrae/projects/macjava/**

The Java Centre is a UK site:

> **http://www.java.co.uk/javacentre.html**

The Java Boutique is a collection of Java Applets. One of the requirements of this site is that, to be listed, the source for the applet must be made available.

> **http://weber.u.washington.edu/~jgurney/java**

Finding a Java Consultant

Since often you won't have the time to develop a custom applet or JavaScript of your own, the following sites can help you find a developer who can perform that task for you. These sites are also a good location to look for Java applications and applets that have already been written and which are free or very inexpensive.

MagnaStar Inc. A Custom Java programming and consulting company:

http://www.magnastar.com

Dimension X. A developer of Java applications:

http://www.dnx.com

Team Java. A resource that boasts a good list of Java Developers:

http://www.teamjava.com

## CHAPTER 14

VB Script and ActiveX Controls

VB Script and ActiveX are two relatively new technologies from Microsoft. They are similar to JavaScript and Java, respectively, in that the former are scripting languages for Web browsers (primarily), and the latter are ways of adding increased functionality to Web browsers. Together, they provide a framework that can be used to make Microsoft's Internet Explorer and other compatible Web browsers, into very capable tools for working over the Internet, as well as an Intranet.

In this chapter, you will learn:

- What Visual Basic (VB) Script is
- How VB Script is related to Visual Basic for Applications and Visual Basic
- How VB Script interacts with Internet Explorer 3
- What the components of the VB Script language are
- What ActiveX is and how it is used on the Web

What Is Visual Basic Script?

Like the JavaScript language, first introduced by Netscape and fully supported by Microsoft in Internet Explorer 3, the Visual Basic Script (VB Script) scripting language enables you to embed commands into an HTML document. When an Internet Explorer 3 user downloads the page, your VB Script commands are loaded by the Web browser along with the rest of the document and are run in response to any of a series of events. Again, like JavaScript, VB Script is an *interpreted* language; Internet Explorer 3 interprets the VB Script commands when they are loaded and run. They do not need to be *compiled* into executable form by the Web author who uses them.

VB Script is a fast and flexible subset of Microsoft's Visual Basic and Visual Basic for Applications languages. It is designed to be easy to program in and for adding active content to HTML documents quickly. The language elements are mainly ones that will be familiar to anyone who has programmed in just about any language, such as `If...Then...Else` blocks, `Do`, `While`, and `For...Next` loops, along with a typical assortment of operators and built-in functions. This chapter attempts to give you an overview of the VB Script language and show you examples of how to use it to add greater interaction to your Web pages.

Why Use a Scripting Language?

HTML provides a good deal of flexibility to page authors, but HTML by itself is static; once written, HTML documents can't interact with the user other than by presenting hyperlinks. Creative use of CGI scripts (which run on Web servers) has made it possible to create more interesting and effective interactive sites, but some applications really demand programs or scripts that are executed by the client.

One of the reasons VB Script was developed was to provide Web authors a way to write small scripts that would execute on the users' browsers instead of on the server. For example, an application that collects data from a form and then posts it to the server can validate the data for completeness and correctness before sending it to the server. This can greatly improve the performance of the browsing session, because users don't have to send data to the server until it's been verified as correct. It also helps to reduce network bandwidth, either over the Internet or an Intranet, by performing data checks locally and not sending it to a server until it has been verified to be correct. The following are some other potential applications for VB Script:

- VB Scripts can verify forms for completeness, like a mailing list registration form that checks to make sure the user has entered a name and e-mail address before the form is posted.

- Pages can display content derived from information stored on the user's computer—without sending that data to the server. For example, a bank can embed VB Script commands in their pages that look up account data from a Quicken file and display it as part of the bank's page.

- Because VB Script can modify settings for OLE objects and for applets written in Java, page authors can control the size, appearance, and behavior of OLE controls and Java applets being run by Internet Explorer. A page that contains an embedded Java animation might use a

VB Script to set the Java window size and position before triggering the animation. VB Script can be used to set properties for Internet Explorer 3 itself, since it supports OLE automation.

What Can VB Script Do?

VB Script provides a fairly complete set of built-in functions and commands, enabling you to perform math calculations, play sounds, open up new windows and new URLs, and access and verify user input to your Web forms.

Code to perform these actions can be embedded in a page and executed when the page is loaded; you can also write functions that contain code that's triggered by events you specify. For example, you can write a VB Script method that is called when the user clicks the Submit button of a form, or one that is activated when the user clicks a hyperlink on the active page.

VB Script can also set the attributes, or *properties*, of OLE controls or Java applets running in the browser. This way, you can easily change the behavior of plug-ins or other objects without having to delve into their innards. For example, your VB Script code could automatically start playing an embedded .AVI file when the user clicks a button.

How Does VB Script Look in an HTML Document?

VB Script commands are embedded in your HTML documents, either directly or via a URL that tells the browser which scripts to load, just as with JavaScript (and other scripting languages). Embedded VB Scripts are enclosed in the HTML container tag <SCRIPT>...</SCRIPT>.

The <SCRIPT> element takes two attributes: LANGUAGE, which specifies the scripting language to use when evaluating the script, and SRC, which specifies a URL from which the script can be loaded. The LANGUAGE attribute is always required, unless the SRC attribute's URL specifies a language. LANGUAGE and SRC can both be used, too. For VB Script, the scripting language is defined as LANGUAGE="VBS". Some examples of valid SCRIPT tags are as follows:

```
<SCRIPT LANGUAGE="VBS">...</SCRIPT>
<SCRIPT SRC="http://www.rpi.edu/~odonnj/scripts/common.VBS">...</
SCRIPT>
<SCRIPT LANGUAGE="VBS" SRC="http://www.rpi.edu/~odonnj/scripts/
common">...</SCRIPT>
```

VB Script resembles JavaScript and many other computer languages you may be familiar with. It bears the closest resemblance, as you might imagine, to Visual Basic and Visual Basic for Applications because it is a subset of these

III

Writing HTML

two languages. The following are some of the simple rules you need to follow for structuring VB Scripts:

- VB Script is case insensitive, so function, Function, and FUNCTION are all the same. Microsoft has released coding conventions that include a recommended naming and formatting scheme for constants, variables, and other aspects of VB Scripts.

- VB Script is flexible about statements. A single statement can cover multiple lines, if a continuation character, a single underscore (_), is placed at the end of each line to be continued. Also, you can put multiple short statements on a single line by separating each from the next with a colon (:).

VB Script Programming Hints

You should keep in mind a few points when programming with VB Script. These hints ease your learning process and make your HTML documents that include VB Scripts more compatible with a wider range of Web browsers.

Hiding Your Scripts

Because VB Script is a new product and is currently supported only by Internet Explorer 3—though Oracle, Spyglass, NetManage, and other companies plan to license the technology for future versions of their Web browsers—you'll probably be designing pages that will be viewed by Web browsers that don't support it. To keep those browsers from misinterpreting your VB Script, wrap your scripts as follows:

```
<SCRIPT LANGUAGE="VBS">
<!-- This line opens an HTML comment
VB Script commands...
<!-- This line opens and closes an HTML comment -->
</SCRIPT>
```

The opening <!-- comment causes Web browsers that do not support VB Script to disregard all text they encounter until they find a matching -->, so they don't display your script. Make sure that your <SCRIPT>...</SCRIPT> container elements are outside the comments, though; otherwise, Internet Explorer 3 ignores the whole script.

Comments

Including comments in your programs to explain what they do is usually good practice; VB Script is no exception. The VB Script interpreter ignores any text marked as a comment, so don't be shy about including them. Comments in VB Script are set off using the REM statement (short for remark) or by using a single quotation mark (') character. Any text following the REM or single quotation mark, until the end of the line, is ignored. To include a comment on the same line as another VB Script statement, you can use either REM or a single quotation mark. However, if you use REM, you must separate the statement from the REM with a colon (the VB Script multiple-command-per-line separator).

VB Script, Visual Basic, and Visual Basic for Applications

As mentioned previously, VB Script is a subset of the Visual Basic and Visual Basic for Applications languages. If you are familiar with either of these two languages, you will find programming in VB Script very easy. Just as Visual Basic was meant to make the creation of Windows programs easier and more accessible, and Visual Basic for Applications was meant to do the same for Microsoft Office applications, VB Script is meant to give an easy-to-learn, yet powerful, means for adding interactivity and increased functionality to Web pages.

The VB Script Language

VB Script was designed as a subset of Visual Basic and Visual Basic for Applications. As a subset, it doesn't have as much functionality but was intended to provide a quicker and simpler language for enhancing Web pages and servers. This section discusses some of the building blocks of VB Script and how they are combined into VB Script programs.

Using Identifiers

An *identifier* is just a unique name that VB Script uses to identify a variable, method, or object in your program. As with other programming languages, VB Script imposes some rules on what names you can use. All VB Script names must start with an alphabetic character and can contain both upper- and lowercase letters and the digits 0 through 9. They can be as long as 255 characters, though you probably don't want to go much over 32 or so.

Unlike JavaScript, which supports two different ways for you to represent values in your scripts, literals and variables, VB Script really has only variables. The difference in VB Script, then, is one of usage. You can include literals—constant values—in your VB Script programs by setting a variable equal to a value and not changing it. We will continue to refer to literals and variables as distinct entities, though they are interchangeable.

III

Writing HTML

Literals and variables in VB Script are all type *variant*, which means that they can contain any type of data that VB Script supports. It is usually a good idea to use a given variable for one type and explicitly convert its value to another type, as necessary. The following are some of the types of data that VB Script supports:

- **Integers**—These types can be 1, 2, or 4 bytes in length, depending on how big they are.

- **Floating-Point**—VB Script supports single- and double-precision floating-point numbers.

- **Strings**—Strings can represent words, phrases, or data, and they're set off by double quotation marks.

- **Booleans**—Booleans have a value of either `true` or `false`.

Objects, Properties, Methods, and Events

Before you proceed further, you should take some time to review some terminology that may or may not be familiar to you. VB Script follows much the same object model as JavaScript, and uses many of the same terms. In VB Script, just as in JavaScript—and in any object-oriented language for that matter—an *object* is a collection of data and functions that have been grouped together. An object's data is known as its *properties,* and its functions are known as its *methods*. An *event* is a condition to which an object can respond, such as a mouse click or other user input. The VB Script programs that you write make use of properties and methods of objects, both those that you create and objects provided by Internet Explorer 3, its plug-ins, Java applets, and the like.

> **Tip**
>
> Here's a simple guideline: An object's properties are the information it knows, its methods are how it can act on that information, and events are what it responds to.

Using Built-In Objects and Functions

Individual VB Script elements are objects; for example, literals and variables are objects of type variant, which can be used to hold data of many different types. These objects also have associated methods, ways of acting on the different data types. VB Script also enables you to access a set of useful objects that represent the Internet Explorer 3 browser, the currently displayed page, and other elements of the browsing session.

You access objects by specifying their names. For example, the active document object is named document. To use document's properties or methods, you add a period and the name of the method or property you want. For example, document.title is the title property of the document object.

Using Properties

Every object has properties—even literals. To access a property, just use the object name followed by a period and the property name. To get the length of a string object named address, you can write the following:

```
address.length
```

You get back an integer that equals the number of characters in the string. If the object you're using has properties that can be modified, you can change them in the same way. To set the color property of a house object, just write the following:

```
house.color = "blue"
```

You can also create new properties for an object just by naming them. For example, say you define a class called customer for one of your pages. You can add new properties to the customer object as follows:

```
customer.name = "Joe Smith"
customer.address = "123 Elm Street"
customer.zip = "90210"
```

Finally, knowing that an object's methods are just properties is important, so you can easily add new properties to an object by writing your own function and creating a new object property using your own function name. If you want to add a Bill method to your customer object, you can write a function named BillCustomer and set the object's property as follows:

```
customer.Bill = BillCustomer;
```

To call the new method, you just write the following:

```
customer.Bill()
```

HTML Elements Have Properties, Too

Internet Explorer 3 provides properties for HTML forms and some types of form fields. VB Script is especially valuable for writing scripts that check or change data in forms. Internet Explorer 3's properties enable you to get and set the form elements' data, as well as specify actions to be taken when something happens to the form element (as when the user clicks in a text field or moves to another field).

Programming with VB Script

As you've learned in the preceding sections, VB Script has a lot to offer Web page authors. It's not as flexible as C or C++, but it's quick and simple. But, since it is easily embedded in your Web pages, adding interactivity with a little VB Script is easy. This section covers more details about VB Script programming, including a detailed explanation of the language's features.

A full description of the VB Script language would take much more space than this one chapter. Instead, you can read about the highlights of the language later. For a complete description of the VB Script language, go to the Microsoft VB Script Web site at **http://www.microsoft.com/vbscript/**.

Variables and Literals

VB Script variables are all of the type *variant*, which means that they can be used for any of the supported data types. Constants in VB Script, called *literals*, are similar to variables and can also be of any type. In fact, VB Script doesn't really have any "constants" in the usual sense of the word, since VB Script treats literals the same as variables. The difference lies in how the programmer uses them. VB Script variables can hold boolean data, one-, two-, or four-byte integers, four-or eight-byte real numbers, dates, strings, and a few specialized types such as objects and error numbers.

Expressions

An *expression* is anything that can be evaluated to get a single value. Expressions can contain string or numeric literals, variables, operators, and other expressions, and they can range from simple to quite complex. For example, the following is an expression that uses the assignment operator (more on operators in the next section) to assign the result 3.14159 to the variable sngPi:

```
sngPi = 3.14159
```

By contrast, the following is a more complex expression whose final value depends on the values of the two Boolean variables blnQuit and blnComplete:

```
(blnQuit = TRUE) And (blnComplete = FALSE)
```

Operators

Operators do just what their name suggests; they operate on variables or literals. The items that an operator acts on are called its *operands*. Operators come in the two following types:

- **Unary**—These operators require only one operand, and the operator can come before or after the operand. The Not operator, which performs the logical negation of an expression, is a good example.

- **Binary**—These operators need two operands. The four math operators (+ for addition, – for subtraction, * for multiplication, and / for division) are all binary operators, as is the = assignment operator you saw earlier.

VB Script supports the = assignment operator, math operators such as +, –, and *, comparison operators such as < and >=, logical operators such as And and Or, and the string concatenation operator &.

Controlling Your VB Scripts

Sometimes the scripts that you write are very simple and execute the same way each time they are loaded—a script to display a graphic animation, for instance. However, in order to write a script that will perform different functions depending on different user inputs or other conditions, you need to add a little more sophistication. VB Script provides statements and loops for controlling the execution of your programs based on a variety of inputs.

If you are familiar with just about any other computer language, you will recognize most of the control structures used in VB Script. They include the following types:

- **Testing Conditions**—You can test conditions in VB Scripts using the If...Then...Elseif...Else...End structure. In use, if would look something like:

```
if (sngX> sngPi) then
    blnTest = TRUE
    intCount = intCount + 1
else
    blnTest = FALSE
    intCount = 0
end if
```

- **Repeated Actions**—VB Script supports several looping constructs, including For...Next, For Each...Next, While...end, Do While...End, and Do...Until. Each of these loops does similar things with its own particular spin. An example of a Do...Until loop is the following:

```
intCount = 1
do
    document.write "Count is " & CStr(intCount) & "<BR>"
    intCount = intCount + 1
until (intCount = 101)
```

III

Writing HTML

> **Note**
>
> Again, we've barely even scratched the surface of VB Script—the language itself, what it can do, and how it interacts with the Web browser and user. For a complete reference on using VB Script, see the VB Script Web site at **http://www. microsoft.com/vbscript**.

VB Script Examples

Microsoft maintains a listing of sites making use of VB Scripts. This list is a great way to find out what is really possible using the VB Script techniques. You can access this list through the VB Script Web site at **http://www. microsoft.com/vbscript/**. Another good list of VB Script sites is given at the Visual Basic Pro Web site located at **http://www.inquiry.com/ techtips/thevbpro/**.

Displaying Real-Time Data Using VB Scripts

One of the sites listed on the Microsoft VB Script Site list shows a good example of what can be done by combining VB Script and JavaScripts is the Investor's Edge Web site, which uses them to show real-time financial information. Investor's Edge is located at **http://www.investorsedge.com/**.

Interacting with Objects

This example shows an example of how to use VB Script to manipulate another Web browser object, the ActiveX Label Control (you'll learn more about ActiveX Controls below). The label control enables the Web author to place text on the Web page, select the text, font, size, and an arbitrary angle of rotation. One of the exciting things about the label control is that it can be manipulated in real time, and produce a variety of automated or user-controlled effects.

In the example shown below, text is placed on the Web page using the label control, and form input is used to enable the user to change the text used and the angle at which it is displayed. Figure 14.1 shows the default configuration of the label, and figure 14.2 shows it after the text and the rotation angle has been changed. This is a good example in that it shows interaction of VB Script, HTML forms, and an ActiveX Control.

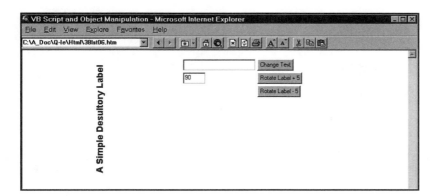

Fig. 14.1
The ActiveX Label Control allows arbitrary text to be displayed by the Web author in the size, font, position, and orientation desired.

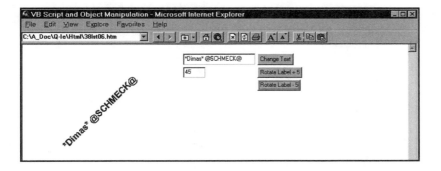

Fig. 14.2
VB Script's ability to manipulate Web browser objects allows the label parameters to be changed dynamically.

Listing 14.1 shows the code used to produce this example. Some things to note about the example are the following:

- The <OBJECT>...</OBJECT> is where the ActiveX Label Control is included, and its default parameters assigned. The classid attribute must be included exactly as shown. The id attribute is the object name used by VB Script to reference the label control object. The other attributes define the size and placement of the control.

- The <PARAM> tags within the <OBJECT>...</OBJECT> container enable the Web author to define attributes of the ActiveX Label Control. The NAME, VALUE pairs are unique to each ActiveX Control, and should be documented by the ActiveX Control author. For the label control, they define various aspects of the appearance of the label. The NAME is also used to manipulate the value with VB Script.

- An HTML form is used to accept input and print output for information about the label control. The first text area is used to set the label text, while the second text area is used to output the current label text angle. The buttons call the appropriate VB Script routine to change the label text or angle.

III

Writing HTML

■ One final note about the placement of the VB Scripts in this HTML document. The functions are defined in the <HEAD> section—this is not necessary, but it is common practice, so that they will be defined before used. The last <SCRIPT>...</SCRIPT> section, though, which initializes the value of the form text area showing the current angle, is placed at the end of the HTML document to ensure that the object is defined and value set before it is called.

Listing 14.1   14LST06.HTM   VB Script Can Interact with Objects

```
<HTML>
<HEAD>
<OBJECT
     classid="clsid:{99B42120-6EC7-11CF-A6C7-00AA00A47DD2}"
     id=lblActiveLbl
     width=250
     height=250
     align=left
     hspace=20
     vspace=0
>
<PARAM NAME="_extentX" VALUE="150">
<PARAM NAME="_extentY" VALUE="700">
<PARAM NAME="Angle" VALUE="90">
<PARAM NAME="Alignment" VALUE="2">
<PARAM NAME="BackStyle" VALUE="0">
<PARAM NAME="Caption" VALUE="A Simple Desultory Label">
<PARAM NAME="FontName" VALUE="Arial">
<PARAM NAME="FontSize" VALUE="20">
<PARAM NAME="FontBold" VALUE="1">
<PARAM NAME="FrColor" VALUE="0">
</OBJECT>

<SCRIPT LANGUAGE="VBS">
<!--
Sub cmdChangeIt_onClick
     Dim TheForm
     Set TheForm = Document.LabelControls
     lblActiveLbl.Caption = TheForm.txtNewText.Value
End Sub
Sub cmdRotateP_onClick
     Dim TheForm
     Set TheForm = Document.LabelControls
     lblActiveLbl.Angle = lblActiveLbl.Angle + 5
      Document.LabelControls.sngAngle.Value = lblActiveLbl.Angle
End Sub
Sub cmdRotateM_onClick
     Dim TheForm
     Set TheForm = Document.LabelControls
     lblActiveLbl.Angle = lblActiveLbl.Angle - 5
      Document.LabelControls.sngAngle.Value = lblActiveLbl.Angle
End Sub
```

```
  -->
  </SCRIPT>

  <TITLE>VB Script and Object Manipulation</TITLE>
  </HEAD>
  <BODY>

  <FORM NAME="LabelControls">
  <TABLE>
  <TR><TD><INPUT TYPE="TEXT" NAME="txtNewText" SIZE=25></TD>
      <TD><INPUT TYPE="BUTTON" NAME="cmdChangeIt" VALUE="Change Text">
      </TD></TR>
  <TR><TD><INPUT TYPE="TEXT" NAME="sngAngle" SIZE=5></TD>
      <TD><INPUT TYPE="BUTTON" NAME="cmdRotateP" VALUE="Rotate Label +
  5">
      </TD></TR>
  <TR><TD></TD>
      <TD><INPUT TYPE="BUTTON" NAME="cmdRotateM" VALUE="Rotate Label -
  5">
      </TD></TR>
  </TABLE>
  </FORM>

  <SCRIPT LANGUAGE="VBS">
  <!--
  Document.LabelControls.sngAngle.Value = lblActiveLbl.Angle
  -->
  </SCRIPT>

  </BODY>
  </HTML>
```

Introducing ActiveX Controls

Microsoft's Object Linking and Embedding technology (OLE) has been one of
the most significant breakthroughs in application development thus far. OLE
itself is derived from the Component Object Model (COM) technology,
which is a standard and defines how OLE components, or objects, interact
with each other. Fortunately, you do not have to understand COM technology to utilize OLE functionality.

When application development was still in the 16-bit phase Microsoft's OLE
controls were in the .VBX format (Visual Basic Control). Since the 32-bit development boom, this has been replaced with its 32-bit counterpart—the
.OCX format. Not long after its introduction, when Microsoft really joined
the Internet race, .OCX file formats were taken to a new level—ActiveX
controls.

ActiveX/OCX—the Difference

Simply put, ActiveX controls are OLE components that can be inserted into Web pages. Therefore, ActiveX controls are in fact .OCX files that have been extended to Internet use. Currently, the new MS Internet Explorer fully supports ActiveX controls, and documents. With the help of a plug-in (NCompass), Netscape also can offer support.

ActiveX versus Java

Like a Java applet, an ActiveX control runs on the client computer within the browser. ActiveX gains its advantage, however, because it's language independent, which means developers can develop in any language supporting the COM technology. ActiveX is also able to support a wider range of GUI components than Java can currently offer.

Java has the advantage of being platform independent, while ActiveX controls can run only on client computers that support OLE 2.0. Java is also more secure; ActiveX controls are free to perform all types of functions on the client machine, while Java implements strict security guidelines for their programs.

How Can You Use ActiveX Controls on the Intranet?

Until the introduction of ActiveX, CGI scripts were used for most of the user interaction on the Internet. This worked fine and there didn't seem to be many complaints at the beginning. However, CGI had its limits. CGI programs ran on the server and would tie up server resources; they also proved to be rather slow, and error prone. CGI scripts were written in languages like Perl, which responded to HTML form events, and were limited to the events passed by the HTML form. Figure 14.3 shows an HTML form with buttons that send events (called actions) to a CGI script.

Note

CGI stands for Common Gateway Interface, and is a protocol that defines the way a Server script communicates with a client program. CGI is not a programming language, and therefore CGI scripts can be written in virtually any language that supports input/output streams. Perl is the most commonly used language for CGI programming because of its simplicity.

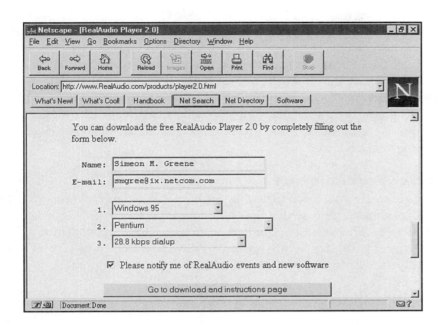

Fig. 14.3
An HTML form
with buttons that
will send an event
(called actions) to
a script on the
Web server.

ActiveX can offer a much richer set of components than CGI. With ActiveX, you can replace simple HTML forms with interactive spreadsheets, smarter buttons, Dialog boxes, and basically any OLE control you can think of. In addition to this, you can also add document objects from your favorite applications, such as MS Word, MS PowerPoint, and so on.

ActiveX Requirements

There are certain requirements that should be addressed before you delve into the world of ActiveX development. Questions that you should ask yourself before you begin are:

- What kind of environment does ActiveX support?
- What would I need to add to my Web server to make it ActiveX compatible?
- What will the clients that will be connecting to my server need in order to view the ActiveX controls on my server?
- What browsers support ActiveX?
- Will I need to distribute any plug-ins?

This section addresses these questions.

III

Writing HTML

The Client-Server Environment

ActiveX supports the client-server environment in this way: A client requests an HTML page through his/her browser from the Web server. If the HTML page contains an ActiveX control, the control is downloaded to the client side if it does not already exist. The ActiveX control, once downloaded, runs entirely on the client computer. Since all Intranet environments are also client-server environments, you need not worry about having to implement client-server architecture.

Server Requirements

A server doesn't need much to be able to serve ActiveX controls to clients. MIME types must be set so that the client program knows what type of data it will be receiving, and how to handle it. Setting the MIME types differs for each type of server. The MIME type for an ActiveX control is application/x-oleobject. See the user's manual of your Web Server to set this value correctly.

Note

MIME stands for Multipurpose Internet Mail Extension, and does more than handle the way mail is sent. MIME is used to define documents on a Web server so that client programs, such as browsers, can use these definitions to determine what application should be executed to display the document. These applications usually come in the form of a plug-in or helper application.

The MIME settings for ActiveX controls will be discussed again later in this chapter.

Client Requirements

Because ActiveX controls are downloaded from the server, and then run on the client machine, there are certain requirements that need to be met on the client machine for the control to be executed.

Required .DLLs

All ActiveX controls require the MFC40.dll in order to function. If the client computer does not have this control, the requested ActiveX control can't be displayed. This means that the .DLL must be downloaded and placed in the Windows\System subdirectory of the client before the ActiveX control. It may be a good idea to provide a link to download this .DLL before giving the user access to the Web page containing the ActiveX control. Any other .DLLs that are used by the control also need to be on the client computer.

For ActiveX documents, all clients being served need to have the viewer files for these documents in order to view them. This means that if you were serving MS Word documents, your clients must have either the entire MS Word application, or at least the viewer files. Viewer files for the MS Application suite are available at **http://www.microsoft.com/msoffice/msword/ internet/viewer/**.

Operating System Requirements

Unlike Java, ActiveX is not platform independent. The clients that you serve must have an operating system that supports the controls you develop or the documents you create.

Supported Browsers

Currently, ActiveX controls and documents are supported by the MS Internet Explorer version 3.0. At the time that this chapter was written, there was not a final version of MS Explorer, but a prereleased version is available with the ActiveX SDK. Unbeknownst to many, Netscape can also display ActiveX controls. The only difference is that Netscape requires a plug-in to do so. I found a great plug-in that supports ActiveX controls. The plug-in is called NCompass and is available at **http://www.ncompasslabs.com/**. NCompass enables you to display ActiveX controls and documents in the Netscape browser Window. It also provides the ability to download multiple .OCX files and dependent .DLLs together with the main control.

Using ActiveX Documents (or Document Objects) on the Intranet

Now that all the theory is over, it's time to put what you learned about ActiveX into action. In this section you learn how to add ActiveX documents (also called doc objects) to the HTML pages that you serve on your corporate Intranet.

Choosing a Suite of Applications

The first step to serving ActiveX documents is to choose a suite of applications to serve. Currently, only MS Office documents are supported as ActiveX documents, so this is the suite of applications discussed throughout this chapter. Once the application suite is chosen, the next step is to provide a means for your clients to view these applications. This means providing access for clients to download the viewer files, or notifying browsers with an HTML page prior to the page containing the document that they need to have the MS Office package (or one of its applications) to view the following

ActiveX documents. Viewers that already have these files ignore this warning and proceed to viewing the files. In order to view these files as ActiveX documents, the servers and clients need to have the correct MIME types configured for serving and receiving them. This is done automatically by the NCompass plug-in for Netscape, or by MS Explorer 3.0. Once this is done, ActiveX documents are available for viewing through the browser window.

Embedding Documents into Your Web Page

Embedding a document into your Web page is as simple as providing a direct link to the document using the HREF tag. For example, if you want to provide a link to a MS Word document, use:

```
<A HREF="http://www.mysite.com/documents/mydoc.doc>
```

and the user sees the specified Word document, appear in their browser window. An example of a MS Word document in a Netscape Browser (made possible by the NCompass plug-in) is shown in figure 14.4.

Fig. 14.4
An MS Word document embedded in a Netscape Browser (made possible by the NCompass plug-in).

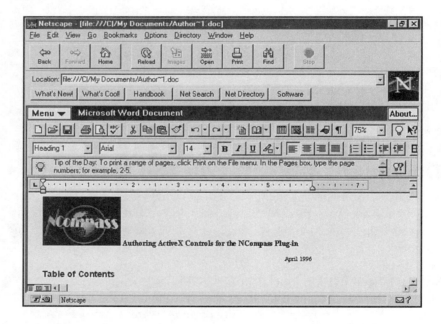

An ActiveX document can also be viewed by Netscape on the local machine. To do this, simply choose File from the menu bar, then Open file... from that menu. From here, you can choose any MS Word, MS PowerPoint, MS Graph, or MS Excel document you wish to view.

A Typical Example

A good example for using ActiveX documents on your company's Intranet can be found at **http://www.ncompasslabs.com/ActiveX,** Office Integration (see figure 14.5). This example shows how using ActiveX documents can save valuable time, and be efficient for use on the corporate Intranet.

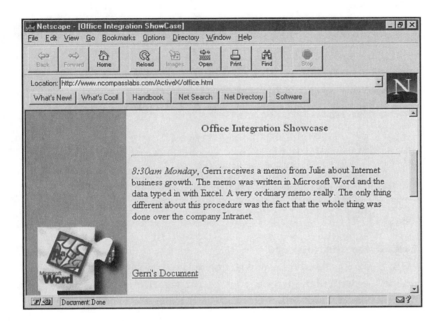

Fig. 14.5
Office integration at Ncompasslabs.com.

Using ActiveX Controls on the Intranet

The power of ActiveX is truly expressed by ActiveX controls. ActiveX controls expand power of plain CGI forms and buttons by providing customizable buttons, list boxes, and other Windows components. ActiveX controls also enable developers to make custom controls that can display movies, connect to databases, and display specialized text (such as vertically positioned).

Embedding Controls into Your Web Page

Embedding controls into your Web page is a little more challenging than pointing to an ActiveX document. ActiveX controls must be embedded using the EMBED tag (for Netscape), or the OBJECT tag (for MS Explorer). Both tags can be used together in a Web page to make the control visible to users with either browser. Also, in order to embed an ActiveX control, you need to have

III

Writing HTML

the MSADK (Microsoft ActiveX Development Kit) and use its STM tool to create a stream file for the control. The STM tool is described later in this chapter. The control that you are attempting to embed must also be insertable. You can check to see if the control is insertable by checking the Insert Object menu choice for its availability in MS Word, or a similar Microsoft application. The following HTML script shows an example of embedding a control for Netscape and MS Explorer—the control will only appear once, as either <EMBED> tag will place it into Netscape or <OBJECT> will put it into Explorer:

```
<html>
<head><title>Sample ActiveX Control</title></head>
Enter some text here
<!Embed an ActiveX control for Netscape (using the Ncompass plug-
➥in)>
<EMBED SRC="filename.stm" code="filename.ocx" width=300 height=250
alt="ActiveX control">

<!Embed the same control for MS Explorer>
<OBJECT DATA="filename.stm" code="filename.ocx width=300
➥height=250>
</OBJECT>
<html>
```

The EMBED Tag for Netscape

The EMBED tag is used in Netscape to notify the browser that a plug-in is needed for the particular references within the tag. In the case of an ActiveX control, the EMBED tag notifies Netscape that it needs to run the NCompass plug-in to display the control. The EMBED tag takes five attributes to describe an ActiveX control to Netscape. Table 14.1 shows these attributes and their description.

Table 14.1 Attributes of the EMBED Tag	
Attribute	**Description**
SRC	Specifies the location (source) of the specified document.
CODE	Specifies the binary code that corresponds to the source.
HEIGHT	Specifies the height that Netscape should use to draw a frame for the control.
WIDTH	Specifies the width that Netscape should use to draw a frame for the control.
ALT	Specifies alternative text for the control should the client not be able to display it.

The Object Tag for MS Explorer

The OBJECT tag is used by MS Explorer to define a specified object for MS Explorer to display. Table 14.2 shows the attributes of the OBJECT tag, and their descriptions.

Table 14.2 The OBJECT Tag Attributes	
Attribute	**Description**
DATA	Specifies the location (source) of the specified document.
CODE	Specifies the location of the binary definition that corresponds to the source.
WIDTH	Specifies the width that MS Explorer should use to draw a frame for the specified control.
HEIGHT	Specifies the height that MS Explorer should use to draw a frame for the specified control.

The source descriptor should point to the .stm file, which contains the Persistent Properties of the specified control. This file is created by using the STM Tool from the MSADK.

The code descriptor should point to the actual control, which should be an .OCX file.

Where to Get More Information on ActiveX

For more information on ActiveX controls and for examples of the different controls available and how they are used, check out the following URLs:

http://www.ncompasslabs.com/ (The NCompass home page)

http://www.microsoft.com/ie/ (Microsoft's Internet Explorer Web site)

http://www.microsoft.com/activex/controls (Microsoft's ActiveX Control Web site)

http://www.dclgroup.com/ (The Data-Core home page)

III

Writing HTML

CHAPTER 15

Search Engines and Annotation Systems

The previous chapters in this book have taught us the virtue of using the World Wide Web paradigm for serving internal documents on the Corporate Network and how to piece together the necessary software and systems that form parts of the whole jigsaw puzzle. The chapters that follow teach us how to use the tools acquired in the first part of the book to build several useful applications that can help the Web serve the Intranet better.

In this chapter, you learn:

- How to build simple search and retrieval scripts for simple databases
- How to setup and use an advanced search engine to search through the entire Intranet
- How to use Web technology as a workgroup tool, including document annotation capabilities and Web conferencing systems

Searching Simple Databases

In this section, we will build a sample search script that can search through a company's phonelist and retrieve the requested information, based on a query. Although this is considered a simple database application, it differs from what is normally thought of as a database because users can only view, but not enter, information. Creating Web database applications that can modify, add, and delete from databases is covered in a later chapter; this chapter is more concerned with search and retrieve applications that are used as guide maps around the vast Web. These applications provide a simple form-query-result paradigm to navigate the Web.

Even though many types of data in an organization are maintained centrally, often they need to be made available to hundreds, or even thousands of users, either internally or externally. Examples of this type of data include a company phone and address book, a product catalog that maps product numbers to titles, or a list of regional sales offices and contacts. All of these types of information can be stored in a relational database, but there's really no need for anything more than a simple text file. If the goal is to make information available, quickly and easily, a simple Web search routine can achieve the desired result without all the headaches of maintenance that is associated with a Relational Database.

> **Note**
>
> The examples in this chapter are written using Perl. Since Perl is an open scripting language, these examples are not limited to any particular Operating System or Web Server.

Example Search Scenario

In our example, we will consider a simple text file containing the names and phone numbers of employees in a fictitious company called ABC Inc. It is not uncommon for companies to store employee names and phone numbers electronically. In a typical scenario, the Human Resources department would print out the document and hand out copies to all the employees. ABC Inc. however, is on the cutting edge of technology, as it has employed an Intranet and intends to post the document on the local Web for its employees' benefit. It is up to us to implement a search functionality on the Intranet to enable the user to search for a specific employee's phone number by the employee's name.

Grepping for data

At the heart of the search is the grep command, which simply looks for pattern matches in a file. One of the benefits of this approach is that the text file need not be in any certain format. Grep just reads each line of the file for a match; it doesn't care how many columns there are or what characters are used to separate fields. Consequently, the phone book script can be used to search any text file database.

Tip

Grep is a native UNIX command. The Windows NT version of grep (grep.exe) is included with the Windows NT Resource Kit.

Listing 15.1   A simple search program to sift through a phone list

```
# search.pl

# Define the location of the database
$DATABASE="\\web_root\\cgi-bin\\phone.txt";

# Define the path to cgiparse
$CGIPATH="\\web_root\\cgi-bin";
# Convert form data to variables
eval '$CGIPATH\\test\\cgiparse -form -prefix $';

# Determine the age of the database
$mod_date=int(-M $DATABASE);

#Display the age of the database and generate the search form
print <<EOM;
Content-type: text/html

<TITLE>Database Search</TITLE>
<BODY>
<H1>Database Search</H1>
The database was updated $mod_date days ago.<p>
<FORM ACTION="/cgi-bin/search.pl" METHOD="POST">
Search for: <INPUT TYPE="TEXT" NAME="QUERY">
<INPUT TYPE="SUBMIT" VALUE="SEARCH">
</FORM>
<p><hr><p>
EOM

# Do the search only if a query was entered
if (length($query)>0) {
  print <<EOM;
Search for <B>$query</B> yields these entries:
<PRE>
EOM

#Inform user if search is unsuccessful
$answer = 'grep -i $query $DATABASE';
if (!$answer) { print "Search was unsuccessful\n" ;}
else { print $answer\n" ; }

print <<EOM;
</PRE>
</BODY>
EOM
}
```

Fig. 15.1
This generalized database search form is used with the search script to search any text file database.

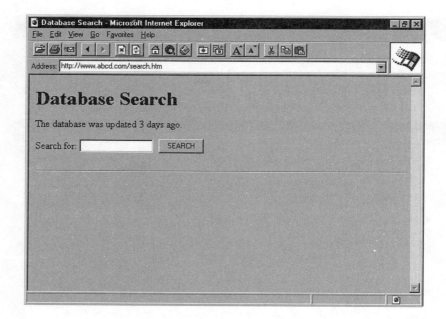

Note

Though the above script assumes a windows based Web server, it can be generalized to suit any operating system. When implementing on a UNIX system, the data path has to be modified to replace "\\" with "/".

To use the script for data other than the phone book, simply change the name and location of the text file containing the desired information. Because the script uses the generic grep command, it can be used with almost any text file for any purpose. This script utilizes the *cgiparse* program to parse the data sent to it. This utility is freely available via anonymous ftp from **ftp.ncsa.uiuc.edu**.

Tip

You can make searches case-sensitive by removing the -i option from the grep command.

Generating Text Files from Databases

To take advantage of the simple search routine above, you must have some text file data to start with. If your data is currently in another format, such as a proprietary database, you must first convert it to an ASCII text file. You can easily create the necessary text file by exporting the data from the native format to ASCII text. Almost all databases include the capability to export to text files.

After the text file has been created, you simply need to specify its path in the search script.

Choosing Between Several Databases

With a few simple modifications, you can use the script generically to search one of many databases that all have different paths. This is done most efficiently in one of two ways. You can allow the database to be chosen by selecting one of several hyperlinks, in which case extra path information in the URL can be used to specify the database. Alternately you can allow the user to choose which database to search in a fill-in form.

Choosing via Hyperlinks

Suppose you want users to be able to choose between several different divisional phone books. One way to do this is to include a pre-search page on which the user selects the database by clicking the appropriate hyperlink. Each link calls the same database search script, but each includes extra path information containing the path to the database. The following HTML demonstrates how the hyperlinks are constructed.

```
<H2>Company Phonebooks</H2>
<A HREF="/cgi-bin/search.pl/db/IAphone.txt">Iowa Locations</A>
<A HREF="/cgi-bin/search.pl/db/CAphone.txt">California Locations<A>
<A HREF="/cgi-bin/search.pl/db/KSphone.txt">Kansas Locations</A>
```

The name of the search script in this example is `/cgi-bin/search.pl` and the databases are named "/db/IAphone.txt," and so on. The search script itself needs to be modified to use the extra path information.

First, the name of the database to search is specified in the extra path information rather than hard-coded into the script. Therefore, the line at the top

III

Writing HTML

of the script, which specifies the path to the data, needs to read the extra path information. This is done by reading the PATH_INFO environment variable. In Perl, the syntax for this is:

```
$DATABASE=$ENV{"PATH_INFO"};
```

Second, the ACTION attribute of the form, which is generated inside the script, needs to specify the path to the database. This way, after the user performs the initial query, the correct database is still in use. This is accomplished by changing the <FORM ACTION...> line to:

```
<FORM ACTION="/cgi-bin/search.pl$DATABASE">
```

> **Note**
>
> No slash (/) is necessary to separate the script name (/cgi-bin/search) from the extra path information because $DATABASE already begins with a slash.

These are the two modifications necessary to implement choosing a database via hyperlinks. The hyperlinks to other databases are now included in the search form. The resulting form is shown in figure 15.2. The complete modified script code is included below. Only new or changed lines have been commented.

Listing 15.2   Choosing databases using URLs

```
# search2.pl

# Get database name from extra path info.
$DATABASE=$ENV{"PATH_INFO"};

$CGIPATH="\\web_root\\cgi-bin";
eval '$CGIPATH\\test\\cgiparse -form -prefix $';

$mod_date=int(-M $DATABASE);

# Show the current database and list other available databases.
# The <FORM ACTION ...> line now includes the database name as extra
path info.
print <<EOM;
Content-type: text/html

<TITLE>Database Search</TITLE>
<BODY>
<H1>Database Search</H1>
Current database is $DATABASE.          Show the current database
It was updated $mod_date days ago.<P>
You can change to one of the following databases at any time:<P>
<A HREF="/cgi-bin/search/db/IAphone.txt">Iowa Location</A><BR>
```

```
<A HREF="/cgi-bin/search/db/CAphone.txt">California Locations</A><BR>
<A HREF="/cgi-bin/search/db/KSphone.txt">Kansas Locations</A><P>
<FORM ACTION="/cgi-bin/search2.pl$DATABASE" METHOD="POST">
Search for: <INPUT TYPE="TEXT" NAME="QUERY">
<INPUT TYPE="SUBMIT" VALUE=" Search ">
</FORM>
<p><hr><p>
EOM

if (length($query)>0) {
  print <<EOM;
Search for <B>$query</B> yields these entries:
<PRE>
EOM

$answer = 'grep -i $query $DATABASE';
if (!$answer) { print "Search was unsuccessful\n" ;}
else { print $answer\n" ; }

print <<EOM;
</PRE>
</BODY>
EOM
}
```

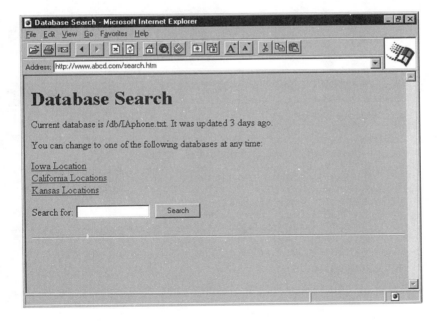

Fig. 15.2
This method uses hyperlinks to select a new search database.

Choosing via a Form

Depending on the application, it may be more convenient for users to choose their database via a form rather than via hyperlinks. The initial form uses

Radio buttons to choose the desired database, and after that the chosen database is active for all searches. Figure 15.3 shows the initial form used to select the database. The form code is included below.

Fig. 15.3
In this form, you select the search database and then proceed to the search form.

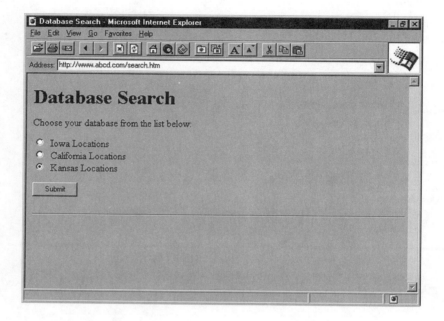

Listing 15.3   Choosing search database via a form

```
<TITLE>Database Search</TITLE>
<BODY>
<H1>Database Search</H1>
Choose your database from the list below:<P>
<FORM ACTION="/cgi-bin/search3.pl" METHOD="POST">
<INPUT TYPE="RADIO" NAME="DATABASE" VALUE="/db/IAphone.txt"
➥CHECKED>Iowa Locations<BR>
<INPUT TYPE="RADIO" NAME="DATABASE" VALUE="/db/
➥CAphone.txt">California Locations<BR>
<INPUT TYPE="RADIO" NAME="DATABASE" VALUE="/db/KSphone.txt">Kansas
➥Locations<P>
<INPUT TYPE="SUBMIT" VALUE=" Submit ">
</FORM>
<p><hr><p>
```

The initial selection form passes the path of the chosen database in the input field named "DATABASE," so only two modifications are necessary to the original search script that receives this information. First, the path to the database is now read from the initial selection form, so a separate line defining

$DATABASE is no longer necessary. Second, the search form must have a way to keep track of the current database. This is conveniently accomplished by including a hidden input field in the search form named "DATABASE." This way, whether the search form is called from itself or from the initial selection form, it always knows the path to the correct database. The code for the search script is included below. Only the new or changed lines are commented. The resulting search form appears in figure 15.4.

Listing 15.4   Passing database name via hidden form fields

```
# search3.pl

$CGIPATH="\\web_root\\cgi-bin";
eval '$CGIPATH\\test\\cgiparse -form -prefix $';
# $DATABASE is now defined as a form variable

$mod_date=int(-M $DATABASE);

# A hidden field <INPUT TYPE="HIDDEN" NAME="DATABASE" ...> stores the
➥database path.
print <<EOM;
Content-type: text/html

<TITLE>Database Search</TITLE>
<BODY>
<H1>Database Search</H1>
The current database is $DATABASE.
The database was updated $mod_date days ago.<p>
<FORM ACTION="/cgi-bin/search3.pl" METHOD="POST">
<INPUT TYPE="HIDDEN" NAME="DATABASE" VALUE="$DATABASE">
Search for: <INPUT TYPE="TEXT" NAME="QUERY">
<INPUT TYPE="SUBMIT" VALUE=" Search ">
</FORM>
<p><hr><p>
EOM

if (length($query)>0) {
  print <<EOM;
Search for <B>$query</B> yields these entries:
<PRE>
EOM

$answer = 'grep -i $query $DATABASE';
if (!$answer) { print "Search was unsuccessful\n" ;}
else { print $answer\n" ; }

print <<EOM;
</PRE>
</BODY>
EOM
}
```

III

Writing HTML

Fig. 15.4
Once the search database is selected in a separate form, this form is used to perform the search.

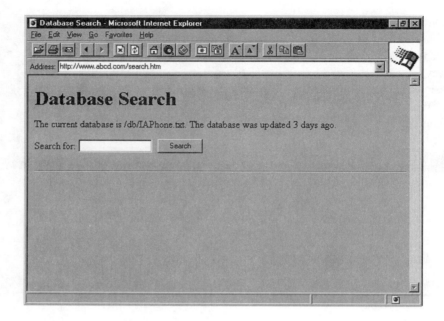

Searching Multiple Files and Directories

The previous examples searched only one file at a time. However, grep is flexible enough to search multiple files and directories simultaneously.

Searching Multiple Files

In the previous example, the user was allowed to choose between several different phone directories. The script is easily modified to search multiple files simultaneously. Instead of specifying one file in the $DATABASE environment variable, specify a path to the directory containing the phone text files (\db). So, the line beginning $DATABASE= in the original script (search.pl) changes to:

```
$DATABASE="\\db\\*.txt";
```

The grep command now searches for the desired information in all files in the \db directory that correspond to the wildcard pattern specified.

Searching Multiple Directories

Taking it a step further, the grep command can also accept multiple files in different directories. For example, you can specify the following database files:

```
$DATABASE="\\db\\phone*.txt \\db2\\address*.txt"
```

Now, the grep command searches all .TXT files in the \db directory beginning with phone and all .TXT files in the \db2 directory beginning with address.

Accommodating Form-less Browsers

Although most Web browsers today have forms capability, not all do. To allow these browsers to search for information, it's common to offer an alphabetical or numerical index of data as an alternative to entering a form-based query. Typically, you create a hyperlink for each letter of the alphabet and specify an URL for each hyperlink that performs the appropriate search. For example, in a phone book listing where last names are listed first, you could search for capital C's at the beginning of a line to get a listing of all last names beginning with C. To create a hypertext index that can submit this type of search automatically, write:

Listing 15.5   Breaking down databases alphabetically

```
<H1>Phone Book Index</H1>
Click on a letter to see last names beginning with that letter.<P>
<A HREF="/cgi-bin/search?A">%26A</A>
<A HREF="/cgi-bin/search?B">%2lb</C>
...
<A HREF="/cgi-bin/search?Z">%26Z</Z>
```

Note

The queries in this example begin with the caret (%26 = "[af]") to force grep to look for the specified character at the beginning of a line.

Searching an Entire Web Server

So far, we have only looked at searching collections of simple text files. This is fine, as long as users are expected to search through specific files only. A good implementation of a Web server, however, is one that includes the capability to search for words anywhere on the server, including plain text and HTML files. It's theoretically possible to simply grep all HTML and TXT files under the document root (and other aliased directories), but this can be very time-consuming if more than a handful of documents are present.

The solution to the problem of searching a large Web server is similar to that used by other types of databases. We maintain a compact index that summarizes the information present in the Web server's content area. As data is

III

Writing HTML

added to the database, we just keep updating the index file. The usual method of maintaining the integrity of the index file is to run a nightly (or more frequent) indexing program that generates a full-text index of the entire server in a more compact format than the data itself.

Indexing with ICE

A popular indexing and searching solution on the Web is ICE, written in Perl by Christian Neuss in Germany. It's freely available on the Internet from **http://www.informatik.th-darmstadt.de/~neuss/** and is included on the Webmaster CD. In the discussion that follows, we cover ICE, how it works, and how it can be modified to include even more features. By default, ICE includes the following features:

- Whole-word searching using Boolean operators (AND and OR)
- Case-sensitive or case-insensitive searching
- Hypertext presentation of scored results
- The ability to look for similarly-spelled words in a dictionary
- The ability to find related words and topics in a thesaurus
- The ability to limit searches to a specified directory tree

ICE presents results in a convenient hypertext format. It displays results using both document titles (as specified by HTML <TITLE> tags) and physical file names. Search results are scored, or weighted, based on the number of occurrences of the search word, or words, inside documents.

Note

Since ICE is written completely in the Perl programming language, the software works under UNIX as well as under MacOS and Windows.

The ICE Index Builder

The heart of ICE is a Perl program that reads every file on the Web server and constructs a full-text index. The index builder, "ice-idx.pl" in the default distribution, has a simple method of operation. The server administrator specifies the locations and extensions (TXT, HTML, etc.) of files to be indexed. When we run ice-idx.pl, it reads every file in the specified directories and stores the index information in one large index file (by default, index.idx). The words in each file are alphabetized and counted for use in scoring the search results when a search is made. The format of the index file is simple:

Listing 15.6   Format of ICE Index file

```
@ffilename
@ttitle
word1 count1
word2 count2
word3 count3
...
@ffilename
@ttitle
word1 count1
...
```

Running the Index Builder

The index builder is run nightly, or at some other regular interval, so that search results are always based on updated information. Normally, ICE indexes the entire contents of directories specified by the administrator, but it can be modified to index only new or modified files, as determined by the last modification dates on files. This saves a little time, although ICE zips right along as it is. On a fast machine, ICE can index 2-5M of files in under 15 seconds, depending on the nature of the files. Assuming an average HTML file size of 10K, that's 200-500 separate documents.

Windows NT users can use the native at command to schedule the indexing utility. UNIX users can use cron for scheduling.

Note

It's often a good idea to schedule at or cron jobs at odd times because many other jobs run on the hour by necessity or convention. Running jobs on the hour that don't have to be run this way increases the load on the machine unnecessarily.

Tip

The Windows NT scheduler service has to be running in order to schedule jobs using the at command.

Space Considerations

Searching an index file is much faster than using grep or a similar utility to search an entire Web server; however, there is a definite space/performance tradeoff. Because ICE stores the contents of every document in the index file, the index file could theoretically grow as large as the sum of all the files indexed. The actual "compression" ratio is closer to 2:1 for HTML because ICE

III

Writing HTML

ignores HTML formatting tags, numbers, and special characters. In addition, typical documents use many words multiple times, but ICE stores them only once, along with a word count.

> **Note**
>
> When planning your Web server, be sure to include enough space for index files if you plan to offer full-featured searching.

The Search Engine

The HTML that produces the ICE search form is actually generated from within a script (ice-form.pl), but calls the main search engine (ice.pl) to do most of the search work. The search simply reads the index file previously generated by the index builder. As the search engine reads consecutively through the file, it simply outputs the names and titles of all documents containing the search word or words. The search form itself and the search engine can be modified to produce output in any format desired by editing the Perl code.

Tips and Tricks

The ICE search engine is powerful and useful by itself. There's always room for improvement, however. This section discusses several modifications you can make to ICE to implement additional features.

Directory Context

A very useful feature of ICE is the ability to specify an optional directory context in the search form. This way, you can use the same ICE code to conduct both local and global searches. For example, suppose you're running an internal server that contains several policy manuals and you want each of them to be searchable individually, as well as together. You could simply require that users of the system enter the optional directory context themselves; however, a more convenient way is to replace the optional directory context box with radio buttons that can be used to select the desired manual.

A more programming-intensive method is to provide a link to the search page on the index page of each manual. The URL in the link can include the optional directory context so that users don't have to enter this themselves. This way, when a user clicks the link to the search page from within a given manual section, the search form automatically includes the correct directory context. For example, you can tell the ICE search to look only in the /benefits directory by including the following hyperink on the Benefits page:

```
<A HREF="/cgi-bin/ice-form.pl?context=%2Fbenefits>Search this
manual</A>
```

> **Note**
>
> The slash (/) in front of benefits must be encoded in its ASCII representation ("%2F") for the link to work properly.

In order for this to work, you'll need to make the following necessary modifications to ice-form.pl:

- Set the variable $CONTEXT at the beginning of the script (using cgiparse or your favorite parsing utility) based on what was passed in from the search URL.

- Automatically display the value of $CONTEXT in the optional directory context box (`<INPUT TYPE="TEXT" NAME="CONTEXT" VALUE="$CONTEXT">`).

Speed Enhancements

If the size of your index file grows larger than two or three megabytes, searches take several seconds to complete, due to the time required to read through the entire index file during each search. A simple way to improve this situation is to build several smaller index files (say, one for each major directory on your server), rather than one large one. However, this means you can no longer conduct a single, global search of your server.

A more attractive way to break up the large index file is to split it up into several smaller ones, where each small index file still contains an index for every file searched, but only those words beginning with certain letters. For example, ice-a.idx contains all words beginning with "a," ice-b.idx contains all words beginning with "b," and so on. This way, when a query is entered, the search engine is able to narrow down the search immediately based on the first letter of the query.

> **Note**
>
> In the event that your server outgrows the first-letter indexing scheme, the same technique can be used to further break up files by using unique combinations of the first two letters of a query, and so on.

In order to break up the large index file alphabetically, you need to modify the ICE index builder (ice-idx.pl) to write to multiple index files while building the code. The search engine (ice.pl) also needs to be modified to auto-select the index file based on the first letter of the query.

Searching for Words Near Each Other

Although ICE allows the use of AND and OR operators to modify searches, it only looks for words meeting these requirements anywhere in the same document. It would be nice to be able to specify how close to each other the words must appear, as well. The difficulty with this kind of a search is that the ICE index doesn't specify how close to each other words are in a document. There are two ways to overcome this.

First, you can modify the index builder to store word position information, as well as word count. For example, if the words "bad" and "dog" each occur three times in a file, their index entries might look like this:

```
bad 3 26 42 66
dog 3 4 9 27
```

In this case, 3 is the number of occurrences, and the remaining numbers indicate that "dog" is the 4th, 9th, and 27th word in the file. When a search for "bad dog" is entered, the search engine first checks if both "bad" and "dog" are in any documents, and then whether any of the word positions for "bad" are exactly one less than any of those for "dog." In this case, that is true, as "bad" occurs in position 26 and "dog" occurs in position 27.

There's another way to search for words near each other. After a search is entered and files containing both words are found, those files can simply be read by the search program word-by-word, looking for the target words near each other. Using this method, the index builder itself doesn't have to be modified. However, the first method usually results in faster searches because the extra work is done primarily by the index builder rather than by the search engine in real-time.

WAIS

Yet another popular freeware search utility for Web and Gopher servers running on Windows NT, is the European Microsoft windows NT Academic Center's (EMWAC) Wide Area Information Server (WAIS). It's included in the Webmaster CD.

WAIS Architecture

WAIS is comprised of three basic components:

- WAISSERV—a protocol handler and search engine
- WAISINDEX—the indexing utility
- WAISLOOK—the search utility

The WAIS Search engine implements features like Boolean (and, or, not) searches and synonym files.

WAIS Operation

Operation of WAIS is similar to that of ICE. It involves creation and periodic updating of the index files.

Note

The configuration information of WAIS is setup using the WAIS Control Panel Applet.

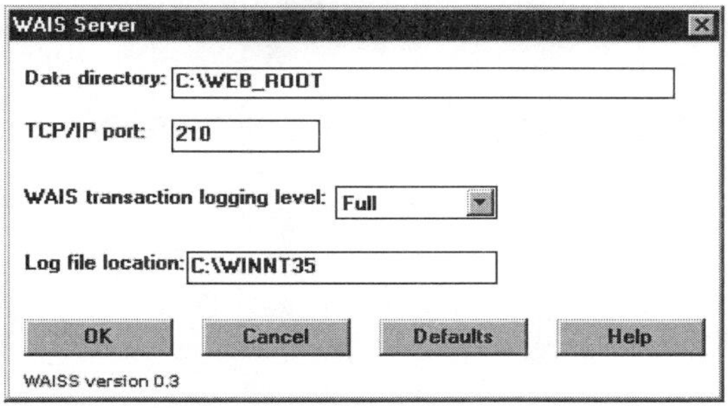

Fig. 15.5
WAIS Server configuration applet in the control panel.

Once the configuration information is setup, the index can then be created using the WAISINDX program. The WAISINDX program can be used to create indexes that are intended to be used internally, within the site, or it can be used with the -export option, which enables us to register it with the database of databases, thus opening our database to public use. To register, send the index.src file to the following e-mail addresses:

```
wais-directory-of-servers@cnidr.org
wais-directory-of-servers@quake.think.com
```

Note

To export a WAIS database and register it with the WAIS Database of databases, check the information in index.src; make sure it contains an IP address and a DNS name, as well as the TCP/IP port under which the WAIS Server is running.

Other Web Search Solutions

While the Net seems vastly endless in its repertoire of solutions to choose from, it becomes more and more incumbent upon us to thoroughly study the feature sets of the various search systems. We must decide on one that best suits our Web site with respect to Operating System, Web Server, volume and value of content, security, and so on. The following list should serve as a basic checklist of things to consider before deciding on any one of the solutions:

- Compatibility with Operating System
- Compatibility with Web Server
- Boolean Searches (and, or, not operators)
- Synonym searches
- Plural searches (a search for "woman" also returns all documents with reference to "women")
- Weighted results
- Ease of installation and integration
- Amount of programming involved

The following table shows a list of available commercial, shareware, and freeware Search systems that can be used on a Web site. It is important to note that this list is, by no means, exhaustive.

Product	Company	Address
Excite	Architext Software	www.excite.com
Livelink Search	OpenText Corp	www.opentext.com
Verity	Verity Inc	www.verity.com
CompasSearch	CompasWare development Inc	www.compasware.com
NetAnswer	Dataware Technologies Inc	www.dataware.com
Fulcrum Search server	Fulcrum Technologies Inc	www.fultech.com

Including Content

A very desirable enhancement to a search system is the inclusion of some sort of summary of each document presented in the search results. The Lycos Web searcher does exactly this by displaying the first couple of sentences of each document on its search results page. This enables users to find the documents most relevant to their topic of interest quickly.

To include summary content, store the first 50-100 words in every document in the index file created by the index builder. Doing this, however, requires yet more storage space for the index file, and therefore may not be desirable.

Web Conferencing—Discussion and Annotation Systems

The World Wide Web was originally developed as a medium for scientific and technical exchange. One of the important elements of that exchange is the sharing of ideas about other people's work. This has been common on UseNet news for many years now, but articles are limited largely to plain ASCII text. The Web, with its superior hypertext presentation, presents opportunities for richer exchange, but has developed as a remarkably one-sided communications medium thus far. This is unfortunate for those who would like to take advantage of the Web's superior document capabilities along with the flexibility and interactivity of UseNet.

Why is the Web one-way?

In spite of various techniques, such as CGI scripting, the World Wide Web is still primarily a one-way medium, with the client issuing requests and the server supplying requested documents. These limitations are not fundamental to either the HTTP or HTML. The ingredients necessary for world-wide annotation of Web documents and posting new documents to servers are already in place, but these have not yet been implemented. There are, however, a few exceptions; we will discuss these in the following section.

Group Annotations

The most notable exception is NCSA Mosaic, which supported a feature called *group annotations* in the first few versions. This feature enables users to post text-only annotations to documents by sending annotations to a group annotation server, which NCSA provided with earlier versions of their Web server. Group annotations, however, have been abandoned in later versions of Mosaic in favor of the HTTP 1.0 protocol, which supports group annotations differently.

CGI and HTTP POST

The second exception is CGI scripting, which enables the server to both send and receive data. The data is usually simple text, such as a query or form information, but it can also be an entire document, such as an HTML file, spreadsheet, or even an executable program. The ability to post documents to CGI scripts, however, is not particularly useful, as of yet, because Web clients don't support it. What would be useful is an introduction of a <FILE> element to forms, which, when selected, would ask the user to specify the name of a local file to be sent to the server when the form is submitted. This would be a convenient way to upload documents to a Web server, similar to the way that documents are uploaded to CompuServe or bulletin board systems.

Because HTTP and HTML already support most (if not all) of the ingredients necessary for a more interactive Web, it's probably only a matter of time before these will be incorporated into browsers and servers alike. In the meantime, however, prototypes of what the future holds have been constructed using news, e-mail, and CGI scripts.

News and the Web

UseNet news makes available today in plain ASCII text some of what the Web will do tomorrow in HTML. News can effectively be used as a private or public tool for information exchange. Public newsgroups are the most familiar; with world-wide distribution, they enable anyone to post articles. By running your own news server, you can also create entirely private newsgroups (as for an internal bulletin board system) or semi-private groups, which the public can read but not post to. The capability to control who can read news and who can post to a local server makes news a useful tool for workgroup discussion.

> **Tip**
>
> Many Web browsers can both read and post news. This simplifies the use of both news and hypertext in an organizational context by providing a common interface for viewing both kinds of documents.

While news is an excellent medium for conducting entirely private (inside a corporate network) or entirely public conversations (UseNet), it's not as well suited for allowing discussions between a select group of individuals located all over the world. It's possible to create a special news server for this purpose and use password security to ensure that only the intended group of people can read or post news to the server. However, users of the system would be inconvenienced because most news readers expect to connect to one news server only. If users were already connecting to another news server to receive public news, they would have to change the configuration information in their news reader in order to connect to the special server. Fortunately, there are other answers to this problem.

Hypermail

E-mail is a more flexible method of having semi-private discussions among people all around a large Intranet. Using a mailing list server (list server), it is possible to create a single e-mail address for a whole group of people. When an item is sent to the mailing list address, it's forwarded to all members of the list. This approach has several advantages over running a news server, in addition to the previously mentioned convenience issue.

> **Tip**
>
> Through various e-mail gateways, it's possible to do almost anything by e-mail that can be done on FTP, Gopher, news, or the Web, only slower.

A very nice complement to a mailing list is a *mailing list archive*, which stores past items on the mailing list. Public mailing list archives can be stored on the Web for the benefit of later reference. A really powerful tool called *hypermail* converts a mailing list archive into a hypertext list of messages, neatly organized to show message threads. Mail archives converted with hypermail can be sorted by author, subject, or date.

> **Tip**
>
> A commercial mail server for Windows NT, which integrates other features such as List Server, Hypermail, and so on, is NTMail. Information on NTMail is available at **http://www.mortimer.com/ntmail/default.htm**.

> **Tip**
>
> Hypermail for UNIX is available free of charge under a license agreement, at **http://www.eit.com/software/hypermail/**.

III

Writing HTML

Annotation Systems

While e-mail and news are both valuable tools for workgroup discussion, they still lack an important feature: the ability to make comments on a document in the document itself. In the paper world, this is accomplished with the infamous red pen. However, the equivalent of the editor's pen in the world of hypertext markup is just beginning to manifest. The ultimate in annotation would be the ability to attach comments, or even files of any type, anywhere inside an HTML document. For now, however, it's at least possible to add comments to the end of an HTML page. Several people are working on annotation systems using existing Web technology. The following sections take a brief look at a few of them.

HyperNews

Not to be confused with hypermail, HyperNews does not actually use the UseNet news protocol, but it allows a similar discussion format and is patterned after UseNet. You can see examples of HyperNews and find out more about it at **http://union.ncsa.uiuc.edu/HyperNews/get/ hypernews.html**. Figure 15.6 shows a sample screen of a browser access to a HyperNews server.

Fig. 15.6
A sample
HyperNews
session.

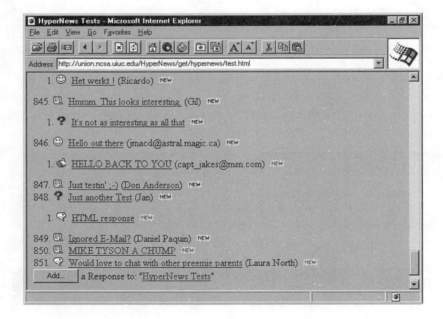

W3 Interactive Talk (WIT)

A similar system originating at CERN allows new "proposals," or comments, to be submitted in response to a given document. This is a practical way for a group of engineers, for example, to discuss a document. Some degree of security is possible by requiring users to have a valid username and password before they can post comments. This can be combined with user authorization procedures to control who can see documents, as well. More information on W3 Interactive Talk is available at **http://www.w3.org/hypertext/ WWW/WIT/User/Overview.html.**

Web Conferencing Systems

The glaring deficiency of the Web, namely, that it has been a one-way drive, has not gone unnoticed, however. There are quite a few systems available that employ the traditional client/server architecture to implement Web conferencing systems.

One commercially available Web conferencing product for Windows NT is WebNotes, a product of OS TECHnologies Corporation. WebNotes is a client/server solution where the "client" is any HTML capable Web browser (Mosaic, Netscape, and so on). The WebNotes server software maintains discussion threads of topics of discussion, remembers "already-seen" messages by users, and enables users to post discussion material, either as text or as HTML documents with inline graphics. It also employs a text search engine that facilitates retrieving discussions based on the result of a search query. Figures 15.7 and 15.8 show sample screens of discussion threads and the general navigation concepts.

> **Note**
>
> More information and a live demonstration of WebNotes can be found on OS TECHnologies' home page at **http://www.ostech.com**.

Yet another powerful freeware Web Conferencing system for UNIX is COW-conferencing on Web.

Other Web conferencing systems that can be found on the Net include, but are not limited to:

- Agora Web Conferencing System—**http://www.ontrac.yorku.ca/ agora**
- WebBoard from O'Reilly and associates—**http://webboard. ora.com/**

III

Writing HTML

- Futplex system—**http://gewis.win.tue.nl/applications/futplex/index.html**
- Cold Fusion Forums from Allaire—**http://www.allaire.com/**
- InterNotes from Lotus—**http://www.lotus.com/inotes**

Fig. 15.7
A sample
WebNotes
discussion thread.

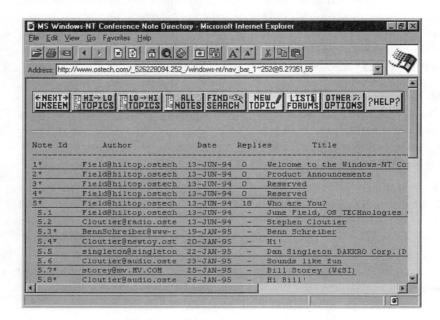

Some of these systems also enable users to upload files to the server, thereby allowing them to upload picture binaries to inline their message content with graphics.

Academic Annotation Systems

Many of the annotation-like systems on the Web today are academic in nature. At Cornell, a test case involving a computer science class allows students to share thoughts and questions about the class via the Web. Documentation on the Cornell system is available from **http://dri.cornell.edu/pub/davis/annotation.html**. The Cornell site also has useful links to related work on the Web. Some of the related systems that have been developed use custom clients to talk to an annotation database separate from the Web server itself, much like the early versions of Mosaic. This architecture may well be the future of annotations and the Web.

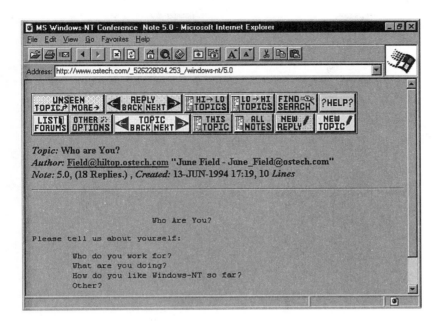

Fig. 15.8
Webnotes
discussion thread
drill down.

On the lighter side, take a peek at MIT's Discuss->WWW Gateway to get a behind-the-scenes look into an American hall of higher education. For a particularly novel and entertaining use of the Web, take a peek at the Professor's Quote Board at **http://www.mit.edu:8008/bloom-picayune.mit.edu/ pqb/**. ❖

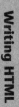

III

Writing HTML

## CHAPTER 16

Database Access and Applications Integration Using Scripts

The explosion of the Internet is being discussed within the business community almost as much as it is in public. Companies are struggling with the meaning of the Internet, how it may be exploited for new business opportunities and what external and internal threats may arise as a consequence of its exploitation by others. One thing is certain, the Internet has fundamentally and irreversibly altered the rules for constructing and delivering business information systems. This chapter explores these issues and provides some insight regarding the construction of Web enabled business systems that can extend a company's reach. In this chapter, you will learn:

- The kinds of business applications to consider for implementation as WWW scripts
- Which Web technologies match your application requirements
- What kinds of information should be stored as rows in a relational database instead of HTML documents in the file system

The Internet as a Public Wide Area Network

Traditionally, only very large corporations had the resources to develop and deploy on-line business systems that reached beyond a campus. Generally, available solutions for wide area communications infrastructure did not exist. Companies were limited to in-house design, construction, and administration of private networks. The cost of these solutions was prohibitively high for all but the very largest and wealthiest corporations.

From a business point of view, the Internet represents a low cost, worldwide data communications utility that has unmatched geographic coverage and an explosively growing population of users. This is the Internet's primary value to businesses. The barriers of entry to worldwide transaction processing are so low that essentially every business can afford to exploit it. With proper designs and a robust security infrastructure, there is now an opportunity to extend existing online business systems directly to consumers. As with any major environmental change, businesses that understand the meaning of the Internet, Web technology and how to exploit it will be more likely to survive. Those that ignore it will find themselves at a serious competitive disadvantage.

How Databases Differ from HTML Files

To understand how a business might exploit the Internet and the World Wide Web, it's important to understand the objectives and limitations of the WWW infrastructure from a business system point of view.

The World Wide Web was conceived of and designed as a mechanism for publishing information in electronic form. HTML is the media of the Web. The fundamental characteristics of the Web are:

- It forms a global library of read-only electronic paper documents.
- It provides a way to locate documents in the library in two ways:
  - by powerful text search engines, and
  - by manual navigation from one document to other related documents.
- It supports better than ASCII but less than "rich" text documents.
- It supports the delivery of multimedia (graphics, voice, and video) documents.

HTML Advantages

HyperText Markup Language is the medium used to construct documents for this library. The advantages to a business for using HTML as an electronic document format are:

- HTML documents are accessible to the entire Internet population because it is a simple ASCII-based language.
- Writing HTML documents is simple. So simple that they can be constructed using an ASCII file editor. Therefore, authoring HTML documents is inexpensive and universally enabled.
- Freely available text indexing and search engines exist that make locating information in the library easy.

- The language directly supports manual document-to-document navigation via hyperlinks.

If publishing a library of HTML documents addresses some portion of your business system requirements, then the Web and HTML documents are the answer for you. It is a great, low-cost, ubiquitous electronic document library system.

Adobe Acrobat

Adobe has extended the Postscript technology to address electronic publishing requirements. Their suite of Acrobat products enables publishers to use high-end publishing tools, such as FrameMaker, Premier, and Illustrator to create magazine-quality publications and deliver them over the Internet as Postscript Display Format (PDF) files. The freely available Acrobat Reader, which operates much like a Web browser, can be used to view these files. A Netscape Navigator Plug-in called Amber is available; it enables you to view PDF files within the Netscape Navigator window, much as any HTML file.

HTML Disadvantages

Even as a document library system, HTML files have some significant disadvantages.

- Very few businesses create formal or informal electronic documents in the form of HTML files. Most businesses create informal electronic documents in the form of OLE objects using desktop word processing applications like Microsoft Word and WordPerfect.

- Most businesses create formal (professional) electronic documents using professional publishing tools, such as PageMaker and its companion tools from Adobe.

Other than as an electronic document library, this technology does not support many traditional business system requirements. It is, in fact, too restrictive for most applications:

- It only supports read access to information in the library. The information is not available for update. There are no services for managing or controlling updates to the library. There is no locking mechanism or concurrency control that would enable a document to be shared for update even if an update capability existed.

- The information is in unstructured electronic paper format. So while there are powerful text indexing and search engines available for HTML documents, data query capabilities are severely limited. For example,

III

Writing HTML

the following query cannot be formulated using an HTML search engine because it cannot understand the meaning of the terms ShipToName, ShipToAddress, and so on.

```
SELECT ShipToName, ShipToAddress FROM Library WHERE ShipToZip IS
BETWEEN
32256 AND 32779;
```

■ Because the information content of the documents is unstructured, specific data content cannot easily be extracted and processed by business applications.

Relational Databases

Most business applications manage the creation, update, delivery, and destruction of data. As can be seen in the preceding section, this capability is not native to Web technology. It must be added.

Relational Databases are the defacto standard for managing business information today. Their success is no accident. Relational databases have been designed to efficiently process high volumes of short transactions involving simple alpha/numeric data. Relational databases have the flexibility to handle ad hoc queries and new data relationships, and they pay a lot of attention to data integrity, availability, and multiuser data sharing (concurrency control) requirements. They provide a robust set of functions for administrating, distributing, accessing, and updating business information. Microsoft provides two low cost, highly capable relational database products: Microsoft Access and Microsoft SQL Server. IBM also delivers its excellent DB2 database product for all IBM Operating Systems and Microsoft NT.

SQL

Relational databases and normalization rules provide a well reasoned structure for analyzing and designing the data aspects of business applications. Once data is structured into these well formed tables, SQL enables applications and end-users reliable access to business information.

Relational databases are today's standard for managing business information and are the preferred database technology choice when extending on-line business systems to the Internet.

Why Use a Database for Web Page Publishing?

WWW server software is fairly simple in concept. It receives a request (GET) for a named resource, finds the named resource, and sends the retrieved resource to the requester. Most WWW server software assumes the resource is a file, and relies on the operating system's file system to resolve the name (path) to the file so that it can be read. A major drawback of this implementation is that the name of the resource is also its address. It cannot be moved without changing its name.

Servers, however, don't need to be implemented this way. For example, the server could assume the name is constructed of three parts:

- A data source name (database)
- A table name
- A field name
- A field value

and use a relational database engine to find and deliver the record. For example, HTML could be stored in a MEMO column in an Access database. This implementation would provide a mechanism for recording additional information (properties) about the document.

Let's use the Microsoft Access/95 Orders sample database as an example. This database consists of eight tables as listed in figure 16.1.

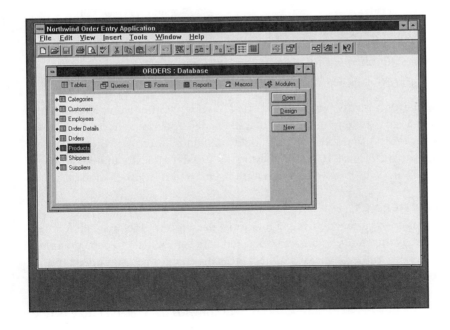

Fig. 16.1
The Microsoft Access/95 sample database consists of eight tables. The layout of the Products table can be discovered by selecting its name and pressing the Design button.

III

Writing HTML

We will use the Products table to illustrate how material could be served from a table instead of a file. Figure 16.2 shows how the Products table has been designed.

Fig. 16.2
The Products table has been designed with ten fields. Field names (beginning with ProductId) are listed in the first column of the Design window.

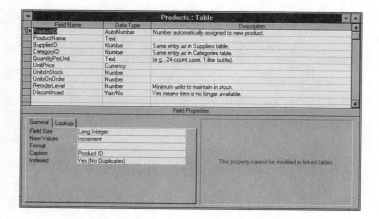

One could publish Product information by accessing this database table instead of an HTML file. An anchor could then be constructed as follows:

```
Information about our <A HREF="Orders/Products/ProductId/
Aniseed_Syrup"> Aniseed Syrup</A> product.
```

The server software would connect to the Orders database and issue the following SQL statement to select the desired record:

```
SELECT * FROM Products WHERE ProductName='Aniseed_Syrup';
```

The question is why would you create a Web server that is implemented on top of a database engine instead of a file system. Several vendors have developed servers that resolve URL's to database tables and rows; you can retrieve inventory information, create guestbooks and dynamically update Web pages. The Web browser becomes a front-end to a relational database.

Advantages

A primary advantage to using a relational database engine, instead of a file system, is the ability to attach structured data (properties) to each document, such as the Author, Version, Subject,etc. This enables you to understand more about the document and to deliver documents based upon the values of the document's properties. For example, a CGI script can easily deliver a list of all documents written by a specific author within a specified time period. No external indexing or search engine is required.

A database can also provide a richer set of functions managing this information. Various levels of authorization, versioning, distribution, replication, and locking can be applied to tables for better control and to ensure data security and integrity.

Disadvantages

An immediate drawback of this approach is that the tools used to create electronic documents are designed to run on top of file systems. When you create an HTML file, image, video clip, etc.,with any existing tool, it will be saved as a file. Therefore, additional work will be imposed on authors to get their material into and out of the database.

Second, database engines have much more limited text indexing and search capability than the WAIS search engines that provide access to HTML files. WAIS indexing utilities are run periodically to analyze the library's text and create compact index files. The WAIS search engine provides support for wildcard characters, Boolean operators and nearness tests. These algorithms do not run against the library files themselves. Rather, they run against the set of indexes built by the off-line utilities. For example, when you search the Yahoo library for "good places to surf," it replies with a list of home pages with ratings of how good they match your search criteria. It rates the results through complex algorithms.

Some of these text search engines enable you to specify even more powerful queries. The Dialog search engines let you specify the distance between key words. Some examples might be:

```
FIND BUDGET(10N)SENATE
```

which would find all documents with the word BUDGET within ten words of the word SENATE;

```
FIND (FEMALE or WOMEN) and (WEIGHT TRAIN? OR WEIGHT LIFT? OR
WEIGHTLIFT?)/ENG
```

which would find English language documents regarding female weightlifting articles. None of these capabilities are offered in Relational database engines.

In contrast, SQL does very well at finding records based upon specific values in small character or numeric fields. However, documents are stored as large variable length character fields in relational database systems. Wildcard characters are very limited and boolean operators are not even available for these types of fields. In fact, you cannot search for anything beyond the first 255 characters of a document stored in a Microsoft Access memo field.

Finally, database engines are optimized to store large numbers of (relatively) small records, while file systems are designed to store (relatively) small numbers of large files. A database implementation could end up being slower than a file system implementation depending on the nature of the information.

Integrating Your Web Page and a Database

Because the use of ODBC as the API between your application to the relational database engine enables you to pick virtually any database product and change database products with minimal impact to your application, we will assume you have made this choice. The steps for accessing a database from a Web page is:

- Define the datasource and the ODBC driver to the ODBC driver manager.
- Use a form on an HTML page to request information from the user
- Create a script to process the form and access the database.

> **Caution**
>
> Microsoft provides a set of object classes (MFC) for implementing ODBC applications. This set of object classes are not thread safe and must not be used to implement Web applications via the ISAP interface.
>
> Also, ISAPI is a multithreaded interface. While the Microsoft Access product can be used as the database system for CGI applications, it can not be used for ISAPI applications. MS SQL Server 6.0 or newer must be used when implementing ISAPI database applications.

Installing ODBC

An ODBC Software Development Kit is available from the Microsoft Developer's Network (MSDN) at a Level 2 subscription. A Level 2 MSDN membership provides you with the latest versions of Windows and Windows NT Workstation, including prerelease versions. It also provides you with the *Development Platform*—a set of CDs updated quarterly that contains all the software development kits (SDKs), device driver kits (DDKs), and Windows and Windows NT Workstation operating systems from Microsoft, both domestic and international versions. For information about subscribing to the MSDN, see **http://www.microsoft.com/msdn**.

The ODBC SDK provides you with the necessary header files, help files, and DLL's to implement ODBC applications. It also provides you with test utilities, trace utilities, administration and setup utilities, and sample application source code.

Setting Up an ODBC Data Source

Use the ODBC/32 administration utility provided by the ODBC/SDK or the ODBC Service Applet on the control panel to set up and identify your database as an ODBC data source. In either case, you will see the ODBC Administration window as shown in figure 16.3. Each driver provides a different setup application. If you're using the Microsoft ODBC driver to connect to an MS Access or SQL Server database, make your database a *System Database*. This means that any user logged into this machine is able to see and potentially use this data source. Because the data source has its own logon ID and password, it is still protected.

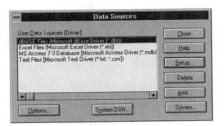

Fig. 16.3
The ODBC applet in the control pane must be used to specify an ODBC data source.

With the Data Source dialog box on the screen, click System Database, then Add, Microsoft Access (.mdb) driver, and OK. This brings you to the Setup dialog box. Use the Select button to find the database on your hard drive (the database must be on a hard drive on the local system of the Web server). Enter the Data Source name. Accuracy is very important because ODBC is case-sensitive. When connecting to ODBC, you define the name of the *datasource*, not the name of the database. Click Advanced and set the password to simple with the Login name admin. Again this is important, ODBC will not connect to a *datasource* unless this information is accurate.

Why Use the Web Technology for Database Applications?

This is a more pertinent question. The Internet offers companies a low cost network utility. Some aspects of the World Wide Web technology enable companies to exploit this utility. What's important is reaching a broader population of potential customers over a wider geographic area. While HTML enables you to construct electronic documents and publish them on the Web, most business applications have nothing to do with publishing. They manage the processing of data to conduct business.

Structured Information

Business applications process structured information. The fields in an HTML FORM structure data values into named fields. The values entered into an HTML FORM can be extracted and stored into a relational table's rows and columns.

When information is named and structured, it can be processed. An application can verify that a field contains numbers when it should and that the numbers are entered in a valid format. Once validated, the value of a field can be added, subtracted, and averaged. These are the kinds of things business applications do.

Complex Queries

It may take a very complex query to locate the precise information a person needs for a business activity; for example, "Find all the people who entered orders for black wingtip shoes in the month of December last year." If the information is stored in an SQL database, the above request might be satisfied by the following SQL select statement:

```
SELECT Name, Address FROM CustomerOrders WHERE Item = 'SHOE' and
Style = 'WINGTIP' and OrderDate >= '#12/01/1995' and OrderDate <
'#1/1/1996';
```

> **Note**
>
> Indexing engines and Web crawlers do not have any visibility to information stored in a database that is reached this way.

Updates

By its nature, a business transaction changes the state of information in the business system. An order is placed, a payment is made, and the order is shipped. HTML and file systems do not provide the necessary structure, concurrency controls, or transaction support to meet these requirements.

Platform Independent User Interface

Traditional business transactions were implemented using dumb terminals, such as IBM 3270's, 5250's, 3101's, DEC VT100's, VT220's and VT320's. These character-based devices were all that was necessary to enable people to retrieve, enter, update, and delete business information. Business transactions were designed and coded specifically to the company's dumb terminal type. An application coded to run on an IBM 3270 could not be delivered to an operator on a DEC VT100.

HTML forms provide an operator interface and level of function similar to the IBM 3270. The primary difference is that an application can be designed and coded to interact with an HTML form rather than any specific piece of hardware. Web browsers interpret the form and present it to the operator regardless of whether it is running on a UNIX workstation, an IBM PC, or an Apple Macintosh. This Web technology isolates the business application developer from hardware implementation concerns. The application is developed to a form abstraction rather than to a hardware implementation.

This makes Web technology attractive to business application developers regardless of whether or not they ever expect to deliver their applications across the Internet. Web browsers and HTML forms provide a low-cost, high-function delivery mechanism that isolates their investment in application code from workstation, operating system, and hardware changes.

User Interface Distribution

Before the advent of Web technology (specifically graphical browsers), a company wanting to present a business application to PC users had only two choices:

- put a dumb terminal emulator on each PC and make them operate like an IBM 3270 or DEC VT100. This approach would allow companies to continue to run the same application code they had. Any off-the-shelf emulator would do.

- develop some PC-based code that would replace the old application, or at least present a new Graphical User Interface (GUI) to the old code. However, this would mean that the company had to deliver its own code to be installed on each PC.

For the most part, the first option isolates applications from the chronic migration to new hardware and operating system levels. PC users, upgrading to Windows 95 or NT, could upgrade or replace the emulator code if necessary, without impact to the business applications at all. The drawback is that users have become unimpressed with the old, dumb terminal user interface. Its "un-usability" and "un-friendliness" are contrasted with ever improving windows based Graphical User Interfaces (GUIs).

The second option brought MIS into a new world of complexity. Programming, configuration management, and control (keeping the distributed application code current and in sync with hardware and OS changes) were significantly more complex.

Web technology is a middle ground that enables a company to present an acceptable user interface to a wide population of users, who have an unknown configuration, in a cost effective way. HTML and the browser provide some elements of a GUI interface. No company application code needs to be installed on the user's configuration and programming to an HTML interface is relatively easy. With extensions like the Java Abstract Windows Toolkit (AWT), user interfaces can be created which approach the sophistication of those created using the Microsoft Windows Foundation Classes.

Multi-media Support

Some business information is graphical in nature (X-rays) and some is best understood when rendered as a graphic (trend charts). Web technology enables applications to deliver these forms of information simply and effectively, something that dumb terminal emulators cannot do.

Business Transactions on the Web

Web technology enables the use of the Internet as a low-cost, wide-area network utility. It provides an acceptable user interface to a broad population of users. It isolates the company's application code from distribution and configuration issues. Are there any drawbacks or inhibitors? To find out, let's explore the nature of a business transaction.

What Is a Transaction?

A computerized business transaction is a dialog between a human and one or more applications; it results in a change to the state of the business system.

Atomic Transactions

An atomic transaction consists of a single exchange of information between an operator and an application:

1. An operator retrieves, updates, and sends (posts) a form to an application.
2. The application processes the form, performs its function, and replies to the operator.

Conversational Transactions

On the other hand, a conversational transaction consists of multiple exchanges of information between an operator and one or more applications:

1. An operator retrieves, updates, and sends a form to the application.
2. The application processes the form, extracts some information, remembers some of the information, retrieves some additional information from persistent storage, and sends it to the operator along with a new form.

3. The operator looks at the new information, makes some decisions, updates the form, and sends it back to the application.

4. Steps 2 and 3 are repeated an undetermined number of times.

5. The application processes the form, performs its function, and replies to the operator.

An example might be an ever-narrowing search for information where the operator enters some broad parameters about lease agreements, the application responds with a list of hits, the operator enters additional search constraints to be applied against the already qualified results, and so on. The operator finally finds the set of interesting lease agreements and wants them deleted.

The application for the atomic transaction does not need to know anything beyond the information contained in the single form it received. It contains the necessary and sufficient information for the application to completely perform its function. In contrast, the application in the conversational transaction is much more complex. It needs to know what state of the conversation it is in and the information it gathered earlier in the conversation before it can determine what it should do next. Additionally, it can be conversing with several users at the same time. In order to hold a conversation with an operator, an application needs three pieces of information when it receives a form to process:

- To which conversation does this form belong?
- What is the current state of the conversation?
- What information do I have from the earlier parts of the conversation?

While HyperText Transport Protocol (HTTP) and CGI can easily support atomic transactions, it does not directly provide the necessary support for conversational transactions.

Maintaining the State of the Conversation.　HTTP coupled with CGI scripts, is a sessionless, stateless protocol. When an application completes processing a form and sends a new form to the operator in reply, the program's database connection is closed and the application terminates. When the new form is posted to the application, a new application (it may or may not be the same program) is started and the new form is processed. The second application has no memory of any prior processing activity or state and neither the server nor the browser provides sufficient information to the application for it to identify which conversation a form belongs to, or even whether or not the form is part of a conversation. Without these vital pieces of information, the application does not have a way to hold a conversation.

Logical Units of Work.   A logical unit of work is a set of changes to the state of business information stored in the database that must be completed entirely, or not completed at all. If the set of changes is only partially completed, the business information in question has lost its integrity and may lead to unpredictable business and business system behaviors, which is clearly an undesirable situation.

Database systems support the concept of a logical unit of work. They provide applications with three operations to manage logical units of work:

- Begin Transaction
- Commit
- Rollback

Begin Transaction marks the start of the logical unit of work. All changes to the state of information from that point forward belong to one logical unit of work. When an application completes a transaction, it can use the Commit operation to commit the state changes to the business system, or the Rollback operation to empty the set, as if the application had never run.

Note

An application must issue one of these closing commands before it ends.

Atomic transactions can exploit these operations in a simple and straightforward manner. Conversational transactions cannot. The problem for conversational transactions is a consequence of the stateless nature of CGI and the implementation of relational database engines. When a CGI application has completed the processing of a form and has replied to the operator, it ends. What happens to data changes it has made during that processing? Relational database engines require an application to either commit or rollback its work before it ends. Let's look at a vehicle purchase application that must update both customer information and mark a vehicle as sold.

1. In the first exchange, the operator retrieves the customer entry form and sends it to the application, including the sale price.

2. The application updates the customer file and retrieves a list of vehicles at the dealer, constructs an option list form, and sends it to the operator.

3. The operator selects the vehicle sold and sends the form to the application.

4. The application marks the vehicle as sold and links it to the customer record. It generates and sends a confirmation page to the operator.

What happens if the customer backs out of the sale between steps 2 and 3, the customer's credit check fails, the sold vehicle is not on file, or the network connection is lost? If anything unusual occurs between steps 2 and step 4, the state of the business information is incomplete. We have a customer record indicating he bought a car for a specific price, but we do not know what car he bought. This is because the application did not have a way to define a logical unit of work to the database that spanned the changes in steps 2 and 4. From the database's point of view, step 2 was one logical unit of work and so was step 4.

Also, because the application was terminated and restarted, any pending updates from the first interaction with the operator must have been committed or rolled back independent of the current interaction. This is a severe limitation on the design and implementation of business applications.

Concurrency Control

Suppose an account manager was looking over delinquent lease customers and came to the conclusion that a car should be repossessed based upon a customer's account history. While the account manager was reviewing the history, someone else was applying payments. The account manager repossesses the car based upon the information he/she reviewed over the past 20 minutes. However, at the time the repossession transaction completed, the customer's account had been posted with sufficient funds to make it current! This company will have one very irate customer on their hands when the car is towed away!

In order to guarantee that the repossession transaction was correct from a business point of view, the transaction should make sure that the information that the operator used during the life of the conversation to base her/his decisions on is still true at the end of the transaction.

Concurrency controls are needed when multiple people want to share the ability to update a set of resources. These controls either prevent the actions of one operator from invalidating the actions of another or they ensure that when an operator's actions have been invalidated, he/she is notified of the fact. There are two concurrency control strategies:

- *Pessimistic Concurrency Control.* Prohibit other applications from modifying information that is being used to base this decision upon until this logical unit of work has completed because it is likely that they will change it before this work is completed. This is useful when there is a high transaction rate against a small number of records—perhaps a pricing table in a catalog order entry application.

■ *Optimistic Concurrency Control.* Allow other applications to modify information that is being used to base this decision upon while this logical unit of work is in progress because it is highly unlikely that they will change it before this work is completed.

A Design for Conversational Transactions

The earlier problems are now partially solved with the new Internet Server Application Programming Interface (ISAPI). ISAPI enables an application to maintain state information and a database connection between interactions with a browser. Therefore, business applications should always be implemented using ISAPI instead of CGI.

An ISAPI application can create a persistent thread for each concurrent conversation. It can also create a reliable conversation identifier using three pieces of information:

■ The Internet address of the operator's workstation

■ A unique conversation identifier

■ A time span

By passing the conversation identifier to the browser as a hidden input field, the reply from the browser can be matched with a conversational thread in the application. The application root can then pass the input stream to the appropriate waiting thread to continue the conversation. Since the ISAPI application never terminates, the relationship between a conversation identifier and an application thread can be maintained across interactions with the browser.

Also, the state of the application's database connection, locks and uncommitted updates are maintained. This enables the application to commit or rollback the entire logical unit of work defined by the conversation.

Internet Draft proposals

There is an Internet Draft proposal to the HTTP Working Group from Bell Laboratories and Netscape Communications Corporation which improves upon the HIDDEN field approach. The proposal specifies how a business application can send a piece of state information in the HTTP response header, which the client browser will store. Included in that state object is a description of the range of URLs for which that state is valid. Any future HTTP requests made by the client, which fall in that range will include a transmittal of the current value of the state object from the client back to the server. The state object is called a cookie. Cookies are a general mechanism which server side connections can use to both store and retrieve information on the client side of the connection.

Simple forms of cookie support have been implemented in Netscape 3.0 and Internet Explorer 3.0.

The heavily annotated pseudo code provided in listings 16.1, 2, and 3 illustrates how a conversational transaction could be implemented based upon an overall OO code framework. First, we will look at the ISAPI entry point code, which uses a *context* class and a *transaction* class. Next, we will review the *context* class, which establishes the processing context for the transaction and an implementation of a transaction. The *transaction* class relies on an overall application framework which we will discuss last.

The ISAPI Entry Points

The code shown in listing 16.1 is provided to illustrate how to set up the ISAPI entry points. Comments are provided for explanation.

Listing 16.1

```
// Simple ISAPI Test Program.
#include <windows.h>
#include "httpext.h"
#include "transact.hpp"

BOOL WINAPI _export GetExtensionVersion (HSE_VERSION_INFO *pVer) {
     pVer->dwExtensionVersion = MAKELONG(HSE_VERSION_MINOR,
HSE_VERSION_MAJOR);
     lstrcpyn(pVer->lpszExtensionDesc,"www.ipworld.com ISAPI sample
code.", HSE_MAX_EXT_DLL_NAME_LEN);
     return TRUE;
}

DWORD WINAPI _export HttpExtensionProc(LPEXTENSION_CONTROL_BLOCK
lpEcb) {
     string      *transactionId;
     TCtransaction *workTransaction;
     TCtransaction *transaction;
     TCcontext *context;
     string    *workstationAddress;
```

(continues)

Writing HTML

Listing 16.1   Continued

```
    context = new TCcontext(lpEcb);
    transactionId = context->IdentifyTransaction();
    workstationAddress = context->IdentifyWorkstation();
    if (workstationAddress == NULL) {
        context->ReportError
            ("500 HttpExtensionProc unable to determine the client
address.");
        return HSE_STATUS_ERROR;
    }

    if (transactionId == NULL)
        transaction = new TCtransaction(workstationAddress->c_str());
    else {
        workTransaction = new TCtransaction();
        transaction = workTransaction-
>GetTransaction(transactionId->c_str());
        delete workTransaction;
    }

    if (transaction == NULL) {
        context->ReportError("500 Unknown transaction.");
        return HSE_STATUS_ERROR;
    }

    int rtnCode;
    rtnCode = transaction->Run(context);
    delete context;
    if (rtnCode == 99) {
        delete transaction;
        return HSE_STATUS_SUCCESS_AND_KEEP_CONN;
    }
    return HSE_STATUS_SUCCESS;
}
```

The Context Class

The code shown in listing 16.1 relies on methods defined for the Context and Transaction classes. The Context class shown in listing 16.2 encapsulates the ISAPI interfaces and hides them from the rest of the classes. Normally, there would be a pure virtual class definition to define the interfaces and the following code would be an ISAPI context subclass implementation. This code also illustrates how to obtain environmental information provided by the http.

Listing 16.2

```
The Context Class Header File
#include <cstring.h>
#include "httpext.h"
```

```
class TCcontext {
private:
     LPEXTENSION_CONTROL_BLOCK lpEcb;
public:
     TCcontext(LPEXTENSION_CONTROL_BLOCK lpE);
     void DebugLog(char *msg);
     void ReportError(CHAR szErrMsg[]);
     string *IdentifyTransaction();
     string *IdentifyWorkstation();
     int WriteClient(CHAR szOutBuff[]);
     string *ReadClient();
     BOOL EchoStream(char *outBuffer);
};

TCcontext::TCcontext(LPEXTENSION_CONTROL_BLOCK lpE) {
     lpEcb = lpE;
     return;
}

void TCcontext::DebugLog(char *msg) {
     fstream ErrLog("isapi.log",ios::app);
     ErrLog << msg << "\n";
     ErrLog.close();
}

void TCcontext::ReportError(CHAR szErrMsg[]) {
     HCONN          hConn;
     DWORD          dwSize;
     LPDWORD        lpdwSize;

     DebugLog(szErrMsg);
     dwSize = strlen(szErrMsg);
     lpdwSize = &dwSize;
     hConn = lpEcb->ConnID;
     lpEcb-
>ServerSupportFunction(hConn,HSE_REQ_SEND_RESPONSE_HEADER,szErrMsg,
          lpdwSize, (LPDWORD)szErrMsg);
     return;
}

int TCcontext::WriteClient(CHAR szOutBuff[]) {
     BOOL           rtnCode;
     HCONN          hConn;
     DWORD          dwSize;
     LPDWORD        lpdwSize;
     int            iSize;
     char           szHeadBuff[1024];
     char           szHeadForm[] = "Content-Type: text/
html\r\nContent-Length: %06i\r\nConnection: Keep Alive\r\n\r\n";

     lpdwSize = &dwSize;
     hConn = lpEcb->ConnID;
     iSize = strlen(szOutBuff);
     sprintf(szHeadBuff, szHeadForm, iSize);
```

(continues)

III

Writing HTML

Listing 16.2   Continued

```
        dwSize = strlen(szHeadBuff);
        rtnCode = lpEcb-
>ServerSupportFunction(hConn,HSE_REQ_SEND_RESPONSE_HEADER,"200 OK",
            lpdwSize, (LPDWORD)szHeadBuff);
        if (!rtnCode) {
            ReportError("500 ContextWriteClient ServerSupportFunction
error.");
            return HSE_STATUS_ERROR;
        }

        DWORD           dwReserved;
        dwReserved = 0;
        dwSize = strlen(szOutBuff);
        return lpEcb->WriteClient(hConn, szOutBuff, lpdwSize,
dwReserved);
}

string *TCcontext::ReadClient() {
        HCONN           hConn;
        DWORD           dwSize;
        LPDWORD     lpdwSize;
        lpdwSize = &dwSize;

// Fill the buffer with new inbound data.
// Request it via ReadClient if necessary.
//
// Copy the inbound data to our buffer
        DWORD       nBytesToCopy;
        string    *inBuffer;
        inBuffer = new string((char *)lpEcb->lpbData);
// Calculate how much is left and go get it.
        nBytes = lpEcb->cbTotalBytes - lpEcb->cbAvailable;
        if (nBytes > 0) { // Let's go get the rest of the data
          work = new char[nBytes];
        if (!lpEcb->ReadClient(lpEcb->ConnID, work, (LPDWORD) &nBytes))
{
            delete work;
            return NULL;
        }
        inBuffer->append(work);
        }
        return inBuffer;
}

string *TCcontext::IdentifyTransaction() {
        char szInBuff[4096];
        char *workptr1;
        char *workptr2;
        strcpy(szInBuff, (char *)lpEcb->lpbData);
        workptr1 = strstr(szInBuff,"SESSIONID");
        if (workptr1 == NULL) return NULL;
        workptr2 = strtok(workptr1,"=");
        if (workptr2 == NULL) return NULL;
```

```
      workptr1 = strtok(NULL,"&");
      if (workptr1 == NULL) return NULL;
      urlDecode(workptr1);
      strcvrt(workptr1, '+', ' ');
      return new string(workptr1);
}

string *TCcontext::IdentifyWorkstation() {
      CHAR          szInBuff[256];
      DWORD           dwSize;
      BOOL           rtnCode;
      LPDWORD      lpdwSize;
      dwSize = sizeof(szInBuff);
      lpdwSize = &dwSize;
      rtnCode = lpEcb->GetServerVariable(lpEcb->ConnID, "REMOTE_ADDR",
szInBuff, lpdwSize);
      if (rtnCode) return new string(szInBuff);
      return NULL;
}

BOOL  TCcontext::EchoStream(char *szOutBuff) {
      BOOL           rtnCode;
      char           szWorkBuff[256];
      CHAR           szInBuff[8192];
      HCONN          hConn;
      DWORD           dwSize;

      LPDWORD      lpdwSize;
      lpdwSize = &dwSize;
      hConn = lpEcb->ConnID;

      strcat(szOutBuff,"<H1 align=center>Form Echo</H1>");
      strcat(szOutBuff,"<PRE>");
      sprintf(szWorkBuff,"Connection handle = %d<BR>", hConn);
      strcat(szOutBuff,szWorkBuff);
      strcat(szOutBuff,"Request Method = ");
      strcat(szOutBuff,lpEcb->lpszMethod);
      strcat(szOutBuff,"<BR>");
      strcat(szOutBuff,"Query String = ");
      strcat(szOutBuff,lpEcb->lpszQueryString);
      strcat(szOutBuff,"<BR>");
      strcat(szOutBuff,"Path Information = ");
      strcat(szOutBuff,lpEcb->lpszPathInfo);
      strcat(szOutBuff,"<BR>");
      strcat(szOutBuff,"Path Translated = ");
      strcat(szOutBuff,lpEcb->lpszPathTranslated);
      strcat(szOutBuff,"<BR>");

      dwSize = sizeof(szInBuff);
      rtnCode = lpEcb->GetServerVariable(hConn, "CONTENT_TYPE",
szInBuff, lpdwSize);
      if (rtnCode) {
            strcat(szOutBuff,"Content type = ");
            strcat(szOutBuff,szInBuff);
            strcat(szOutBuff,"<BR>");
      }
```

III

Writing HTML

(continues)

Listing 16.2 Continued

```
        rtnCode = lpEcb->GetServerVariable(hConn, "SERVER_PROTOCOL",
szInBuff, lpdwSize);
        if (rtnCode) {
            strcat(szOutBuff,"Server protocol = ");
            strcat(szOutBuff,szInBuff);
            strcat(szOutBuff,"<BR>");
        }

        dwSize = sizeof(szInBuff);
        rtnCode = lpEcb->GetServerVariable(hConn, "HTTP_ACCEPT",
szInBuff, lpdwSize);
        if (rtnCode) {
            strcat(szOutBuff,"HTTP Accept = ");
            strcat(szOutBuff,szInBuff);
            strcat(szOutBuff,"<BR>");
        }

        dwSize = sizeof(szInBuff);
        rtnCode = lpEcb->GetServerVariable(hConn, "REMOTE_ADDR",
szInBuff, lpdwSize);
        if (rtnCode) {
            strcat(szOutBuff,"Remote address = ");
            strcat(szOutBuff,szInBuff);
            strcat(szOutBuff,"<BR>");
        }

        dwSize = sizeof(szInBuff);
        rtnCode = lpEcb->GetServerVariable(hConn, "REMOTE_HOST",
szInBuff, lpdwSize);
        if (rtnCode) {
            strcat(szOutBuff,"Remote host = ");
            strcat(szOutBuff,szInBuff);
            strcat(szOutBuff,"<BR>");
        }

        dwSize = sizeof(szInBuff);
        rtnCode = lpEcb->GetServerVariable(hConn, "REMOTE_USER",
szInBuff, lpdwSize);
        if (rtnCode) {
            strcat(szOutBuff,"Remote user = ");
            strcat(szOutBuff,szInBuff);
            strcat(szOutBuff,"<BR>");
        }

        dwSize = sizeof(szInBuff);
        rtnCode = lpEcb->GetServerVariable(hConn, "SERVER_NAME",
szInBuff, lpdwSize);
        if (rtnCode) {
            strcat(szOutBuff,"Server name = ");
            strcat(szOutBuff,szInBuff);
            strcat(szOutBuff,"<BR>");
        }
```

```
        dwSize = sizeof(szInBuff);
        rtnCode = lpEcb->GetServerVariable(hConn, "SCRIPT_NAME",
szInBuff, lpdwSize);
        if (rtnCode) {
            strcat(szOutBuff,"Script name = ");
            strcat(szOutBuff,szInBuff);
            strcat(szOutBuff,"<BR>");
        }

        dwSize = sizeof(szInBuff);
        rtnCode = lpEcb->GetServerVariable(hConn, "CONTENT_LENGTH",
szInBuff, lpdwSize);
        if (rtnCode) {
            strcat(szOutBuff,"Content length = ");
            strcat(szOutBuff,szInBuff);
            strcat(szOutBuff,"<BR>");
        }

        dwSize = sizeof(szInBuff);
        rtnCode = lpEcb->GetServerVariable(hConn, "HTTP_CONNECTION",
szInBuff, lpdwSize);
        if (rtnCode) {
            strcat(szOutBuff,"HTTP connection = ");
            strcat(szOutBuff,szInBuff);
            strcat(szOutBuff,"<BR>");
        }
        strcat(szOutBuff,"<BR>");

        strncpy(szInBuff,(char *)lpEcb->lpbData,8192);
        char *p;
        p = strtok(szInBuff,"&");
        while (p!=NULL) {
            urlDecode(p);
            strcvrt(p, '+', ' ');
            strcat(szOutBuff,p);
            strcat(szOutBuff,"<BR>");
            p = strtok(NULL,"&");
        }
        strcat(szOutBuff,"</PRE>");
        return TRUE;
    }
```

The Context class encapsulates the ISAPI interfaces so the transaction code can be written without knowledge of them.

The Transaction class shown in listing 16.3 encapsulates the logic of the application program. When the ISAPI entrypoint gets control, it determines whether the input is a continuation of an existing conversation, or the start of a new conversation. If it is the start of a new conversation, it creates a new instance of the transaction class. There would normally be an abstract class definition for transactions which would implement all Transaction methods except the Run() method. Each application transaction would be a subclass of the abstract transactions and would implement its specific Run() method logic.

Listing 16.3

```
The Transaction Class Header File
class TCtransaction {
private:
    static TCtransaction* head;
    TCtransaction      *next;
    string            *transactionId;
    int               state;
public:
    TCtransaction(const char *ipAddress = "000.000.000.000");
    ~TCtransaction();
    void     Purge();
    void     SetState(int newState);
    int      GetState(const char *sid);
    int      State() const;
    TCtransaction      *GetTransaction(const char *sid);
    const char *TransactionId() const;
    int      Run(TCcontext *context);
};
TCtransaction* TCtransaction::head =0;

// Transaction constructor.
TCtransaction::TCtransaction(const char *ipAddress) {
    TTime    now;
    string sep("^");

    if (0 == strcmp("000.000.000.000",ipAddress)) return;
    transactionId = new string(ipAddress);
    transactionId->append(sep);
    transactionId->append(now.AsString());
    TCtransaction *cursor = head;
    if (cursor == 0) {   // If the list is empty, then set the head
to
        head = this;       // point to this transaction.
    } else {              // Otherwise, run the list and add this one
to
        while(cursor->next != 0) cursor = cursor->next;
        cursor->next = this; // the end.
    }
    state = 0;  // Initialize the state to zero and
    next = 0;   // the next pointer to zero.
    return;
}

TCtransaction::~TCtransaction() {
    // Remove the transaction from the list.
    // Delete the transaction.
    return;
}
```

```
// Return the state of the transaction.
int TCtransaction::State() const { return state; }
// Return the transaction ID.
const char *TCtransaction::TransactionId() const { return
transactionId->c_str(); }

// Get a transaction pointer by specifying it's ID.
TCtransaction *TCtransaction::GetTransaction(const char *sid) {
    TCtransaction *cursor = head;          // Start at the head.
    if (cursor == 0) return NULL;     // Nothing on the list!
    if (*cursor->transactionId == sid) return cursor; // Found it at
the head.
    while(cursor->next != 0) {          // Run down the list looking
for it.
        cursor = cursor->next;
        if (*cursor->transactionId == sid) return cursor; // Found
it.
    }
    return NULL; // No such transaction was found.
}

// Set the state of the transaction.
void TCtransaction::SetState(int newState) {
    state = newState;
    return;
}

// ********************************************************************
// Normally TCtransaction::Run() would be defined as a pure virtual
function
// and this example would be defined as a subclass. The ISAPI entry
// point would create a new instance of the subclass. But for brevity
// we defined the example logic right here.
// This code is dependent on the resto of the www.ipworld.com frame-
work.

int TCtransaction::Run(TCcontext *context) {
    string     *inStream;  // Borland string class.

// Send the HTML prolog out.
    ClassifiedProlog(context, szOutBuff);
// Read in the data from the client
    inStream = context->ReadClient();

    switch(state) {
        case 0: // Manufacture and send a record entry form to the
client.
        // Create an instance of the Classified Record entry form
which
            // is defined as a subclass of HTML forms.
        TCclassifiedEntryForm entryForm(context, "Classified
Entry");
            // There maybe something of interest in the input stream
that should
            // go back out.
        entryForm.Input(inStream->c_str());
```

(continues)

III

Writing HTML

Listing 16.3 Continued

```
            // Manufacture the entry form html based upon it's defini-
tion.
                entryForm.SendEntryForm(szOutBuff);
                // Send the epilog.
            ClassifiedEpilog(szOutBuff);
            // Write it back to the client.
                if (!context->WriteClient(szOutBuff)) return
HSE_STATUS_ERROR;
                SetState(1);   // Set the next state of this transac-
tion.
                return 1;
            case 1:
               // The entry form should now be filled out and full of
values.
            // Read in the data from the client
                inStream = context->ReadClient();
            // Create an instance of the Classified Record entry form
which
                // is defined as a subclass of HTML forms.
              TCclassifiedEntryForm entryForm(context, "Classified
Entry");
              TCattribute *workAttribute;
            // Ask the entry form to load itself from the stream.
              entryForm.Input(inStream->c_str());
            // Process the form.
            // If requested, perform the action.
              workAttribute = entryForm.FindAttribute("ACTIONCODE");
              if (workAttribute == 0)
                 context->ReportError(
                    "Internal error. No action code specified in this
form.");
              if (*workAttribute == "Store") {
                 // Create an instance of the classified record object
class whic
                    // is defined as an odbc subclass of record objects.
                    TCclassifiedRecord classifiedRec(context, "ipworld",
"Public",
                    "Open", "Classified");
                    // Ask the form to copy its values to the record.
                    entryForm.CopyTo(classifiedRec);
                    // Ask the record to create itself (inserts a record
into the database).
                    if (classifiedRec.Create()) {
                        workAttribute =
classifiedRec.FindAttribute("OID");
                        if (!workAttribute)
                            context->ReportError("Internal Error. No OID
for this record.");
                        strcat(szOutBuff,"<p>Your event has been suc-
cessfully added to the database.\n");
                        strcat(szOutBuff,"Thank you.\n");
                        strcat(szOutBuff,"<b>Your record ID is: ");
```

```
                                strcat(szOutBuff,workAttribute->Value());
                                strcat(szOutBuff,"</b>.\n");
                                strcat(szOutBuff,"Please record this number
and the password you supplied in case\n");
                                strcat(szOutBuff,"you want to update or delete
this item in the future.\n");
                                strcat(szOutBuff,"Thank you.\n");
                    } else {
                                strcat(szOutBuff,"Oops... Something bad
happened.\n");
                    }
            } else {
                // Assume the operator wants to preview the entry.
                // Create an instance of the classified display form.
                    TCclassifiedDisplayForm displayForm("Display Classi-
fied");
                    // Ask the entry form to copy its values to the
display form.
                    entryForm.CopyTo(displayForm);
                    // Ask the display form to construct HTML based upon
it's definition.
                    displayForm.SendDisplayForm(szOutBuff);
            }
            // Send the epilog.
            ClassifiedEpilog(szOutBuff);
            // Write it back to the client.
                if (!context->WriteClient(szOutBuff)) return
HSE_STATUS_ERROR;
                SetState(0);
                return HSE_STATUS_SUCCESS;
            default:
                context->ReportError("500 Unrecognized state in main
routine.");
                return HSE_STATUS_ERROR;
        }
    return 99;
}
```

The Transaction class implements the application logic. Multiple instances of the transaction could be running concurrently, each with its own thread.

The Browser's Back Control

When it saves a page to its cache, some browsers identify the HTML "page" by its URL. This enables it to retrieve a page out of its cache when referenced again. However, responses generated by applications do not have a complete URL. There is no file name. Some browsers use the application's name in lieu of a file name. This leads to a design problem for conversational transactions. Suppose you create one application that manages the entire conversation. Each form in the conversation is posted to the same application and each reply comes from the same application. Most

(continues)

(continued)

browsers overlay the prior reply with the current one. If part of your application relies on the browser's "Back" control to allow the operator to return to earlier generated HTML pages, you are in trouble. It will not work. For these browsers, each generated reply must come from a different application in order to keep the browser from overlaying earlier generated pages. The Netscape Navigator browser does not have this design flaw.

An OO Application Architecture for the Web

There is nothing so dynamic in the computer industry today as the explosion of Internet technologies. If it is true that designing business applications for change is a primary objective of software development, then it is especially true for designing business applications that use Internet technologies.

Object Technology

Object technology promises you the ability to deliver high quality, low cost, low maintenance applications that are resilient to change. This promise, however, is conditional upon the "proper" exploitation of the technology.

Application Architecture Options

Many developers use case tools that enable them to exploit technology objects (such as buttons, frames, and so on) to create nice GUI interfaces. They then write procedures that run when certain events occur. These procedures are variously called *callbacks*, or *event handlers*. The entire application is designed within the framework provided by the case tool's technology objects. This, however, is not constructive object-oriented application development. It is procedural application development that is designed to operate within a specific object-oriented GUI framework.

The Object Management Group (OMG—the largest software consortium in the world) believes that by exploiting the constructive capabilities of the technology one can achieve its promises. That is, the characteristics and behavior of objects should be abstracted to provide a general capability over a wide range of specialized sub-classes. The abstract interface can then be used by all clients, regardless of specialized implementations.

This paradigm is generally accepted for technology objects. That is, it's accepted that there should be a general interface to buttons that enables you to put a label on them or re-size them, regardless of whether they surface as a Motif button or a Microsoft Windows button. For the most part, this philosophy has not been internalized to the point of affecting how you design business objects.

Object-oriented Application Design

Suppose you want to create a business application that uses HTML forms for its user interface. Suppose you want your application to be able to dynamically determine if the browser is Java enabled, and use a Java form instead of an HTML form. When a posted Java form is received, it will require a different kind of processing. You want this technology change to occur without changing more than one or two lines of code.

In order to make this a reality, you need to write your application to an abstract object class called something like TCform. One specialized type of form might be an HTML form class called TChtmlForm, and another might be a Java form class called TCjavaForm. If the application is written to the abstract TCform interface, it has the ability to dynamically switch between an HTML user interface and a Java user interface. The code might look like:

```
rtnCode = lpEcb->GetServerVariable(hConn, "HTTP_ACCEPT", szInBuff,
lpdwSize);
if (strloc(szInBuff,"Java")) myForm = new TCjavaForm;
else myForm = new TChtmlForm;
```

From that point on, all the code is the same.

Creating a Constructive Environment

Under the OMG design concept, developers first design the basic building blocks of an application and then they use these building blocks to construct applications. Using Legos as an analogy, first you need to design the Legos pieces, and then you can use the pieces to construct things. When Legos first came out, they were designed to be used to construct houses and buildings. You had about six basic pieces which enabled the construction of any building design (except round ones).

Embracing the OMG concept of objects and exploiting this technology successfully means you need to create a set of abstract classes that can be assembled to construct any business application. You must ask the questions, what is the nature of a business application, and what building blocks are essential to its construction?

III

Writing HTML

Developing an Abstract Application Model

The following is a generalized model of business applications:

Characteristic	Definition
Static Model	The state or characteristics of a business object.
Algorithms	The business algorithms used to perform calculations.
Constraint Logic	The business logic employed to regulate state changes in the object space; sometimes known as integrity rules.
Operations	The business object's methods and interfaces to those methods.
Transactions	A controller that prescribes a dialog with an operator to accomplish a logical unit of work.
Workflows	A process for completing a set of transactions.

This chart corresponds roughly to understanding that an abstract house is composed of a roof, a floor, walls, doorways, and window openings. It does not necessarily tell you what fundamental blocks are needed, but it does outline the abstract requirements you are trying to satisfy. The next step is to identify a set of abstract classes that can be used to construct this abstract application. They might include:

Component	Definition
Domains	Responsible for verifying values, rendering values in various formats and units of measure, relational operations, algebraic operations, and so on.
Attributes	Responsible for its state or value.
Objects	Responsible for knowing characteristics or attributes of some real world entity or event and for the persistent storage of their state.
Rules	Enforces constraints.
Events	Can be used to trigger the execution of rules.
Forms	Responsible for rendering themselves to operators and for verifying their validity.
Transactions	Responsible for controlling the operator dialog and completing or rolling back a logical unit of work.
Workflows	Responsible for managing the process to complete a set of transactions.

This object analysis has shown that these are a sufficient set of basic abstract classes that enable the construction of Web-based business transactions.

OO Patterns

The next step is to take this analysis into object design. You used the patterns described in *Design Patterns, Elements of Reusable Object-Oriented Software* by Gamma et. al. to help design a highly reusable abstract application model. ❖

CHAPTER 17

Commercial Applications

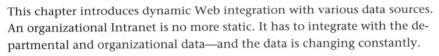

This chapter introduces dynamic Web integration with various data sources. An organizational Intranet is no more static. It has to integrate with the departmental and organizational data—and the data is changing constantly.

All the major players such as Microsoft, Oracle, Informix, and so on have tools to publish data from their client/server database systems. In the client/server world, Oracle is the most popular database. Oracle is in the forefront of Intranet applications and has a superior Internet strategy covering small to large institutional databases. Microsoft Backoffice and their SQL server database is growing in its popularity especially with its close integration with Windows NT and the Internet Information Server. Illustra, now part of Informix, has some innovative products. We can say that they are pioneering object-based relational databases, which are the main focus in this chapter. As we cover the data integration, we will touch upon some of the related tools from these vendors.

Lastly, this chapter discusses the database access from the Java language and covers the JDBC the database access classes that are a part of the Java language in some detail. The JDBC is important from a client/server perspective to develop custom 3-tier or n-tier applet-based applications.

In this chapter, you will learn about:

- Data integration tools from Microsoft covering the Microsoft BackOffice
- Oracle's Web system
- Illustra's DataBlade concept
- JDBC (Java Database Connectivity) APIs, which are a part of Java 1.1

Microsoft BackOffice

Microsoft BackOffice product is the enterprise level solution from Microsoft that includes components from a database to a proxy server. The current BackOffice version is 2.0 with Windows NT 3.51, which will be soon replaced by Windows NT 4.0 and IIS 2.0. Microsoft has already a proxy server code named Catapult and an Index server code named Tripoli in beta, which will become part of the BackOffice suite. It is informative to take a look at the last couple of versions of BackOffice as outlined in Table 17.1. to see the progression of the various products and the influence of the Intranet.

Table 17.1 Microsoft BackOffice Versions				
Version	**Messaging**	**Database**	**Internet**	**Other Components**
1.5	Mail Server 3.51	SQL Server 6.0	NA (Can down download IIS from WWW)	SNA Server 2.11, Systems Management Server 1.0
2.0	Exchange 4.0	SQL Server 6.5	IIS 1.0c	SNA Server 2.11, Systems Management Server 1.1
Future (4 to 6 months)	Exchange 4.0 built-in	SQL Server 6.5	NT 4.0 with IIS 2.0	SNA Server (Internet access/Middleware component) Systems Management Server (Updated to allow over the Internet) Catapult Proxy server Tripoli Index Server

BackOffice Integration with WWW

The Microsoft BackOffice is an integrated solution for enterprise on the Windows NT platform. With the increasing popularity of the Intranet as the basis for corporate information systems, the BackOffice suite is becoming an integrated Intranet system. Let us look at some of these integration features from various points of view.

First and foremost is that all the components share the Windows NT security system. In a multi-server, multi-location enterprise, the BackOffice provides a single sign-on facility. Domains, trusts, users, and groups are part of the NT security system. Users can login from any workstation including anywhere on the Intranet and have a secure access to resources. They do not have to logon many times with different passwords and usernames. As explained in Chapter 5, users can use FTP and WWW services with their username/password combination. This suite also provides the encrypted username/password security as well as SSL support for the WWW/http protocol.

The second integration is in the administration and monitoring areas. The BackOffice components from the SQL server to the IIS share the Windows NT logging and alert subsystem as well as the performance monitoring subsystem. The Windows NT server runs and manages the applications and services; and, the administration and monitoring tools available in NT provide global functionality across all the BackOffice components.

Looking at data integration, of all the BackOffice components, the IIS and the SQL server are closely integrated on the data sharing level. As the products evolve, Microsoft is adding more and more data level integration between the IIS and SQL server.

The SQL server can be accessed directly from the corporate Intranet using the standard development tools (such as Visual J++, Visual Basic, C++, and Delphi) using ISQL/Transact-SQL and also client applications based on ODBC or DB-Library. The SQL server uses TCP/IP protocol and also the Multi-Protocol Network Library called *netlib*, which establishes encrypted connections over the Intranet with users and servers. Figure 17.1 shows how to install the network protocol support for the SQL server.

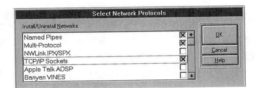

Fig. 17.1
SQL server multi-protocol network setup.

Other than the traditional full-fledged client/server development using the SQL library interfaces, there are three major interfaces to the Web through IIS: IDC, dbWeb, and the SQL Web Assistant.

III

Writing HTML

As we have seen earlier, the ISAPI allows you to write DLLs for the Internet Information Server. The Internet Database Connector Driver is an ISAPI program that handles ODBC data sources.

DbWeb is a point-and-shoot interface for publishing databases.

The SQL server has the Web assistant that can publish data to the Web. Actually, this can be used with any Web server. The following sections give an overview about these strategies.

Internet Database Connector

The Internet Database Connector allows the publishing of ODBC compliant databases on the Intranet/Internet. This means, with the IDC you can publish data in SQL Server, Access, ORACLE, Informix, SYBASE, and other ODBC-compliant databases. Microsoft positions IDC as a developer technology that serves as a foundation for developing custom database applications with IIS. Basically, it provides a way to use SQL statements through ODBC drivers and connect the results to a Web page.

The Internet data connector is an ISAPI DLL named httpodbc.dll. It converses with the Web browsers through the IIS with the http protocol and with the databases on the backend using the ODBC. The steps are as follows:

1. Create an Internet data connector file—with .IDC extension—on the IIS server. This file is a text file that specifies an ODBC data source and login information, as well as queries programmed in SQL to retrieve and/or update data.

2. Create an HTML extension file—with .HTX extension—on the IIS server. This file also is a text file that acts as a formatting template for any retrieved results. The IDC file references the .HTX file so that the database information can be formatted to display in an HTML page.

3. Now create the Web page that passes a reference to a specific .IDC file in order to connect to and access the database from a Web browser. The Web page (HTML document) can include a form so that users can enter search or update information that will be used by the IDC file when executing the SQL statements. If results are returned, they are returned in an HTML page that is formatted based on the rules set up in the .HTX file.

Using Internet Database Connector

The HTML Web page document has the HREF link filled with the .idc file name. For example,

```
<A HREF="http://www.astrix.com/samples/sample1.idc">Sample IDC</A>
```

As .idc extension is associated with httpodbc.dll, the .idc file is passed to the httpodbc.dll. This .idc file has ODBC data source details including username, password and data source name, the .htx template file name, and the SQL query at minimum.

> **Tip**
>
> There are many more fields possible in the .idc file. Please refer to the IIS product documentation for the .idc field details.

The httpodbc.dll issues the ODBC query/statement. The result is then formatted using the .htx file as the template. The now HTML-formatted ODBC result is sent to the IIS and the IIS sends the HTML document to the client. The IDC is capable of creating interactive forms that can create, modify, and delete SQL data.

SQL Server Web Assistant

The SQL Server Web Assistant is positioned as a tool to publishing SQL server data in the HTML format. The main distinction is that this is a non-interactive process. That is the IDC uses the ISAPI gateway to "pull" data from the SQL server. The Web Assistant uses the "push" method to deliver data. It updates the Web page as scheduled by the configuration.

The Web Assistant can handle Transact-SQL queries, stored procedures, and extended stored procedures. On a functional level, the Web assistant is an interface to a stored procedure named sp_makewebtask. The HTML Web page file can be updated whenever relevant data changes (by using a trigger) or updated at scheduled intervals (by using the SQL Enterprise Manager scheduling).

dbWeb

The Microsoft dbWeb is implemented through ISAPI DLLs. In that respect, it is similar to IDC. The difference is that dbWeb is an end-user tool with a graphical, point-and-click, query-by-example (QBE) interface. Similar to IDC, dbWeb connects the Web to ODBC data sources. The dbWeb runs on a Windows NT server and requires IIS and ODBC 2.5 drivers for the database you want to publish.

The dbWeb is a very flexible product and is not limited to only Microsoft databases. It can connect to any data source that supports 32-bit ODBC, and so dbWeb can be used on all the major databases including Oracle, Sybase, and Microsoft Access in addition to SQL server. Even Lotus Notes has an ODBC driver! And dbWeb supports dynamic data queries and basic row manipulation which means you cannot only publish data but can manipulate (create, update, and delete) that data, too.

Installing dbWeb

As of now, dbWeb is a downloadable product and is free from Microsoft. Download a copy (the file is named dbweb11.exe and is about 7.7 MB) from www.microsoft.com/intdev/dbweb. The current version is 1.1.

> **Note**
>
> The dbWeb was developed by Aspect Software Engineering Inc., and the company was taken over by Microsoft.

Run the dbweb11.exe to install the dbWeb. Figure 17.2 shows the installation screen with component options. If you want to install only certain components, the choice can be made here. Figure 17.3 shows the directory options window for WWW publishing of the data through dbweb.

Fig. 17.2
dbWeb installation shows the selection screen for the components to install.

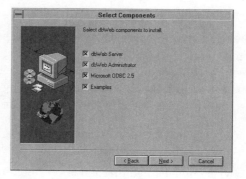

Fig. 17.3
dbWeb Installation—II. Shows the directories for WWW publishing of data through dbWeb.

Using dbWeb

The dbWeb consists of two components—the dbWeb service and the dbWeb administrator.

The dbWeb service runs as a 32-bit multithreaded NT service. The functionality includes processing data retrieval requests and formatting and displaying the results. The results are displayed based on the configurations done using the dbWeb administrator. The data display including the query fields, the actions permitted (insert, delete, or update records), and so on, can be controlled.

The dbWeb service gets the user requests from the WWW browser, communicates with the ODBC data source, and returns the results to the IIS which, in turn, send to the client browser.

The dbWeb administrator is a very powerful GUI front-end for configuring the system. It uses schema to control how the database information is published on the Intranet. Schema defines the query and resulting HTML pages that are displayed on the Web.

The main advantage of dbWeb is that no HTML or ISAPI programming knowledge is necessary to create the dbWeb schema. The dbWeb administrator provides an interactive Schema Wizard for this purpose. Figures 17.4 and 17.5 show two representative dbWeb Administrator screens.

III

Writing HTML

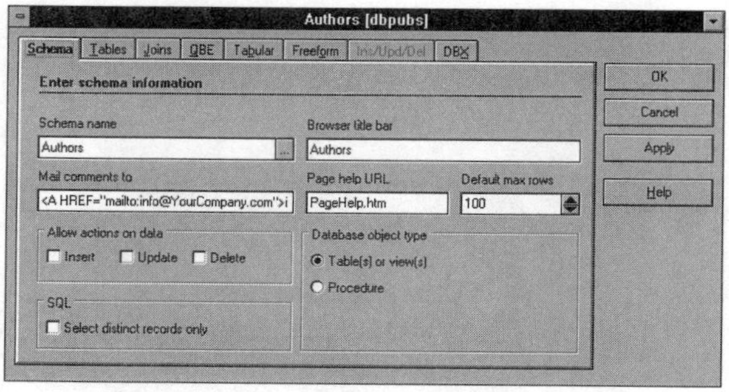

Fig. 17.4
The dbWeb
Administrator
Schema shows the
configuration for a
table to be
published.

Fig. 17.5
The dbWeb
Administrator
QBE.

The following list summarizes the main capabilities of dbWeb administrator:

■ Specify search fields for a Query-by-Example (QBE) Web page
(see figure 17.5).

■ Choose the data fields that will appear on a tabular Web page showing
a list of the records.

■ Specify jumps from the list of records to a single record displayed on a
Freeform Web page.

■ Schema GUI to choose data sources, set properties for fields on the
Query-by-Example (QBE) Web page, and set properties such as Automatic Links to jump to data displayed in other schema or to quickly
drill down from a tabular results page to a single record page
(as in figure 17.4).

■ DBX editor to fully customize your Web pages by entering HTML code
directly into the specification for the Web page.

■ Control which tables and fields are available for display or update. In
the Schema window, you choose which fields appear on your Web
pages.

- Set properties to allow updates, deletes, and inserts on your database.
- Write procedures to enforce business rules.

Oracle Universal Server and Web System

Oracle is the most widely used RDBMS and as we all know the company is committed to the Web in more than one way. From the less expensive Network Computers to the multi-site transaction processing applications, Oracle has solutions either in place or in development. We describe a few of them in this section and, as is the true nature of the Web, by the time you read this, Oracle will have released more tools and ideas!

Oracle's solution for the WWW and for Intranets is the Oracle WebSystem which is a part of the Oracle Universal Server. Oracle specs Universal Server as a complete solution for managing any data—relational, spatial, text, image, video, and audio—in any application, at any scale.

Oracle's flagship database server coupled with SQLNet and secure network services (now Advanced Networking Option) enable one to leverage the power of networked databases. When integrated with the Oracle Webserver, the Oracle servers become a powerful World Wide Web server with the potential for enabling a whole new generation of Web applications. Oracle's features include scalability, industrial strength, mission-critical applications support, and security.

Universal Server—Components

The Oracle Universal Server Suite consists of an Oracle Database server, interoffice Message Server, and the WebServer. (The Oracle RDBMS server comes in three flavors—Personal Oracle7, Oracle7 Workgroup Server, and the Enterprise Oracle7.) There are also components such as File and Print Manager for Windows Clients, Operating System Manager for remote monitoring and server management, User Manager to add, modify, delete users, and Backup Manager for remote backup and restore services, and some optional CPU-specific components.

Client Components

The client components provide the functions necessary to access information from the clients. They include Toolbar with Secure Single Login, InterOffice Client for messaging, Oracle PowerBrowser, Objects for OLE, and ODBC Drivers.

III

Writing HTML

Oracle PowerBrowser is a WWW browser that supports Java, JavaScript, Oracle BASIC script, version 2.0 of HTML, and all the major extensions to HTML, including frames, HTML 3.0 tables, and backgrounds.

The ODBC drivers can be used in conjunction with Microsoft IIS IDC and dbWeb for interactive publishing of data in Oracle databases. Also the ODBC drivers can be used with JDBC for connecting with Java applets.

Hardware and Software Requirements

The following table gives a general idea of the requirements for the server, manager, and client components. You can use the following table as an estimate. Please refer to Oracle Web site as well as spec sheets for the latest requirements.

Server	Initially be available on Solaris—Intel and Microsoft Windows NT. The recommended configuration is an Intel-based machine with a 100MHz Pentium processor, 64MB RAM, and 2GB of disk space.
Oracle Enterprise Manager Suite Pack	Microsoft Windows NT and graphical environment with 32 MB of RAM and 1 GB of disk space.
Client	Microsoft Windows 95 or Microsoft Windows NT graphical environment with 16 MB of RAM and 500 MB of disk space.
Toolbar, secure single login, login,and local GUI administration tools	Windows 3.11, Windows 95, or Windows NT. However, the InterOffice Server's Web client and Web-based local database administration tools may be accessed from any system with an HTML 2.0- compliant World Wide Web Browser.

In this section, our focus is on the Oracle WebSystem, which consists of the Web server and client products. The Oracle WebSystem is capable of reliably managing a high volume of online dynamic data.

The current Oracle WebSystem components are as follows. Bear in mind that the version numbers and operating systems almost surely will change by the time you read this chapter. You will find the latest information at the Oracle Web site at **www.oracle.com**.

Oracle WebServer 3.0	Announced
Oracle WebServer 2.0	SPARC Solaris 2.4
Oracle WebServer 1.0	Windows NT
Oracle WebServer Option 1.0	For integration of earlier versions (7.1.6 or higher) of Oracle Databases
Oracle PowerBrowser	All supported OSs

The Oracle WebServer is included with Oracle7 Server Release 7.3. In the following section, we will cover the Oracle WebServer product in some detail.

The Oracle WebServer

The Oracle WebServer, integrates the Intranet to Oracle's database, enabling developers to build powerful dynamic Web applications with HTML pages reflecting current information from the database servers. The WebServer product went from version 1.0 to 2.0 to now 3.0 in a matter of six months. Let us look at the architecture and some of the tools available from Oracle.

Oracle WebServer 1.0

The WebServer 1.0 consisted of two components: the Oracle Web Listener and the Oracle Web Agent. The Oracle Web Listener/HTTP Listener is a process running on the Web Server computer supporting hundreds of concurrent users and is suitable for high-traffic and mission-critical applications on wide-area networks. It has file caching algorithms including asynchronous read-ahead and sharing between multiple connections. It supports CGI version 1.1. The Oracle Web Agent is a gateway that invokes Oracle stored procedures, passes parameters to the procedure, and provides an output mechanism for the result set. I agree with Oracle's statement that it provides an object-oriented, user-extensible framework for producing dynamic HTML pages using PL/SQL. The Web Agent enables users to dynamically pull information and post transactions into corporate databases from their Web browser.

Oracle WebServer 2.0

Oracle did a lot of improvement and redesigned the WebServer 1.0 to develop Web Server 2.0. This product is a robust, secure, and multithreaded architecture.

The WebServer 2.0 is centered around the Web Request Broker (WRB), the multithreaded, multi-process HTTP server. The Web Listener in 1.0 is enhanced to a high-performance Web Listener, which hands over the HTTP

III

Writing HTML

requests to the Web Request Broker. The WRB is a component-based extensible architecture. The extensions can be business logic or special processing or general purpose modules such as the Java Virtual Machine or credit card processing, and so on. In fact, one of the cartridges is the PL/SQL Agent (which is a high-performance replacement for the Web Agent in WebServer 1.0), which performs a two-way data communication with stored procedures in Oracle databases.

The WRB has dynamic load-balancing capabilities which are essential for large-scale applications. The WRB is supported by SDK for development and management tools for administration and performance monitoring.

Internally, the Web Listener is the front-end HTTP processor. It gets the incoming HTTP requests and delivers them to the Web Request Broker. The Web Request Broker has a WRB Dispatcher (WRBD). The WRBD has a registry of currently running object processes, which are encapsulated with callbacks to the WRB Execution Engines (WRBX), and routes the incoming requests to one of them.

> **Note**
>
> The object processes are developed using the WRB Software Development Kit. These object processes are called cartridges. The inter-cartridge API, which will be fully developed in WebServer 3.0, will enable the cartridge modules to communicate with one another.

Oracle has developed the PL/SQL agent as a cartridge. There are third party vendor cartridges such as the Verifone Virtual Point of Sale cartridge. Intranet developers can develop their own cartridges encapsulating business rules and common logic and connect them to the WRB.

Another important advancement in the cartridge development is the implementation of Java Virtual machine as a cartridge. So, now, any Java program can interact with other cartridges, thus enabling the developer to design and implement powerful Java applications. Oracle has extended the Java language by adding three packages: oracle.plsql.*, oracle.html.*, and oracle.rdbms.*. These packages add the oracle database access, dynamic HTML generation, and PL/SQL access functionalities to the Java language.

In the security area, it supports SHTTP and SSL. Also the advanced networking option features are extended to the Web. (The Advanced Networking option even gives fingerprinting security.) It also supports IP-based and domain-based restriction—which is a good feature for Intranets—and also Oracle Secure Network Services (SNS)—which gives capability for secure access across firewalls.

PowerBrowser

The PowerBrowser is the Oracle client-side Web browser. It also includes a Web server (called "personal server," which falls under the peer-to-peer Web server category), an integrated BASIC scripting environment, Java support, and Network Loadable Objects.

The BASIC scripting environment is similar to JavaScript and VBScript and follows the Oracle's Power Object's syntax. The Network Loadable Objects are similar to and compatible with Netscape plug-ins, which are third-party extensions.

The Advanced Networking Option

This option is very important from a security point of view. This component provides single sign-on services, network encryption and user authentication, and OSF DCE integration for Oracle databases. The Oracle spec sheet characterizes the SQLNet integrated with the advanced networking option as any protocol, any application, and any data capability.

Oracle7 Advanced Networking Option also provides technology for encrypting data traffic. This supports MD4/MD5 RSA digest algorithms and DES 40-bit key encryption. This supports token authentication and also biometric authentication. The biometric authentication uses fingerprints to authenticate users! This option can be integrated with the WebServer to provide secure access to corporate information. (Using fingerprints for an Intranet application inside a firewall would be too much security. But if you work with the CIA or have very sensitive data, it is worth it. Also, this feature could be used for access into buildings, and so on.)

One point of interest to Intranet practitioners is that in conjunction with third-party firewall vendors, the security can be extended to Web browsers outside the firewall.

Informix Illustra

Illustra is an Object-oriented database management system (ORDBMS) developed by Illustra Information Technologies, Inc., now merged with Informix. The Illustra products consist of a core database server, "snap-in" modules called DataBlade modules, and application development tools.

The radical concept is the DataBlade module—conceptually similar to objects in Java or C++—which is a collection of data structure definitions and methods or functions that manipulate the data plus new access methods to these

III

Writing HTML

objects. The aspect which makes this suited for the Web is that the architecture is extensible to media-rich objects like audio and video clips, time series, maps, text, images of various kinds like VRML, PDF, JPEG, GIF, or even data types that have yet to be invented! With Illustra's merger with Informix, these products will incorporate the object orientation with the transaction processing capability of Informix software.

We can predict the future direction of Illustra knowing that their mission statement is to enable businesses to manage any kind of information—including traditional, new, and future data types in a completely integrated system that best suits their particular needs.

The Illustra Object Relational Database Management Server

The Illustra Server is an object-oriented relational database. It handles a variety of data as data types with query, analysis, and intelligent selection capability.

The Illustra server supports traditional relational technologies including standard SQL, data integrity and security, and transaction processing including recovery and scalability. It adds the object technology to extend data types, access, display, and storage. The Illustra documents call this an object-relational concept—powerful enough to store and manipulate richly structured data and enforce the complex business rules that define its integrity, and flexible enough to handle novel data structures effectively.

The Illustra Server when combined with DataBlade modules adds unprecedented power to the relational model—extending the SQL query language to process rich data. It provides content-based queries, optimized query plans, and high-performance storage and retrieval tailored to any data type including new ones. The Illustra supports UNICODE for internationalization of the Web site. Table 17.2 lists the platforms and operating systems supported by the Illustra ORDBMS.

Table 17.2 Illustra-Supported Platforms	
DEC Alpha	OSF-1 3.0
HP 700/800	HP/UX 10.x
Intel	NT 3.5/3.51
Silicon Graphics	IRIX 5.2/5.3
Sun	SunOS 4.1.3
Sun	Solaris 2.3

> **Note**
>
> Many of the DataBlades from Illustra are not supported on all platforms and operating systems. I am sure they will port the DataBlades to other OSs. So check with the Illustra Web site for availability.

The DataBlade Concept

As described earlier, the DataBlades are extensible intelligent modules for a particular data type with data interpretation, storage, access, and possibly display capabilities. They can be viewed as "smart objects." For example, the time series DataBlade implements the time series as Data Type and extends the relational model to support repeating time-based data like financial, scientific, and so on. It supports storage, access, and modeling of time series data. Figure 17.6 shows the general modules in the Illustra ORDMBS design.

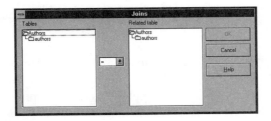

Fig. 17.6
Illustra ORDBS overview.

The following table (see Table 17.3) summarizes some of the most important DataBlades available. More details including white papers can be obtained from the Illustra Web page **http://www.illustra.com**.

Table 17.3 List of Illustra DataBlade Modules	
Image DataBlade Module	The storage and manipulation of raster images. It includes functions that crop, scale, rotate, and otherwise manipulate images.
PLS DataBlade Module	Mechanisms to search, store, and manage text.
S-Plus DataBlade Module	Adds support for over one thousand statistical functions to the Illustra Server. Example applications include Financial Risk Management, Modeling Equity Returns, Analysis of the Residual Returns of Stocks, and so on.

(continues)

III

Writing HTML

Table 17.3 Continued	
Sybase Gateway Module	Integrate data from a Sybase database with information stored within Illustra.
Text DataBlade Module	Provides text analysis and matching capabilities. The text is stored in native format using a high-performance storage mechanism known as D-Tree.
TimeSeries DataBlade Module	Supports the definition and manipulation of time series data such as stock market information. The applications include portfolio analysis, trend determination, and so on.
VIR (Visual Information Retrieval)	Content-based search and retrieve of DataBlade Module images and videos from multimedia databases by using searches based on the actual content of the image. The searchable attributes include color, shape, texture, and composition.
Web DataBlade Module	To support Web interactively from an Illustra Server.

Web DataBlade

One of the most interesting and most useful DataBlades from an Intranet practitioner's point of view is the Web DataBlade. The Web DataBlade is a collection of tools, functions, and examples for the development of intelligent, interactive, and Web-enabled database applications. The Web DataBlade pioneers the "remote authoring" capabilities where authors can securely submit contents and the HTML pages will automatically show the new information.

And naturally the Web DataBlade works with other DataBlades which enables one to interactively publish data like time series, statistical, and so on.

Using Web DataBlade

The HTML pages—containing HTML, embedded SQL statements, conditional logic, and error handling—are stored in an Illustra server database. The Web DataBlade adds the following (see Table 17.4) set of database-oriented markup tags to the normal HTML tags:

Table 17.4 Illustra Web DataBlade-Specific HTML Tags	
<?MISQL> <?/MISQL>	Specifies the SQL formatting instructions. Provides an optional conditional flag.
<?MIVAR> <?/MIVAR>	Manages variables within the Application Page.
<?MIERROR> <?/MIERROR>	Manages error processing within the Application Page.
<?MIEXEC> <?/MIEXEC>	Enables the application designer to call system services from within the HTML page.
<?MIBLOCK> <?/MIBLOCK>	Enables you to delimit logical blocks of HTML based on a conditional statement.

The Web DataBlade module dynamically generates HTML pages from these templates stored inside the database.

The Web DataBlade module consists of two components: the WebExplode function and the Illustra CGI driver called Webdriver.

When a link is clicked by a user, the browser client sends the associated CGI query to the Web server. The Web server launches the Illustra CGI driver Webdriver. This driver connects to the database and extracts the Web page—which is a row in a table issuing the SQL command. Now the WebExplode parses the extracted pages and executes the embedded queries in the <?MISQL> <?/MISQL> block. The results are "exploded" (hence the name WebExplode) and formatted onto the page in the form of text, images, video, or any other selected data type from other DataBlades. The WebExplode process runs in the Illustra database server. The resultant Web page is passed to the Webdriver which, in turn, sends it to the client browser via the Web server.

For example, at the Illustra site, a title page comes up when we get to **http://www.illustra.com**. From that page, there are links to other pages.

For the "Corporate Overview" page, when we click the link, the query **http://www.illustra.com/cgi-bin/Webdriver?MIval= about_corporate_overview** is fired, which fetches the required page.

The "About Illustra Web" page was generated by the query **http://www.illustra.com/cgi-bin/Webdriver?MIval=about**.

III

Writing HTML

For the "Illustra server," the query was **http://www.illustra.com/ cgi-bin/Webdriver?MIval=products_software_browse&name=I llustra+Object+Relational+Database+Management+System**.

Webdriver handles all aspects of database interface and customizes the applications based on information obtained from a configuration file, the CGI environment, URLs, and HTML forms. Webdriver also manages the database connection and retrieval of the Application Page from the database. The Webdriver also has a GUI page builder to create, edit, delete, and execute HTML pages in Web applications.

To optimize the connection management and handle peak loads between the Web server and Illustra database, especially for high-load applications, the Web DataBlade module provides the Webclient as an alternative to Webdriver. Using the Webclient, Intranet administrators can configure a predefined number of database connections to be established to manage all CGI process requests.

A few applications possible with the Illustra Web DataBlade are as follows. Please refer to the Illustra Web site for more applications and links to demo pages.

- Online catalog management including product inventory levels, reorder points, account transaction histories, and updating the catalog for product additions, deletions, and so on.

- Directory publications like third party vendors directory where the directory vendors can "remotely author" their information on products and services and the changes will be reflected dynamically on the list. Illustra has the Sun Catalyst demo.

- Digital Photo Library where users can do intelligent queries like "show me similar looking products" that will aid in online shopping.

- Another good application is the corporate document library. This application can be developed by linking the Web DataBlade with the Text DataBlade. The result is a searchable electronic library for manuals, policy documents, reports, and so on across the organization. Again, one can use the "remote authoring" concept for the providers to author these documents.

Unique features of Illustra:

In addition to the concepts like Web DataBlades, object extensions, remote authoring, and so on, there are two more concepts which make Illustra unique.

They are:

- *Rules System.* Illustra has a means to analyze application usage based on frequency and location of user selections (typically by mouse "clicks"). This is done by analyzing the click stream. Click stream analysis means that you can track where and how often a user clicks a particular application area. With the feedback gathered through click stream analysis, you can build a business model around the usage of an application.

  Rules also enable specified events to trigger notification messages. By monitoring the ordering quantities, we can trigger an inventory-low event to possibly alert or even place an order with the supplier.

- *Time Travel.* This relates to versioning capability. One can query past versions of objects using this feature.

Java Database Access

No Intranet book—especially the database access topic—will be complete without a discussion on Java and database access. Java Database connectivity is aimed at developing client/server applications either as a stand-alone application (which is composed of many Java classes and packages and could consist of some components which are downloaded from the Intranet) or as applets. The stand-alone application is more suited for Intranets. The future Intranet applications will be a set of Java objects involving multi-tier, multi-sourced data and possibly applets. Figure 17.7 shows the general scheme for a Java applet as well as a Java stand-alone application. Even though applets access is restricted to their server, this scenario will change once signed applets and other security schemes become prevalent.

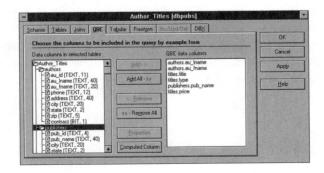

Fig. 17.7
Java applets versus Java applications.

Applets access the database through the Web server from where they were downloaded. Applications can access data on any database server.

Java is suited for Intranet client/server applications because of its platform independence, robust language constructs, downloadable applets (easy installation and software maintenance), tight coupling to Internet/Intranet, and so on. To effectively implement a 3-tier or multi-tier intranet client/server application, JDBC is an essential component. There are other new classes like the commerce API, security API, multimedia API, and so on, which are a part of Java 1.1 which will enhance the attractiveness of Java as a viable client/server database access development platform.

There are at least three major ways in which databases can be accessed from Java. They are:

1. *JDBC (Java Database Connectivity)*. JDBC is the relational SQL API classes for Java applets and applications. In the following subsection, we will go into more details.

2. *Wrapper classes and Relational APIs*. These are class libraries and packages provided by database vendors and third party developers to interact with specific databases. This category also includes the proprietary class libraries for multiple data source access.

   The RMI and object serialization APIs fall in this category. There are initiatives from the OMG (Object Management Group) to interface CORBA and Java. There are products like Orbix from Iona Technologies to interface Iona's ORB and Java. Microsoft will (if not already in alpha stage!) certainly have a Java-ActiveX classes/API.

3. *Object Databases*. As we have seen in the earlier section, products like Illustra, which fall under object databases, have Java applet interaction through their own proprietary classes. This technology is still in its infancy stage. The ODMG (Object Database Management Group) is working on an API specification. The specs will work with other object initiatives like the OSQL transaction processing.

JDBC

The JDBC—Java Database Connectivity—is a set of classes to connect Java programs and applets to relational databases. The API enables a Java program to issue SQL statements and process the results. The API specification is developed by JavaSoft. The JDBC is database- and platform-independent. The JDBC specification and more details are available at **http://splash.javasoft.com/jdbc**. The JDBC spec underwent a 90-day public review that ended in June 1996. The current version, 1.00, dated June 12, 1996, has all the comments incorporated and is frozen.

JDBC Internals

The JDBC design was influenced by XOPEN SQL CLI and Microsoft's ODBC. The JDBC API consists of the java.sql class which one imports into the program using the import java.sql.* statement. The JDBC Driver/Manager implements the classes either in Java language or as a native library. Let us look at the sample implementation—JDBC-ODBC Bridge from Sun-Intersolv. Figure 17.8 shows the data flow for the JDBC-ODBC bridge implementation.

The JDBC classes consist of database connections, SQL statements including stored procedures, result sets, and database metadata (which is information about the underlying result set to be interpreted with methods like getColumnName and getTableName). The main classes are as shown in Table 17.5.

Fig. 17.8
Data Flow for JDBC-ODBC reference implementation.

Table 17.5   JDBC Main Classes (java.sql.)

Type	Class Name (java.sql.)
Implementation	Driver
	DriverManager
	DriverPropertyInfo
Database Connection	Connection
SQL Statements	Statement
	PreparedStatement
	CallableStatement
Data	ResultSet
	ResultMetaData
	DatabaseMetadata
Errors	SQLEXception
	SQLWarning
Date/Time	Date
	Time
	Timestamp
Misc.	DataTruncation
	Numeric
	Types

The DriverManager creates the connection object— usually one per database. The connection objects have methods to create statement objects which have methods to create ResultSets. The SQL statements are executed from the statement object, and the data rows are read from the ResultSet.

The JDBC API is a specification (or interface in Java terms) and the driver manager is the OS- and hardware-specific implementation. Currently, most of the JDBC drivers are implemented with OS-specific components (like DLLs for the Windows environment). But they can also be implemented in Java for platform independence and possibly be downloaded as an applet.

To test the compatibility and standardize the JDBC API, JavaSoft and Intersolve are developing a JDBC compliance suite. The companies are also developing a reference implementation for the popular ODBC interface.

Vendor List

As of writing this chapter, the JDBC Web page lists about 28 companies that have endorsed the JDBC database access API. The list is growing and, when you are ready to do some evaluation, get the latest list from the JDBC Web page of JavaSoft **http://splash.javasoft.com/jdbc/jdbc.vendors.html**. I have listed the major players in Table 17.6. But I am sure there will be more innovative companies who will develop fast and easy drivers for JDBC. Please treat this list as a starting point and follow the links surfing the net.

Table 17.6   JDBC Vendor List

Company	Product/Implementation
Borland International Inc.	JDBC & Interbase
IBM	Database-2(DB2)
Informix Software Inc.	Informix Database, Illustra
Intersolv	JDBC,SequeLink
Oracle Corporation	PL/SQL connection
Sybase Inc.	JDBC Links to SQL Server 11
Symantec	JDBC and more
Visigenic Software Inc.	OpenChannel
WebLogic Inc.	T3 Server, dbKona, and Kona Line
XDB Systems Inc.	JETConnect

III

Writing HTML

## CHAPTER 18

Groupware Applications

Groupware is almost as popular a term as Intranet or client/server. It is also as ambiguous as the other terms. Groupware applications basically allow groups of people to share and discuss ideas electronically.

This chapter focuses on the benefits of groupware in the Intranet. Groupware applications such as Lotus Notes are discussed and some shareware/freeware applications such as Usenet News and mailing lists are discussed. A sample installation of a Usenet server, mailing list and archiver is covered.

WWW applications such as chat scripts and bulletin boards are also covered.

In this chapter, you will learn the following:

- What groupware is
- How to incorporate Lotus Notes into your Intranet
- How to setup Usenet News servers
- How to setup mailing lists

Groupware and the Intranet

Groupware is a term used to describe applications that allow groups of people to discuss documents or ideas. This discussion may be in real time but does not have to be.

Some examples of groupware applications would be:

- **Document markup or group revisions.** Lotus Notes is a commercial application that handles document markup and revisions control. Some free applications that allows groups to mark up documents would be mailing lists and Usenet. These systems do not handle revision control but by quoting what other people say and adding your own comments you can have a discussion on a document.

- **Group whiteboards.** These are versions of the classic "whiteboard" or "chalkboard" that is so common in meeting or conference rooms. This allows one or more people to comment on a drawing or sketch.

- **Chat rooms or discussion area.** These are areas for people to share ideas. These programs usually allow real time discussion.

- **Bulletin boards.** These are similar to chat rooms but are usually not in real time. They allow a message to be posted and receive comments from other users.

The next section discusses how these applications fit into an Intranet.

Groupware and the WWW have long been thought of as competitors but recently they have been considered more as allies. Groupware and Intranets fit together quite well since they both help to make groups work more closely together without having to actually get together.

Intranets normally allow documents to be shared but without groupware they can't be commented on and discussed. Once you add groupware to the picture, the Web can be used to help users collaborate on projects.

Some ideas on how to use groupware combined with the Intranet server would be:

- Discussion areas for different groups to share ideas or to act as a virtual meeting area.

- Bulletin boards for asking questions on company products, policies, or procedures.

- Document management. Specifications and designs are always in review processes. Using groupware can allow users to make changes and suggestions to the current document so that the next review can have all the requested changes incorporated into it.

- Design reviews. By using a group whiteboard, designers can discuss project ideas and effectively communicate ideas to the entire group across the network.

Many different groups can benefit from a groupware addition to the Intranet. This includes:

- Salespeople can discuss new products with other sales members, engineers, and marketing people, to help come up with a selling strategy.

- Marketing can discuss new ideas with sales and engineers to decide which product features are most important to customers.

- Engineering can use the discussion area to discuss new ideas or ways of working around a problem.

- The design process can go more smoothly by discussing problems with manufacturing people as well as engineers.

- Hardware and software groups can discuss what features should be handled by hardware and which ones make more sense to perform in software.

- Human Resource groups can discuss new policies or existing procedures with employees to get a feel for what people think of the policy or what benefits can be added to make a more enjoyable place to work.

- Customer service can discuss common problems with engineers to figure out a workaround or a better way of implementing products to better meet the customers' needs.

- Purchasing can discuss different products and pricing with engineers or office personal to decide which products can be substituted or changed to reduce costs.

As you can see, many different groups can use groupware and discussion servers to improve processes and reduce costs. Groupware or discussion areas can also reduce travel costs since "virtual meetings" can take place over the network. This allows employees to take place in meetings across the globe without leaving their desks.

Lotus Notes

Lotus Notes is unique among groupware products in that it is the only *complete* groupware solution. It is the only software product that addresses a comprehensive definition of what groups of office workers have to accomplish and how computers can facilitate those activities. Some groupware products facilitate communication between workers; for example, e-mail programs. Other products facilitate collaboration; for example, bulletin board discussion software. Yet other products help people coordinate their activities; for example, form routing products. Only Lotus Notes addresses all of these aspects of group activity.

Lotus Notes combines three key ingredients. It starts with shareable, distributed, document-oriented databases. It adds messaging in the form of fourth-generation (hypertext-enabled) electronic mail and the ability of Notes databases to pass messages to each other. It tops the sundae off with a rich, integrated, easy-to-master set of programming tools with which Notes users can combine the first two features into flexible solutions to their business problems.

Shared Document Databases. The heart of Notes is its shared document database technology. Notes databases consist of collections of documents contributed by users or added automatically by the system in response to various events. The documents are content-rich, in the sense that they can include highly formatted text and embedded objects, such as spreadsheet ranges, references to records in external databases, graphic images, sound bites, and video clips. Notes databases are shareable in the sense that multiple users can add to and access them simultaneously.

Messaging. All Notes databases can be mail enabled, meaning that they can be made to send documents to each other via Notes' built-in store-and-forward messaging capability. A by-product of this is Notes Mail, which is Notes' built-in e-mail system. Each Notes Mail user has his or her own mail database. Notes users can communicate with each other by Notes Mail and with non-Notes users through mail gateways and message transfer agents.

Development Tools. In addition to its document databases and messaging capability, Notes provides a rich programming environment that offers you a selection of programming languages, from simple (the Notes @function language) to more powerful and complex (LotusScript™, an ANSI BASIC compliant language similar to Visual BASIC™; the Lotus Notes API, a library of C functions; HiTest Tools™ for Visual BASIC™; HiTest Tools for C++; numerous third-party programming tools; and, due to be available in Notes Release 4.5, an implementation of Java™).

Notes Applications

These three features of Notes—shared document databases, integrated messaging, and application development tools—combine to permit the quick creation and customization of Notes applications to accomplish a variety of purposes, including publication of information, tracking of projects, and workflow. Notes applications can be classified as follows:

- Broadcast databases
- Reference libraries
- Discussion databases
- Tracking databases
- Workflow applications

Broadcast Databases and Reference Libraries

Notes is an ideal vehicle for storing masses of information, available to masses of users. Notes documents can store virtually any type of information, including embedded files created in other applications. Notes provides powerful tools for locating information in its databases. These include multiple, easily defined, user-customizable views of databases and a full-text indexing and search engine. These databases might be populated by people adding individual documents or by Notes programming that converts incoming data from, say, a news feed into Notes documents. In this capacity Notes duplicates the capabilities of World Wide Web servers.

Discussion Databases

Notes documents can be defined as main documents or responses. One resulting type of Notes database is the discussion database, in which one person starts a discussion by creating a main document and other people continue the discussion by creating responses. The responses appear in Notes views indented beneath the documents to which they respond, making it easy for the reader to follow a discussion thread. In this capacity, Notes duplicates the functions of bulletin board systems, discussion forums in CompuServe, and Usenet News Groups and List Servers on the Internet.

Tracking Databases and Workflow Applications

This is where Notes stands out from the groupware crowd. In a tracking database, a group of people collaborating on a project add documents describing their activities. Every member of the group can keep track of the progress of the project by referring to the database. In a workflow application, programming and messaging are added to the tracking database so that the members of the group can be notified by Notes when they have to perform some activity crucial to the project.

For example, a salesman might fill out an expense report. When the salesman saves and closes the expense report, Notes mails it automatically to an expense tracking database on a Notes server, and mails a message to the appropriate manager notifying her that the expense report requires her review and approval.

The message received by the manager includes a link to the expense report in the tracking database. By double-clicking the link, the manager opens the expense report. When the manager approves and saves the expense report, Notes generates another message and mails it to the accounting clerk responsible for paying the expenses, and so the cycle continues.

III

Writing HTML

If either the manager or the accounting clerk neglects a pending task, Notes may send a reminder. If the person designated to complete a task is unavailable for any reason, Notes might automatically send the notice to a substitute.

Because all of the evolving information is stored in a central tracking database, anyone involved in the transaction can see its status simply by looking there. In form routing programs, the salesperson who submitted the expense report has no way of checking the status of his expense check other than to ask his manager and the accounting clerk. In Notes, he merely opens the expense report in the tracking database. If his manager has approved it, the report will reflect that fact. If the clerk has not issued the check, the report will reflect that fact as well.

Other Features of Notes

Standing alone, the features listed above make powerful tools available to small groups of people all of whom have constant computer access to the same database server. Several other features of Notes combine to make these capabilities available to groups of hundreds or thousands of people who may be located all over the world. Some of them may be only occasionally or never connected to the company network. Others may not be employed by our company at all, but rather may work for our customers or suppliers or business partners.

Client/Server Technology

Notes is a client/server system. Notes servers store Notes databases, provide multiple levels of security, and make information in the databases available to people and other servers according to their access rights.

People use the Notes client to access the data on the servers. The Notes client can access Notes servers via network connections or remotely by modem. Notes Release 4 makes connection to servers a no-brainer for the user by allowing Notes administrators to predefine connection procedures from different locations.

For example, if a salesman is in the office, he connects to the LAN, tells Notes he is in the office, and Notes automatically uses the LAN to connect to the server. Then the salesman goes on the road, arrives in a hotel room, connects his modem to a telephone line, and tells Notes he is located in a hotel. Notes automatically calls the server using the modem and a standard hotel phone system dialing sequence. All the user had to know was how to tell Notes his current location. The location profile, predefined by the Notes administrator, did all the hard work of reconfiguring Notes to connect properly using the available mode of connection.

Distributed Data

Notes databases can be fully replicated, meaning that full copies of them can be maintained in multiple locations, either on Notes servers or on Notes clients. Workers located in offices scattered all over the world may access copies of a database located on their local Notes servers. They don't have to suffer slow response times by accessing remote databases over narrow-bandwidth links in real time. The company does not have to bear the expense of high bandwidth wide area network connections.

Users use the local copy of the database, adding documents, editing existing documents, and reviewing others. Periodically—hourly, daily, or weekly, depending on the nature of the application—the servers replicate with each other. All changes in each copy of the database are replicated with the other copies of the database, so that, over time, the workers see not only their local changes but also those made by remote workers.

Likewise, home-based workers or workers who are on the move, flying or driving from appointment to appointment, can carry replica copies of relevant databases on their laptops. They can work locally, reviewing project status and adding new documents to reflect their own activities. From time to time, they can connect to a Notes server by modem or by connecting to the network, and replicate their copy of the database with the server copy, sending their changes and receiving those made by their coworkers.

Connectivity

Notes was designed from the ground up to work with whatever other software tools you may use. You can pull information into Notes documents from all of your desktop productivity applications as well as from databases located on PCs and mainframes. You can also export information to your back-end databases. Also, Notes runs on a variety of platforms including Windows, Windows 95, Windows NT, Macintosh, OS/2, NetWare, and several varieties of UNIX. It can use all major networking protocols including TCP/IP, SPX/IPX, NetBEUI, NetBIOS, AppleTalk, and Banyan VINES.

Robust Security

All of this versatility would be of limited use if Notes did not have the ability to secure Notes databases against intruders. In fact, Notes has robust, multi-layered security features. To read or contribute to Notes databases, you must first positively identify yourself to the Notes server. Notes uses public/private key encryption to accomplish this. After the server knows who you are, it can block you out at the server, database, document, or field level. That is, you can be excluded from the server's access control list, each database's access control list, view, form, and document access lists, and from access to fields by field-level encryption.

III

Writing HTML

Notes Documents and Fields

Lotus Notes databases bear only the most superficial resemblance to standard computer databases. They do have records and fields in them, as do standard databases, but the resemblance ends right about there. In a standard database, all records in a table have the same set of fields and each field is the same, fixed length, whether it contains data or not.

Notes records, known as *documents* or *notes*, look and feel more like word processor documents than database records. Notes fields do not have a fixed length and the length of any one field varies from document to document depending on the field's actual contents. No two documents in a database need incorporate the same array of fields. Document A might have fields one, two, and three, while document B has fields one, two, and four. And a document might acquire fields one and two when created, then have fields three and four added at a later date.

Notes Forms

When you create, edit, or read a Notes document, you do so using a template known as a *Form*. Forms define what fields may be added to a document when created or edited. They define what fields may be seen when reading the document. They also define how the document will be formatted.

You may use one form to create a document and another to read it. Or I may read a document with Form A while you read it with Form B. The result might be that I, the salesperson, would see some fields and you, the manager, would see others. Notes databases typically have multiple forms.

Notes Views and Full Text Search

To find information in a Notes database, you could either browse Notes views or you could use Notes' full text search engine to locate documents. A Notes view is a tabular listing of documents. The documents appear in rows, and information from the documents appears in columns. Most Notes databases include multiple views, allowing you to use the one most suited to your search. For example, in a training department database, you might view course offerings by date in one view and by subject in another view. A third view might show only a subset of documents. For example, a view might show only the classes scheduled for this week.

Notes Costs and Connectivity

Until Notes Release 4 arrived in January 1996, Notes was a closed system. You had to have a Notes client, available only from Lotus, to gain full access to Notes databases, or you could gain limited, customized access to Notes databases with some of the Notes add-in tools, such as Notes ViP (currently Revelation ViP 2.0 for Lotus Notes, available from Revelation Software, Cambridge, MA). Also, until Notes Release 4 arrived, these tools were much more expensive than the browsers necessary to implement a company Intranet.

Of course, with Releases 4 and 4.5, all this has changed. Lotus has dramatically increased Notes' functionality and its interconnectivity with non-Notes systems. The Notes client can now function as a Web browser. The Notes server can either publish Notes databases to your Web server or it can function as a stand-alone Web server. The Notes server can also serve as a backend to non-Notes mail clients including cc:Mail and MAPI mail clients such as the Windows 95 mail client.

Lotus has also slashed Notes' pricing to bring Notes servers and clients in line with Internet servers and browsers. For example, a single Notes server now costs about $700. InterNotes Web Publisher (which cost $7500 when first released in January 1995) is now included in the box with the server software. And a Notes Desktop™ client, which includes all Notes functionality except server administration and application design, runs as low as $69 per desktop if purchased in quantity.

Notes and the Intranet

Like just about everyone else, Lotus recognizes the value that the Internet, Intranets, and the World Wide Web offer to businesses seeking connectivity within the enterprise and between the enterprise and the outside world. Lotus also recognizes that the Internet/Intranet is a perfect extension of Notes's own connectivity, and that Notes is the perfect development and deployment platform for Web applications. Therefore, Lotus has developed several products to integrate Notes with the Internet and your Intranet, and has integrated Web protocols including HTML, HTTP, and Java directly into Notes.

Notes-to-Internet/Intranet products include two—InterNotes Web Navigator and Lotus InterNotes News—that are designed to bring Internet/Intranet resources to Notes users. They include two—InterNotes Web Publisher and Domino Web Server—that make Notes resources available to the Internet/Intranet. Finally, there are Lotus NetApps, designed to streamline the development of Web-enabled Notes applications.

InterNotes Web Navigator is a Web browser integrated into Notes. The Notes 4.0 version of InterNotes Web Navigator resides on the Notes server and requires you to browse by way of your Notes server as proxy server. In Notes 4.5, the Notes client can either browse via the Notes server, as in Notes 4.0, or browse the Web directly.

III

Writing HTML

InterNotes News is a Notes server-based interface to UseNet News Groups. It converts News Groups into Notes discussion databases and transmits Notes users' contributions back to the News servers.

InterNotes Web Publisher and Domino Web Server both publish Notes data to the Web. InterNotes Web Publisher works with any third-party Web server. Domino Web Server is a stand-alone, Notes server-based Web server. Both products simplify the authorship of Web documents by allowing anyone who can fill in a form to author Web documents. Both products simplify Web site management by automating the maintenance of documents and the links between them. Both products allow people who don't otherwise have access to data on Notes servers to access Notes data in their Web browsers via the Internet/Intranet.

Finally, Lotus NetApps are what Lotus calls "application frameworks". They are generic Notes applications that you can customize to meet your needs. Lotus plans to release several of them and released the first one, Net.Presence, concurrently with the release of Notes 4.5. Net.Presence is available for download from Lotus' Web site (**www.lotus.com**) and consists of a set of Notes database templates designed to streamline the design, creation, and management of Web sites. You can use the templates as is or you can customize the templates or borrow from them to generate content databases made to your order. Lotus has announced the future release of Net.Marketing and Net.Service, which are sets of templates and tools for building marketing capabilities and customer service capabilities, respectively, into your Web site.

For years, Lotus Notes has been *the* tool for automating group interactivity. With Domino and the InterNotes tools, Lotus provides the back-end tools for integrating Notes and your Intranet. With the NetApps, Lotus provides the front-end applications. Altogether, Lotus Notes provides about the most comprehensive approach to designing, creating content for, maintaining, and making generally effective use of a Web site of any set of products on the market today.

Usenet

Earlier, we discussed implementing Usenet in conjunction with a Web server to add discussion areas to the Intranet. Usenet news is based on the Network News Transport Protocol (NNTP). Usenet is the term used to describe the global network of systems that share news articles, though NNTP can be set up for internal use only.

Most current browsers can read and post news articles. This make the addition of Usenet a simple, seamless addition.

Some ideas for local groups might be:

- **company.eng.** This group could be used to discuss engineering issues.
- **company.windows.** This group might allow users to discuss Windows applications and help each other solve problems.
- **company.policies.** This might be an area for employees and managers to discuss company policies.
- **company.outages.** Power or network shutdowns could be placed in this group. This group might want to be moderated since it is used to inform only.
- **company.specs.** This might be used to discuss specifications that are being worked on.
- **company.misc.** This group might be for miscellaneous discussions.

One of the good things about Usenet is its hierarchical nature. This means that groups can be broken down further if one group gets too busy. For example, the group "company.eng" might get too busy with hardware and software engineers talking. If this happens, the group can be split into "company.eng.hw" and "company.eng.sw."

There are different Usenet News servers available for many different platforms. This includes INN, Netscape News Server, and Interware from Consensys.

INN

INN, The InterNet News server originally written by Rich Salz. INN runs on most UNIX platforms and comes in source code form. INN is one of the more popular news servers since it is available free of charge.

INN can be downloaded from:

- **ftp://ftp.uu.net/networking/news/nntp/inn**
- **ftp://ftp.msen.com/pub/packages/inn**

Installing INN

Once you have downloaded and unpacked the INN distribution, you should read the documentation available in Install.ms.*. This will give you a good idea of how INN works and what can be done. Installation requires running BUILD; usually "sh BUILD" will do this. BUILD will ask a few site-specific questions. If you don't know the answer, hitting return will usually do the right thing. BUILD needs to be run as root.

Once BUILD configures the source, it will run make. This might take a while to finish. It will also make the directories and install the program. If INN doesn't build and install with BUILD, then you should look at the installation instructions in Install.ms.*.

Running INN

Once it is built and installed, there is some configuration that may need to be done. You should read the Install.ms.* files for instructions on what needs to be configured. At a minimum, you may need to edit:

- **expire.ctl.** How often to expire articles. The syntax is groups:modflag:keep:default:purge. Groups define which groups you are talking about; modflag is either M for moderated, U for unmoderated or A for all. Keep, default, and purge are the number of days to keep articles. Keep is the minimum number of days, default is the default number, and purge is the maximum number.

- **hosts.nntp.** Access list of who sends us news articles. For a stand-alone site, this may be blank. The syntax is host:password. This allows you to force a site to use a password for security reasons.

- **inn.conf.** Configuration file for INN. This file allows you to define the local domain name (domain), what to put in the From line (fromhost), default moderator address (moderatormailer), what to put in the path and Xref header (pathhost), Organization name (organization), and the default NNTP server (server).

- **moderators.** Can be used to set groups up as moderated. The syntax is newsgroup:pathname. Newsgroup is the group and pathname is the address to send the posting to. %s in the pathname is replaced with the newsgroup name.

- **newsfeeds.** For defining whom to send and receive articles from. The syntax is site:pattern:flag:param. The site is the remote sitename, pattern is the list of groups to send, flags can be used to limit which types of articles to send, param is for any parameter needed. More information on the newsfeeds file is in the man page.

- **nnrpd.access.** Who can read articles from this server. The syntax for a line is host:perm:user:pass:groups. This can be used to only allow certain machines or people to read or post articles.

- **passwd.nntp.** Password file for NNTP access. This is the file that tells INN what password to use when it connects to a remote site. The syntax is host:name:pass:style. Host is the remote host name, name is the username to use, pass is the password, style is used to define optional authentication formats.

> **Caution**
>
> Be careful when editing the newsfeeds file that you do not send any local groups to outside hosts. Also, make sure if your machine is not sending and receiving articles, you don't put any hosts in the hosts.nntp file.

Once you have configured INN, you can start it up and test it. This is done by running rc.news script. If you want INN to start on reboot, you will need to add this to the startup scripts.

> **Note**
>
> INN is a very complicated system. You should read the man page entries for the commands and make sure you understand what the different files do.

Once INN is running, you need to add your local groups and decide whether they are moderated or not. To add new groups, you can use the command:

```
ctlinnd newgroup [groupname] [rest] [creator]
```

groupname is the name of the group. rest is one of the following:

- **y** Local postings are allowed.
- **n** Local postings aren't allowed; remote postings are allowed.
- **m** This group is moderated and articles must be approved.
- **j** The articles are not kept but are junked. They will be passed on to other newsfeeds.
- **x** No articles can be posted to this group.
- **=other.group** Used to make articles appear to be sent to a different group.

Intranets will probably either want to use y for discussion groups or m for moderated groups.

The creator is the person who created or requested the group.

Netscape News Server

Netscape sells a commercial News server called Netscape News Server. It is available from **http://www.netscape.com/** and sells for $995.

Netscape News Server runs on the following platforms:

- OSF/1 version 2.0
- HP/UX version 9.03 and 9.04
- AIX version 3.2.5 and 4.1
- IRIX version 5.2 and 5.3
- SunOS version 4.1.3
- Solaris version 2.3 and 2.4
- BSDI version 1.1 and 2.0

Netscape News Server is a very easy-to-administer news server for UNIX machines. Netscape has built on the news server idea and added an HTML front-end. This allows Netscape News to be administered from any Web browser.

Using a browser, you can:

- Add or remove local or remote newsgroups.
- Add access control to limit who can read or post articles.
- Add servers to distribute news articles to or receive articles from.
- Shut down or start the news server process.
- Change how long news articles remain on the server.

InterWare

Consensys has developed a suite of Intranet/Internet applications called InterWare. This includes a Usenet server that runs on 32-bit windows such as NT or 95. It is available from **http://www.consensys.com/interware/ intrware.htm/** and can be ordered for $795.

The News Server has a graphical user interface to make administration easier. This graphical administration interface allows you to:

- configure upstream and downstream sites.
- add new groups.
- remove groups.
- limit who can access different groups.
- start or stop the server.

Mailing Lists

Mailing lists are similar to Usenet News with one major difference: Mail is sent to the user, news requires the user to go read it. This makes news less desirable; since users are required to check in and see if there are any new news articles. For messages that are required to be read, mailing lists sometimes make better choices.

Most e-mail packages can be set up to handle mailing aliases; in fact, most companies already have aliases in place. Some aliases might be for:

- **All.** This would go to everyone in the company. It would be used for important announcements.
- **Geographic.** This could be used for a specific building. This might be used if, for example, someone left his headlights on.
- **Departmental.** This would be for a specific department. It could be used for departmental discussions.

A simple mailing list can be maintained by the e-mail administrator. It would involve the administrator creating a company alias that goes to a group of people. For sites running UNIX, this would involve adding a line to the aliases file. This file is normally located in "/etc" or in "/usr/lib." Once a change has been made, you will have to run the command "newaliases" to re-create the sendmail alias database. Other e-mail packages may have other ways of creating a global alias. Check your documentation for more information.

Note

If your site runs NIS, then you will have to also remake the NIS alias maps. This is usually done by cd'ing to /var/yp and running "make."

One disadvantage to this procedure is the fact that the administrator must make all changes to the mailing lists. Other mailing list packages may not require this. Let's look at another way to have mailing lists set up. This program is called majordomo.

Majordomo

Majordomo is one of the most popular mailing list managers available. It was written by Brent Chapman of GreatCircle Associates. It is available from **ftp://ftp.greatcircle.com/pub/majordomo**. Majordomo will run on most versions of UNIX.

Once it is downloaded and unpacked, it can be installed with just a few steps. The installation instructions are included with the distribution. The major steps to install Majordomo are:

- Create a majordomo account for this to run under. Also, create a majordomo group for this.

- Create the directories where majordomo will be installed and make them mode 775.

- Edit the Makefile and make any changes that are required.

- Make the code. This is done by using "make" and then "make install."

- As root install the wrapper program, "make install-wrapper."

- Install the majordomo.cf file in /etc.

- Add the majordomo aliases to the alias file.

Once majordomo is installed and running, you can start creating lists. The majordomo list owner must create new lists but once they are created, users can subscribe and unsubscribe without the administrator's help.

To create a new list, you need to do the following:

- cd to $listdir and create an empty file called <listname>. listname is the name of the mailing list.

- create a file called <listname>.password and put the approve password in it. See the instructions if you don't understand this.

- create a file called <listname>.info with the introductory list information.

- Add the aliases to the alias file. See the install instructions for details.

- Optionally create the archive directory in $file_dir.

- Optionally create the digest word directory in $digest_work_dir.

Users can subscribe and unsubscribe to lists by sending e-mail to majordomo with the body of the message containing: "subscribe listname," or "unsubscribe listname." For help on majordomo, you can send the command "help" in the body of the message to majordomo.

LISTSERV

LISTSERV is one of the first mailing list managers available. It is currently available for most versions of UNIX as well as VMS and Windows NT. It is available from Lsoft (**http://www.lsoft.com/**).

Once a mailing list is created with LISTSERV, it can be maintained remotely via e-mail. This makes LISTSERV easy for moderators and users alike. Lists can be set up to be public, where anyone can subscribe and unsubscribe, or private, where the administrator must approve or make all subscription changes.

LISTSERV is very popular and chances are good that if you subscribe to any mailing lists, they will be running LISTSERV.

Hypermail

Hypermail isn't a mailing list manager, but it is an HTML front-end for a mailing list archive. This allows a mailing list to be browsed through a Web browser.

This is different than reading mail from a browser because Hypermail actually sorts the messages by threads. Most browsers do not allow this, plus not all browsers can be used to read e-mail. Messages can also be sorted by date and author.

Hypermail is available from **http://www.eit.com/software/ hypermail/hypermail.html**. It is free for both non-commercial and commercial uses though the licenses differ. It is available in binary form only and is available for the following platforms:

- Sun OS 4.1.3
- Solaris 2.3
- Irix 5.2
- OSF/1 2.0

Once the binary file is downloaded, it can be run with the following options:

- **u** This option is used to add a single message to the archive.
- **p** This is used to show the progress of the Hypermail run.
- **i** This tells Hypermail to read from stdin.
- **x** This is used to overwrite an existing archive.
- **m** This is used to specify the mail archive to create an HTML index for.
- **l** This is the name of the archive. This will be used as the title for the HTML files.
- **d** This is the directory that the HTML files should be placed in. If this is blank, the files will be created in a directory called archive in the current directory.
- **a** This is a link to other related archives.
- **b** This is used to add a link to information about the archive. For example, subscription information.
- **c** This is used to define a configuration file to use.
- **z,h,?** These options print the usage or help page for Hypermail.

The easiest way to use Hypermail is to create a directory for each mail archive you are using in the DocumentRoot or other directory in the Web server. Then, run Hypermail with the following command line:

```
hypermail -m <archive-file> -d <directory> -l <archive name>
```

III

Writing HTML

This will read in the archive file and store the HTML files in the directory you created for it. It will also add a title to the HTML pages.

Once you run Hypermail for the first time, you can run with this same syntax to update the archive. If, for some reason you need to re-create the archive, you can add the "-x" option and overwrite the old archive files. Figure 18.1 shows a Hypermail page.

Fig. 18.1
Hypermail is an HTML front-end for mail archives.

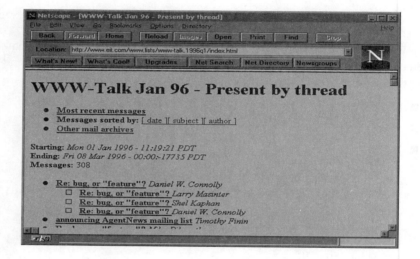

Bulletin Boards and Chat Scripts

Bulletin boards are pages that can be written to and read by a number of people at once. This can allow someone to post a question and receive numerous answers. This sounds much like Usenet and it is quite similar. That's part of the reason Usenet and the WWW work so well together. WWW bulletin boards, however, aren't limited to text articles like Usenet is, though the documents can be any valid HTML page.

Chat scripts are similar to bulletin boards but are designed to be used in real time. As you type a comment everyone else sees it and can reply. This is similar to the Internet Relay Chat (IRC). Much like bulletin boards differ from Usenet because of the advantages of HTML, chat rooms differ from IRC because of the ability to handle HTML documents.

Web technology is rapidly being developed to allow more two-way communication such as chat rooms and bulletin boards and, by the time this book is published, things may have changed drastically. To keep current, you should monitor the page **http://union.ncsa.uiuc.edu/HyperNews/get/www/ collaboration**.

It is possible to use existing Usenet protocols and mail servers to act as Web-based bulletin boards. This can be done by simply sending HTML files instead of simple text files. This allows documents to contain hyperlinks to other messages and graphics. Usenet servers and mailing lists, however, don't normally have links to previous and next messages and they also don't handle inlined images very well. Still, many companies find using this already deployed technology is enough to get them by.

There are a few other bulletin board based products available and one we will discuss is HyperNews. This is available from NCSA, the original creators of Mosaic.

HyperNews

HyperNews is a WWW bulletin board-like system that runs on most UNIX systems that have Perl5.001m or Perl5.002 ported to them. There is currently no port to NT, Windows or Macintosh. HyperNews is available from **http:// union.ncsa.uiuc.edu/HyperNews/get/hypernews.html**. Figure 18.2 shows a page from a HyperNews server.

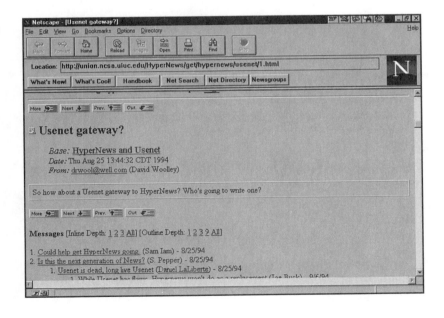

Fig. 18.2
HyperNews allows threaded discussions.

Once you download and unpack the distribution, you should see a directory called HyperNews1.9. Under this directory is another directory called ".scripts." Hiding underneath there is all the code for HyperNews. This includes:

- **README** What is included in the distribution.
- **Makefile** Used to package a release. Not needed by users.
- ***.html** Documentation for the HyperNews system.
- ***.pl** The actual programs used by HyperNews.
- **fixPerlPath** This is a script that can be used to change where the program looks for perl.
- **Icons** This directory contains all the icons used in HyperNews.

To install HyperNews, you need to make sure you have CGI scripts enabled for your server. You also need to create a directory writable by the server. Others should not be able to write in this area. This should be called HyperNews/SECURE by default.

Once you have that set up, you are ready to go. You can read the file "installation.html" if you have any problems or questions. It explains this in detail.

- If you untarred the distribution in a directory that doesn't allow CGI scripts, then it must be moved to one that does. The default area is /cgi-bin/HyperNews.
- Make sure your server is enabled to follow symbolic links in the HyperNews directory.
- Create e-mail aliases for HyperNews and HyperNews-Owner. These should point to the HyperNews administrator.
- Open a browser to the document called "HyperNews/.scripts/ setup-form.pl." You might need to change the name to end in ".cgi" depending on your server configuration.
- After filling out this form, you can submit it and it should configure itself. You may have to change the permissions on the HyperNews directory tree so that changes can be made by the server user.
- Once HyperNews is installed, you need to create the base articles. This is outlined in the "base-articles.html" file. Basically, you need to run the "http://www.server.com/HyperNews/edit-article.pl" script.
- Read the "instructions-html" page for instructions on how to become a member, read a message, add a message, submitting a message, and administration of messages.

WWWBoard

WWWBoard is a script written by Matthew M. Wright. Matt makes many very useful scripts available free of charge at **http://www. worldwidemart.com/scripts**. He does ask for credit for writing the programs and would like to hear from users of the software.

WWWBoard is a standard Perl script and should run on any platform that has Perl available. It may require some minor changes to work on Perl systems other than UNIX. Installation for WWWBoard is covered in detail in the README file that comes with the distribution.

WWWBoard also has an HTML administration interface to make it even easier to manage. This is called WWWAdmin and it is also shipped with the distribution.

WWWAdmin allows you to delete messages by message number, by date, or by author. You can also change the administrator password from this interface.

Other Options

In addition to HyperNews, there are also other software packages available. Some of these include:

- Futplex System. This is available from **http://gewis.win.tue.nl/ applications/futplex/index.html**.
- Interaction/IP. This is a commercial package that runs under Mac OS. It allows for threaded discussions and chat rooms. More information is available at **http://www.ifi.uio.no/~terjen/interaction/ index.html.**
- WebBoard from O'Reilly and Associates. This is available from **http:// webboard.ora.com/.** WebBoard is a 32-bit windows applications, so it can be run on Windows 95, as well as NT. Unfortunately, WebBoard does not currently run with IIS since it requires CGI standard 1.2 and password pass through. It does run with WebSite, also from O'Reilly and Associates.

  WebBoard can be used for private or public conferences and can have up to 255 separate conferences set up on each machine.
- The book *Webmaster's Expert Solutions* also has a nice section on Chat Scripts and bulletin boards. This book is available from Que.

III

Writing HTML

Part IV

Maintenance and Security

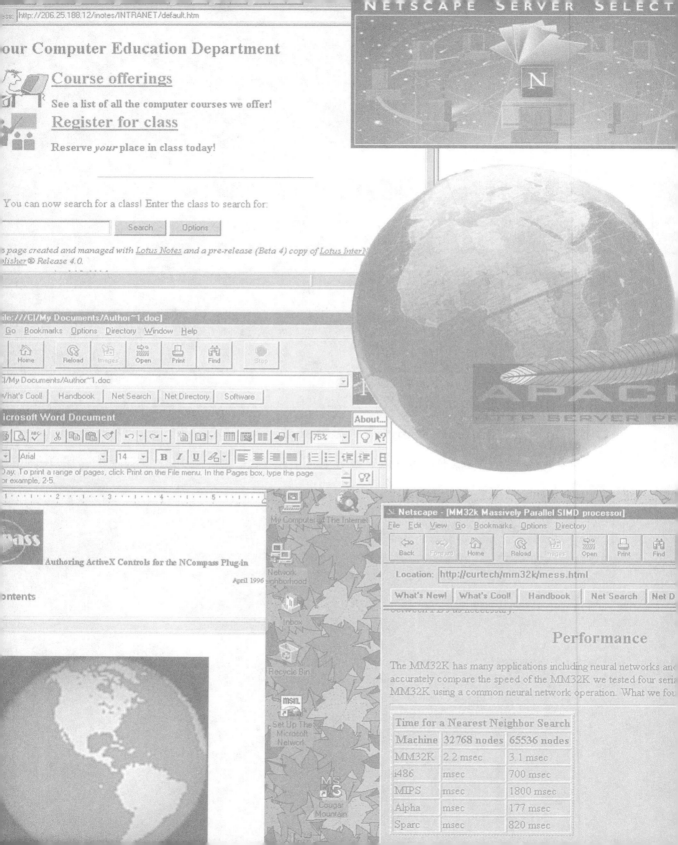

http://206.25.188.12/inotes/INTRANET/default.htm

our Computer Education Department

Course offerings

See a list of all the computer courses we offer!

Register for class

Reserve *your* place in class today!

You can now search for a class! Enter the class to search for:

[Search] [Options]

s page created and managed with *Lotus Notes* and a pre-release (Beta 4) copy of *Lotus InterN*
lisher ® Release 4.0.

le:///C|/My Documents/Author~1.doc]

Go Bookmarks Options Directory Window Help

| Home | Reload | Images | Open | Print | Find | Stop |

/My Documents/Author~1.doc

What's Cool! | Handbook | Net Search | Net Directory | Software

icrosoft Word Document   About...

Arial   14   **B** *I* <u>U</u>   75%

Day: To print a range of pages, click Print on the File menu. In the Pages box, type the page
or example, 2-5.

Authoring ActiveX Controls for the NCompass Plug-in

April 1996

ntents

My Computer / The Internet

Network eighborhood

Inbox

Recycle Bin

msn.

Set Up The Microsoft Network

MS S

Cougar Mountain

Netscape - [MM32k Massively Parallel SIMD processor]

File Edit View Go Bookmarks Options Directory

| Back | Forward | Home | Reload | Images | Open | Print | Find |

Location: http://curtech/mm32k/mess.html

What's New! | What's Cool! | Handbook | Net Search | Net D

Performance

The MM32K has many applications including neural networks and
accurately compare the speed of the MM32K we tested four seria
MM32K using a common neural network operation. What we fou

Time for a Nearest Neighbor Search		
Machine	32768 nodes	65536 nodes
MM32K	2.2 msec	3.1 msec
i486	msec	700 msec
MIPS	msec	1800 msec
Alpha	msec	177 msec
Sparc	msec	820 msec

CHAPTER 19
Using Multimedia

Multimedia is the fusion of communication streams that affect different sensory modalities. Multimedia is a powerful tool for computing information systems, enabling you to convey ideas via mechanisms, such as graphics, 3-D modeling, motion, and sound.

With multimedia, you are better able to communicate meaning to your audience; these techniques more directly interface with an individual's real-world perceptions. Some examples of multimedia may merely provide flash, attempting to amaze users with technical wizardry; however, the best use of these devices enables your Intranet to illustrate concepts that can't be sufficiently explained through the textual medium.

In this chapter, you will learn:

- What multimedia technologies are readily available for integration with your Intranet
- How to create and incorporate multimedia into your Intranet
- How to enable your audience to utilize multimedia
- What the concerns are of using multimedia
- What Intranet applications are best suited for multimedia

Using Sound

The primary means through which humans communicate is sound. Early PCs were limited to producing simple beeps and buzzes, but most desktop machines today can re-create speech, music, and advanced sound effects. This medium adds a whole new dimension to your audience's experience as they use your Intranet.

Sound File Characteristics

Sound is a perception created by pressure waves that are sensed by the ear. This real world phenomenon must be translated into data understood by a computer. Two very different types of sound files available to desktop computers accomplish this, MIDI files and waveform files.

Musical Instrument Digital Interface (MIDI) is a format that is used to reproduce music. It tells a music synthesizer when to start and stop playing certain notes and instruments. MIDI is a very compact and efficient format, but it doesn't attempt to precisely reproduce a prerecorded, real world auditory experience.

Waveform files are much less compact, but attempt to describe the wave corresponding to a sound. These files can replicate voices and reproduce specific musical presentations. For these reasons, most Intranet applications are best suited to waveform versus MIDI data. Sound information in these files is characterized by three parameters:

- Sampling rate. A continuous sound wave is broken down into discrete "slices," known as samples, and then stored as digital information. These values are referred to in terms of kilohertz (kHz) or "samples per second" (samples/sec). 8,000 samples/sec is sufficient to re-create most sounds, but many sound cards allow for rates up to the CD quality 44,100.

- Bits per sample. A greater number of bits per sample allows a sound wave's amplitude to be more precisely measured. Basic sound data is stored in 8 bits, but more advanced computer configurations use 16.

- Number of channels. Mono sound corresponds to a single channel, while stereo information is stored as two.

All of these parameters affect the quality and compactness of the digitized sound.

Sound File Formats

Waveform audio data is usually stored in one of many file formats, which make up a confusing array of schemes. It is useful to incorporate previously recorded sounds into your Intranet. Understanding the commonly available formats assists you in developing a consistent collection. The formats you commonly find are shown in table 19.1.

Table 19.1   Common Sound File Formats

Format Type	Extension
NeXT/Sun	au, .snd
RIFF WAVE (Microsoft)	.wav
Creative Voice	.voc
Macintosh/SGI AIFF	.aiff
Macintosh HCOM sound	none

Playing, Creating, and Editing Sound Files

In order to work with sound files, your desktop computer must have suitable hardware. Macintosh and most UNIX workstations are constructed with the minimum necessary hardware. The basic speaker on a PC, however, is suited to playing simple beeps and not much more; drivers have been written to demand more from this little piece of hardware, but the reproduced sounds are very poor in quality and the speaker has no ability to record sounds. Thus, to support multimedia sound, PCs should be equipped with one of many available sound cards, the most common being the Creative Labs SoundBlaster series.

Caution

Sounds can be very distracting in an office environment. When using audio files on an Intranet, make sure that you make it clear to the individual viewing the page that a sound will be played if he proceeds. Use sounds judiciously.

Many good sound applications are available on the Internet for different platforms. *WHAM* for Windows can play and record many sound formats, including all listed in table 19.1. *SoundApp* for Macintosh plays a similarly impressive array of formats. Enabling your Web browser to utilize these applications is a two step process that is similar for all "helper" applications:

1. Download the software, unpack it, and install it onto your computer.

2. Configure your Web browser to use the application as a helper. This is done through your helper application preferences menu and configuring your browser to launch the application for "audio/basic," "audio/x-wav," and "audio/x-aiff" formats.

Recording sound files may require additional hardware, such as a microphone or an interface to a CD. You need to choose a file format and the characteristics that make the most sense to your Intranet. You need to record the most compact files with the necessary level of quality. For speech and simple sound effects, a rate of 8,000 samples/sec and saved in the ubiquitous NeXT/Sun .au format is probably the best idea. For high-fidelity music, choosing a higher sampling rate and a format like WAVE makes more sense. Realize that such files require a significant amount of space and take a considerable delay in downloading.

For more advanced sound file editing, Cool Edit for Windows (see figure 19.1) is a high-quality application that is available on the Internet. With Cool Edit, you can record sounds, retouch files, add special effects, merge files, and work with many sound file formats. If you work a great deal with sound and find this program's capabilities limiting, more advanced commercial packages are available at greater costs.

Fig. 19.1
Cool Edit allows you to manipulate waveform sound files.

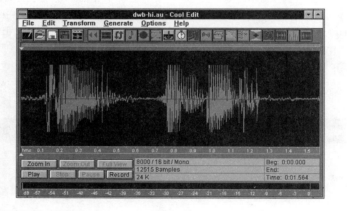

Note

WHAM is available from URL: **http://www.winsite.com/pc/win3/sounds/wham133.zip**

SoundApp is available from URL: **http://hyperarchive.lcs.mit.edu/HyperArchive/Archive/gst/snd/sound-app-202.hqx**

Cool Edit is available from URL: **http://www.netzone.com/syntrillium/**

RealAudio

RealAudio is a commercial audio delivery system developed by Progressive Networks. While other sound file formats require large storage space and a significant delay to transmit from the server, RealAudio is designed to provide efficient, on-demand audio. RealAudio provides a good solution for audio-intensive Intranets.

The RealAudio system consists of three components: The RealAudio Player enables Windows, UNIX, and Macintosh computers to play RealAudio sounds and is freely available. The RealAudio Server enables an Intranet to transmit audio information, and a license must be purchased from Progressive Networks. The RealAudio Encoder enables you to encode standard audio formats into the RealAudio format.

Once the RealAudio Player has been installed on a desktop computer, it can receive and play RealAudio files. The Player contacts the server with a TCP connection to control the transmission, while the sound data is sent back as a stream of UDP datagrams. The Player reproduces the sound as it receives the stream of data, meaning that perceived download time is minimal. Sound quality is generally good, though over a busy network, datagrams will be lost and quality will degrade.

Audio content is provided by installing the RealAudio Server and then creating links in your HTML page to RealAudio metafiles. A metafile is a simple text file; it contains the URL to the sound file and should be transmitted with a MIME type of "audio/x-pn-realaudio." When the browser receives the metafile, it passes it to the Player, which then receives the RealAudio sound identified by the URL. The steps to setting up the RealAudio server are:

1. Download the RealAudio Server archive file from Progressive Networks as per the instructions provided by them. For Windows NT systems, the file will be a PKZip archive. On UNIX systems, the file will be a UNIX compressed TAR archive. If you are installing the server from a CD-ROM, mount the CD and copy the directory structures to your machine. Ensure that the permissions are appropriate and skip to step 3.

> **Tip**
>
> You need a special utility to extract PKZip archive files. The PKWare utilities are available from URL: **http://www.pkware.com/**

2. Move the file into the directory where the server should reside. Under Windows NT, "`C:\win32app`" may be a good choice. Under UNIX

systems, "/usr/local" may be most appropriate. The following examples assume these directories. Uncompress the file.

3. Configure the server by editing the file called "server.cfg," located within the "pnserver" directory. Ensure that all defaults are appropriate. You will need to add values for the "CustomerName" and "LicenseKey" settings with the information provided by Progressive Networks in order to use your licensed server.

4. You will want to have the server start up automatically during your machine's boot process. To do this under Windows NT, you will need to use a utility provided by Progressive Networks, invoked as so:

```
C:\win32app\pnserver\bin\crtsvc
C:\win32app\pnserver\bin\pnserv20.exe
C:\win32app\pnserver\server.cfg
```

This utility will add the RealAudio server into your Services Control Panel. You can now use that utility to configure the startup characteristics of the PNServer service. Ensure that the Startup Type is set to "Automatic."

To start the server automatically under UNIX systems, you will need to add the following lines to an appropriate startup script, depending on the UNIX platform you use. Consult your system administrator for assistance.

```
if [-f /usr/local/pnserver/bin/pnserver ]; then
    echo "Starting RealAudio server..."
    /usr/local/pnserver/bin/pnserver /usr/local/pnserver/
    server.cfg
fi
```

5. You've now successfully setup your RealAudio server. Reboot your machine to start the server. Now you need to create RealAudio content. Refer to the Real Audio Content Creation for detailed instructions on creating RealAudio data files, which end in the .ra extension. Place them into the server's BasePath directory.

6. You must create a metafile which points the RealAudio player to the appropriate RealAudio data file. For example, the metafile "test.ram" intended to play "test.ra" would contain:

```
pnm://myserver/test.ra
```

7. Configure your HTTP server to serve .ram metafiles as the content type "audio/x-pn-realaudio".

8. Create an HTML page which links to the metafile. For example:

```
<A HREF="test.ram">test RealAudio file</A>
```

Maintenance

9. Ensure that your browser has the RealAudio player properly installed and try out the HTML page created in step 8.

The RealAudio Player has a Netscape Plug-in feature which is supported by Windows and Macintosh systems. If you use the Netscape Navigator as your browser, the Plug-in enables you to embed RealAudio files within your Intranet's HTML pages, and place the controls to the Player directly alongside the rest of your content. You can customize the interface by placing certain controls within specific parts of your pages.

With the Netscape Plug-in, a powerful multimedia presentation feature is possible. With the special events tool, you can create a control file that directs the Plug-in to guide the user's browser through a series of Web pages while RealAudio content is provided. For instance, a series of HTML pages could be leafed through while a narrator provides additional information.

RealAudio makes another type of presentation possible—live events. Users can connect to your Intranet and experience RealAudio content in real-time as it is being recorded. Individuals who arrive late join the presentation in progress. As data is captured from a source, such as a microphone, the RealAudio system passes it on to all connected clients, enabling you to set up Intranet-based events such as speeches and lectures.

The major drawback to implementing RealAudio on your Intranet is the cost for the Server. Special Intranet pricing is available, but you need to decide if the powerful Intranet applications possible with RealAudio are worth the price. As of this writing, a single Intranet server with support providing five simultaneous connections costs $790, while one providing unlimited access costs $5,990.

> **Note**
>
> Information regarding RealAudio products is available at URL: **http://www.realaudio.com/products/**

Video and Animation

Few visual cues grab your audience's attention better than motion. A casual surf through the Net demonstrates that this fact hasn't been overlooked by Internet Web developers. Scattered bits of flash may liven up a page, but Intranets demonstrate the real value of moving pictures, which convey information and communicate ideas.

Basic Animation Techniques

The simplest Web animations consist of a series of static image files, usually GIFs or JPEGs, which when displayed sequentially create the perception of motion. These are the most commonly seen techniques for animation, since the technology required for authoring and display is minimal. All of these techniques are adequate for simple moving pictures, but are inappropriate for complex multimedia data.

The easiest and most limiting technology is *client-pull*. This technique uses a special HTTP header, which can be mimicked by an HTML element, to tell a Web browser to load another page after a certain delay. Listing 19.1 shows the implementation of this technique by using the META tag as indicated.

Listing 19.1   A Client-Pull HTML Document

```
<!DOCTYPE HTML PUBLIC "-//IETF//DTD HTML//EN">
<HTML>
<HEAD>
<META HTTP-EQUIV="refresh" CONTENT="1; http://www.company.com/
➥page2.html">
<TITLE>Client Pull</TITLE>
</HEAD>
<BODY>
<H1>Client Pull</H1>
<P><IMG SRC="image1.gif" ALT="animation"></P>
</BODY>
</HTML>
```

Netscape defined this technique, and it is supported by their browser and Microsoft's Internet Explorer. This technique is easy to implement, since you only need to create a series of Web pages with embedded images that, when displayed in order, appear animated. Only HTML knowledge is required. Client-pull drawbacks stem from the fact that the browser must initiate a new TCP connection, with its associated overhead, for each frame. The delay caused can be quite noticeable, usually spoiling the illusion of animation.

A slightly more complex mechanism is *server-push*, where the Web server sends a multipart document that encapsulates a series of images. Again, this technique was defined by Netscape and is supported by both the Netscape Navigator and the Microsoft Internet Explorer.

Server-push allows the animation data to be much more focused than with client-pull. Only one connection is maintained, making this more efficient for the client and allowing for smoother animation of in-line images. Server-push, however, presents certain problems relating to long-term network connections and places a significant burden upon the Web server. Furthermore, most implementations require that a CGI application be written and supported on the server to maintain the server-push sequence. Finally, the delay between each frame is determined by download time, and leads to jerky animation at times.

By far, the most elegant implementation of simple animations is based on technology defined in 1987. The GIF87 specification enabled a GIF image file to contain a series of snapshots. The GIF89a specification enabled this feature to be extended through Application Extension Blocks (AEBs), allowing for application-specific information to be included in the file. Netscape has defined such an AEB, which allows for a specific delay time to be defined between the display of each snapshot, as well as looping capabilities throughout the series of images.

The latest versions of Netscape Navigator and Microsoft Internet Explorer support these images, and many advantages of this technique are readily apparent. The GIF89a animation file is transmitted as a single, compact unit, and requires no ongoing network connections that burden server, client, or network. These images can be displayed as easily as in-line images on HTML pages in an efficient manner. In fact, most popular Web sites on the Internet use GIF89a images exclusively, abandoning client-pull and server-push.

Most GIF file editing environments don't support these file formats, but many tools are quickly filling the void. On Windows systems, you can utilize the bookware Gif Construction Set; Macintosh computers have GifBuilder to use, while gifmerge is available for UNIX workstations. The editing environment is currently spartan with these tools, though you will witness quick results.

Note

The Gif Construction Set is available from URL: **http://www.mindworkshop.com/alchemy/alchemy.html**

GifBuilder is available from URL: **http://iawww.epfl.ch/Staff/Yves.Piguet/clip2gif-home/GifBuilder-0.3.2.sit.hqx**

gifmerge is available from URL: **http://www.iis.ee.ethz.ch/~kiwi/gifmerge.html**

Embedding and Linking Video Files

While the previously described techniques are suitable for cartoon-like animations, experiences which approach video-quality on an Intranet rely upon video file formats. Commonly used formats include: *AVI*, whose background is based on Microsoft Windows; QuickTime, developed on Apple Macintosh systems; and MPEG, a platform-independent solution from its inception.

Viewers are available across platforms to handle these and other video file formats. It makes sense to enable your Intranet audience to accept as many as possible. NET TOOB (see figure 19.2) is a shareware utility for Windows that supports AVI, QuickTime, and MPEG. Sparkle is freely available for Macintosh computers, supporting both QuickTime and MPEG files. XAnim for UNIX plays QuickTime, AVI, and MPEG files.

Fig. 19.2
NET TOOB allows you to play many video formats.

> **Note**
>
> NET TOOB is available from URL: **http://www.duplexx.com/dl_nt.html**
>
> Sparkle is available from URL: **http://hyperarchive.lcs.mit.edu/HyperArchive/Archive/gst/mov/sparkle-245.hqx**
>
> XAnim is available from URL: **http://www.portal.com/~podlipec/home.html**

It is probably best for an Intranet to standardize on one video file format, and MPEG is probably the best solution. It's cross-platform support is superior and it enables high-resolution, high-compression video and audio data.

MPEG's basic design is to predict motion from frame to frame, using three types of frames. Intra frames serve as reference points, coding an entire still image. Predicted frames are decoded from the most recently reconstructed intra or predicted frame. Finally, there are bidirectional frames, which are conceptually similar to intra frames, except that they are predicted from two frames, one in the past and one in the future.

Creating video scenes from scratch requires hardware to which many individuals don't have access, but entry-level technologies are inexpensive. Digital cameras enable you to capture live scenes, while video capture cards enable you to create digital video files from other sources like prerecorded video tapes and television transmissions. Simple digital cameras for Windows and Macintosh computers cost only one to two hundred dollars, while many SGI UNIX workstations arrive with a camera already attached.

Developing your own video data is no longer the realm of high-tech design studios and well-funded hobbyists. With a little work, Intranet applications can be greatly enhanced by capitalizing upon this technology.

Real-Time Video

Transmitting real time video data presents some very significant challenges, and most solutions available for Intranet uses are still somewhat immature. A few real time and broadcasting video systems are available, such as Xing StreamWorks and SGI's WebFORCE Media Server. The most widespread technology is Enhanced CU-SeeMe from White Pine.

Enhanced CU-SeeMe has multiplatform support and enables up to 8 individuals to interact with appropriate hardware. Of more usefulness to the Intranet is the Reflector, which can broadcast a single video stream to many clients on the network. White Pine currently makes available demo versions of all server and client software, so that you can determine if these applications meet your Intranet needs.

The real-time video market will mature rapidly, and more Intranet solutions will soon be tenable. Any attempt to incorporate video into an Intranet should be carefully thought out: Video can be slow to transmit, uses a significant portion of available bandwidth, and places considerable demands on workstations.

Note

Information regarding StreamWorks products is available at URL: **http://www.xingtech.com/streams/index.html**

Information regarding the WebFORCE MediaServer is available at URL: **http://www-europe.sgi.com/Products/cosmo/media_base/index.html**

(continues)

(continued)

Information regarding CU-SeeMe products is available at URL: **http:// goliath.wpine.com/cu-seeme.html**

Other Moving Picture Techniques

A few other technologies, which may make sense depending on your Intranet development resources, present themselves today. Java applets are commonly used to create simple animations. These applets require a significantly greater overhead than GIF89a animation's, but enable users to interact and control the animation's progression.

Other third party animation formats are being released for use with Intranets. One premier technology is Macromedia Director, a professional quality animation studio system. The *Shockwave for Director Plug-in*, supported by the Netscape Navigator, enables Director files to be embedded directly into Web pages. As other vendors capitalize on the potential of the Intranet, additional quality solutions will become available.

Tip

"Shockwave" is a general term Macromedia uses for all of its plug-ins which support a variety of their products. For example, Shockwave for Director allows you to view Director animation files embedded within Web pages, while Shockwave for Authorware allows you to utilize files from that multimedia authoring system.

Note

Information regarding Java is available at URL: **http://java.sun.com/ allabout.html**

Information regarding Director and Shockwave for Director is available at URL: **http://www.macromedia.com/Tools/Studios/DMS/index.html**

Creating 3-D Worlds with VRML

Virtual Reality Modeling Language (VRML) is a language that enables developers to create three-dimensional (3-D) worlds. The original goal of VRML was to change the Web from a text-based interface to a 3-D-based interface. For instance, instead of reading pages and clicking on links to get information, users walk down corridors and grab books off a shelf. While current browsers and authoring software aren't up to the task of creating such experiences, VRML provides many capabilities for an Intranet.

Perhaps the most exciting use of VRML for an Intranet is to model objects that cannot be adequately described with just text and 2-D graphics. VRML empowers you to create a model that can be viewed from any perspective in the three dimensional virtual space. Your users can zoom in, rotate, and move through your objects. Generating a complex model may take a great deal of effort, but even simple models can illustrate concepts in a powerful manner.

Language Overview

VRML's basic design defines objects in virtual 3D-space. The basic set of objects are *nodes*, which create or transform items in the virtual world. Nodes form the basis for all VRML worlds, and the 36 instances fall into seven groups:

1. Nodes that define geometric shapes (e.g. spheres, rectangular solids, arbitrary shapes)
2. Nodes that define the properties and appearance of shapes
3. Nodes that transform the virtual working space
4. Nodes that define the user's perspective on the world
5. Nodes that define the lighting in the world
6. Nodes that group other nodes for certain purposes
7. Nodes that import other objects from the network

Listing 19.2 shows a simple VRML scene which defines a light source, creates a blue sphere at the origin, and then creates a red cube centered two meters from the origin. If you save this file with a ".wrl" extension and load it into one of the VRML viewers described on the following page, you will be able to view and move about this simple model.

Listing 19.2   Simple VRML Scene

```
#VRML V1.0 ascii
Separator {
  DirectionalLight {
    direction 0 0 -1     # Light from observer into scene
  }
  Separator {          # Create an example blue sphere
```

(continues)

```
Listing 19.2   Continued

    Material {
      diffuseColor 0 0 1  # Use blue color
    }
    Sphere {}          # Draw spehere of default radius
  }
  Separator {          # Create an example of a red cube
    Material {
      diffuseColor 1 0 0  # Red color
    }
    Transform {
      translation 0 2 0  # Move it up 2 meters (y-axis) from origin
    }
    Cube {}            # Draw cube of default dimensions
  }
}
```

Limitations and Future of VRML

Before delving into VRML, it is useful to understand its limitations. The current VRML 1.0 specification defines three-dimentional shapes, lighting effects, surface properties, and hypertext links to other resources on the network. It doesn't provide audio capabilities, animation, or complex interactions between the user and the virtual scene.

There is a proposal for VRML 2.0 known as Moving Worlds, created by SGI in collaboration with Sony and Mitra. Moving Worlds has been chosen by the VRML Architecture Group as the basis for the creation of a final VRML 2.0 draft. Moving Worlds not only extends VRML's static modeling features, but adds animation, user interactions, scripting, and prototyping so that objects can be reused. VRML 2.0 will make truly encompassing virtual experiences possible.

VRML Viewers

Many VRML viewers are available for various platforms, and the ability of these products to render virtual worlds in an efficient manner is steadily increasing. The Netscape Navigator on Windows platforms supports Netscape's Live3D Plug-in, so that VRML scenes can be viewed directly within the browser. For the Internet Explorer, Microsoft has created the Microsoft VRML Add-in, extending VRML support to Windows 95 systems.

Helper applications are available for UNIX and Macintosh systems. For UNIX workstations, VRWeb is a good utility that is freely available and can be compiled on many platforms. VRML Equinox provides Macintosh PowerPC computers with VRML capabilities. These helper applications should be configured to be launched by a browser for files of the "x-world/x-vrml" MIME type, the content type all Web servers should use to transmit VRML files.

VRML Authoring Applications

Listing 19.2 illustrates the simple design of VRML, but creating complex worlds by hand is tedious and time consuming. Fortunately, many 3-D authoring tools, which support the VRML specification, are available. If you are just setting out to create virtual worlds, the freely available ClayWorks can provide great assistance in developing your Intranet's 3-D models. ClayWorks is a DOS application, but runs without problems on Windows NT.

If you need professional quality 3-D design systems for your Intranet applications, two good systems are Lightwave 3-D Modeler and WebSpace Author. (See figure 19.3.) Lightwave runs on Windows NT, SGI, and Amiga, while WebSpace Author runs on SGI platforms only.

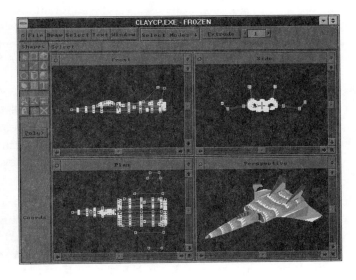

Fig. 19.3
ClayWorks provides a convenient interface for creating 3-D objects.

Note

Live3-D is available from URL: **http://home.netscape.com/comprod/products/navigator/live3d/index.html**

The Microsoft VRML Add-in is available from URL: **http://www.microsoft.com/ie/addons/vrml.htm**

(continues)

(continued)

VRWeb is available from URL: **http: //hyperg.iicm.tu-graz.ac.at/vrweb**

VRML Equinox is available from URL: **http: //www.northplains.com/ EquiInfo.html#EquiDownload**

ClayWorks is available from URL: **http: //cent1.lancs.ac.uk/tim/clay.html**

Information regarding Lightwave 3-D Modeler is available at URL: **http: // www.newtek.com/medium/lw-info.html**

Information regarding WebSpace Author is available at URL: **http: // webspace.sgi.com/WebSpaceAuthor/index.html**

Other Multimedia Experiences

As the Web matures, new technologies are used as vehicles for multimedia systems, while established technologies are adapted to the new Web paradigm. Intranets will become the proving ground for these new multimedia applications and systems.

Java Multimedia Applets

Java's true multimedia potential is a great deal more than custom-coded image-flipping applets. Furthermore, an emphasis on Java application development may be misplaced with Intranet implementations. Most Intranet developers do not have the resources to create and support complex Java programs.

The Java market is progressing at an extremely aggressive pace, and soon third-party applets will support video, sound, and other forms of multimedia. Java will enable your audience to interact with these multimedia experiences. Importantly, these solutions will not demand programming resources for your Intranet implementation, but merely the ability to install and support a Java applet.

These applets will leverage off of Java's strengths. They will be distributed on-demand from your Intranet to your audience's Web browsers, requiring no end-user interaction. Multimedia Java applications will execute on all Java-capable browsers, which are available for UNIX, Macintosh, and 32-bit Windows systems. Windows 3.1 Java implementations will be arriving in the near future. Perhaps most importantly, Java's design places heavy emphasis on security, allowing for an increasingly convenient method of transparent network distribution to be safe in your business environment.

CADIS KrakatoA is one Java product that is already available. KrakatoA allows you to set up a powerful search engine for your Intranet, and includes a user-friendly Java interface for browsers. The Java interface is convenient, presenting information more understandably than an HTML-based search interface. However, for clients which cannot run Java, the KrakatoA product includes a pure HTML front-end.

> **Tip**
>
> For other examples of Java applets and applications to use within your Intranet, visit the Gamelan directory, available at URL: **http://www.gamelan.com/**

ActiveX Technology

The Microsoft Internet Explorer introduces the ActiveX technology to the Web. With ActiveX controls, formerly known as OLE controls or OCX, dynamic content and application linkages can be developed. For instance, ActiveX controls with Internet Explorer can provide an in-line animation or allow an Excel spreadsheet to be embedded within a Web page.

In many ways, Java applets and ActiveX controls provide similar capabilities to the Web. Java provides an innovative, secure architecture, while ActiveX draws strength from Microsoft's market control and enables companies to build off of their existing OLE development investments. Time will tell which provides a more lasting solution.

Professional Multimedia Systems

Companies developing multimedia authoring systems have not missed the tremendous potential of the Web. Two major players in this market have recently released Plug-ins for the Netscape Navigator that can bring advanced capabilities to your Intranet. Multimedia authoring systems have been firmly established in the desktop market for years, but only now are making a transition to Web-based information schemes. These authoring systems have traditionally been targeted toward computer-based training, on-line documentation, simulations, electronic publications, and kiosks, all of which dove-tail nicely with Intranet goals.

Macromedia Authorware, available for Macintosh and Windows systems, is a professional tool for developing interactive multimedia systems. It supports many external media types, styles, and navigation techniques. Authorware content can be loaded onto an Intranet, and your audience can use the freely available Macromedia Shockwave for Authorware to utilize your information.

Another major player in this market is AimTech IconAuthor. IconAuthor has a good editing environment and powerful data handling. A Netscape Plug-in for IconAuthor is available, allowing this system to be smoothly integrated with your Intranet.

Note

Information regarding Authorware and Shockwave for Authorware is available at URL: **http://www.macromedia.com/Tools/Studios/AIS/index.html**

Information regarding IconAuthor is available at URL: **http://www.aimtech.com/lia.htm**

Concerns About Delivering Multimedia Content

Integration of multimedia content into your Intranet creates a number of challenges. Recognizing the issues you will face, and developing a plan for dealing with them, minimizes the time you spend troubleshooting problems and developing work-arounds.

Configuring Desktop Machines

Your Intranet physically resides on one, or a relatively small set of machines, so you can develop a fine degree of control of the machine's configuration. Loading multimedia content that you develop onto your Intranet won't present too many obstacles. However, unlike standard Web technologies, such as HTML, in-line images, and hypertext links, browsers don't come automatically configured to handle multimedia content.

For each new multimedia technology, identify the hardware and software requirements for all desktop machines you support. Things to consider include:

- What is the minimum hardware necessary to present the multimedia content? Sound cards, memory, and video resolutions can all limit what your end-users experiences.

- What helper applications or plug-ins are necessary to view the multimedia content? Do these applications integrate with the Web browser(s) that your users utilize?

- Are there any associated costs or licensing agreements necessary to use helper software?
- Are solutions provided for all of your desktop operating systems, such as Windows 3.1, Windows 95, Windows NT, Macintosh, and any of the many flavors of UNIX?
- What are the installation and configuration procedures for all required software?

Once you fully understand all of these issues, develop a plan for rolling out new multimedia content to your audience. Depending on the level of sophistication of your users, you may need to provide documentation that can be located on the Intranet itself, create installation scripts, or even allocate resources to load software for each user.

Problems with Network Restrictions

Most Web communications occur through well-defined protocols that have been in place for many years. One of the goals of most secure network environments is to ensure that only those known protocols are allowed and no more. Unknown protocols could potentially provide an access hole from the Internet into your internal environment. *Firewalls* are a way of addressing these concerns.

If your internal network is spread throughout several physical locations, firewalls may be in place to establish the security of the intervening links. Furthermore, many areas of your internal network may need to follow different security policies, and thus firewalls may be placed between departments in an internal network. Thus, even in a seemingly homogenous internal environment, network access throughout that environment can be closely controlled.

One of the problems that multimedia presents to these types of environments is that some technologies define their own application protocols and standards. For instance, RealAudio relies upon the server's ability to send UDP datagrams to the client machine. Until a standard firewall is reconfigured, RealAudio content is unavailable to a user, if the server lies beyond the firewall.

Unless you already know what you might be dealing with, troubleshooting these problems can be extremely frustrating. Table 19.2 shows some multimedia applications and what modifications must be made to firewall configurations. Enabling these protocols can compromise your site's security stance, so careful, well-informed decisions must be made before acting.

Table 19.2 Multimedia Applications that Affect Firewalls	
Application	**Network Protocols to Enable**
RealAudio	7070/TCP (outgoing), 6970/UDP through 7170/UDP
CU-SeeMe	7648/UDP, 7649/UDP
StreamWorks	1558/UDP
WebFORCE Media Server	unknown at this time

Limitations of Network Bandwidth

One of the most pressing concerns about delivering multimedia content is in the area of network bandwidth. Networks are designed to handle a certain threshold of traffic and as usage approaches that limit, response times degrade, connections are refused, transmissions are cut off, and, in the case of streaming protocols like RealAudio, the content's resolution is degraded. In other words, the quality of your Intranet suffers as the pipeline becomes congested.

Multimedia applications are particularly susceptible to these problems, since most of them require a great deal of digital information in order to encode their data. As you integrate more and more multimedia technologies, your network usage will rapidly increase. Before your Intranet's success becomes its own downfall, it's a good idea to consider ways of dealing with congestion.

The simplest mechanism for reducing network load is to ensure that your audience is using a sufficiently large disk cache. Disk caches allow browsers to retrieve and store data from the Intranet once, only retransmitting the data when the file has been modified from the reference source. While large caches limit a user's remaining disk space, small caches mean that stored data is quickly overwritten and the benefit of the cache disappears.

There are steps that the Intranet content provider can take, such as limiting the resolution and amount of multimedia data. For audio data, reduced granularity means lower sampling rates, fewer bits per sample, and less sampling channels (e.g. mono versus stereo sound). For graphical information, techniques such as reduced pixel dimensions and fewer colors may reduce the file sizes. Limiting the number of multimedia files that are downloaded by your users at once will improve the situation. Consider a single page with four large GIF89a animations, that cause four simultaneous downloads per browser. Using multimedia with a prudent and deft hand prevents congestion problems before they start.

Another mechanism to consider is compression. Many multimedia solutions define complex compression schemes that greatly reduce the number of bits sent over your network; MPEG and RealAudio are two good examples. However, other applications could benefit from additional compression techniques.

For instance, large VRML files can be compressed with the GNU Zip scheme. Most Web servers support the "Content-Encoding" HTTP header; this allows for nearly seamless transfers of compressed data between server and browser. The VRML file is identified by the server as GNU Zip encoded, but the media content type is still shown as the usual "x-world/x-vrml". The Web browser, when receiving such a file, decompresses the file and smoothly passes it on to the normal VRML viewer. One concern is that appropriate decompression software may need to be loaded on some Web browsers. Furthermore, while this technique alleviates some burden from the network, it places a greater burden on the desktop machine, which must use its processing power to decompress data.

The most complicated, but ultimately most scaleable solution is proper network design. Development of an organization's infrastructure is a critical issue to its continuing to perform the necessary function. Whenever the topic is visited, it is crucial to consider how your Intranet will affect the internal network and vice-versa. The three primary ways of avoiding network congestion with an Intranet application are faster networks, intelligent network design, and distributing network load.

A faster network infrastructure is the easiest solution to arrive at when congestion becomes a problem. While it requires a significant product investment, more bandwidth to work with is not going to exacerbate the current situation. Congested subnets that are using old technologies can be upgraded, relieving the strain in critical areas. Unfortunately, throwing hardware at the problem isn't the only solution.

Your Intranet should be placed onto a network segment that is readily visible to the key members of your audience. If possible, it should be isolated from busy services that compete for network resources. Your company's data center, if it has one, probably would provide the best environment, but that fact should not be taken for granted.

If an Intranet solution continues to deplete network resources, you may need to consider distributing the network load. A series of caching proxy servers placed at strategic locations in the infrastructure will greatly improve the situation. Caching proxies obtain Web data for clients, storing the static content for future requests. Thus, a large image would be transmitted from the

Intranet to the proxy only once, though many Web browsers may receive the same data through the proxy.

Another load distribution technique is mirroring the Intranet servers throughout the network. Instead of having one Intranet server that serves the entire company, separate servers with identical content can be placed at key locations. Smoothly redirecting users to the most appropriate mirror is a problem, but soon intelligent DNS-based systems, like Cisco's Distributed Director may be most successful. Mirroring software itself still needs development, but for large companies that place a great demand on their Intranets, this may be a necessary tactic.

> **Note**
>
> Information regarding Distributed Director is available at URL: **http://cio.cisco.com/warp/public/751/advtg/swww_wp.htm**

Applying Multimedia to Your Intranet

The usefulness of multimedia has been stressed throughout this chapter, but any Intranet implementation of these technologies should be done with prudence. Many examples on Internet Web sites are simply inappropriate on an Intranet. Internet sites use glitter to attract individuals from a passive audience.

On an Intranet, availability and usefulness of information are key. Multimedia should only be used when it is essential to communicate certain concepts, not as window-dressing for other information. Following are few examples.

First Example—VRML Object Modeling

When describing a physical object, few techniques are more powerful than allowing your audience to directly examine its shape and structure. With VRML, representations of complex objects can be created and placed on the Intranet. Your audience can then view the object from various angles and distances, and rotate the object to see how all of the pieces fit together. They can even travel into the object, viewing any internal structure you decide to include.

Second Example—RealAudio Presentations

If your company is typical of many others, high-profile presentations by corporate executives are a regular occurrence. A company's visionaries need a means of communicating that vision and sharing their enthusiasm. Unfortunately, workers can't always be physically present.

RealAudio allows for real-time playback for anyone who has access to the Intranet during such presentations. Such data could be stored, so that other workers could listen to the data at a later time. If Web versions of any slides are available, the RealAudio system can use its synchronized multimedia capabilities to playback the slides in time to the audio.

Third Example—Multimedia Training Courses

Every company must develop a means of training its workforce. Hands-on training and lectures are very effective, but have a great deal of ongoing overhead to maintain. Unfortunately, even well written documentation usually falls short of meeting all of the necessary training goals.

Multimedia can make up for this deficiency. Interactive multimedia enables users to exert control over the flow and presentation of the learning experience. A fusion of different media, tailored to specific tasks, can teach ideas that prose could never accomplish. Finally, as part of the Intranet, these materials will have high-visibility and ready access. ❖

## CHAPTER 20

Usage Statistics and Log Analysis

There will come a time when someone wants to know that the Intranet is being used to make the company more efficient. This may be as simple to prove as showing how much less paper is being used or how many people answered their own questions using the online help desk.

However you convince management that the Intranet has paid off will require you to keep track of the usage statistics. This chapter will show you what sort of information can be reported and some utilities to use.

In this chapter, you will learn:

- What statistics are logged
- How to run reports to get usage statistics
- How to find out who is using the Intranet
- How to find which browsers are being used

Hits versus Visits

When people talk about Web sites and how popular they are, the term commonly used is *hits*. Some big sites may get hundreds of thousands of "hits" per day. This does not mean hundreds of thousands of visitors or even hundreds of thousands of pages; it means hundreds of thousands of connections.

A single HTTP connection may download one graphic, one text page or one file; the key word here is one. Each page that shows up in a browser may contain many separate pieces. Each piece causes a new connection to be established. Figure 20.1 shows a simple HTML page that contains three graphics. This would cause four hits to be made on the server.

Fig. 20.1

This page would cause four hits. One hit for the text and one for each icon.

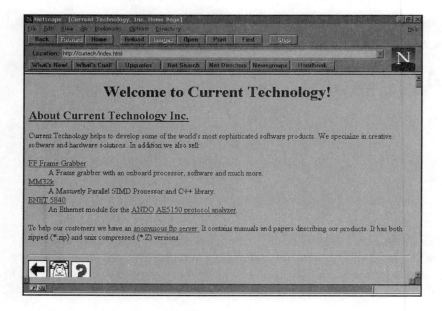

Since HTTP is a connectionless protocol it isn't possible, using normal means, to accurately track the number of unique visitors. It is possible, however, to estimate by looking at unique hosts and log files.

Log files list the hostname along with the username, if you are using authentication. Using authentication enables you to follow a user through a site, but some users find it inconvenient to log in to a site and leave. Intranets, however, can force a user to log in and can use the username to track a user.

Some log files also record the HTTP_REFERER variable. This tells the page that the user was on the page before. It's possible to follow HTTP_REFERER variables back through the log files and create a path that a specific user followed. This has pitfalls, though, since a user might type in an URL in the browser, also not all browsers support the HTTP_REFERER variable.

It is also not possible to count just the number of hits on the home page; some users might go to a specific URL in the site and not go to the home page at all. Accurately counting the number of visitors versus the number of hits is one of the more daunting tasks for Web site administrators.

Why Analyze?

Gathering useful statistics from the Internet is one of the main goals of many Web administrators. Because of this, there are many tools available that analyze the log files and generate statistics.

Common statistics include:

- Number of hits
- Bytes transferred
- Number of unique hosts
- Percent of each type of browser
- Percent from each country

For an Internet site these are all very important statistics but for an Intranet some of these don't make any sense. Still, Intranets can benefit from a log analysis program.

Some reasons for an Intranet to analyze the access logs include:

- Convincing management the Intranet is worth the time and money spent to get it going and to keep it running. Showing the number of times a day it is accessed can convince most managers the Intranet server is a useful addition.

- Deciding which features are important can help decide which features get worked on the most. If everyone is looking at the phone list page, then maybe that should be the first one to get a search engine added.

- Determining if there are flaws in the business system. If everyone in the order entry department is going back three pages to get to a screen in the accounting section, then the page should be moved or a link added on the order entry section.

- Helping the departments that need it most. If no one in the sales department has even looked at the sales page, then they may not realize it is there. They may also not know how to get there or may not have the software setup. Analyzing the logs would show that no one has accessed this section.

Log Files

All Web servers generate log files or at least have the option to create log files. The log file contains information, such as the URL name, the status of the request, the date and time, and the hostname. Some logfiles also contain the

HTTP_REFERER and the browser type. This can be useful when tracking a user through a site or deciding which features to add.

Each server has a slightly different log file format though most of them support the common log format. Netscape's proxy server has two additional formats; InterNotes logs its information to a Notes database and Microsoft IIS can be setup to log to a backend database such as SQLserver.

There are many tools available to gather statistics from the log files. These are covered later on in this chapter. Before seeing what information can be found using these tools we need to understand the different log file formats.

Common Log Format

The common log format is the standard log format. Most servers can support this log format. Most tools understand this format as well. This makes it a good choice for use as a log file format.

The common log format logs various standard information such as:

- Remote hostname. This is the host requesting the document. If the server can't resolve the name, it places the IP address here instead.
- The username if known, otherwise a —. This is unknown unless you are using ident lookups to find out the remote username.
- The login name if authentication is being used, otherwise a —.
- The date the request was made.
- The request. This includes the method, such as GET or POST, the URL, and the protocol.
- The return code. If the document was returned okay, this should be 200.
- The size of the document in bytes. If the document was not returned due to an error, this will be —.

Using the common log format enables you to get many statistics including:

- Reports on the number of unique hosts that connected
- Reports on the number of documents retrieved
- Reports on the number of bytes sent out
- Reports on the number of errors. This is useful for reactive maintenance of the document tree.
- Reports on number of users, if using authentication or remote lookups (identd). Identd is a protocol that allows a site to query who has connected to it. Normally HTTP doesn't allow the real username to be sent

but if the client site is running indentd, it is possible.

■ Reports on most popular documents

The common log format doesn't enable the server to log where people come from (HTTP_REFERER), or what browser they used. Some servers log this information in a separate file or in the same file. If this is logged in the same file, it is referred to as the combined common log format. With these two fields you can:

■ Receive reports on the number of unique browsers

■ Receive reports on most popular browsers

■ Track where people are coming from

■ Track a user's path through the site

Here is a sample common log file:

```
client - rich [09/May/1996:13:43:20 -0400] "GET / HTTP/1.0" 200 477
client - rich [09/May/1996:13:45:11 -0400] "GET /product1.html
➥HTTP/1.0" 404 -
client - rich [09/May/1996:14:01:41 -0400] "GET /product.html HTTP/
➥1.0" 200 204
client - rich [09/May/1996:14:02:02 -0400] "GET /images/product.gif
➥HTTP/1.0" 200 9534
client - rich [09/May/1996:14:04:49 -0400] "GET / HTTP/1.0" 200 477
```

This simple example shows a user who authenticated himself as rich connecting in from a host called client, on May 9, 1996 at 1:43 PM. He first got the servers home page "GET /". This document was 477 bytes long and was returned OK.

He received the next page two minutes later, but got an error. The 404 means that the document was not found. This probably means we have a bad link on the home page. Sixteen and a half minutes later he tried to get product.html, which is 204 bytes long, and also seems to include product.gif. This was retrieved 21 seconds later and was 9534 bytes long.

It looks like he read it for almost three minutes before going back to the home page. Then he left the site.

This is all guesswork; since we don't have the HTTP_REFERER logged, "rich" could have gone to other documents in his hotlist between our pages and came back. There could also be two people using the same machine both authenticating themselves as "rich."

InterNotes NSF Files

InterNotes writes its logs into the normal Notes server log "LOG.NSF". This enables the administrator to create custom Lotus Notes views for the database. Since InterNotes is a WWW gateway rather than a server, the logs only contain information on files that users access.

This is not to say that this information is not useful, rather that this is information on client activity rather than server activity. The logs can still tell which files users are accessing and which ones aren't being used.

Microsoft Logs

The Microsoft server can log its messages to a log file or to an ODBC capable database. To setup logging you use the Internet Server Manager.

In the Server Manager, click the service you are interested in and go to the "logging" tab. You need to check the box next to Enable Logging for the server to log messages.

> **Note**
>
> When logging to a file, the maximum line length is 1200 bytes and the maximum field length is 150 bytes. When logging to a database, the maximum field limit is 200 bytes.

In this screen you can also set the server to use a new log file every day, week, month, or when it reaches a certain size. You can also specify a log file directory to use.

Alternatively, you can set the messages up to go to an SQL or ODBC database server. This requires you to enter the data source name, the table name, the username, and password.

Once the server is setup to log messages, you can look at them by using the Internet Server Manager. You can also use standard database tools, if you sent the messages to a database.

It is also possible to use standard log analysis tools that understand the common log format. This is because Microsoft includes a program to convert the Microsoft log file format to the common log format.

This program is called convlog.exe. It is located in \Inetsrc\Admin. The more popular options for convlog are:

- ■ -sf -sg -sw. Process FTP logs, Gopher logs, or WWW logs respectively.
- ■ -t type. Type is either ncsa for common log file format, or emwac for

the emwac format.

- ■ -o directory. This allows you to store the output in a separate directory.
- ■ -h. This displays the help screen.

Error Logs

In addition to the access log, there is also the error log. This is where the Web server logs any errors that it encounters. These errors can be very useful in debugging problems and spotting bad links.

The error log file is a simple file. It contains a line for each error. This line contains the date, the time stamp, and the error message.

Some of these error messages are warnings such as:

- ■ "send timed out for www.client.com, /index.html"
- ■ "send lost connection to client 123.123.123.123"
- ■ "read timed out for browser.machine.com"

These errors mean that, for some reason, the connection never finished. This usually means the network is too slow. If you get a lot of these messages, you may need to increase the amount of bandwidth to your ISP. These messages might also mean the client's network is too slow or has problems. Don't worry if you see occasional warning messages like these.

There are some errors that you should look at right away. These include:

- ■ "access to /usr/local/http/htdocs/index.html failed for client.machine.com, reason file does not exist"
- ■ "access to /usr/local/http/cgi-bin/phone.cgi failed, reason malformed header from script"
- ■ "/usr/local/http/cgi-bin/phone.cgi: perl not found:"

The first error message means someone tried to access a document that is not there. This could mean there is a bad link or someone typed in the wrong URL.

The second and third error messages indicate a problem with a CGI program. The second message looks like the script didn't return the correct header information, while the third error is fairly obvious. The perl executable is missing or the script is looking in the wrong place.

One other message you may see often refers to a file called /robots.txt. This is used by Web robots to figure out what on your site should be indexed and what directories to avoid indexing. More information on the robots.txt file is available at **http://info.webcrawler.com/mak/projects/robots/norobots.html**.

> **Caution**
>
> If your site is strictly for Intranet use and should not be connected to the Internet, investigate this access. If you are running a spider internally, this may be all it is, but if you aren't, then it is possible your Web server is accessible from the Internet. You can check your log files for clients that are not part of your network to verify if anyone has connected. If you see connections from outside your site, you need to check your security very carefully.
>
> Other security considerations are failed CGI scripts. Some CGI scripts have holes in them that may allow a cracker to read any file from the machine. Check out any failed connections to CGI scripts.

Analysis Tools

We have examined the reasons that we want to look at our log files and we know what is in them; this section covers some basic tools used to get the information out of the log files and into a useful format.

Some servers have analysis tools included; others can send the information to a database for analysis. Even servers that don't have the ability to analyze or extract data from the log files can yield information.

One of the quickest ways to get statistics out of the access_log is to use the native system tools. UNIX machines have the "grep" program and DOS machines have "FIND." These two programs enable you to get information out of the log file quickly. Windows users can also open a DOS window and use FIND. Macintosh users can download macgrep, a Macintosh version of the UNIX grep command, from **ftp://software.unc.edu/pub/mac/utils/macgrep.hqx**.

Some of these statistics include number of hosts, number of hits, and the number of times a particular host or network accessed the Web server. For example, to list all the hosts from nasa.gov that have accessed your Web site, use the following, in UNIX:

```
grep -i nasa.gov access_log
```

DOS and Windows users can use:

```
FIND  /i nasa.gov access_log
```

Macintosh users can use macgrep to find the phrase nasa.gov. This lists all occurrences of the phrase nasa.gov. This means if you have a page called nasa.gov.html, every time someone accessed that page, regardless of where he came from, it would get listed. The "i" option tells FIND and grep to ignore case. In this way, Nasa.Gov is listed.

There are many freeware or shareware log file analysis tools. These are usually written in PERL or another scripting language. This makes them easier to adapt to your specific needs.

The first one we will look at is Analyze from Netscape. This is included with the Netscape servers. We will also look at wwwstat, a common log format analyzer, IIStats, which allows statistics to be generated from native Microsoft IIS log files, and wusage, another common log format analyzer.

Netscape Analyze

Netscape includes some extra programs with the server package. One of these is Analyze, a logfile analyzer. This program is stored in the ns-home/extras/log_anly directory. In this directory you find:

- analyze. This is the Analyze program.
- a_form.html. This is an HTML form that you can use to submit analyze requests to from any Web browser.
- a_form.cgi. This is the cgi program that the form uses to generate the HTML page.

The Analyze package can be run two different ways, from the command line, or from the Web server.

The Analyze has the following options:

- -n name. This enables you to define the name of the server.
- -x. This tells the program to output HTML instead of straight text.
- -p. This is the output order. This can be c, t, or l. The order these are in determines what order the count, time stats, and lists are displayed. The default is ctl.
- -i filename. This is the input filename. The default is standard input. (stdin).
- -o filename. This is the output filename. The default is standard output or stdout.
- -c. This is a list of what to count. The default is hnreuokc. The default tells it to count number of hits (h), Not modified codes (n), redirect codes (r), server errors, total unique URLs (u), total unique hosts (o),

total kilobytes (k), number of kilobytes saved by caching. You can also use f to get number of not found errors. This is also covered in the next list.

- ■ -t. This determines which time stats to display. The default is s5m5h24. This corresponds to 5 seconds, 5 minutes, and 24 hours. There is also the z option, which doesn't list any time statistics.

- ■ -l. This is used to generate a list of the most popular URLs, or the clients who access the most often. This can also be used to list any URL or hosts that have been accessed more than a number of times. For example -l c+5h5, the default, shows any URL that has been accessed more than 5 times and the top 5 hosts. -z doesn't show any lists.

The count option, -c, has a number of things that can be counted. These include:

h	the number of hits
n	the number of 304 accesses (not modified, use local copy)
r	the number of 302 (redirects) accesses
f	the number of 404 (document not found) accesses
e	the number of 500 accesses (server error)
u	the total number of unique URLs accessed
o	the total number of unique hosts
k	the total kilobytes transferred
c	the total kilobytes saved by caches
z	don't count anything

The easiest way to use the analyze program is to create a Web page for it. This allows statistics to be gathered without having to remember the syntax of the Analyze program.

To set up the Web page you need to perform the following:

- ■ Copy the a_form.html document to somewhere in the document area of the Web server. If you don't want anyone else to get statistics, you can use access control to restrict access to this page.

- ■ Copy the Analyze program and the a_form.cgi script to the cgi-bin directory. If you don't have a cgi-bin, you need to create one and enable CGI programs to be run from there.

- ■ You might need to edit the a_form.html file and change the ACTION tag to point to the correct URL for the a_form.cgi program.

■ Now you can load the a_form.html page in the browser and fill it out and submit it (see fig. 20.2).

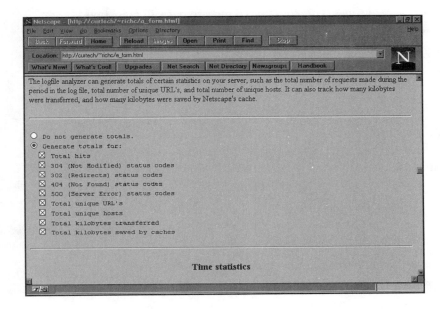

Fig. 20.2
This form can be used to get usage statistics.

wwwstat

wwwstat is a Perl script that can be used to generate usage summaries. It can generate reports based on:

■ Monthly statistics

■ Daily Statistics

■ Hourly statistics

■ Total transfers by domain

■ Total transfers by file

These statistics include the following:

■ Percent of total requests

■ Percent of total bytes

■ Number of requests

■ Number of bytes transferred

wwwstat is available from **http://www.ics.uci.edu/WebSoft/wwwstat**. Once you download and unpack the program you should see:

- README. This contains information on the wwwstat package.
- CHANGES. This is a list of changes.
- country-codes. This contains country to domain mappings.
- example.html. This is a sample output from wwwstat.
- oldwwwstat. Older httpd servers generated different logs. If you are running an older version of NCSA https (before 1.2), you can use this program.
- wwwstat. This is the actual PERL program

It may be necessary to edit the wwwstat program before you run it. This is covered in the README file. You will probably have to change the location of the PERL executable and the locations of various files. These changes are all in the first part of the code and are easy to make.

You can run wwwstat with no options to get some nice output or you can use options to get specialized reports. These options are covered in the README file. Some of the more useful options are:

- -x. list non-existant files. Can be used to find bad links.
- -a hostname. List all entries from hostname.
- -A hostname. List all entries not from hostname.
- -c code. List all entries with a stauts of code.
- -C code. List all entries without a status of code.
- -d date. List all entries that happened on date.
- -D date. List all entries that didn't happen on date.

Figure 20.3 shows the output from a wwwstat run.

There is also a package called gwstat that can take the output from wwwstat and create graphs of the statistics, as shown in figure 20.4. This program is available from **http://dis.cs.umass.edu/stats/gwstat.html**.

IIStats

IIStats is a program that can analyze the Microsoft IIS logs. It doesn't need to have the log files converted to the common log format like some statistics programs do.

IIStats can be downloaded from **http://www.cyber-trek.com/iistats/iistats.zip**. It is free software and is covered under the usual GNU General Public License.

IIStats requires the Perl5 for Windows NT program. This program is available from **http://www.perl.hip.com/**.

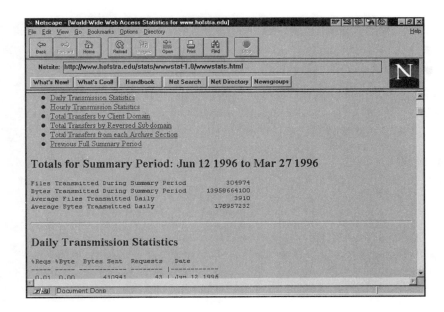

Fig. 20.3
wwwstat can generate pages like this one.

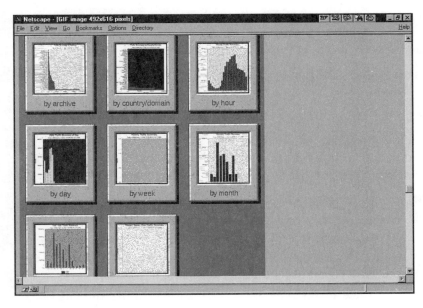

Fig. 20.4
gwstat creates graphs like these from the wwwstat output.

IV

Maintenance

IIStats generates the following information from the log file:

- Total hits per server
- Total bytes transferred

IIStats also generates an HTML page with a table containing detailed summaries. This tables gives number of hits and bytes transferred per page as well as by site. This makes a nice way to add site statistics to your Web site.

wusage

wusage 4.1 is another statistics package that can analyze common log format server files. wusage also gives analysis of IIS logs and EMWAC style logs. It can generate graphs in gif format, as well as normal HTML tables.

It is available from **http://www.boutell.com/wusage/**. This is a shareware package. For commercial sites it costs $75, for educational or non-profit organizations it costs $25. You can download the 30-day evaluation copy from the above site and try it. If you like it, you can register it and pay for it then.

wusage is available for many UNIX versions, as well as OS/2, Windows 95, Windows NT, and DOS. This makes it nice since any machine can be used to generate the statistics, as long as it has access to the access_log file.

wusage requires configuration before it can run properly. Fortunately there is a command, called makeconf, in the wusage directory, that automates this.

After makeconf finishes, you are ready to run wusage. You can specify the config file by adding -c configfile. Otherwise, wusage prompts you for it.

After running wusage you will find that the program has placed some files in the directory you previously specified. These files include:

- index.htm or index.html. This is the HTML output from wusage.
- database.dat. This is the database file. It can be read into most spreadsheets. The format is tab delimited.
- *.htm. These are broken down reports. They may be by day, week, or month, depending on how the configuration is set up.
- *.gif. These are the graph images that are used in the *.htm files.

wusage is a very nice statistics package that allows many different reports to be run. Figures 20.5 and 20.6 show reports created with wusage.

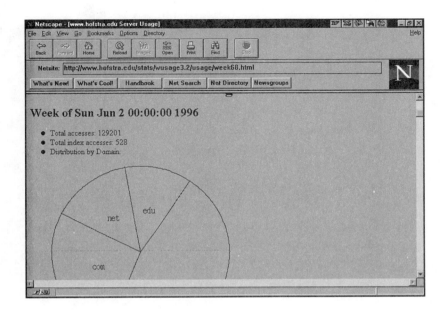

Fig. 20.5
A weekly report
from wusage.

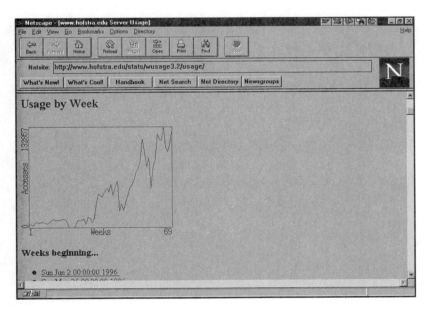

Fig. 20.6
A yearly report
from wusage.

IV

Maintenance

## CHAPTER 21

Maintaining the Server and Documents

Setting up the initial Web server can be a challenge. It can also be a lot of fun. Once the server is up and running though the job is not over. Intranets are constantly changing to add new information and to keep existing documents in order.

Maintaining the site requires dedication from all the people working on the project. Links must be kept in order, site maps must be kept current, and new files must be added in an organized manner.

In this chapter, you will learn the following:

- How to organize your site
- How to use tools to verify links automatically
- How to create a site map using tools
- How to use Server Side Includes to make maintenance easier

Organizing Hierarchy

After the Web server is up and running, you must decide how to organize the documents on the Web server. It's a good idea to have a file system layout that somewhat mirrors the links in the files. This makes the server almost maintain itself.

Most Web sites have a central home page that splits up into different topics. By choosing the right topics, you can keep the document structure organized and still allow the server to grow and expand. The different topics may be departments, projects, or ideas. These topics may be controlled by one person, or by different people for each topic. In whatever way it is managed, it's easier to understand if the files are organized in a hierarchical order.

Each major topic should be a separate subdirectory of DocumentRoot. This allows the Web server to be split up at a later date if the load gets to be too much for one server. This also makes it easier to find HTML documents when you are looking for them in the file system. Figure 21.1 shows a layout for a Web server.

Fig. 21.1

Each major topic should be a located in a separate directory. This makes it easier to follow when you are editing the files.

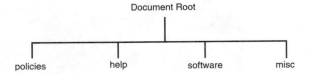

For each main topic, you can use the DirectoryIndex, or equivalent directive, to define the home page or each topic. Scripts that tell where in the file system they are can then be written.

It may be desirable to have more than one layer of directories in which to organize files. This allows, for example, a directory tree to have a major topic for software engineering then a subtopic for each project the software group is working on.

> **Note**
>
> When deciding on a layout for the server it's often a good idea to map out on paper how the server will be organized. This map should be given to anyone adding documents to the server to help it stay organized.

Once the layout has been decided on, the next step is to decide who will be responsible for the different parts of the server.

Access Control

When a Web server is first created, there is almost always a nice concise plan of how the documents will be structured, how the site will look, and what can and can't be placed on the server. As time goes on, though, the plan is forgotten or ignored and the Web server tends to become a maze of broken links and loops.

Companies often have certain individuals who are responsible for the organization of the server. They make sure people don't add links that don't work and only add what is appropriate for the server. These Web developers often find it easier to define a policy about who can add what, and then use technical solutions to enforce the policy.

These policies are usually one of three types:

- Open. This means anyone can do anything. There are no restrictions on who can edit, remove, or add links.
- Distributed. This assigns a person to be responsible for a certain area of the Web server.
- Central. One person is responsible for adding links, changing documents, and verifying the structure.

Each access policy has its advantages and disadvantages. Some make it easy to add documents and are not as strict; others are very limiting and can be too much of a burden. Commonly, more than one type of access policy is needed for an Intranet. It's important to try to choose the right policy for your company. By choosing an appropriate access policy, the Web server can be easy to update, while order and reason are maintained.

Open

The open model of access control is the easiest to setup. It allows anyone to add, remove, or change any document in the tree. This includes links, pages, and images.

The open model makes it very easy for developers and users to change documents. This ease of change often seems like a good idea at the start, but can quickly turn the site into a maze of disorganized links.

> **Note**
>
> The open model may be a good choice in a small company or group, since users can make their own changes without having to bother a developer. Larger organizations, however, might find the open model doesn't afford enough control so that the server quickly becomes disorganized.

To setup the open model, simply set the permissions on the files and directories in DocumentRoot. This enables anyone to make changes. In UNIX this is done by setting the modes to 777, "chmod 777 <name>". NT, Netware, and

Notes all use GUI interfaces to set the permissions. In the open model the important thing is to enable anyone to read, write, delete, and create files or directories.

Caution

The open model makes it very easy to make changes to the server, but it can be dangerous if an intruder gets in since they can also change any file or directory.

Distributed

The distributed model enables certain people to change certain sections of the Web server. Unlike the open model, only selected people can change the documents or directories. This allows more control over where things are placed and how they look.

The distributed model can be setup to enable different developers to be responsible for separate areas or to jointly manage the entire server. Most companies choose to have each department manage their own document tree.

Note

The distributed model gives more control to individual groups. Then each group can add their own documents without having to worry about the entire site becoming disorganized.

When using the distributed model, permissions that allow certain group members to change the files must be set. Most systems make it easy to create a new group and add members. Simply create a group of users who have been approved to make changes. Once the group is set you need to make the files owned or managed by this group.

Note

It may be desirable to have more than one group manage a directory. In UNIX you can only have one group managing a directory or file. To get around this you can create a larger group that contains the groups you want to manage the documents.

Central

In the central model, a person or group manages the entire server. This group is required to make all changes to the document tree. Using this method creates centralized control over the server that can reduce the incidents of bad links or poorly placed documents.

The central model, however, makes it hard for users to get documents changed or added, since they must find a developer anytime there is a change. This can cause a bottleneck when many changes are required and take developers away from other job duties.

> **Note**
>
> Central access gives companies tight control over what goes on the Web server, but it can make it difficult to get documents changed.

To setup the central access model, simply setup the document tree so only the person responsible can make changes. This is easy to do in any operating system; check your documentation if you aren't sure how to do it.

> **Note**
>
> When setting permissions, make sure the server user can at least read all the files. If not, it will return an error when it tries to access them and they won't be displayed in the user's browsers.

Multiple Access Methods

Most organizations require more than one access method. It is common for the server's home page to be maintained using the central access method. This keeps anyone from adding new higher level topics.

In order for users to get changes done easily, the different groups are controlled using the distributed method. This allows groups to contact a local developer when making changes.

The open model may be used for groups as well, although this can lead to that section of the server becoming difficult to navigate.

Whichever model your company decides to use, make sure that the permissions are setup to properly enforce the policy. It is also necessary to make sure the server user can still read the documents.

Tool Features

As a Web server grows, it gets harder and harder to make sure all the documents have HTML tags and that all the links go somewhere. Small Web servers may have a person who checks the links on a daily or weekly basis, but with larger sites this may not be possible.

Fortunately there are some tools that can automatically check the site for you. These tools can be used to check the HTML syntax, or to check for broken links and images. Some tools also allow the site to be indexed and an HTML page to be generated showing the site map. Other tools contain simple ways to change and replace words, or check the spelling in the document.

HTML Validators

HTML validators are used to verify the syntax in an HTML document. This includes checking for misplaced tags, incorrectly nested tags, or tags that aren't closed properly.

Some browsers may handle problems in the HTML properly so checking the document using a browser is not the best way to verify the HTML syntax. If you are using a standard browser in the Intranet and never plan on allowing other browsers to be used, then you can just make sure it looks okay in the standard browser.

Most HTML editors can be used to validate HTML in a document, they can also be used to generate correct HTML. A few limitations are outlined in the following list:

- Documents can't be automatically checked. If your site only has 20 or 30 documents, it might be okay to have to view each one in an HTML editor to verify it. If your site has 10,000 documents, this is out of the question.

- HTML editors can't check the output of ServerSide Includes. If your site uses SSI, then you can't use an HTML editor to check the output of the program since the server creates it on the fly.

There are a few HTML validators that automatically check the documents that the server generates. They do this by performing a GET on the file, from the server. Not all validators will do this.

Link Checkers

All Web servers have many links. These links sometimes get changed or removed and not all the pointers get updated. Link checkers enable the Web administrator to verify that all the links on the Web server point to a valid document.

Link checkers normally work by getting the first document and then every included document. They do the same for each document. Any errors they receive are reported to the administator.

Note

It's possible to check the www log files for errors and fix the broken links that are reported. This is an example of reactive maintenance, fixing the problem when it is a problem. Running a link checker enables you to use proactive maintenance, or fix the problem before ay one notices it. Proactive maintenance is better than reactive maintenance.

If your site has many links to servers not under your control, you should run a link checker frequently. If there are no external links, you only need to run a link checker when documents change.

Most link checkers can be setup with different configurations, for example, to look for local broken links or to check a certain number of links deep. This saves time because the link checker can be setup to verify only the parts of a site you specify.

Site Mappers

Some tools can be used to create a Web index of a site. This is handy for users to be able to get a view of the site. The index generated may not be quite what you are looking for and some changes might be required.

Tools

We have discussed some of the features ueful in a site maintenance package. This section will discuss some commercial and non-commerical tools available today.

NetCarta WebMapper

NetCarta WebMapper (**http://www.netcarta.com/**) is a commercial Web site tool that allows Web maps to be created and distributed. WebMapper can be used to allow users to graphically navigate a site by displaying a tree view of the site. When the user selects a page, WebMapper automatically starts a Web browser and displays the page.

WebMapper can also be used to help maintain a site. It allows checking of all links in a site. Using WebMapper can not only verify that a link points to another page, by viewing a graphical map of the site you can verify that the links point to the right page. This involves some human intervention but greatly simplifies checking the site.

WebMapper can run on a 486 with at least 8MB of RAM. Like most Windows programs, more memory means faster performance. It also requires 7MB of disk space. WebMapper runs on 32-bit windows systems such as Windows 95 and NT.

WebMapper also allows you to generate statistics on the number of links, images, audio files, video files, CGI scripts, applications such as java apps, Word documents or PDF files, and Internet services such as FTP or gopher servers. These statistics can help spot links that you were unaware of; for example, if someone added a link to an FTP site or added a CGI script.

WebMapper can also be used to generate an HTML map of the site. Simply map the site and export the map as HTML. This can be done by using the Export as HTML link under the File menu.

WebMapper has many nice features such as the graphical viewing and mapping of a site. It does not, however, check the HTML for correctness. Even without this ability though WebMapper is a very nice utility.

Incontext WebAnalyzer

WebAnalyzer from Incontext (**http://www.incontext.com/**) allows you to graphically view a site much like WebMapper. It runs on Windows 95 systems. WebAnalyzer also allows you to filter for certain characteristics such as link type or size. WebAnalyzer can also check that links are pointing to another document.

When you start WebAnalyzer you will see a blank screen with a spot to enter an URL. Enter the URL of the site you want to analyze. This will cause WebAnalyzer to start mapping and checking your site.

Once it is finished you should have a nice view of your site. You can see a page's properties by selecting it and choosing URL, Properties. This displays the name, MIME type, last modified date, size, also the number of links to the page and from the page and the depth, or number of links it took to get there.

WebAnalyzer also allows you to filter for certain types of files. This features is very handy since it allows you to find any image bigger then 10KB. Then you can go to those images and try to reduce the size. You can also search for unresolved links, text-only links, or define your own search filter.

WebAnalyzer has a row of menus across the top. These include: File, for opening, closing, and saving maps; URL, for finding information about a page; Project, for starting or stopping a search, as well as making or viewing a report. Another menu is the tools menu. This allows you to customize how WebAnalyzer looks and runs. This is also where you define the Web browser and editor you are using. You can also define your filters under this menu.

WebAnalyzer is very nice for finding large images and for graphically viewing your site. Like WebMapper, WebAnalyzer doesn't check the HTML for correctness.

htmlcheck

htmlcheck can be used to check the syntax of HTML 2.0 or 3.0 documents. It can also be used to verify local links. htmlcheck can be run on any machine with either Perl or awk. This includes UNIX, DOS, Windows, and Macintosh.

htmlcheck can also handle Netscape extensions. htmlcheck may report errors or warnings on some HTML that is actually legal but doesn't work well on some browsers. This means it checks for viewability more than adherence to the specification.

You can get ftp htmlcheck from **ftp://ftp.cs.buffalo.edu/pub/ htmlcheck**. There are three versions available:

- htmlcheck.tar.Z. This is the compressed tar file containing the distribution. It requires uncompress and tar to unpack.
- htmlcheck.tar.gx. This is the gzipped tar version. It requires gunzip and tar.
- htmlcheck.zip. This requires Pkunzip or unzip to get at the files.

No matter which version you download and unpack, you should end up with a directory full of files. The HTML validator is made up of the following files:

- htmlcheck.awk. This is used if you are using awk for the interpreter.
- htmlcheck.pl. This is the Perl version of the validator.
- htmlcheck.sh. This is a shell script that picks the best available interpreter.

To run the program you can use one of the following syntaxes:

- awk-htmlcheck.awk [options] infile.html
- perl htmlcheck.pl [options] infile.html
- sh htmlcheck.sh [options] infile.html

The sh version requires a UNIX machine, but the other two versions can be run on any machine, as long as Perl or awk are available.

> **Note**
>
> Awk can be replaced with *nawk* or *gawk;* both are newer versions of awk and can be run on different platforms, such as NT or DOS.

The infile.html can be replaced with any HTML file or files. To test all HTML files in a directory, use *.html or *.htm. The output is sent to standard output and can be saved to a file by using normal redirection, such as appending `> outputfile` to the command.

The options that can be used are described in the manual page for htmlcheck. The most popular ones are:

- netscape=1. If this option is given, Netscape tags do not generate an error.
- html3=1. This option is used to check HTML3 files. It causes htmlcheck to not give an error when it sees an HTML3 tag.
- cf=filename. This can be used to define a configuration file. This is useful when there are many options.

htmlcheck can also be setup to automatically generate a table of contents for an HTML document. This is done by using the makemenu program that is shipped with htmlcheck.

If the makemenu program is run with toc=1 as an option, it tries to generate a table of contents for the document. This is done by looking at the headers (H1-H6).

makemenu can be run one of three ways:

- awk-f makemenu.awk [options] infiles
- perl makemenu.pl [options] infiles
- sh makemenu.sh [options] infiles

makemenu does a good job of indexing a single file, but can't handle an entire site yet.

MOMspider

MOMspider stands for MultiOwner Maintenance spider. It's designed to make it easier to maintain a Web space where multiple servers aren't all maintained by the same person. This describes a large Intranet quite well, since in a large Intranet each department might have its own server.

MOMspider is normally setup to run on a nightly basis from the UNIX *cron* program. This enables the Web administrator to keep abreast of changes. MOMspider is careful not to overload a Web server and only sends a few requests before pausing for a few seconds. This way the server can keep managing requests without any noticeable performance problems.

MOMspider requires Perl version 4.036 or higher to run, but should run on any UNIX machine that has PERL. In addition to the Perl interperter, MOMspider also requires the libwww.perl library version 0.30 or higher.

PERL can be downloaded from **http://www.cis.ufl.edu/perl** and libwww-perl can be downloaded from **http://www.ics.uci.edu/libwww-perl**. Once you have these two packages downloaded and installed, you are ready to get MOMspider.

MOMspider can be downloaded from:

- **http://www.ics.uci.edu/WebSoft/MOMspider**
- **ftp://liege.ics.edu/pub/arcadia/MOMspider**

Once it is downloaded and unpacked, you should have a number of files and directories:

- MOMspider. This is the MOMspider main program.
- *.pl. These are modules that help MOMspider run properly.
- docs/*. This is the documentation for MOMspider. It also contains the postscript version of the WWW94 paper on MOMspider.
- examples/*. These are example configuration files for MOMspider.

The first step is to edit MOMspider and make sure the correct pathname for perl is in the first line. The default is /usr/local/bin/perl.

You also need to define the MOMSPIDER_HOME environment variable. Csh users can use "setenv MOMSPIDER_HOME /path/to/momspider". Sh or Ksh users can use "export MOMSPIDER_HOME=/path/to/momspider".

Next you need to edit the configuration file. You have to change the LocalNetwork name so that MOMspider knows which links are local and which are remote. This should be all you need to change. If your server is slow, you might also want to check out the rest of this file. There are some options that set the max depth, max number of consecutive hits without a pause, and how long to pause.

Once the configuration file has been changed, you need to edit the instruction file. The instruction file is made up of several global directives and traversal tasks.

The global directives are:

- SystemAvoid. The name of the systemwide avoid file.
- SystemSites. The name of the systemwide sites file.
- AvoidFile. The name of the users avoid file.
- SitesFile. The name of the users sites file.
- SitesCheck. The number of days between checking the /robots.txt file. Normally 15.
- ReplyTo. Who should get e-mail about the spiders actions.
- MaxDepth. The maximum number of links deep to traverse. Used to keep MOMspider from getting stuck in a loop.

There are three types of traversals. These are:

- Site. This searches an entire site. It doesn't follow links off site, but checks to make sure they exist.
- Tree. This checks a tree in a server. It doesn't follow links out of the directory tree but verifys that they exist.
- Owner. This looks at the metainformation to check the links owners. It only checks links that are owned by the correct group. This is not normally used.

The other directives that we will look at include:

- Name. The owner of the spider is used in owner traversals. This is a required field and must be a single word.
- TopURL. This is where to start the traversal.
- IndexURL. Where the index file will be for this traversal. Must be a full URL and must be included.
- IndexFile. The actual filename for the IndexURL file.

- IndexTitle. This is an optional field that is used for the title of the index file.
- EmailAddress. This is who the report will be e-mailed to.
- EmailBroken. If this is in the file, a mail message will be sent when a broken link is found.
- EmailRedirected. If this directive is specified, then an e-mail message will be sent when a link is a redirected link.
- Exclude. This is a URL prefix that should not be traversed. This might be something that is already checked or out of your control.

A properly organized Web site can probably use an instruction file, similar to the following:

```
AvoidFile    /path/to/momspider/momspider-avoid
SitesFile    /path/to/momspider/momspider-sites
<Site
    Name          Company
    TopURL        http://www.company.com/
    IndexURL      http://www.company.com/siteindex.html
    IndexFile     /webserver/htdocs/siteindex.html
    IndexTitle    MOMspider Index for Company.com
    EmailAddress  admin@company.com
    EmailBroken
    EmailRedirected
>
```

This tells MOMspider to check all links in www.company.com and e-mail admin@company.com, if any broken or redirected links are found. It will also generate an index file and put it in /webserver/htdocs/siteindex.html.

The index MOMspider creates is more useful for reference than an actual drop in site map. It contains the following information:

- The date the index was started.
- Who ran the index.
- A table of contents for the index. This is at the top of the page.
- A section of links and documents in the index. These links contain the return code, the title of the file, and the last-modified date.
- A summary table. This lets the administrator see statistics on how many links were checked, avoided, broken, redirected, and changed.
- A list of broken links.
- A list of redirected links.
- A list of changed link destinations.
- A list of expired documents.

SSI as a Maintenance Tool

Server Side Includes (SSI) can be used to make a site easier to maintain. Scripts can be written to automatically generate links to the last referred document, the document up a layer, a help screen, or any information that should be on each document.

SSI can be used to create a systemwide template. This can automatically add a header and footer to all the pages. It allows the look and feel of the document to be changed easily.

A sample header might add the <HTML>, <BODY>, and <TITLE> tags. A footer may have the company information, copyright information, and links to the index, help, and home pages.

Using SSI to add headers and footers to a page makes it easy to change how a site looks and to add new features as they are developed. Since every page uses these headers and footers you can easily change the entire document by editing one simple file.

> **Note**
>
> Using SSI adds some CPU overhead since the server must parse the file each time it is accessed. Some sites may find this to be too much CPU processing for the server to handle without slowing down.

Below is a sample header program that can be used to automatically add the title and opening tags to a document. It's written in a shell script, but can be written in any language.

```
echo '<html>'
echo '<head>'
echo '<title>'"$*"'</title>'
echo '</head>'
echo '<body>'
```

This script simply adds the header information and uses the arguments for the title. When called like this:

```
<!--#exec cmd="header Company Web Site" -->
```

It will prepend the following to the HTML document when it sends it:

```
<html>
<head>
<title> Company Web Site</title>
</head>
<body>
```

Here is a sample footer SSI, which can be used to append the generic information to the bottom of every page:

```
echo '<A HREF="/phone.number.html"><img src="/images/phone.gif"
➥alt="Phone"></a>'
echo '<A HREF="/readme.html"><img src="/images/question.gif"
➥alt="?"></a>'

echo '<HR>'
echo 'This page, and all contents, are Copyright  1995 by Company'
echo '</BODY>'
echo '</HTML>'
```

This would append the following to the end of every script that called it:

```
<A HREF="/phone.number.html"><img src="/images/phone.gif"
➥alt="Phone"></a>
<A HREF="/readme.html"><img src="/images/question.gif" alt="?"></a>
<HR>
This page, and all contents, are Copyright  1995 by Company
</BODY>
</HTML>
```

You can organize your document tree to contain navigational links, which make it easier for users.

Let's assume that we created a main directory with a separate directory for each main topic. In each directory the main page is called index.html. Any subdirectories are also set up this way. This gives our script the following information about navigation:

- If the name of this document is index.html, up a level would be referenced by ../index.html.

- If the name of this document isn't index.html, then up one would be index.html.

- If the name of this document is /index.html, we are already at the home page.

- Some browsers send a HTTP_REFERER header, which tells the server where they came from. If HTTP_REFERER is set, we can use that to generate a back page.

Our script can now generate links to up one page, Home (if we aren't already there), and back (if our browser supports it).

The finished footer script is follows:

```
#!/bin/sh
echo '<HR>'
# Are we already home?
#If so then we don't send an up or a home icon
```

```
if [ x"$DOCUMENT_URI" != x"/index.html" ]
then
        echo '<A HREF="/index.html"><img src="/images/logo.gif"
➡alt="Home"></A>'
        echo '<A HREF="../index.html"><img src="/images/up.gif"
➡alt="Up"></A>'
fi

# If this is not called index.html then up one would be index.html
if [ x"$DOCUMENT_NAME" != x"index.html" ]
then
        echo '<A HREF="index.html"><img src="/images/up.gif"
➡alt="Up"></A>'
fi

# This checks to see if we know where the user came from if so we
#    can generate a back icon.
if [ x"$HTTP_REFERER" != x"" ]
then
        echo '<A HREF="$HTTP_REFERER"><img src="/images/back.gif"
➡alt="Back"></A>'
fi

#everyone gets this part
echo '<A HREF="/phone.number.html"><img src="/images/phone.gif"
➡alt="Phone"></a>'
echo '<A HREF="/readme.html"><img src="/images/question.gif"
➡alt="?"></a>'
echo '<HR>'
echo 'This page, and all contents, are Copyright  1995 by Company'
echo '</BODY>'
echo '</HTML>'
```

Using CPP Instead of SSI

If your server doesn't support SSI, you can perform some of the same functions by using the CPP program. CPP is a program that the C compiler uses. It handles such things as #include filename.h. It can also be used as an HTML pre-processor to include static footers and headers. This requires two files: the Source file and the HTML file. In order to make changes you edit the Source file and run it through CPP to create the HTML file. The HTML file is the file that the server sends.

For example, instead of using an SSI to append our original static footer, we could create a file called footer.html. In it place the following:

```
<A HREF="/phone.number.html"><img src="/images/phone.gif"
➡alt="Phone"></a>
<A HREF="/readme.html"><img src="/images/question.gif" alt="?"></a>
<HR>
This page, and all contents, are Copyright  1995 by Company
```

```
</BODY>
</HTML>
```

Then in all the HTML source files you put:

```
#include "footer"
```

This gets replaced with the contents of the footer file when you ran it through CPP. CPP is not available on all systems and requires two files instead of one. It does not, however, have the CPU overhead that SSIs have and for large sites the trade-off might be worth it. ❖

## CHAPTER 22

Sharing the Intranet with the World

After your Intranet has been in use a while you might realize that allowing customers to query the Intranet server directly can help to reduce support staff. Much of the information on the Intranet may be used for support services such as a database of common questions. By allowing external access many calls can be averted. It is also possible to setup remote offices with access to the corporate Intranet over the Internet.

Many times information that would be useful to an Intranet is already available on the Internet. Rather then duplicate this information it is possible to link in external sites with your Intranet.

In this chapter, we will discuss the following:

- How to safely allow customers access to certain parts of the Intranet
- How to only allow authorized users access to an area
- How to link in other Internet sites
- How to query external sites

Allowing Internet Users Access to Your Site

Many popular Internet sites started out as test sites used internally. These Intranets were such successes that the company decided to make the software available to any customers connected to the Internet.

This is very common and quite likely to happen more often as Intranets become more useful. Allowing Internet users to access part of your Intranet can be a formidable task, especially with security being a major concern, but the WWW is designed to be very flexible and can be used by both internal and external users without too many problems.

There are basically two different approaches to allowing Internet users to get to part of your Intranet: Using the Web server access controls and dedicating a separate machine to Internet access.

Using Software to Share Certain Directories

Because most Web servers allow you to specify who can access different directories, this is one of the easiest ways to allow some external access to the Intranet server. Using the access directive already supported by the server is simply a matter of changing the access file—usually access.cfg—and restarting the server. Some servers such as IIS allow you to change access permissions via a graphical user interface.

However, your permissions allow you to specify restrictions based on two criteria: IP address and username. IP address permissions allow the administrator to only allow certain machines to access the site or parts of the site. Using usernames and passwords to restrict access allows certain users to get to parts of the site. Using a combination of these two permissions allows fairly selective control.

Restricting by IP

The first way we will look at is to restrict which IP addresses or address ranges can connect to a directory. This works well if you know the IP addresses that should have access and you trust the security of the remote site. If someone gains access to the machine you are allowing, they can access your machine.

The easiest way to split the Web server is to have one directory tree that is public and one that is private. This is shown in figure 22.1.

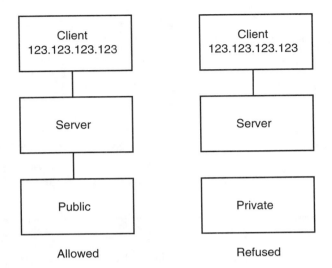

Fig. 22.1
123.123.123.123 can view the public directory but not the private one.

Using Apache or Netware Web Sever it is necessary to edit the access.cfg file, which is located in the configuration directory—usually /usr/local/etc/httpd/conf for Apache or in SYS:\WEB\CONFIG for Netware. It is also possible to use the override file—usually .htaccess—for Apache and acess.www for Netware, in the directory itself. You need to check the Limit directive for the different directories that the Web server uses. The private directory should have a Limit directive that looks like the following:

```
<Directory private>
<Limit GET >
order allow deny
allow 123.123.123.0
deny from all
</Limit>
</Directory>
```

Line one defines what directory we are describing. If we were using the .htaccess file instead of the global file, this directive would not be necessary. The Limit defines what can be done to files in this directory, in this case GET. The order tells Apache to allow first and then deny. The allow 123.123.123.0 tells Apache that anyone coming from a machine on the 123.123.123 network can have access. The deny line refuses access to everyone else. The next two lines finish the directives.

For the public directory everyone should have access so the directives should look like the following:

```
<Directory public>
<Limit GET >
order allow deny
allow all
</Limit>
</Directory>
```

This is similar to the directive used to deny except in this example we say allow all and don't have a deny line. We could limit access, say from a competitor or a harassing machine by adding a deny line with the IP addresses we want to refuse access to.

Note

More details on the Limit directive are available in Chapter 3, "Installing and Configuring HTTPD for UNIX."

After changing the access.cfg file you must restart the server or send it a hangup (HUP) signal.

The Netscape server can be configured to block access by IP addresses as well. To do this you use the server manager program located in the admserv directory in the server root directory. If the admin server is not already running, then run start-admin to start the admin server program. Then point your Web browser to **http://intranet.server.name:aport/**.

Next perform the following:

1. Choose the link for "Restrict access from certain addresses," under "Access Control and Dynamic Configuration." This will bring up a new form.

2. Enter the pathname and files to protect. You can use wildcards to allows certain groups of files. To protect the private directory you would enter **/private/***.

3. Enter the hosts that should have access. This can use wildcards as well. For the network 123.123.123 you would enter **123.123.123.***.

4. Submit the form.

Using wildcards also allows you to limit different type of files. For example, you might allow remote users to access all the files except .cgi files. If so, you would enter **/private/*.cgi**.

Using Microsoft IIS you can only allow or deny access to the entire server using IP restrictions. If you need to allow users to only part of your site, you will need to use user-based security, which is discussed in the next section.

Passwords and Usernames

There may be times when you need a finer granularity than restricting access by IP address. This might happen if you only want selected customers to have access to a particular part of your Intranet. This would allow, for example, a support contract-only area.

> **Tip**
>
> Since many people have Internet access at home it is possible to allow them to access the Intranet from home. This can allow a form of telecommuting over the Internet. Using passwords and usernames helps to make sure only valid users can connect over the Internet.

HTTP allows for basic authentication only. This allows servers to require passwords but the passwords are sent in the clear. This allows anyone sitting on a network that the traffic passes through to use a network sniffer to see the username and password. If this is not enough security for your site, you will need to use some sort of encryption, such as SHTTP or SSL. SHTTP and SSL are covered in Chapter 1.

Using usernames and passwords with Apache requires editing either the directory directive in the access.cfg file or the file .htaccess file in the directory you want to protect. The Limit directive needs to contain:

```
<Limit>
require valid-user
AuthName [Auth-domain]
AuthType Basic
AuthUserFile [user-file]
AuthGroupFile [group-file]
</Limit>
```

The `require` directive tells the server what users to allow access to. `valid-user` tells it to allow anyone with a valid account to be able to access it. You could also list which users can have access to this directory.

`AuthName` defines the security domain the password is good for. This is normally the same for the entire machine, but it is possible to have more then one security domain per server.

`AuthType` has to be `Basic` because that is all Apache uses. `AuthUserFile` and `AuthGroupFile` define what files contain the usernames and passwords.

The Limit directive is covered in more detail in Chapter 3 "Installing and Configuring HTTPD for UNIX".

Netscape's server also allows username and password authentication. To enable it you will need to go into server manager (see previous section or Chapter 5 for details) and select the "Restrict access to part of your server through authentication" link.

Netware Web server allows either file-based authentication, like Apache, or NDS-based (Netware Directory Services based) authentication. The most common way is to use file-based authentication if you are going to be sharing the server with external users.

To restrict directory access you must manually edit the per directory access control file, normally ACCESS.WWW. Before the Limit directive you must add three directives:

- `AuthType Basic`—This tells it what type of authorization type to use.
- `AuthName [name]`—This is the name of the security domain. It is used to tell the user which password to enter.
- `AuthUserFile [filename]`—This is the filename that contains the encrypted passwords.

Inside the Limit directive you need to add a Require directive telling the server which users can have access to the directory. This can be a list of usernames or "valid_user." Using valid_user allows any user listed in the `AuthUserFile` to have access as long as he or she enters the correct password.

The encrypted file is created using the command `pwgen`. It takes as arguments the input file and the output file. The input file is a file containing usernames and clear text passwords. For example:

```
Rich:secret
Tom:quiet
Al:ring
```

After running `pwgen` and copying the encrypted file in ServerRoot, usually SYS:WEB, you should copy the unencrypted file to floppy disk and remove it from the system. This is added protection to keep the passwords from being accidentally discovered.

If you choose to use NDS passwords, you can use the webmgr.exe program to configure the access restrictions. To do this perform the following:

1. Start webmgr.
2. Click File/ Select Server.
3. Select the correct server directory (probably a drive mapped to SYS:\WEB).
4. Select the Directory from the drop-down list.
5. Select Directory Services from the Authorization list.
6. Type the NDS context name that contains the user object that should have access.
7. Select the user.
8. Click Add to Authorized users list.
9. Click OK.
10. Click Save and restart.
11. Enter the Web server password and OK for your changes to take effect.

Microsoft IIS can also be used for username authentication. This can be done by performing the following:

1. Open the Web server properties box.
2. Select the service tab.
3. Choose Basic under Password authentication.

This will force users to supply a username and password. This username must be a valid account for the machine running IIS or in an accessible NT domain.

> **Caution**
>
> Using Basic authentication sends the username and password in clear text. This will allow anyone on the network or on a network that the traffic passes through to see the username and password with a network sniffer.

If your users are using Microsoft Internet Explorer for Windows 95, you can choose Windows NT Challenge/Response instead of Basic. This does not send unencrypted passwords in the clear.

Running Two Servers on One Machine

It is also possible to run two separate WWW servers on one machine. This is useful to allow tighter restrictions on the private server while allowing looser restrictions on the public one.

You must first choose an alternate port for one of your servers to run on. Normally the externally accessible server runs at port 80 because this is the default. The internal server can run on any free port. Ports range from 1 to 65535.

Note

You can use any port between 1 and 65535 to run a Web server on. It is important to make sure the port is free before trying to use it. Ports less then 1024 are considered reserved. On UNIX machines this means you must have root permissions to run a server on these ports.

Configure one server to run on one port and the other to run on a separate port. This will require two separate configuration directories and may require two licenses.

Using Separate Machines

A better alternative to sharing an Intranet server with Internet users is to have a separate machine dedicated to the Internet. Because the WWW is distributed it is very easy to split the server into separate pieces and have links from the private Web server point to the public server. This adds a layer of protection in case the public Web server is compromised.

Running a separate machine allows looser controls to be placed on the internal server while still protecting sensitive data from intruders. It also provides a layer of protection because the external server doesn't need to have full network access.

When running with two servers it is desirable to separate them with a firewall or other protective measures. This helps to eliminate crackers getting access to the internal server using other means then the WWW software. Firewalls are covered in Chapter 23, "Intranet Security."

There are different ways to split the Web servers such as:

- ■ Separate mirrored directories of information. This way uses two identical directory trees, one for external access and one for internal access. This, in conjunction with a firewall, can be used to totally isolate the two machines as in figure 22.2. Every night, or as often as needed, simply copy the mirrored directory to tape, or over the network to the external machine.

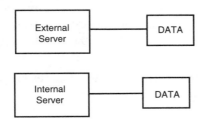

- Data on the external server. This allows less administration than two identical copies with a slight sacrifice on security. The data and directory resides on the external machine and links are made from the internal machine to the directory on the external machine. This unfortunately, leaves the data mostly unprotected as opposed to having it stored behind a firewall.

- Store the data on the internal server. It is also possible to store the data and directories on the internal server and allow the external server access to run commands on the internal server. This also has slight security concerns because the external server can be compromised and used to attack the internal machine.

Having a separate server separated by a firewall and mirroring the required data is the most secure solution. It is also the most costly, both in hardware costs and maintenance costs. It is important to decide how much security is enough for your company.

Remote Access

It is common for users to want to access corporate information while they are on the road. Sales people and field support personnel frequently need access to sensitive company data while out of the office. This data though may need to be kept private and not released to the Internet community.

The following are several ways for people to get access to an Intranet:

- Dial-in PPP or SLIP links. PPP and SLIP allow remote machines to act as if they were directly connected to the LAN.

- Internet access. Internet Service Providers are available almost everywhere. Allowing users to access the Intranet over the Internet has security concerns that must be addressed.

- Dial-in Accounts. UNIX machines allow users to dial-in and act as a serial terminal such as a VT100. This would allow them access to non-GUI based tools such as Lynx or e-mail.

- Dial-in to the server. NT allows users to dial directly into the NT machine, using Remote Access Service (RAS), and not have access to the network. This allows access to the Intranet without having free rein of the network.

- Private network link. This can be used if, for example, a remote office wants access to the corporate Intranet.

Dial-in IP

Dial-in IP connections such as PPP or SLIP allow remote machines to connect over standard phone modems and act as if they were directly connected to the network. This allows them to use standard network tools such as Netscape Navigator, InterNotes, or Microsoft Internet Explorer.

PPP and SLIP access is distributed with Windows 95 and NT as well as with OS/2. It is available for Windows 3.x and above from many commercial sources as well as shareware. UNIX machines can download software to allow them to connect over modem lines as well. Some UNIX operating systems have PPP or SLIP already available. Check your documentation.

> **Note**
>
> PPP software for PCs is available from many commercial sources as well as a shareware package called Trumpet Winsock. Trumpet is very popular and can be downloaded from **ftp://ftp.trumpet.com.au/ftp/pub/winsock**.

PPP and SLIP require either a dedicated communication server, or a server package running on a server machine. PPP/SLIP servers are available for UNIX machines. Windows 95 and Windows NT have PPP servers shipped with them. See the documentation on setting up PPP or SLIP links.

Dial-in IP connections should be protected using strong security. Basic security such as usernames and passwords is the minimum security you should have on dial-in connections. There are even more secure ways to protect your dial-in lines, such as the following:

- Caller ID information. Some software packages support checking the Caller ID (CID) information and comparing it to a defined list. If your users commonly call in from the same number, CID may be a good idea. However, if your users don't call in from predictable numbers, then administration will be more difficult.

■ Callback security. Callback security is a good way to save cost and make your site more secure. The user dials-in to a modem or rack of modems and logs in with a username and password and sometimes a phone number to call back. This number can either be entered here or recorded in a file. If your users are frequently changing numbers, they may need to be able to enter the number themselves. Then the connection is closed and the modem calls back the user.

■ One-time passwords. One-time passwords frequently require either a card that displays a random password, or a list of passwords that are generated beforehand. Once the user logs in using a password it is no good and a new one is used next time he or she logs in.

Once a PPP or SLIP link is established, normal IP-based networking programs should work. Because most modems are under 28.8 Kbps—as opposed to the 4 Mbps or higher used in most LANS—performance will be much slower.

Internet Access

If employees are often calling in long distance, then the phone costs can add up very quickly. It is possible for remote users to connect to the Intranet over the Internet. Internet Service Providers, such as AT&T, Sprint, and Uunet have local numbers in most large cities. CompuServe and America Online also have local numbers in most cities.

Using the Internet opens many security problems but most of them can be limited by using a few server access lists, such as restricting to known IP addresses or forcing users to login using a username and password. To be even safer you should probably use a secure protocol such as SSL or S-HTTP.

Caution

When using the Basic authentication passwords are sent in the clear. This allows other network users to sniff the password and username if they are attached to the same network or a network that the traffic passes through.

IP Restrictions

If your employees often connect from a certain customer site, or if your remote offices also have Internet connections, it might be possible to use Internet address restrictions to only allow certain addresses to connect.

> **Caution**
>
> IP Spoofing is fairly easy to do. It involves using another machine's IP address to send commands or requests to a third machine. Allowing access by IP address only is asking for trouble.

There are several ways to enforce IP restrictions. We have covered how to do this on a per directory level using Apache, Netscape, and Netware. Using the same instructions you only need to restrict access to each directory in your Web server tree.

> **Note**
>
> There is also a UNIX package called TCP Wrappers that can be used to only allow access to certain IP addresses. It can also be used to start separate servers for internal and external users. TCP Wrappers are covered in Chapter 23, "Intranet Security."

To allow IP restrictions in Microsoft IIS you need perform the following steps:

1. Bring up the WWW service properties page.
2. Select the Advanced tab.
3. Click the button labeled Denied access. This disables everyone and only allows certain hosts. This is the best way to handle security.
4. Click the Add button.
5. Choose either single computer or Group of Computers.
6. Enter the IP Address or IP Address and subnet mask as required.

Password Authentication

It is also possible to force users to login whenever they access the WWW server. This is done in the same manner as per directory.

Simply follow the directions to setup password authentication for a directory and apply it to all directories.

Note

It is also possible to apply these restrictions on just the Document Root directory but check your documentation to make sure the permissions will follow from there.

This forces users to supply both a username and a password to access documents from the Intranet server.

Caution

Using Basic authentication passwords are sent in the clear. This allows anyone with access to a network segment that your traffic passes over to sniff your password and username. The only way to defeat this is to use encryption or one-time passwords.

Using the Web server protections only protects against attacks to the Web server. If users can get access via other means, it is necessary to secure those as well. This is shown in figure 22.3

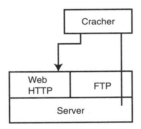

Fig. 22.3
Crackers may be able to get documents using other protocols than HTTP.

Dial-In Accounts

Allowing users to dial-in and have full network access makes it easy for them to get work done, but it is sometimes complicated to set up and use. There also is no real way to track what a remote user is doing using dial-in IP.

If someone breaks in, one of the most important tasks (after fixing anything he broke and closing the security hole that allowed him in) is to find out what the cracker did. Using dial-in accounts helps to keep track of what users are doing just in case their account is ever stolen.

Dial-in accounts are often much easier to set up than a PPP or SLIP server. Most UNIX machines allow a modem to be hooked up to a serial port for remote access. There are often few changes that need to be done except for telling the system to allow logins on the remote port.

This is generally done in one of the following ways:

- Adding a getty process in inittab. In some UNIX versions, based on SystemV, there is a file called inittab that controls startup processes. It is necessary to add a line telling inittab to start a getty process on the serial port. You must reboot the server or send a HUP signal to init for these changes to take effect.

- Add a tty entry to the ttytab file. BSD-based UNIXs usually have a file called /etc/ttytab. This is used to start programs on certain terminal devices. After these changes are made, you will need to reboot the server or send a HUP signal to init to get it to re-read the file.

Software is also available to allow a remote user to take over a PC. This software allows a remote user to enter commands just as if he were located at the keyboard. This can be used to allow remote users to connect to and use the Intranet. A dedicated PC, however, is required.

Remote Access Server

Microsoft Windows NT contains a package called RAS (Remote Access Server). This package allows remote logins to the NT server itself.

RAS allows the access to be restricted to the NT server only or to the entire network. Configuring RAS is fairly simple to do:

1. Add the software by selecting Add Software under the network settings dialog box located in the Network area of Control Panel. Then click on Remote Access Software.

2. In the Add Port box, click the port on which you intend to use RAS.

3. You can either enter the modem type manually by clicking cancel, or click OK to have it automatically detected.

4. In Port Usage you can define the port to be used as dial-in only, dial-out only, or both. For a RAS server you probably want to set this to dial-in only. Click the Receive Calls Only option.

5. In the RAS setup box you can define the network settings. These include limiting access to just the server or allowing network access.

After RAS is setup you need to grant users permission. This is done by performing the following:

1. Open the Remote Access Admin icon.
2. Select the server or domain to use.
3. Under the Users menu click permissions.
4. In the remote access permissions box select the permissions this user should have.

Encrypted Tunnels

It is possible to use special encryption equipment to link remote offices over the Internet without having to worry about someone seeing your traffic.

These devices can be hardware devices such as routers or software devices that act as proxy servers to the remote network. These links are configured to automatically encrypt traffic to a specific network before sending the traffic over the Internet.

Unfortunately these devices normally require the same sort of equipment on both ends of the link. It is sometimes problematic exporting encryption outside of the United States.

External Links

One of the main reasons for having an Internet connection is to be able to access the many sources of information. Finding the information however can be very frustrating.

Some search engines will return hundreds of links on almost any search. While this is very good for finding arcane bits of knowledge, this is often times too overwhelming to be useful.

Some companies will either dedicate someone to be an Internet researcher, or more often, whoever is most familiar with finding information acts as a contact person. Either way, having a separate page on the Intranet for useful links can be very helpful.

There are many books available that can act as reference books on where to find information on the Net, but this information is often general reference only. Companies often need more specific information related to their specific product lines, such as a construction company having links to lumber yards or distributors. It is very useful to have links to the competition as well to keep abreast of what they are doing.

Finding all this information can require many hours of time. That's why having a global bookmark or hotlist available for users of the Intranet makes such sense.

There are many Internet sites that will be useful to your company. Some will be very specific to your company's needs and some will be generic. This section covers a few of these generic links and shows how to integrate external links into the Intranet.

Linking in Remote Forms

As we learned earlier in this book, forms require an action item. In our examples we used local scripts, but it is possible to use remote scripts as well. The basic form is still the same:

```
<form method="POST" action="script">
```

The method is either GET or POST depending on how the script is expecting the data. The action is the script that receives the data. The action item can also be a remote form as long as you give it the complete URL of the form. This would allow a form to be local to your machine and send a request to a remote machine.

For example, to send a tracking request to the FedEx site you would have a fill out form that uses the FedEx script to actually query the site. This allows your users to only use bandwidth when sending the request and sending the answer.

> **Note**
>
> You should always check with the Webmaster at the remote site before using one of their scripts in your forms. They will probably be flattered that you find their site so useful, but some sites may not want you to link to them.

CUSI

CUSI stands for Configurable User Search Interface. It is used to build a page of search engines. It uses the remote script function to submit queries to different search engine depending on what you are looking for.

CUSI has search engines for software, RFCs, index sites, and general search engines. It is very customizable—as the name implies—and if maintained, is very useful as a building block for a company search page.

More information on CUSI is available from **http://pubweb. nexor.co.uk/public/cusi**. ❖

## CHAPTER 23

Intranet Security

Intranet security means not only keeping unauthorized users from reading, changing and deleting company information. It also means keeping employees from wasting time on the Internet and also from making the company look bad by posting sensitive or inappropriate information.

There are, fortunately, some things that can be done to improve the security of your Intranet. These are both technical solutions and policy decisions that can be put in place to help make things safer and more productive.

In this chapter, we will learn:

- How to write a security and access policy
- How to enforce policy decisions
- How to install software and hardware to limit exposure from the outside
- How to keep internal users from abusing the Internet
- How to spot something wrong

Security and Access Policies

One of the most important—and most overlooked—part of implementing network security is to have a written policy. A policy is a document that describes what you are trying to protect and what you are trying to protect it against, as well as describing what should and shouldn't be done over the network. Having a policy allows you to measure how effective any procedures you have implemented are. Policies also help explain to users and management why some things need to be done differently or not at all.

Writing polices is not easy and this book will not go into detail on how to do it. We will discuss generally what needs to go into a policy and discuss where to get some sample polices.

Writing Policies

Writing policies is a complicated task because it requires keeping ideas general enough to be flexible but specific enough to be useful. There are normally two different parts to the policy. The first part is the security portion, which describes what needs to be protected and how to protect it. The second part is the access part. This part describes what can be done over the network.

The first step in writing the security portion is to define what needs to be protected. This is the hardest part to determine because most users don't know what they use or how important it is. It is often better to work with each group, determine what they use for files and programs, and compile a list of who uses what.

> **Caution**
>
> When writing the policy, you should not use specific filenames because they may change. Instead it should be kept general, such as a statement reading "Payroll files should only be viewed or changed by payroll employees." Keeping the model general allows flexibility and changes to occur without having to rewrite the document.

Next you need to determine who shouldn't be able to get to what. Often security is implemented in layers or tiers. The top tier is for very sensitive machines such as those that create accounts or that enforce security. This could be the NT domain controller, NIS master, or Kerberos master. The NT domain controller handles security and accounts for NT based networks, while the NIS master and the Kerberos master handle accounts for mainly UNIX-based accounts.

The second tier of information should be allowed to be changed by only certain groups. It may need to be viewed by more than one group. Define what those groups are and what access they need.

The third tier is usually readable by everyone and writable by only certain groups. The last tier is information that can be written or read by everyone. The Internet usually falls under one of these tiers. Some companies may only allow certain people or groups of people to post information. This helps to eliminate inaccurate information from being sent out from the company.

> **Note**
>
> This security model does not specifically deal with the accesses from the Internet. It is assumed that Internet users can get access to the network, and any document that is readable by everyone can be read by these users as well. Hopefully this is not true, but if you assume it is, then you can prepare for it.

Once the part of the policy describing who can change what files is determined, usage is usually discussed. An example might be a section determining that passwords are required, must be hard to guess, and also that passwords should not be given to anyone or written down. It is common to refer to other documents that explain password procedures or other site specific requirements. This allows specific requirements to be documented and changed without having to rewrite the security policy.

Once the access policy is determined, it is common to put in a section describing what will happen if it is not adhered to. This is often a touchy issue and it will be necessary to get the personnel department or manager involved as well as legal assistance.

Once the policy is written, it should be reviewed by either a lawyer or a legal department. Upper management needs to be informed of what the policy means and how it needs to be enforced. If upper management doesn't understand or agree with the security policy, it is not useful.

Sample Policies

Policies are general guidelines, and it is common for a template policy from another company or institution to be used as a guideline. Sample policies can be downloaded from the following sites:

- **http://delphi.colorado.edu/~pubs/draft9.html**
- **gopher://gopher.eff.org/11/CAF/policies**
- **http://www.crmwc.com/aup.htm**
- **http://chico.rice.edu/armadillo/acceptable.html**
- **http://all.net/books/policy/top.html**

Again these policies are guidelines and may not describe the requirements of your specific site. They should help explain how the document should be worded and what should be included.

Policy Pitfalls

When writing policies it is important to use careful wording and expressions. In case of disputes, this policy may need to be taken into a court and it should be reviewed by a legal department or lawyer who understands computer laws.

One of the important things to remember when writing either this policy or the security policy is to be consistent in everything you allow or deny. For example, if the access document says no access to online stock quotes, and one of the upper managers has access, then your policy is no good. There should be a way for someone to get access, even if it will not be allowed. A good way to do this is to have a clause that says "No access to online stock quotes without permissions from _____". This allows some people to have it and not others.

Employees' feelings must also be taken into account, especially in companies where employee morale is important. Improper or harsh wording can cause employees to feel "Big Brother" is watching and may get bad feelings about the company. This is not to say that employees should be allowed to do whatever they feel like on the Internet, but a little trust can go a long way.

User Education

One of the most important steps in allowing employees to access the Internet or Intranet is to teach them how to use it. There should be a document or required training class that employees must take before being unleashed on the Internet. This class or document needs to cover a few issues. Among them are:

- Netiquette. This is like etiquette in the network world. This section of the document should discuss the simple issues like not posting blatant advertisements to groups that don't allow them, the proper way to subscribe and unsubscribe from mailing lists, and not forwarding personal e-mail to mailing lists. There is a frequent posting in news.answers that discusses netiquette. This posting is a good reference to use when developing a user education program.

- How the software works. This is simply sitting down and teaching users what hypertext is, how it works, what is available and how to find that which is not readily available. This section should cover any Internet tools the company uses including News readers, WWW browsers, FTP clients, and E-mail.

- Security. This includes basic security guidelines including e-mail insecurities, choosing good passwords, and not sending company sensitive documents to mailing lists.

- Accountability. Explaining to users that connections can be logged is a way to reduce the amount of time wasted on the Internet. This is only possible in certain network configurations where the access is through a particular point, such as with InterNotes, Socks, or proxy servers.

If the document, or class, covers these basics and teaches the users how to act responsibly on the Internet, many problems can be avoided.

A good example to show employees that what they post is reflected back on the company is to search one or two of the major search engines for the company name and see what comes back. Everyone might be surprised!

Accountability

In our list of topics users need to be educated on, we mentioned accountability. This can be used to help deter employees from spending too much time on personal projects.

Many companies have logs files that contain statistics on user accesses. These may include:

- Size. This is the number of bytes downloaded per connection. This statistic allows departments or users to be billed, or help account for bandwidth usage.

- Name. This is the document name, such as index.html or button.gif. This name might give clues as to what the document contains.

- Time and date. This tells when the file was downloaded. The policy might allow personal use after work hours or during lunch.

- Site name. This is the remote site connected to. This might also give clues as to whether it is work related or not.

- Destination port. This may be FTP, HTTP or any other port. This usually gives a as to clue what protocol was used to download the file.

> **Caution**
>
> Filenames and destination ports may be misleading. Files can be called anything and do not have to end in particular extensions if the server is configured properly. Servers can also be configured to run at non-standard ports.

Many sites institute a billing procedure to hold departments accountable for supplies, and consider billing for network bandwidth. This will at least have the effect of allowing management to see who is using the bandwidth.

Other sites have a "Top Ten Users" or "Top Ten Sites" list. Employees don't want their managers to see their names on the top ten users connecting to www.wastetime.com, and may limit their usage.

Using accountability to convince employees not to abuse the Internet is usually better than trying to use technical tricks to block certain accesses. It often allows for better employee relations since the company is showing that they trust their employees not to waste time, and are only trying to keep track of where the bandwidth is being used.

Security Through Obscurity

One of the easiest ways to prevent casual users from accessing your Intranet is to make it hard to find. This will not prevent someone who is trying to break into your site, but it may keep out some people.

Security through obscurity isn't real security. It is more like camouflage and, like camouflage, once your site is seen it is extremely vulnerable. Obscurity is a good way to make intruders spend time poking around and hopefully do something to set off alarms and alert someone that they are trying to get in. The best defense, though, is to use a combination of security measures, such as server security or firewalls, in conjunction with obscurity. Hopefully this will alert you to intruders knocking at the door before they can get in.

There are a few ways to hide your Intranet. The following ways are covered in detail in the next few sections:

- Using non-standard ports. The standard port is 80. Using a different port will make it harder to find.
- Using hard to guess names. Most companies use WWW for the Web server machine name. Using something different can make it harder to find.
- Hiding your server's name. This can be done by not listing it in the DNS tables for your site, and not using it to browse the Web, send e-mail, or post to Usenet.

Using Non-Standard Ports

Using non-standard ports is one of the easiest ways to hide your site from prying eyes. Most Web servers have a simple configuration that allows the administrator to change which port to listen on.The default port is 80. Changing the port from 80 to something else will make it harder to find.

Changing the Port Number with Apache

Changing the default port is fairly easy to do. For Apache, there are two ways to do this—depending on how it is run. If you run Apache via inetd, then you simply need to edit /etc/inetd.conf and change the port to something other than 80. Then restart inetd by sending it a HUP signal, for example kill-HUP pid (pid stands for *Process ID number*).

If you run Apache from a startup script such as rc.local, you need to edit the httpd.conf file, which is usually found in the httpd/conf directory. There is a line in this file that contains a port directive. By default it uses port 80. Simply change this to a different port and restart HTTPd.

Changing the Port with Netware Web Server

Changing the port for Netware Web server can be done using the Web server manager program. Simply choose file and select server. Type in or select the drive that has the Web server tree mapped to it. Change the TCP port number to something other then 80. Next click OK, and then click save and restart. Enter the Web server password when prompted and click OK.

Changing the Port with Netscape Server

To change the port in Netscape enterprise server, you need to use the server manager program. You can start this process by running start-admin and then pointing a forms capable browser at **http://intranet.server.name: aport/**. Intranet.server.name is of course the Intranet server, and aport is the administrator port.

Your browser should come up to the administrator server page. Go to the line under Global URL Configuration that lists Server Port Number and change it from 80 to a different port number. After you submit the form and restart the server it will be running at the new port.

Using Hard to Guess Names

Most companies want people to be able to find their Web sites so they usually name them **www.company.com**. This also makes it easy to remember.

However, there is nothing saying that the Web server has to be called **www.company.com**. It can be named something as obscure as **udu33rf.company.com**. There is not much of a chance of someone guessing a name like that.

Hiding Your Server's Name

Using a hard-to-guess name is useless if it is listed in the Domain Name Service (DNS), or shows up in public access logs. This section discusses how to setup your machine so it cannot be found easily.

> **Note**
>
> DNS is the system that allows machines on the Internet to know who they are talking to. It is a hierarchical, distributed naming system that allows each site to maintain its own list of hostname to IP address mappings. DNS stands for Domain Name Service.

Hiding Via Separate Name Servers

Some sites run separate internal and external name servers to allow internal machines to connect to the Intranet server by name, but not give out information to the rest of the Internet.

Basically it works like this. When an internal user wants to talk to a machine by name, queries go to the internal name server, which does one of two things. If it is a local machine, it replies with the correct answer. If it is an external machine, it queries the external name server to resolve it.

External users can only connect to the external server, which doesn't know about all the internal machines. Because it doesn't have internal names listed, it reports back an error whenever someone asks for them.

Setting up and maintaining two separate name server machines can be cumbersome and costly. Experts disagree on whether running separate name servers gains anything or not, but all experts agree that simply hiding your Intranet is not enough to protect it.

Keeping Your Name from Other Sites' Log Files

It is also important to keep your server name from appearing in other sites' access logs. Some sites don't adequately protect their access logs from being read from Internet users and this can allow your hard-to-guess name to be found out.

The best way to keep your server's name out of other sites' access logs is simply not to use it for Web surfing, Usenet posting, sending e-mail, or any other Internet access.

Whenever someone connects to a Web server it makes an entry in the log file. Some sites, either on purpose or by accident, make their log files publicly readable. If you use your secret Web server for browsing, it might get listed in one of these public log files and get indexed at a search engine site. All a hacker has to do is connect to a major search engine and search for **yourcompany.com** and look for strange names.

The same is true for Usenet postings and e-mail lists, which are usually archived on a Web site and indexed. It makes sense to occasionally search for your company name on search engines, to check for security problems such as this.

Pitfalls with Security Through Obscurity

Unfortunately there are many programs available that can search for open ports on a machine or a range of machines. These port scanners are available for downloading from the Internet and can run very quickly. In TCP/IP there is a limit of 65,535 different port numbers that can be used so it is not very hard for a hacker to scan all the ports on a host and find any hidden servers.

> **Note**
>
> Port scanning software is a hacker's friend, but it can also be a network manager's friend as well. Port scanning software can detect unauthorized servers running that can cause security problems. Port scanners are available from several places, including "strobe" from **ftp://suburbia.net/pub/** and "netcat" from **ftp://avion. org/src/hacks**.

It is possible to booby trap your machine to catch people running port scanning software. You can set up dummy servers that report when someone connected to them and where he or she connected from. Analyzing the logs from these servers may allow you to detect an attack before someone breaks in.

> **Note**
>
> TCP Wrappers (**ftp://ftp.win.tue.nl/pub/security**) are a set of programs written by Wietse Venema. They work by verifying and logging connection information before starting the server. For example, by setting wrappers around your httpd server you can detect what IP addresses have connected, if they really are who they say they are, and accept or refuse the connection. If it is accepted, then it connects with the Web server normally. (See figure 23.1.)
>
> TCP Wrappers also can be used to set up dummy servers. They can be set up to send e-mail, send something to the printer, or send a page if someone tries to connect to a trapped port. Even if you don't need to set up wrappers around your servers, this notification feature makes TCP Wrappers worth downloading.

Fig. 23.1
TCP Wrappers checks the connection before allowing the server to talk to the client.

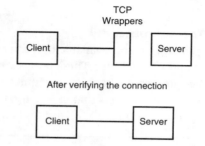

Using the Server Security

If simply hiding the site is not enough, what better defensive measures are available? Most WWW servers offer a layer of protection called access controls.

These access controls may be used to allow you to define IP address ranges that can retrieve documents from your Web server. Most Web servers also allow you to specify a username and password before allowing any documents to be retrieved.

These two ways of protecting the Web server from being abused and the problems with using them are covered in the next few sections. For specific server configurations see the chapter in Part II related to your Web server, or consult your Web server documentation.

There are two security models you can use to secure your Web server:

- All that is not allowed is denied. This means that you start out denying everyone access and only allowing certain machines access. This can usually be done by placing an * (or all) in the deny field and placing the local network number in the allow field.

- All that is not denied is allowed. This means that you allow everyone and deny those sites that are known to be bad. This would be done by placing an * (or all) in the allow field and listing out any site that shouldn't be allowed access to the deny field.

Security experts agree that it is best to deny everything and only allow in what is needed. This reduces the chance of the administrator overlooking something. In an Intranet it is better to deny everyone and allow local IP addresses, rather then try to list everyone who can't see what is on the Intranet.

> **Caution**
>
> Using the Web server security may stop a hacker from getting information from the Web server, but there are other ways to get information out of a machine, such as shared or exported drives. For more explanation, see the section on "Other Access Methods" later in this chapter.

Restricting by IP Address

Almost all Web servers have an access list that defines what machines or networks are allowed to retrieve documents or submit forms. This access list is usually made up of a list of allow and deny fields.

Using Apache, you can restrict access by IP address. This requires you to create a Limit directive in the access.cfg file. This file is usually in the httpd/conf directory.

The Limit directive should look like the following:

```
<Limit>
order deny, allow
Deny *
Allow 123.123.123.*
</Limit>
```

To deny access by IP address to the entire server using Netware Web server, you also need to edit the ACCESS.CFG file and add a Limit directive. The syntax will be the same as Apache uses. The ACCESS.CFG file is located in the \WEB\CONFIG directory.

Setting up access control for Netscape is done via the server manager page. Point your browser to the administration page. See the section on "Changing the Port with Netscape Server" for instructions. Go to the link under Access control labeled "Restrict access from certain addresses." This should bring up a new page. On this page you need to specify what resource you want to protect. To protect the entire server enter *****. Then enter the IP addresses that are allowed access. This should be your local network number followed by an *****. For example, if the local network is 123.123.123, then you would enter **123.123.123.*** to allow all the hosts in your network to have access.

> **Note**
>
> TCP Wrappers also can be used to limit access to the Web server by IP address range. They can also be used to send an error message to external users notifying them of where the external server really is.

IP Spoofing

Restricting access based on the IP address of the requesting machine is a good start toward security; however, that security is only as good as the security of the IP protocol. The IP protocol was designed with ease of use, not security, and allows people to masquerade as other hosts. This is called IP Spoofing.

IP Spoofing is, in a nutshell, telling your machine to use someone else's IP address. This also requires some modifications to get the response to go back to the malicious site, but it can be done.

> **Caution**
>
> In some cases it isn't even necessary to get a response. For example, if a form automatically creates an account, then all a hacker would have to do would be to pretend to be a trusted host and send the URL to add an account to the Web server. Then simply wait for the account to be created. The hacker doesn't need to see a response; he just needs to be able to send commands.

IP Spoofing can be fixed using router access lists. All that is required is to tell the router not to allow any machines using your IP address in from the Internet. (See figure 23.2.) This way your Web server never sees the packets and doesn't have to worry about them. This won't work, though, if you are sharing your Web server with another company over the Internet because the hacker could pretend to be the other company.

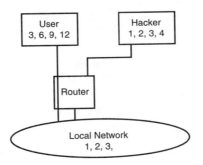

Fig. 23.2
Routers can be used to prevent IP Spoofing attacks.

Usernames and Passwords

Using IP addresses as security protection is a good start but doesn't handle all cases. The most obvious case is when multiple people use the same machine but only one person should have access to your Intranet. This can happen if your users use Internet Service Providers (ISPs) to gain access when they are out of the office.

ISPs generally allow multiple people to log in to one machine or allow dial-up users to share an IP address. Either way it can be disastrous to a security policy based on IP addresses for access decisions.

In this case, it is required to use usernames and passwords. Most Web servers allow username security. (See Part II for specific server configuration information.) Setting up username security is covered in later sections.

When a user encounters a page that is protected, a box appears asking for username. After the username is entered, the password is required. Once the password has been entered, it is checked to make sure it is the correct one. If so, the document is sent to the user; otherwise, an error is sent back. Users usually only need to authenticate once per site, per session. Figure 23.3 shows a password prompt.

Fig. 23.3
Users are prompted for a username and password for secure pages.

One of the problems with username and password protection has to do with the HTTP protocol itself. HTTP sends text "in the clear," which means exactly as you type it. This would allow anyone with a network sniffer on a network segment your traffic goes through to see your username and password.

In Chapter 1 we discussed HTTP as well as the secure versions of HTTP (HTTPS and SSL). Using these protocols or an encrypted link will protect against sniffers, however not all servers support SSL and HTTPS. Check the server documentation in Part II before trying to use this security feature.

> **Note**
>
> Using the Web server security only limits what files can be retrieved through the HTTP protocol. Other ways to retrieve files must be protected as well. For example, a hacker may be able to use anonymous FTP to get to the protected documents.

Configuring Basic Authentication

Using usernames and passwords with Apache requires editing either the Directory directive in the access.cfg file or the file .htaccess file in the directory you want to protect. The Limit directive needs to contain the following:

```
<Limit>
require valid-user
AuthName [Auth-domain]
AuthType Basic
AuthUserFile [user-file]
AuthGroupFile [group-file]
</Limit>
```

The Limit directive is covered in more detail in Chapter 3, "Installing and Configuring HTTPD for UNIX."

Netscape's servers also allow username and password authentication. To enable it you will need to go into server manager and select the link under Access Control that reads, "Restrict access to part of your server through authentication." Follow the directions on this form. Once it is filled out and submitted you need to restart the server for changes to take effect.

Netware Web server allows either file-based authentication, like Apache, or NDS-based authentication.

To restrict server access, you must manually edit the global access.cfg file. Before the Limit directive for the DocumentRoot directory you must add the following three directives:

- AuthType Basic—This tells it what type of authorization type to use.
- AuthName [name]—This is a name telling the user which password to enter.
- AuthUserFile [filename]—This is the filename that contains the encrypted passwords.

Inside the Limit directive you need to add a Require directive telling the server which users can have access to the directory. This can be a list of usernames or "valid_user". Using valid_user allows any user listed in the AuthUserFile to have access as long as he or she enters the correct password.

The encrypted file is created using the command pwgen. It takes as arguments the input file and the output file. The input file is a file containing usernames and clear text passwords. For example:

```
Rich:secret
Tom:quiet
Al:ring
```

After running pwgen and copying the encrypted file in ServerRoot (usually SYS:WEB) you should copy the unencrypter file to floppy disk and remove it from the system. This is added protection to keep the passwords from being accidentally discovered.

If you choose to use NDS passwords, you can use the webmgr.exe program to configure the access restrictions. To do this, perform the following:

1. Start webmgr.
2. Click File/ Select Server.
3. Select the correct server directory (probably a drive mapped to SYS:\WEB).
4. Select the Directory from the drop-down list. To secure the entire server select \.
5. Select Directory Services from the Authorization list.
6. Type the NDS context name that contains the user object that should have access.

7. Select the user.

8. Click Add to Authorized users list.

9. Click OK.

10. Click Save and Restart.

11. Enter the Web server password and OK for your changes to take effect.

Microsoft IIS can also be used for username authentication. This can be done by opening the Web server properties box and selecting the service tab. Choose Basic under Password authentication. This will force users to supply a username and password. This username must be a valid account for the machine running IIS or in an accessible NT domain.

Other Access Methods

Earlier we mentioned other ways for hackers to get files without going through the Web server. This effectively gets around any security the Web server may be using.

Different operating systems have different ways to get files from the server, UNIX servers have FTP, NFS, TFTP, and others, while NT may have shared drives as well as FTP and TFTP. Netware users may also have FTP, TFTP, and shared drives. It is necessary to determine any way that a file can be retrieved from the server and protect against it.

TCP wrappers can be used to allow only certain IP addresses access to the servers that you know about, but there may always be a server you have missed. Hackers will, if possible, place servers running on high ports to allow themselves a way to get back in, just in case their initial break-in is discovered. Running port scanning software against your machines on a regular basis is a recommended practice to help catch these backdoor servers.

The other alternative is to place your Intranet server behind a firewall. This effectively blocks access to all services except the ones you allow. It is possible to use the other security models and disallow access to any servers that you know are bad, but you may miss some. It is always more secure to disallow everything and allow only what you know is needed.

In order to be sure all services are protected, the network must be told to refuse all connections and only allow through certain ones. This is a job for a firewall. Firewalls are covered in the next section.

Firewalls

Almost every company connecting to the Internet needs a firewall. The Web server software security is just not enough, because there are too many other ways to get information, such as FTP, TFTP, or shared file systems.

Firewalls are a system or group of systems that enforce a policy between two networks. In most cases one of the networks is the Internet; however, firewalls can be placed between any two networks.

> **Caution**
>
> Firewalls can protect against many types of attacks by limiting what sorts of protocols can be passed into the company network. However, a firewall doesn't solve all the security problems. User education is required to teach users about security problems such as someone calling them on a phone and asking for a password. Dial-in modems are also a major concern.

Firewalls are split into two different categories: network-level and application-level firewalls. Both have their strengths and weaknesses and it is possible, and often desirable, to use a combination of the two type of firewalls, depending on your security requirements.

Network-level firewalls look at the packet header and see where it is trying to connect to, it then decides if it can pass or not. Application-level firewalls look at the packet and decide what the packet is trying to do and whether it is permitted or not.

Network-Level Firewalls

Network-level firewalls are devices or systems that look at the IP packet header and decide whether the address and port are allowed to pass through or not. It does not look at the data portion of the packet and does not understand what is going through.

The most common network-level firewall is simply a router with an access list defined on it. Machines with two network cards can also be used using special filtering software.

Network-level firewalls are very fast, because they only have to look at the IP header to decide whether the packet can pass or not. Network-level firewalls are also transparent. Because they don't interfere with the packet, users don't need to learn any special commands.

Network-level firewalls however have shortcomings. The logging they use is often not as sophisticated as application-layer firewalls. Network-level firewalls also don't understand what they are passing and can only refuse or deny the protocol. For more sophisticated logging, or finer access control, application-level firewalls are needed. They are discussed later in this chapter.

Benefits of a network-level firewall are:

- Easy to configure
- Transparent to users
- Very fast
- Cost effective

Disadvantages of a network-level firewall are:

- Access control is based only on address/ports
- Logging is fairly simple
- Must have a valid address range

Router Access Lists

Many routers allow the administrator to define an access policy. These access policies tell the router what packets are allowed to pass and which ones are to be dropped.

A simple access policy would say:

- Rule 1: Allow port 25 (e-mail) from anyone into the mailhost.
- Rule 2: Allow port 80 (WWW) from anyone into the external Web server.
- Rule 3: Allow users from 123.234.123 network log in to port 23 (telnet) to mailhost.
- Rule 4: Don't allow anything else in.

This simple access list allows anyone to send e-mail to the mailhost (Rule 1), and allows customers to get to the external WWW server (Rule 2). It also allows people on the network 123.234.123 to log in to the machine mailhost. The most important line is the last one, which says no one else can get in.

Access lists can and will be much more complex than this. Some routers allow you to define what to do if a packet is refused, such as log the attempt to a host or printer. You can also use other keywords to allow traffic out from the internal network to the rest of the world.

Access lists generally can be placed on the external port, on the internal port, or both, depending on the router.

Allowing traffic to a specific set of machines is commonly referred to as a screened-host firewall. This means that traffic is allowed to a specific host or set of hosts but only if it fits through the screen. Our access policy is an example of a screened-host firewall. (See figure 23.4.) The machines that external machines are allowed to talk to are called *bastion hosts*. Bastion hosts are hosts that are secured to (hopefully) resist attack.

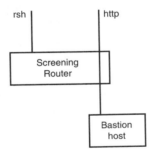

Fig. 23.4
Screened host firewalls allow certain types of traffic to a bastion host.

In addition to the screened-host firewall is a screened-subnet firewall. This allows a defined set of traffic through to an entire network. These configurations are covered in more detail later in the chapter.

Packet Filters
Packet filters are usually machines with two network cards running special software to allow or disallow packets based on their address and destination port.

Packet filters are similar to routers and can be used to build screened-host or subnet firewalls. Packet filtering software can be downloaded from the following sites:

- **IP Filter—ftp://coombs.anu.edu.au/pub/net/kernel**
- **KarlBridge—ftp://ftp.net.ohio-state.edu/pub/kbridge**
- **Screend—ftp://decuac.dec.com/pub/sources**

Packet filter software is available for both DOS machines and UNIX machines and supports many different network cards. Packet filters are often used to act as firewalls because they can run on very cheap hardware. A 386 processor-based machine has more than enough CPU power for a 56 Kbps line to the Internet and can handle T1 speeds, depending on the exact configuration.

Application-Level Firewalls

Application-level firewalls are very secure hosts with two network cards: one set up on the internal side and one setup to run on the hostile side. This bastion host runs proxy servers for each protocol that needs to get through the firewall. This allows no traffic to pass between the two networks and the proxy must instead interpret and relay data back and forth.

Application-level firewalls must understand the protocol they are proxying for and thus can do very sophisticated logging and access controls. For example, a proxy for HTTP may be set up to allow getting pages but not images. It could also be configured to disallow running a CGI program as in figure 23.5.

Fig. 23.5
Application level gateways can be configured to disallow certain parts of a protocol. Here we allow GETtin pages but not POSTing scripts.

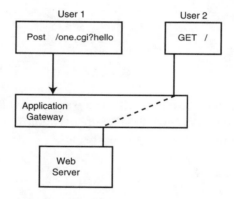

Benefits of an application-level firewall are:

- Very fine access control
- Better logging
- Can be used with reserved or unregistered IP address ranges

The disadvantages of application-level firewalls are:

- Harder to implement
- Performance isn't as good as with a network level firewall
- Special software required for each protocol
- Not always transparent to the user

Address Translation

Because application-level firewalls relay messages instead of passing traffic through, they can be used as Network Address Translators (NATs). NATs are useful for IP networks that are using unregistered address ranges or reserved ranges.

> **Note**
>
> With the explosive growth of the Internet it was realized that there were not enough addresses for everyone who used IP to have a registered address. As a result, RFC 1597 was written. It advised setting aside different ranges of addresses not to be used on the Internet, but to be used only on internal networks. Of course some people who started out using reserved numbers decided to get on the Internet and now must use NATs to perform address translation for them.

Because the Internet is designed not to route traffic to any reserved IP address ranges, using them for internal networks can help to prevent attacks from the Internet. This added security is not without a cost, though, because every external connection may require a network address translator to work properly.

Proxy Gateways

Most popular applications have proxy servers written for them. For example, Trusted Information Systems (TIS) has written a firewall toolkit that contains proxy servers for rlogin, telnet, FTP, X-windows, HTTP, and NNTP (Usenet). These proxies understand the protocol and can be used to safely allow these applications through the firewall.

Whether or not you choose to allow these protocols into your network requires looking at the security policy and deciding if they are required. Just because a protocol can be safely allowed through the firewall doesn't mean it should be allowed into the networks.

For a proxy to work it must understand the protocol it is trying to proxy. This means new protocols may not have a proxy written for them yet. These protocols either need to be passed through a network-level firewall or a generic proxy, also known as application forwarders.

Application Forwarders

Application forwarders are sort of emergency measures for firewall administrators. They allow proxy-like support for protocols that do not have special proxy software written for them yet. Application forwarders are also called generic proxies.

TIS includes a software package called plug-gw, which allows any protocol to be forwarded through an application level firewall without having to use a special proxy package.

Plug-gw may not allow as fine control as a special proxy, because it does not necessarily know what the protocol is doing. It can, however, log connection attempts, times, and hosts. It is a sort of compromise between network level firewalls and full proxy support for a protocol.

Socks

Socks is a generic application forwarder that is often used to allow access out to the world. Using Socks allows IP connectivity to hosts that are normally blocked by a firewall. Socks basically accepts connections from the internal network and relays these connections to the Internet hosts. It also relays data back and forth after the connection has been allowed and established.

Socks comes in source code form and must be compiled for each server platform. Socks is fairly easy to compile and can be done in a short amount of time. You can download socks from **ftp.nec.com/pub/security/ socks.cstc**.

Socks is supported for SunPS, Solaris, AIX, SCO, and Linux.

Firewall Configurations

Firewalls are configured in different ways, depending on how your company decides to balance the cost versus security issue. The most secure firewalls often use a combination of security layers to offer the most protection.

There are three types of basic firewall configurations in use today. They are:

- Dual-homed gateways
- Screened-host gateways
- Screened-subnet gateways

Each configuration has a different tradeoff among between security, cost, and performance. For example, dual-homed gateways are easier to configure and set up then screened hosts, but at a slight loss in security.

Dual-Homed Gateways

Dual-homed gateways are hosts configured to support two network interfaces. One faces in toward the secure network and one faces out toward the hostile network. They are configured not to route traffic between them. (See figure 23.6.)

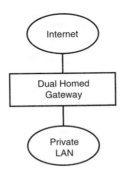

Fig. 23.6
Dual-homed gateways are built with two interfaces—one on each network. They don't allow routing.

The dual-homed machine is also called a bastion host. This machine needs to be as secure as possible, because it is the way a hacker will try to get in from the Internet.

The bastion host is the host that would normally run the external WWW server and FTP server as well as act as a mailhost for the Internet. It also will be the host that runs proxy servers for the users to get access to the Internet.

Dual-homed gateways are the cheapest of the three basic firewalls. However, they have one disadvantage over the other types of firewalls. They have a single point of failure. If any piece of software allows a hacker in, the entire network is exposed.

Screened-Host Gateways

Screened-host gateways are built using a screening router to block traffic to the internal network and to allow traffic to a bastion host. This host has one network interface as opposed to the dual-homed gateway that has two. (See figure 23.7.)

Fig. 23.7
Screened-host
gateways are made
up of a router and
a bastion host.

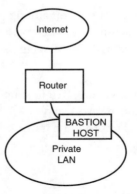

Because most Internet service providers provide a router at the site, it is easy and often economical to use this configuration. Screened hosts have the advantage of being able to allow certain applications in to the network easily.

The ability to poke holes in a firewall can be a major disadvantage if the firewall administrator is forced to open holes for unsafe protocols.

Another disadvantage to screened-host gateways is the fact that this system relies on two separate security devices: the router and bastion host. If either of these fail, the network is exposed.

Screened-Subnet Gateways

A screened subnet is made up of two screening routers with the bastion in the middle. This makes a small isolated network between the secure and hostile networks. The bastion host sits in this isolated network. (See figure 23.8.)

It is possible to have multiple hosts in this isolated network, also called De-militarized Zone or DMZ. This can help to alleviate performance problems.

This configuration is the most expensive but it is also the most secure because two devices need to fail to allow the network to be exposed.

Like the screened-host gateway, it is possible to poke holes through both routers to allow protocols in. This should only be done if the protocol is safe and there is no proxy available for it.

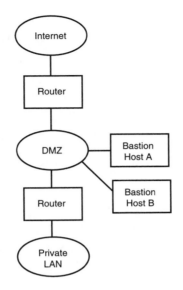

Fig. 23.8
Screened-subnet gateways have an isolated network separated from both networks via routers.

General Security

Many times network administrators put a firewall in place and assume that they are safe. However, this is very rarely the case. This is similar to putting a large steel door on the front of your house, and not paying attention to the glass windows scattered around the building.

Modems

Many companies have modems on their employees' machines. These can be for transferring files, connecting to online services, or might not be used at all. Many of these modems might be set to Auto Answer when called.

Auto Answer modems by themselves aren't a problem, especially on PCs that usually don't allow logins. However, UNIX machines are normally configured to allow remote logins on modem ports. This allows people in without going through the firewall.

UNIX machines aren't the only ones with remote capabilities, though. Many PC modem packages allow a remote user to take over a PC just as if he were sitting at the keyboard. This includes any network access that the machine may have.

Even worse than a login session is a PPP or SLIP connection. Many newer systems, such as Windows 95 or Windows NT, come with PPP software built in. It is possible for a user, knowingly or not, to enable this access. This allows the hacker to access any machine on the network virtually untraced.

It is important for a security administrator to be aware of these potential security holes. Hackers have access to many phone number scanners. These scanners work much like port scanners or network scanners. They start dialing numbers until they get a modem tone and then try to break in. Knowing which phone lines are connected to modems and securing them is as important as configuring a firewall.

Other Remote Networks

In addition to the Internet link, your company may have other remote networks that can be a source of attack. These may be something like Tymnet or Telenet, or a dedicated or dial-up link to another company.

Regardless of where these links go, you should always assume they connect to a hostile network and security should be in place on them. This may include a firewall or another safety device.

Physical Security

Physical security is usually not overlooked because this is the part of security most people are familiar with. Still some security teams spend more time looking for large-sized items rather then high importance items.

Many companies use 8mm or 4mm tape drives for backups. These tapes can easily fit in a shirt pocket. This is one way for data to leak out right past the firewall. Of course, employees need to be trusted to a point in any company.

Another problem can be unshredded confidential documents. One effective trick of a system hacker is to go trashing, which is basically going through a company's dumpster for information that may allow a hacker to get in. People often jot down usernames and passwords as well as telephone numbers and other security information. These notes often end up in the trash after they have been used. Shredding documents is a cost effective way of eliminating the usefulness of trashing.

If users and administrators understand the importance of securing the Intranet, many of these problems are taken care of. Having a secure Intranet can make the difference between people using the Intranet for work or for a toy. Making sure people realize they are accountable for the amount of time they spend on the Internet can also help to keep the Intranet from being abused. ❖

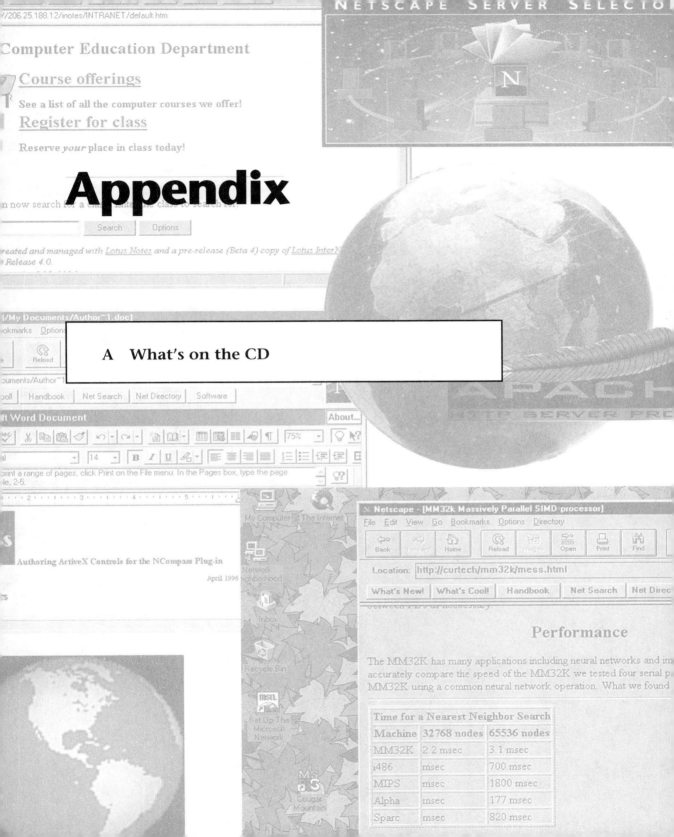

Appendix

A What's on the CD

Computer Education Department

Course offerings

See a list of all the computer courses we offer!

Register for class

Reserve *your* place in class today!

n now search for a class. Enter the class to search for:

Search   Options

reated and managed with *Lotus Notes* and a pre-release (Beta 4) copy of *Lotus InterN*
Release 4.0.

Authoring ActiveX Controls for the NCompass Plug-in

April 1996

Performance

The MM32K has many applications including neural networks and im
accurately compare the speed of the MM32K we tested four serial p
MM32K using a common neural network operation. What we found

Time for a Nearest Neighbor Search		
Machine	32768 nodes	65536 nodes
MM32K	2.2 msec	3.1 msec
i486	msec	700 msec
MIPS	msec	1800 msec
Alpha	msec	177 msec
Sparc	msec	820 msec

ess: http://206.25.188.12/inotes/INTRANET/default.htm

our Computer Education Department

Course offerings

See a list of all the computer courses we offer!

Register for class

Reserve *your* place in class today!

You can now search for a class! Enter the class to search for:

[Search] [Options]

s page created and managed with *Lotus Notes* and a pre-release (Beta 4) copy of *Lotus InterN*
lisher® Release 4.0.

---

le:///C|/My Documents/Author~1.doc]

Go Bookmarks Options Directory Window Help

| Home | Reload | Images | Open | Print | Find | Stop |

/My Documents/Author~1.doc

| What's Cool! | Handbook | Net Search | Net Directory | Software |

crosoft Word Document

About...

Arial   14   **B** *I* U   75%

ay: To print a range of pages, click Print on the File menu. In the Pages box, type the page
r example, 2-5.

Authoring ActiveX Controls for the NCompass Plug-in

April 1996

ntents

Network
eighborhood

Inbox

Recycle Bin

msn.
Set Up The
Microsoft
Network

My Computer

Cougar
Mountain

Netscape - [MM32k Massively Parallel SIMD processor]

File Edit View Go Bookmarks Options Directory

| Back | Forward | Home | Reload | Images | Open | Print | Find |

Location: http://curtech/mm32k/mess.html

| What's New! | What's Cool! | Handbook | Net Search | Net D |

Performance

The MM32K has many applications including neural networks an
accurately compare the speed of the MM32K we tested four seri
MM32K using a common neural network operation. What we fou

Time for a Nearest Neighbor Search		
Machine	32768 nodes	65536 nodes
MM32K	2.2 msec	3.1 msec
i486	msec	700 msec
MIPS	msec	1800 msec
Alpha	msec	177 msec
Sparc	msec	820 msec

NETSCAPE SERVER SELECT

N

APACHE
HTTP SERVER PF

What's on the CD-ROM?

The CD-ROM included with this book is packed full of valuable programs and utilities. This appendix gives you a brief overview of the contents of the CD. For a more detailed look at any of these parts, load the CD-ROM and browse the contents.

Source Code

Here, you'll find examples from the book. Simply click the chapter number of interest and read the code or cut and paste as desired.

Plug-Ins

Plug-ins are great, but finding and downloading them can be a hassle and it is definitely time consuming. We have supplied over a dozen of some of the hottest plug-ins available.

- Acrobat
- Corel CMX
- DWG/DXF
- Envoy Reader
- Fig Leaf Inline
- INSO Word Viewer
- Intercap Inline
- Look@Me
- Scream
- Shockwave for Director
- Sizzler
- VDOLive
- ASAP Web Show
- ASAP Word Power

Helpers

The following are a collection of programs to aid you in the creation of multi-media Web pages. You'll find graphics editors, video editors, sound editors, and so on.

Audio

- Cooledit
- Goldwave
- Midigate
- Mod4Win
- Real Audio
- WHAM
- WPLANY

Multimedia

- Working Model Macromedia Director 5.0

Video/Image

- ACDSee
- GraphX
- LViewPro
- MPEGPlay
- PolyView
- QuickTime
- SnapCAP
- StreamWorks
- VuePrint
- WebImage
- WinECJ
- WinJPEG

HTML Editors and Utilities

Save yourself the trouble of creating HTML pages with Notepad and pick your choice of HTML editor or special purpose utility from the following.

- HotDog
- HTML Assistant
- HTMLed
- HTML Notepad
- HTML Writer
- Live Markup
- WebEdit
- Webber
- Color Manipulation Device
- CrossEye
- EasyHelp/Web
- FrameGang
- Map This!
- WebForms
- Webmania

Java

Here, you'll find Java tools that will help you create animated applets and design scrolling marquees. You'll also get the HotJava browser and the Java Development Kit.

- Clikette
- Java
- Egor
- Ewgie
- Flash
- Swami
- HotJava Browser
- Java Development Kit

CGI and Perl

Perl, the Practical Extraction and Report Language, is the language of choice for scripting CGI interfaces into the World Wide Web. If you don't find a version of Perl for your operating system here, check CPAN or the Perl Language Home Page, and you'll probably find what you're looking for.

- Perl 4
- Perl 5
- CGI Library and Sample Scripts

VRML

Included here are VRML browsers to enable you to build "home worlds" and navigate 3D worlds.

- NAVFlyer
- Pioneer
- VRScout
- Worldview

Web Utilities

Here, you'll find mailing list engines, the popular Excite search engine, Spiders, validation programs, Web stats, security programs, and compression utilities.

- Engine Mail
- HyperMail
- LISTSERV™
- Get Stats
- iView
- WebPlot

Appendix

- LSMTP™
- LWGate
- MailServ
- Majordomo
- MHonArc
- Excite
- MOMspider
- WebLint
- freeWAIS
- Swish
- WWWWAIS
- ARJ
- BinHex
- UUCode
- WinCode
- WinZip
- COPS
- CRACK
- SATAN
- SSLeay
- Tiger
- xinetd

HTML Utilities

- Color Manipulation Device
- CrossEye
- EasyHelp/Web
- FrameGang
- Map This!
- WebForms
- Webmania
- Clip Art, online resources links

Index

Symbols

$DATABASE environment variable, Perl, 346
& string concatenation operator, VB Script, 323
= assignment operator, VB Script, 323
=~, pattern binding operator, Perl language, 278
14LST06.HTM, VB Script for object interaction (listing 14.1), 326
3-D worlds with VRML, 454

A

abend errors, Netware Web Server, 123, 137
abstract application model development, 392
academic annotation systems, 360
Access Control, Netscape Enterprise Server, 105
access
  controls
    Intranet servers, 32
    site content, 484-487
    Web servers, 526-532
  permissions for Internet visitors to Intranet sites, 502
  policies for Intranets, 518-522
  rights for Lotus Notes databases, 173
  usernames, Netscape Enterprise Server administration, 96

access.cfg file, editing for public and private directories, 503
access.conf file, Apache servers, 58
ACCESS.LOG file, Netware Web Server, 134
accountability and Intranet/Internet usage, 521
accounts, dial-in, 513-514
ACLs (Access Control Lists), MS IIS server security, 86
Acrobat Reader (Adobe), reading PDF files, 365
ACTION attribute, FORM tags, 252
Action form, S-HTTP security, 19
ActiveX (Microsoft)
  browser support, 331
  client-server interaction, 330
  controls, 327-329
  doc objects, 331
  documents, adding to Web pages, 331
  embedding into Web pages, 333
  Intranet uses, 328, 333-335
  multimedia, 459
  Web browser support, 331
addresses (e-mail) for groups
  with Hypermail, 357
  see also IP addresses
administering
  IIS servers, 81-83
  Netscape Enterprise Server, 91
  Netware Web Server, 126-127
Administration Server (Netscape Enterprise Server), port assignments, 97

Administration Utility (Netware Web Server), 126-127
  Logs Page, 128, 134-135
  Server Page, 127-129
  System Access Page, 128, 133-134
  User Access Page, 128, 131-132
administrative interfaces, 33
administrator, dbWeb, 401
Adobe Acrobat Reader
  external viewer, 183
  reading PDF files, 365
Advanced Networking Option (Oracle), 407
advantages
  HTML as electronic document format, 364
  relational database engines used with Web servers, 368
AEBs (Application Extension Blocks), animations, 451
AimTech IconAuthor, 460
AllowOveride directive, Apache server user rights, 60
alphabetic breakdown of database (listing 15.5), 347
alphabetical indexes for searches, 347
Amber plug-in, PDF file viewer, 184, 365
American Internet Corp.
  SiteBuilder Web server, 51
  Web site, 51
Amovie external player, 184
analysis of log files
  Netscape Analyze, 475-477
  Web site statistics, 474-480

X

Check out Que® Books on the World Wide Web
http://www.mcp.com/que

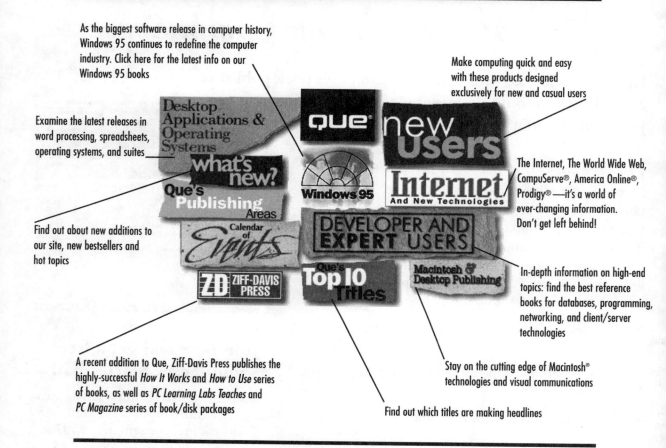

As the biggest software release in computer history, Windows 95 continues to redefine the computer industry. Click here for the latest info on our Windows 95 books

Make computing quick and easy with these products designed exclusively for new and casual users

Examine the latest releases in word processing, spreadsheets, operating systems, and suites

The Internet, The World Wide Web, CompuServe®, America Online®, Prodigy® —it's a world of ever-changing information. Don't get left behind!

Find out about new additions to our site, new bestsellers and hot topics

In-depth information on high-end topics: find the best reference books for databases, programming, networking, and client/server technologies

A recent addition to Que, Ziff-Davis Press publishes the highly-successful *How It Works* and *How to Use* series of books, as well as *PC Learning Labs Teaches* and *PC Magazine* series of book/disk packages

Stay on the cutting edge of Macintosh® technologies and visual communications

Find out which titles are making headlines

With 6 separate publishing groups, Que develops products for many specific market segments and areas of computer technology. Explore our Web Site and you'll find information on best-selling titles, newly published titles, upcoming products, authors, and much more.

- Stay informed on the latest industry trends and products available
- Visit our online bookstore for the latest information and editions
- Download software from Que's library of the best shareware and freeware

Complete and Return this Card
for a *FREE* Computer Book Catalog

Thank you for purchasing this book! You have purchased a superior computer book written expressly for your needs. To continue to provide the kind of up-to-date, pertinent coverage you've come to expect from us, we need to hear from you. Please take a minute to complete and return this self-addressed, postage-paid form. In return, we'll send you a free catalog of all our computer books on topics ranging from word processing to programming and the internet.

r. ☐　Mrs. ☐　Ms. ☐　Dr. ☐

ame (first) ☐☐☐☐☐☐☐☐☐☐☐　(M.I.) ☐　(last) ☐☐☐☐☐☐☐☐☐☐☐☐☐

ddress ☐☐☐☐☐☐☐☐☐☐☐☐☐☐☐☐☐☐☐☐☐☐☐☐☐☐☐☐

☐☐☐☐☐☐☐☐☐☐☐☐☐☐☐☐☐☐☐☐☐☐☐☐☐☐☐☐

ty ☐☐☐☐☐☐☐☐☐☐☐☐☐☐☐☐　State ☐☐　Zip ☐☐☐☐☐ ☐☐☐☐

one ☐☐☐ ☐☐☐☐☐☐☐　Fax ☐☐☐ ☐☐☐ ☐☐☐☐

ompany Name ☐☐☐☐☐☐☐☐☐☐☐☐☐☐☐☐☐☐☐☐☐☐☐☐☐☐☐☐☐

mail address ☐☐☐☐☐☐☐☐☐☐☐☐☐☐☐☐☐☐☐☐☐☐☐☐☐☐☐☐☐

Please check at least (3) influencing factors for purchasing this book.

ont or back cover information on book .... ☐
ecial approach to the content .... ☐
mpleteness of content .... ☐
uthor's reputation .... ☐
blisher's reputation .... ☐
ok cover design or layout .... ☐
dex or table of contents of book .... ☐
ice of book .... ☐
ecial effects, graphics, illustrations .... ☐
her (Please specify): _____ ☐

How did you first learn about this book?

w in Macmillan Computer Publishing catalog .... ☐
commended by store personnel .... ☐
w the book on bookshelf at store .... ☐
commended by a friend .... ☐
ceived advertisement in the mail .... ☐
w an advertisement in: _____ ☐
ad book review in: _____ ☐
her (Please specify): _____ ☐

How many computer books have you purchased in the last six months?

is book only .... ☐　　3 to 5 books .... ☐
ooks .... ☐　　More than 5 .... ☐

4. Where did you purchase this book?

Bookstore .... ☐
Computer Store .... ☐
Consumer Electronics Store .... ☐
Department Store .... ☐
Office Club .... ☐
Warehouse Club .... ☐
Mail Order .... ☐
Direct from Publisher .... ☐
Internet site .... ☐
Other (Please specify): _____ ☐

5. How long have you been using a computer?

☐ Less than 6 months　　☐ 6 months to a year
☐ 1 to 3 years　　☐ More than 3 years

6. What is your level of experience with personal computers and with the subject of this book?

	With PCs	With subject of book
New	☐	☐
Casual	☐	☐
Accomplished	☐	☐
Expert	☐	☐

Source Code ISBN: 0-7897-0823-x

7. Which of the following best describes your job title?

Administrative Assistant .... ☐
Coordinator .... ☐
Manager/Supervisor .... ☐
Director .... ☐
Vice President .... ☐
President/CEO/COO .... ☐
Lawyer/Doctor/Medical Professional .... ☐
Teacher/Educator/Trainer .... ☐
Engineer/Technician .... ☐
Consultant .... ☐
Not employed/Student/Retired .... ☐
Other (Please specify): _____ ☐

8. Which of the following best describes the area of the company your job title falls under?

Accounting .... ☐
Engineering... ☐
Manufacturing .... ☐
Operations... ☐
Marketing .... ☐
Sales .... ☐
Other (Please specify): _____ ☐

9. What is your age?

Under 20 .... ☐
21-29 .... ☐
30-39 .... ☐
40-49 .... ☐
50-59 .... ☐
60-over .... ☐

10. Are you:

Male .... ☐
Female .... ☐

11. Which computer publications do you read regularly? (Please list)

_____
_____
_____
_____
_____
_____
_____
_____
_____
_____

Comments: _____
_____
_____

Fold here and scotch-tape to mail